Regional and Global
Capital Flows

NBER–East Asia Seminar on Economics
Volume 10

National Bureau of Economic Research
Tokyo Center for Economic Research
Korea Development Institute
Chung-Hua Institution for Economic Research
Hong Kong University of Science and Technology
National University of Singapore

Regional and Global Capital Flows

Macroeconomic Causes
and Consequences

Edited by **Takatoshi Ito and
Anne O. Krueger**

The University of Chicago Press

Chicago and London

TAKATOSHI ITO is professor at the Institute of Economic Research at Hitotsubashi University, Tokyo, and a research associate of the National Bureau of Economic Research. ANNE O. KRUEGER is the Herald L. and Caroline T. Ritch Professor of Economics, senior fellow of the Hoover Institution, director of the Center for Research on Economic Development and Policy Reform at Stanford University, and a research associate of the National Bureau of Economic Research.

The University of Chicago Press, Chicago 60637
The University of Chicago Press, Ltd., London
© 2001 by the National Bureau of Economic Research
All rights reserved. Published 2001
Printed in the United States of America
10 09 08 07 06 05 04 03 02 01   1 2 3 4 5

ISBN: 0-226-38676-7 (cloth)

Library of Congress Cataloging-in-Publication Data

Regional and global capital flows : macroeconomic causes and
    consequences / edited by Takatoshi Ito and Anne O. Krueger
        p.   cm.—(NBER—East Asia seminar on economics ; v. 10)
    Includes bibliographical references and index.
    ISBN 0-226-38676-7 (cloth : alk. paper)
        1. Capital movements—East Asia—Congresses   2. Bank
    loans—East Asia—Congresses.   3. International finance—
    Congresses.   I. Ito, Takatoshi, 1950–   II. Krueger, Anne
    O.   III. NBER–East Asia seminar on economics ; v. 10.
    HG3891 .R447   2001
    332′.042—dc21   00-053246

Contents

Acknowledgments

This volume contains edited versions of papers presented at the NBER's East Asia Seminar on Economics tenth annual conference, held in Kona, Hawaii, on 10–12 June 1999.

We are indebted to members of the program committee who organized the conference, and to Chung-Hua Institution, Taipei; the Hong Kong University of Science and Technology; Korea Development Institute, Seoul; and the Tokyo Center for Economic Research.

The National Bureau of Economic Research was the local host. The conference arrangements were made by Kirsten Foss Davis and Brett Maranjian, and were superb. All the participants enjoyed the venue and the wonderful facilities in which the conference was held.

The Center for Global Partnership of the Japan Foundation provided major financial support for the conference, which is gratefully acknowledged. The National Bureau of Economic Research provided logistical support. We are greatly indebted to the NBER, the Center for Global Partnership, and the Asian institutions which supported the research and the conference.

Introduction

Takatoshi Ito and Anne O. Krueger

Over the past few years, the word "globalization" has increasingly been used to characterize the "new international economy." The term seems to imply a quantum leap from an earlier state of relative isolation of countries to a current situation in which all economic activities are very sensitive to events in distant corners of the world. In some regards, that implication is misleading: Increasing interdependence has been an ongoing phenomenon over many centuries as transport costs have fallen, communications links have improved, and times necessary to cover distances have diminished. In one fundamental regard, however, things have altered dramatically in the very recent past.

That regard is the flows of private capital between nations. After the collapse of the international economy in the 1930s, the architects of the Bretton Woods system presumed that private international capital flows would never again be significant, and they built their postwar architecture (of the International Monetary Fund and the World Bank) on that premise.

That premise was largely valid during the 1950s and 1960s, and most capital flows in that era were from official origins to governments in receiving countries. By the late 1960s, however, private capital flows (in addition to short-term trade credits) had resumed in significant proportions between the United States and Western Europe. By the 1970s, private capital

Takatoshi Ito is professor at the Institute of Economic Research at Hitotsubashi University, Tokyo, and a research associate of the National Bureau of Economic Research. Anne O. Krueger is the Herald L. and Caroline L. Ritch Professor of Economics, senior fellow of the Hoover Institution, director of the Center for Research on Economic Development and Policy Reform at Stanford University, and a research associate of the National Bureau of Economic Research.

flows from industrial countries to a select group of newly industrializing countries were beginning to increase. As late as the early 1980s, however, it was widely assumed that official capital flows would continue to be the main source of longer-term financing between industrial and developing countries.

All that changed in the 1990s, however, as the flow of private capital burgeoned. It is estimated that net private capital flows to emerging markets rose from US$47.7 billion in 1990 (equal to 0.8 percent of their GDP) to a peak of $212 billion, or 3.0 percent of their GDP) only six years later in 1996 (International Monetary Fund [IMF] 1999, table 3.1). In a real sense, the magnitude of capital flows has increased so dramatically, there is no question but that there has been a major change in the economic environment.

The very magnitude of these flows raises important questions as to their effects. Issues arise concerning the differential impact of different types of private capital flows—bank lending, bonds, portfolio investment, and foreign direct investment. Questions also have been put regarding the spillover effects, if any, from various types of capital inflow to the domestic economy in terms of technology transfer, learning by doing, and competition.

The fact that large-scale flows are of such recent origin implies that we know much less than we would like to regarding their effects. To contribute to our increasing understanding of these flows, the National Bureau of Economic Research–East Asia Seminar in Economics (NBER-EASE) agenda has, for the past two years, been focused on aspects of capital flows. At the ninth annual seminar, analysts assessed the microeconomic impacts of some capital flows originating in, or destined for, the various countries of East Asia. At the tenth annual seminar, focus was on the macroeconomic aspects of these flows.

Understanding the determinants and consequences of private capital flows is important for its own sake at any time. But in light of the financial crises taking place in Asia and other countries over the past several years, where the behavior of private capital flows was deemed by most to be an important part of the story of crises, understanding the macroeconomic impact of capital flows and their behavior has become a central concern of policy makers everywhere.

Many questions arise. Private capital flows rose sharply prior to the crisis in most crisis-affected countries. They then reversed abruptly, as investors sought to get their money out. These reversals in themselves constituted huge macroeconomic shocks: In the Asian crisis-affected countries, net private capital inflows constituted 6.3 percent of GDP in 1995, and 5.8 percent of GDP in 1996. They then abruptly reversed (after being positive in the first half of 1997) to a negative 2.0 percent of GDP in 1997 and 5.2

percent of GDP in 1998—a swing of more than 10 percent of GDP in a very short span of time.

Why did capital inflows rise and then fall so sharply? And why did the crises happen in such rapid succession in 1997? What determined the timing of the first (Thai) crisis? Why did the crisis spread to neighboring countries? And why were some economies hard hit into crisis while others (such as Taiwan) were able to weather their difficulties with much less strain and no crisis? As economists have debated this question, two broad schools of thought have emerged. On one hand, there are those who believe that economic fundamentals (the exchange rate regime, the rate of domestic credit expansion, or other key policy parameters) were at fault in the crisis-affected countries. On the other hand, there are those who believe that investors are, at least to a degree, irrational, subject to "herd behavior" or otherwise changing behavior sharply in response to events little related to underlying economic prospects.

A second set of questions arises as to the differences between the 1990s crises and earlier, balance-of-payments crises, experienced by many developing countries. At a superficial level, the difference is obvious: In earlier years, balance-of-payments crises took place in countries with little or no capital mobility and largely inconvertible currencies. In the 1990s, by contrast, the fact that there was substantial capital mobility meant that capital flows were a major part of the payments crisis. Yet in fact, a second—perhaps even more important—difference resulted from capital mobility. That is, a change in the exchange rate (a universal part of the policy response to crisis) not only affected importers and exporters and their profitability contrasted with the producers of nontradable goods (such as wholesale and retail trade, construction, and domestic transportation), it also affected the balance sheets of the banks. Once banks (or major borrowers from the foreign banks) had liabilities denominated in foreign exchange, a change in the exchange rate almost inevitably meant that banks' liabilities rose more than their assets. Under these circumstances, when banking and financial systems were already weak, as was the case in many of the crisis-afflicted countries, the fact that there had to be a sizable change in the nominal exchange rate implied that the financial sector of the economy was greatly weakened.

The consequence was the "financial crises" of the 1990s. These crises combined the old-fashioned balance-of-payments crisis with new difficulties associated with a weakened financial system. Worse yet, recovery from crisis could not really begin until the banking system and financial sector were recapitalized, which in turn often required restructuring of the balance sheets of domestic producers. Any financial crisis—such as those in the United States (S&L crisis) in the late 1980s, in Sweden in 1992, and in Japan in 1997—creates major difficulties and challenges for policy makers;

so, too, does a balance-of-payments crisis. The interaction between the two, however, makes the crisis manyfold more difficult to resolve than were each to be faced alone.

In addition to questions concerning the role played by key policy variables in crisis, and the "rationality" of capital flows, the timing of the Asian crises raised another, related, question: that is, whether crises are contagious. Contagion itself could be rational or irrational: It could be rational if the onset of one crisis serves as a "signal" to market participants who cannot otherwise coordinate that a successful attack on another currency (where fundamentals are weakening but where any one individual getting out of the currency is likely to lose) is now possible; it would be irrational if market participants choose to get out of other countries (without regard to their fundamentals) once one country experiences a crisis.

One way or another, all of the papers in this volume address issues pertinent to understanding the macroeconomic dimensions of capital flows, the origins of the 1990s-style crises, the linkages between the foreign exchange variables and the financial variables, and the key questions associated with efforts to solve the crises.

The first several papers cover macroeconomic aspects of capital flows that are relevant for understanding the causes of crisis. The first paper, by Corsetti, Pesenti, and Roubini (CPR), directly addresses the relative importance of financial fragility and external imbalances in the Asian financial crises. In their view, weak fundamentals explain why countries went into a crisis. They contribute to rapidly growing literature on this subject by using "cross-variables." CPR thus find that large current-account deficits significantly increase the probability of a crisis when a country's reserves are low (but do not do so when they are high). They likewise find that real exchange rate appreciation, associated with large current-account deficits, is a significant fundamental. Even more significantly, their results suggest that neither current account deficits nor financial fragility alone seem to cause a financial crisis, but that the presence of a large current-account deficit combined with financial fragility does.

Measures of financial fragility, including the extent of nonperforming loans in the banking system prior to the crisis, and the estimated magnitude of the costs of restoring the banks to solvency are all statistically significant. As Corsetti, Pesenti, and Roubini note, however, "Per se, these results cannot discriminate across alternative explanations of currency crises based on self-fulfilling speculative attacks, as opposed to fundamental factors. They do, however, identify a set of variables that appear to enhance the vulnerability of an economy to a crisis."

In the second paper, Aaron Tornell also examines the linkages between currency and financial crises, and then examines the similarities between the Asian crises of 1997 to the "tequila" crisis in Mexico at the end of 1994. Tornell starts by noting that there are two issues: On one hand, there is a question as to which countries are hit by crises; on the other hand, there is a question as to the timing of the crisis. He recognizes that forecasting the timing of any crisis is difficult, but seeks to ask whether, once there is a crisis somewhere, fundamentals determine which countries are affected.

He finds that countries with "sound fundamentals" (real exchange rates that have not appreciated, the strength of the banking system, and the liquidity of the central bank) are not likely to be vulnerable to crises even when one occurs somewhere else in the world. However, countries whose fundamentals are weaker are vulnerable to crisis, in the sense that if one country is in crisis, the other countries will be attacked if investors turn pessimistic (as they may after a crisis has occurred in one country). Tornell notes that this conclusion implies that, once fundamentals are weak, the risk of crisis is linked to investors' expectations. To the extent that those expectations shift abruptly, countries may experience crisis. Insofar as investors' expectations cannot be explained, the timing of crises cannot be explained.

Two papers examine the role of bank lending in contagion. In the first, Kaminsky and Reinhart calculate the conditional and unconditional probabilities of crisis based on the usual economic variables but including the existence of crisis elsewhere. They conclude that contagion is more regional than global; i.e., that if an Asian country experiences a crisis, other Asian countries are more likely to be attacked than Latin American countries. They also conclude that susceptibility to contagion increases rapidly as more countries go into crisis: If only one country has a crisis, the likelihood of contagion is reasonably small; if two countries are in crisis, however, the odds of contagion increase dramatically. Kaminsky and Reinhart also examined the extent to which trade ties and financial ties between a crisis country and other countries affected the likelihood of crisis in the other countries. They found that close financial ties are more likely to result in contagion than close trade ties. This was the case with Argentina and Mexico, where trade links are very small while financial links are significant, and between Thailand and Indonesia, where the same pattern prevails.

In his paper, Shin-ichi Fukuda attempts to understand the behavior and role of banks and bank lending in the crisis. He develops a model of asymmetric information, in which borrowers know whether they are creditworthy but lenders cannot distinguish between them until there is some difference in their behavior. Lenders can lend for either one or two periods, and bank monitoring can reveal the creditworthy borrowers after one period. In Fukuda's model, creditworthy borrowers seek to reveal their own type, while other borrowers attempt to conceal theirs. The result, in the model, is that there is a trade-off: Efforts to borrow short-term on the part of creditworthy borrowers, and monitoring of loans by banks, can increase the efficiency of the financial system. However, there is also a risk of liquidity problems, and a higher proportion of debt with short maturity increases the likelihood of significant costs associated with periods of illiquidity. As Fukuda recognizes, his model provides one step in understanding bank behavior and the possibility that there can be more than one equilibrium position (and therefore that there can be a rapid shift between good and bad states).

The next two papers examine various aspects of exchange rate behavior as they related to the crises. It was already seen that both Corsetti, Pesenti, and Roubini and Tornell found that vulnerability to crisis was increased with an appreciating real exchange rate and a widening current account deficit. This calls into question the role of the exchange rate regime in making countries vulnerable to crisis. Certainly, the Asian and Tequila crises came about after a substantial period during which the exchange rate regime had had a de facto dollar peg, at least implicitly. On one hand, the dollar peg made the currency more overvalued as the yen depreciated relative to the dollar; on the other hand, for countries whose rate of inflation was above that of the United States and Japan, there was real appreciation on that account.

Moreover, the dollar peg system seemed to reduce currency risk for investors, and thus attracted large capital inflows. These inflows in turn resulted in "overheating" of the Asian economies or a large accumulation of short-term liabilities which made the countries vulnerable for a crash. A central question is whether an alternative currency regime would have made the Asian economies less vulnerable to crisis.[1]

The first of the papers that bear on this issue is by Ogawa and Sun. They first used actual data to estimate regression equations with instrumental variables such as the interest rate, the exchange rate, the rate of export growth, and the rate of change in stock prices to estimate capital flows. They then developed a simulation model to estimate what would have happened under alternative exchange rate regimes in which exchange rates moved as a weighted average of the yen and dollar rates (i.e., had adopted a currency basket peg). According to their model, capital inflows into Thailand and Korea would have been significantly reduced in the period from 1986 to 1997 under the currency basket, and those to Indonesia would have declined somewhat. Interestingly, although both Japanese investors (in yen) and American investors (in dollars) are sensitive to exchange rate swings, American investors appear to respond more strongly, so that in the period when the dollar was constant in nominal terms, foreign investment was attracted to a greater extent than it would have been under a currency basket system. Ogawa and Sun conclude by noting that,

1. There is a growing consensus among the policy making community that the only defensible exchange rate regimes are floating or dollarization. There is, however, less empirical evidence to support this conclusion than would be desirable, and the papers in this volume represent significant progress in providing empirical support for that proposition.

although the exchange rate regime was a factor inducing large capital inflows, other factors (such as deregulation of capital flows) may also have contributed, and that further research is called for to estimate the importance of these factors in surges of capital inflows.

The second paper is by Takagi and Esaka, who investigate how monetary authorities responded to large and rapidly increasing capital inflows. They note that foreign direct investment constituted about half of the East Asian capital inflows in the 1980s, but that by the 1990s, short-term borrowing by banks and corporations was the bulk of capital inflows in most countries (Malaysia was an exception) and were, as already noted, very large. While there are significant benefits to capital inflows, they can impose costs because rapid monetary expansion, inflationary pressures, real exchange rate appreciation, and widening current account deficits can result. And, of course, large outstanding indebtedness increases vulnerability to capital outflows.

Takagi and Esaka question the extent to which monetary management in the capital-receiving countries was appropriate. They note that official foreign exchange reserves rose significantly during the period of capital inflow, indicating that the current account deficits were smaller than the capital inflows by about a third. This means that there was sterilization of capital inflows, which in turn implies that monetary policy was tighter, and interest rates higher, than they otherwise would have been. That, in turn, was undoubtedly a factor in increasing the size of the inflows, contrasted with what they would have been at lower interest rates. Takagi and Esaka then estimate a quarterly model for determinants of monetary aggregates. They conclude that capital inflows into the Asian countries were significantly larger than they would have been in the absence of sterilization.

One economy that escaped the crisis was that of Hong Kong, although the currency was attacked during the summer of 1998. Hong Kong has had a currency board under which there is no independent monetary policy and the exchange rate is rigidly fixed. Since the Asian crisis, many observers—noting the difficulties associated with the fixed nominal exchange rate, or dollar peg, system—have advocated currency boards. In their paper, Kwan, Lui, and Cheng analyze how the currency board system in Hong Kong functioned. They start by examining the policies used by the Hong Kong Monetary Authority (HKMA), which started with a period during which it operated according to set rules. It then switched to a regime in which it used more discretion. Now, finally, it has switched back to a rules-based regime.

In their paper, Kwan, Lui, and Cheng provide a valuable history of the operations of the HKMA and, in addition, attempt to measure the credibility of the system in each of the periods, using methods developed in the target zone literature. They find that the HKMA was far more credible in the period during which it followed rules than when there was more discretion in its operations, and conclude that the use of discretion at the time of the Asian crisis contributed to the erosion of market confidence and made a speculative attack on the currency more likely. While results for Hong Kong would not necessarily hold for other countries if they were to adopt currency boards, the paper provides valuable insights into the functioning of the Hong Kong board.

One of the issues arising out of the financial crisis has been differences in types of capital flows. As suggested by the Fukuda model (and in much other work), many analysts have been suspicious of bank lending—especially short-term bank lending—as making countries much more vulnerable to crisis than they would be if capital inflows were more heavily weighted toward foreign direct investment (FDI), long-term bonds, and equity investments. Three papers at the conference addressed aspects of these issues. Many policy makers and analysts have argued that FDI and equity investments are much less susceptible to sudden departures in times of crisis, and thus are much less volatile than short-term capital flows and especially bank lending.

In his paper, Fukao analyzes the behavior of manufacturing subsidiaries of Japanese companies located in Asia, in an attempt to ascertain how these firms (which were presumably either established by the parent company through FDI or acquired through equity investment) behaved during the crisis. He finds that, in the months following the Asian crisis, Japanese subsidiaries did not reduce employment, although they did not undertake any further new investments. The greater the profitability of the parent company, the greater the likelihood that a subsidiary would maintain employment, suggesting that subsidiaries receive support from their overseas owners during periods of crisis, which may offset part of the impact of the crisis on the economy in which the subsidiary operates. Fukao also found that subsidiaries with strong export positions were able to fare quite well after crises, especially contrasted with subsidiaries whose sales were directed largely toward domestic markets. These latter experienced much more difficulty than their trade-oriented counterparts.

In their paper, Razin, Sadka, and Yuen (RSY) raise some questions about the relative superiority of FDI. They note that FDI has two types of effects. It is beneficial in that it can promote technology transfer, permit the importation of new intermediate goods, and lead to more competition. RSY also point to the stability of FDI in times of financial crisis, and note that FDI may constitute the only remaining link between domestic and international capital markets in times of crisis. However, if there are asymmetric information issues resulting from FDI, those effects can—in their model—result in underperformance of the domestic equity market and thus offset part or all of the benefits of FDI.

In their model, this result comes about because FDI combines foreign and domestic savings, and gives managerial control and inside information about firms' prospects to foreigners (in the firms in which they have invested). With their inside information, foreigners keep equity in firms with good prospects but sell off equity in firms that are likely to be less profitable. Domestic residents do not have insider information, but because of adverse selection their average returns on investment are smaller than they would be if they could choose across the entire range of firms. RSY then proceed to develop a simulation model to attempt to quantify the relative magnitude of the beneficial and the distorting effects of FDI. They find that, for plausible values of the parameters, it is possible that the adverse selection problem may dominate.

In addition to the types of evidence brought to bear on capital flows in the papers already discussed, issues arise with respect to individual countries. In many ways, South Korea's crisis was the most surprising of them all: The country had had an outstanding record of economic growth and rising living standard continuously since 1960. Exports had grown from miniscule levels to make South Korea one of the leading exporters in the world; savings rates had risen; the government budget had been balanced; and inflation had been tamed.

With that enviable track record, researchers have focused a great deal of effort on analyzing the Korean experience. The final paper in the volume examines capital inflows and their role in the crisis from the perspective of the Korean economy. Dongchul Cho and Kiseok Hong try to assess the relative importance of internal factors as contrasted with the external environment (and especially the crisis that had already engulfed Indonesia, Malaysia, and Thailand) in triggering the crisis in South Korea. Cho and Hong examine the various factors that are regarded as important in the fundamentals and in contagion. They conclude that the crises in other countries weakened the Korean economy, but that they alone could not have caused the crisis. Instead, Cho and Hong believe, Korean economic policies, especially in the financial sector, were weaker than was generally perceived. Moreover, they assert that Korean investors believed that the government would bail out the *chaebol,* and continued acting on that belief until the crisis came. Foreigners, by contrast, were more skeptical that a bailout was certain, and hence were the ones who tried to get out of won and Korean investments first. When the first signs of imminent trouble appeared, policy responses were inappropriate and made the onset of the crisis. Cho and Hong thus see the Korean crisis as based on fundamentals, but made worse by contagion effects and policy mistakes in initial efforts to cope with it.

There is, of course, a great deal more to be learned about the interaction between foreign exchange and financial markets in crises, about the timing of crises, about the degree to which contagion can make even countries with sound policies vulnerable, and about the most promising policy approaches to mitigating crises. Yet despite the differences in emphasis across these papers, the reader will recognize a strong consensus on a number of things: the importance of fundamental economic policies, the role of financial and exchange-regime weaknesses in contributing to crisis, and the role of different types of capital flows in contributing to them. It is doubtful whether analysis can yield sufficiently conclusive results that crises can be a thing of the past. Lessons learned and research results such as these, however, can make future crises less severe when they do happen, and can make their onset less likely.

Reference

International Monetary Fund (IMF). 1999. *International capital markets: Developments, prospects, and key policy issues.* Washington, D.C.: IMF.

1

Fundamental Determinants
of the Asian Crisis
The Role of Financial Fragility
and External Imbalances

Giancarlo Corsetti, Paolo Pesenti, and Nouriel Roubini

1.1 Introduction

Episodes of speculative attacks on currencies in the 1990s (such as the 1992–93 crisis in the European Monetary System, the 1994 Mexican peso collapse, and especially the Asian turmoil of 1997–98) have generated a considerable—and finely balanced—debate on whether currency and financial instability should be attributed to arbitrary shifts in market expectations and confidence, rather than to weaknesses in the state of economic fundamentals.[1] Yet, advocates of both the "fundamentalist" and the "nonfundamentalist" views agree in principle that a deteriorating macroeco-

Giancarlo Corsetti is professor of economics at the University of Rome III, visiting professor at Yale University, and research fellow of the CEPR. Paolo Pesenti is senior economist at the Federal Reserve Bank of New York and a faculty research fellow of the National Bureau of Economic Research. Nouriel Roubini is professor of economics at the Stern School of Business, New York University, and a research associate of the National Bureau of Economic Research.

The authors wish to thank Takatoshi Ito, Anne Krueger, Carmen Reinhart, Aaron Tornell, one anonymous referee, and participants at the tenth annual NBER–East Asia Seminar on Economics for helpful comments and suggestions. Michele Cavallo and Scott Nicholson have provided excellent research assistance. Giancarlo Corsetti acknowledges financial support from Ministero dell'Universitae della Ricerca Scientifica e Tecnologica (MURST). The views expressed here are those of the authors, and do not necessarily reflect those of the Federal Reserve Bank of New York, the Federal Reserve System, or any other institution with which the authors are affiliated.

1. Among recent studies focusing on the large-scale speculative episodes in the 1990s before the Asian crisis, see Eichengreen and Wyplosz (1993) and Buiter, Corsetti, and Pesenti (1998a, b) on the European Monetary System crisis of 1992–93, and Sachs, Tornell, and Velasco (1996) on the Mexican peso crisis of 1994. A number of recent contributions on financial and balance-of-payments crises provide a discussion of the issues introduced in this paper—among others, see Dornbusch, Goldfajn, and Valdes (1995), Milesi Ferretti and Razin (1996), Mishkin (1997), Kaminsky, Lizondo, and Reinhart (1998), and Roubini and Wachtel (1998).

nomic outlook increases the degree to which an economy is vulnerable to a crisis.

The problematic economic and financial conditions in Southeast Asia in the years preceding the crisis have been documented in a number of recent studies (including our own contribution in Corsetti, Pesenti, and Roubini 1999c).[2] A widespread view holds that, regardless of whether the plunges in asset prices after the eruption of the crisis were driven by self-fulfilling expectations and panic, weak economic fundamentals were a crucial element in the genesis of the crisis and in its spread across countries. In support of this thesis, in this paper we present some preliminary formal evidence on the links between indicators of currency instability in 1997 and a number of indicators of real and financial fragility at the onset of the crisis. The proposed tests do not aim at discriminating among alternative explanations—rather, the goal here is to provide a set of baseline results to complement and integrate previous analyses pointing to the fragile state of the Southeast Asian economies before the eruption of the crisis.

One of the interesting pieces of evidence that corroborates a fundamental interpretation of the crisis is that well-performing Asian countries were spared its most pervasive consequences. Taiwan, Singapore, and Hong Kong were, relatively speaking, less affected by the regional turmoil. The Hong Kong currency parity was maintained despite strong speculative attacks. Taiwan and Singapore decided to let their currency float rather than lose reserves by attempting to stabilize the exchange rate; however, the depreciation rates of their currencies were modest, and, most importantly, these countries did not experience drastic reversals in market sentiment, financial panic, and large-scale debt crises.

The three countries that were only mildly affected by the turmoil shared a number of characteristics: First, their trade and current account balances were in surplus in the 1990s and their respective foreign debts were low (Taiwan was a net foreign creditor toward Bank for International Settlements [BIS] banks); second, they had a relatively large stock of foreign exchange reserves compared to the crisis countries; third, their financial and banking systems did not suffer from the same structural weaknesses and fragility observed in the crisis countries; and finally, they were perhaps less exposed to forms of so-called "crony capitalism"—that is, from the system of intermingled interests among financial institutions, political leaders, and the corporate elite characteristic of Korea, Indonesia, Malaysia, and Thailand.[3] China also falls in the category of countries that

---

2. A partial list of analyses of the Asian crisis includes Dornbusch (1998), Feldstein (1998), Goldstein (1998), IMF (1998), and Radelet and Sachs (1998). A large number of contributions on the crisis are available online on Nouriel Roubini's Asian Crisis homepage at www.stern.nyu.edu/~nroubini/asia/AsiaHomepage.html.

3. Note that the crisis of the Philippines, a country with better fundamentals and a less fragile financial system than other countries in the region, was also relatively contained. Even

were not subject to disruptive speculative pressure—the Chinese currency did not depreciate in 1997; however, the presence of constraints on capital mobility makes it difficult to compare the performance of this country with the others.

Conversely, as a group, the countries that came under attack in 1997 had the largest current account deficits throughout the 1990s. While the degree of real appreciation over the 1990s differed widely across Asian countries, with the important exception of Korea all the currencies that crashed in 1997 had experienced a real appreciation.

The literature has pointed out several factors that contributed to the deterioration of fundamentals in East Asia. The region experienced significant negative terms of trade shocks in 1996, with the fall in price of semiconductors and other goods. For most countries hit by the crisis, the long stagnation of the Japanese economy had led to a significant slowdown of export growth. Close to the onset of the crisis, the abortive Japanese recovery of 1996 was overshadowed by a decline in activity in 1997. Last but not least, the increasing weight of China in total exports from the region enhanced competitive pressures over the period.

On the financial side, a large body of evidence shows that the corporate, banking, and financial systems of the crisis countries were very fragile: poorly supervised, poorly regulated, and already in shaky conditions before the onset of the crisis (see, e.g., International Monetary Fund [IMF] 1998; Ito 1998; Organization for Economic Cooperation and Development [OECD] 1998; Pomerleano 1998). The evidence suggests a sustained lending boom in the Philippines, Thailand, and Malaysia—strikingly, these were also the first countries to be hit by currency speculation in 1997. It also suggests a severe mismatch between foreign liabilities and foreign assets of Asian banks and nonbank firms. Domestic banks borrowed heavily from foreign banks but lent mostly to domestic investors.[4]

By the end of 1996, a share of short-term foreign liabilities above 50 percent was the norm in the region. At the same time, the ratio between M2 and foreign reserves in most Asian countries was dangerously high: In the event of a liquidity crisis—with BIS banks no longer willing to roll over short-term loans—foreign reserves in Korea, Indonesia, and Thailand were insufficient to cover short-term liabilities, let alone to service interest payments and to repay the principal on long-term debt coming to maturity in the period. One could certainly hold the view that the creditors' panic in Korea and Indonesia resulted purely from a standard "collective action" problem faced by a large number of creditors in their deci-

---

though the exchange rate plunged and the stock market dropped by over 30 percent in 1997, this country did not experience the extent of the turmoil and financial panic that hit Korea, Thailand, Indonesia, and Malaysia.

4. On the role of moral hazard in generating such an overborrowing syndrome, see McKinnon and Pill (1996), Krugman (1998), and Corsetti, Pesenti, and Roubini (1999a).

sions whether to roll over existing credits or call in their loans (see, e.g., Chang and Velasco 1998, 2000). It should also be recognized that market reactions took place under conditions of extreme political uncertainty, low credibility of the existing governments, and skepticism about the direction of (and the commitment to) structural reforms.

Although Asian countries were characterized by very high savings rates throughout the 1990s, the deficiencies of their financial sectors placed a severe burden on the fiscal balances of the affected countries. Such costs represented an implicit fiscal liability not reflected by data on public deficits until the eruption of the crisis, but large enough to affect the sustainability of the precrisis current account imbalances. The size of this liability contributed to expectations of drastic, but uncertain, policy changes (a fiscal reform required to finance the costs of financial bailouts) and currency devaluations (as a result of higher recourse to seigniorage revenues) (see, e.g., Corsetti, Pesenti, and Roubini 1999b and Burnside, Eichenbaum, and Rebelo 1998).

This paper reports and discusses a number of tests of the empirical relevance of the set of macroeconomic factors recalled above. In our tests we compare the performance of all the Asian countries subject to pressures in 1997 with the performance of other emerging economies, for a total sample of twenty-four countries whose selection has been determined by data availability.[5]

The paper is organized as follows. In section 1.2, we present a summary of the analytical model that is the basis of the empirical tests in the paper. In section 1.3, we present the results of our empirical analysis. Next, in section 1.4, we elaborate on the role played by the banking-sector weaknesses and the financial distress of over-leveraged firms in explaining the financial crisis in Asia in the late 1990s. Section 1.5 concludes.

1.2   A Model of the Asian Crisis

After the outburst of the currency and financial crises in Southeast Asia in the summer of 1997, many observers noted that the traditional conceptual and interpretive schemes[6] did not appear, prima facie, to fit the data well and fell short in a number of dimensions.

One reason is the role of fiscal imbalances. At the core of "first-generation" (or "exogenous-policy") models of speculative attacks (á la Krugman 1979 and Flood and Garber 1984), the key factor explaining the loss of reserves that led to a crisis is the acceleration in domestic credit

---

5. The countries are Argentina, Brazil, Chile, China, Colombia, Czech Republic, Hong Kong, Hungary, India, Indonesia, Jordan, Korea, Malaysia, Mexico, Pakistan, Peru, the Philippines, Poland, Singapore, Sri Lanka, Taiwan, Thailand, Turkey, and Venezuela.
6. See Buiter, Corsetti, and Pesenti (1998a), Calvo (1998), Calvo and Vegh (1999), Cavallari and Corsetti (1996), and Flood and Marion (1998) for recent surveys.

expansion related to the monetization of fiscal deficits. In the case of Southeast Asia, the precrisis budget balances of the countries suffering from speculative attacks were either in surplus or limited deficit.

In "second generation" (or "endogenous-policy") models of currency crisis, governments rationally choose—on the basis of their assessment of costs and benefits in terms of social welfare—whether to maintain a fixed rate regime. A crisis can be driven by a worsening of domestic economic fundamentals, or can be the result of self-validating shifts in expectations in the presence of multiple equilibria,[7] provided that the fundamentals are weak enough to push the economy in the region of parameters where self-validating shifts in market expectations can occur as rational events. The indicators of weak macroeconomic performance typically considered in the literature focus on output growth, employment, and inflation. In the Asian economies prior to the 1997 crisis, however, GDP growth rates were very high and unemployment and inflation rates quite low.

In Corsetti, Pesenti, and Roubini (1999b) we have suggested a formal interpretive scheme that, while revisiting the classical models, brings forward new elements of particular relevance for the analysis of the 1997–98 events. Specifically, we have analyzed financial and currency crises as interrelated phenomena, focusing on moral hazard as the common factor underlying the twin crises.[8]

At the core of our model is the consideration that, counting on future bailout interventions, weakly regulated private institutions have a strong incentive to engage in excessively risky investment. A bailout intervention can take different forms, but ultimately has a fiscal nature and directly affects the distribution of income and wealth between financial intermediaries and taxpayers: An implicit system of financial insurance is equivalent to a stock of contingent public liabilities that are not reflected by debt and deficit figures until the crisis occurs.

These liabilities may be manageable in the presence of firm-specific or even mild sector-specific shocks. They become a concern in the presence of cumulative sizable macroeconomic shocks, which fully reveal the financial fragility associated with excessive investment and risktaking. While fiscal deficits before a crisis are low, the bailouts represent a serious burden on the future fiscal balances. The currency side of a financial crisis can therefore be understood as a consequence of the anticipated fiscal costs of fi-

7. See, among others, Obstfeld (1986, 1994), Cole and Kehoe (1996), and Sachs, Tornell, and Velasco (1996). If investors conjecture that a country's government will eventually devalue its currency, their speculative behavior raises the opportunity cost of defending the fixed parity (for instance, by forcing a rise in short-term interest rates), thus triggering a crisis in a self-fulfilling way.

8. Among the contributions to the literature on the twin crises see, e.g., Velasco (1987), Kaminsky and Reinhart (1999), Goldfajn and Valdes (1997), and Chang and Velasco (1998, 2000). The role of moral hazard in the onset of the Asian crisis has been discussed by a number of authors; see, e.g., Krugman (1998), Greenspan (1998), and Fischer (1998).

nancial restructuring that generate expectations of a partial monetization of future fiscal deficits.

It is important to stress that the financial side of the crisis likely results in a severe fall in economic activity induced by the required structural adjustment. This is because implicit guarantees on investment projects lead the private sector to undertake projects that are not profitable. In the tradables sector, the scale and type of technology adopted are not optimal. In the nontraded sector, the profitability of investment suffers from changes in the real exchange rate accompanying the devaluation—changes that do not necessarily depend on the presence of nominal rigidities. Even in the absence of a self-fulfilling panic at the root of the crisis, the adjustment to the existing fundamental imbalance may take more than a correction in the level of the real exchange rate. The economy must pay the cumulative bill from distorted investment decisions in the past.

In addition, political uncertainty about the distribution of the costs from the crisis, and about their effect on the political stability of the leadership, may dramatically increase the risk premium charged by international and domestic investors—Indonesia being a striking example. A deterioration of the financial conditions may therefore deepen and prolong the recession accompanying the crisis. These considerations are important in assessing the relative merits of fundamentalist and nonfundamentalists views of the Southeast Asian events. The first view is not necessarily associated with a quick recovery after a devaluation, since the correction of fundamental imbalances due to moral hazard takes more than a relative price change.

In assessing the role of moral hazard in a financial crisis we should note that investment-distorting expectations of a future bailout need not be based on an explicit promise or policy by the government. Bailouts can be rationally anticipated by both domestic and foreign agents even when no public insurance scheme is in place and the government explicitly disavows future interventions and guarantees in favor of the corporate and banking sectors. In his celebrated analysis of currency and financial crises of the early 1980s, Carlos Diaz-Alejandro (1985) stresses the time-consistency problem inherent in moral hazard:

> Whether or not deposits are explicitly insured, the public expects governments to intervene to save most depositors from losses when financial intermediaries run into trouble. Warnings that intervention will not be forthcoming appear to be simply not believable. (374)

This is because no ex ante announcement by policy makers can convince the public that, ex post (that is, in the midst of a generalized financial turmoil), the government will cross its arms and let the financial system proceed toward its debacle. Agents will therefore expect a bailout regardless of "laissez-faire commitments"—in the words of Diaz-Alejandro—"which a misguided minister of finance or central bank president may occasionally utter in a moment of dogmatic exaltation" (379).

To summarize, in our model, private agents act under the presumption that there exist public guarantees on corporate and financial investment, so that the return on domestic assets is perceived as implicitly insured against adverse circumstances. To the extent that foreign creditors are willing to lend against future bailout revenue, unprofitable projects and cash shortfalls are refinanced through external borrowing. Such a process translates into an unsustainable path of current account deficits.

While public deficits need not be high before a crisis, the eventual refusal of foreign creditors to refinance the country's cumulative losses forces the government to step in and guarantee the outstanding stock of external liabilities. To satisfy solvency, the government must then undertake appropriate domestic fiscal reforms, possibly involving recourse to seigniorage revenues through money creation. Speculation in the foreign exchange market, driven by expectations of inflationary financing, causes a collapse of the currency and brings the event of a financial crisis forward in time.

Financial and currency crises thus become indissolubly interwoven in an emerging economy characterized by weak cyclical performances, low foreign exchange reserves, and financial deficiencies, eventually resulting in high shares of nonperforming loans. Our empirical exercise below is cast within this conceptual framework. Adopting the methodology suggested in previous studies (e.g., Eichengreen, Rose, and Wyplosz 1996; Sachs, Tornell, and Velasco 1996; Kaminsky, Lizondo, and Reinhart 1998), in the next sections we first construct a crisis index as a measure of speculative pressure on a country's currency. Then, we compute a set of indexes of financial fragility, external imbalances, official reserves adequacy, and fundamental performance. Finally, we report the results of the regressions of the crisis index on the above indexes.[9]

1.3 A Preliminary Empirical Assessment

1.3.1 The Crisis Index

Our crisis index (IND) is a weighted average of the percentage rate of exchange rate depreciation relative to the U.S. dollar—if such depreciation can be deemed as abnormal, as explained below—and the percentage rate of change in foreign reserves between the end of December 1996 and the end of December 1997.[10] The logic underlying the index IND is quite

9. Recent empirical studies of the causes of the Asian crisis include Berg and Pattillo (1999) and Alba et al. (1999).

10. This section is based on Corsetti, Pesenti, and Roubini (1999a). The weights assigned to exchange rate and reserves changes in IND are, respectively, 0.75 and 0.25. For the purpose of sensitivity analysis, we consider alternative crisis indexes with different weights and find that the choice of the weight coefficients is not crucial to our results. Also, alternative tests with different samples of shorter size provide similar results. All tests are available upon request.

simple. A speculative attack against a currency is signaled either by a sharp depreciation of the exchange rate or by a contraction in foreign reserves which prevents a devaluation.[11] We present the values for IND in table 1.1: A large negative value for IND corresponds to a high devaluation rate and/or a large fall in foreign reserves, i.e. a more severe currency crisis.[12]

In evaluating the crisis index we need to control for the fact that, in some countries, a high rate of depreciation in 1997 may reflect a past trend rather than severe speculative pressures. For example, the fact that the Turkish currency depreciated by over 50 percent in 1997 should not be interpreted as a signal of crisis, as chronically high inflation rates in Turkey over the 1990s have been associated with normally high depreciation rates.[13]

There is no obvious way to purge the sample of the effects of trend depreciations not associated with a crisis. In this study, we take the following approach: If a currency in 1997 has fallen in value by less than its average depreciation rate in the 1994–1996 period, we consider this as being part of a trend depreciation and set the 1997 depreciation rate equal to zero in constructing the index.[14] In our sample, such a screening procedure leads to a significant resizing of the crisis index for two high-depreciation countries: Turkey and Venezuela.

As table 1.1 shows, in 1997 the countries that appear to have been hit by the most severe crises are, in order, Thailand, Malaysia, Korea, Indonesia, the Philippines, and the Czech Republic.[15] Among Asian countries, the currencies of Singapore and Taiwan were also moderately devalued in 1997, but these two countries were not subject to such extensive and dramatic financial turmoil as that affecting other East Asian economies. Conversely, outside the Asian region, the Czech Republic appears as a crisis country[16] because its currency, which had been pegged since 1992,

11. While, of course, an increase in domestic interest rates may also signal a frustrated speculative attack, our crisis index excludes changes in interest rates. This is because an increase in interest rates in the presence of speculative pressures is highly correlated with nonsterilized foreign exchange intervention, leading to a fall in reserves.

12. In principle, IMF official loans should be subtracted from official reserves in computing the index IND. However, our results would not significantly change if we accounted for IMF disbursements in 1997.

13. Note that Turkey exhibited a satisfactory economic performance in 1997, with GDP growing over 6 percent and its stock market being a leading performer among emerging countries.

14. Other authors use a different approach to the same problem. For example, Sachs, Tornell, and Velasco (1996) control for the variance of the exchange rate and reserves in the last ten years.

15. Latin American countries included in the sample were hit by crises in 1994–95. We refer the reader to the paper by Tornell in this volume for an analysis of the 1994–95 episode and a comparison with our results.

16. The Czech Republic shared many symptoms with the Asian crisis countries: a fixed exchange rate regime maintained for too long, a severe real appreciation, a dramatic worsen-

Table 1.1 Percentage or Percentage Change

Country	Crisis Index (IND)	Real Appreciation (RER)	Current Account (CA)	Lending Boom (LB)	Nonperforming Loans (NPL)	Reserves Adequacy (M2/reserves)	(M1/reserves)	(STD/reserves)
Argentina	4.9	38.6	-1.9	16.5	9.4	351.0	108.2	147.8
Brazil	-0.5	75.8	-2.0	-26.3	5.8	345.9	66.8	78.3
Chile	-1.4	37.5	-1.7	24.1	1.0	188.2	41.9	53.3
China	7.6	4.9	0.8	6.9	14.0	828.9	334.0	26.7
Columbia	-9.1	26.6	-5.0	35.0	4.6	209.4	104.3	73.9
Czech Republic	-19.5	50.7	-4.4	22.7	12.0	356.9	139.5	42.9
Hong Kong	5.7	31.8	-1.6	25.5	3.4	411.9	34.2	20.0
Hungary	-1.6	-38.8	-6.5	-56.5	3.2	167.1	83.3	52.3
India	5.7	-29.1	-1.2	-2.3	17.3	860.0	296.5	37.2
Indonesia	-38.3	17.5	-2.9	9.6	12.9	614.8	114.3	188.9
Jordan	9.8	6.1	-4.5	1.4	6.0	437.8	141.4	33.9
Korea	-38.6	11.1	-2.5	11.2	8.4	665.4	147.6	217.0
Malaysia	-38.8	19.9	-6.4	31.1	9.9	364.8	115.6	45.3
Mexico	10.9	8.9	-2.7	-10.9	12.5	444.8	129.3	142.9
Pakistan	11.4	-2.0	-5.3	-3.7	17.5	3,369.9	1,822.8	399.0
Peru	0.7	-20.4	-6.2	177.2	5.1	123.6	32.4	61.6
The Philippines	-29.8	38.9	-4.6	150.8	14.0	465.6	91.8	849.3
Poland	3.5	30.0	0.9	38.5	6.0	262.3	95.9	14.2
Singapore	-15.7	4.7	16.5	16.7	4.0	103.5	25.0	20.0
Sri Lanka	-1.0	17.7	-5.7	28.4	5.0	236.4	72.9	26.8
Taiwan	-11.4	-7.0	2.9	43.4	3.9	575.1	141.0	22.8
Thailand	-47.8	20.0	-7.2	58.0	13.3	380.5	43.3	121.5
Turkey	4.3	-16.1	-0.1	43.2	0.8	302.6	48.9	76.0
Venezuela	4.9	2.2	6.8	-51.5	3.8	102.4	58.5	28.2

Note: See appendix for explanation of variables.

suffered a severe speculative attack in the spring of 1997, leading to a devaluation.[17]

1.3.2 Indexes of Financial Fragility

Measures of banking system weakness are provided by the stock of nonperforming loans as a share of total assets in 1996 (NPL)[18] and an index of "lending boom" (LB), defined as the growth of commercial bank loans to the private sector (as percentage of GDP) in the period 1990–96. The latter is an indirect measure of financial fragility suggested by Sachs, Tornell, and Velasco (1996).[19] Both variables (NPL and LB) are reported in table 1.1.

We adopt two indicators of domestic financial fragility. The first one encompasses the information in both NPL (nonperforming loans) and LB (lending boom) and is defined as follows: If the sign of the lending boom in the 1990s is positive, we assign to the new indicator NPLB the original value of NPL; if the lending boom in the 1990s is negative, we set NPLB equal to zero.[20]

$$NPLB = \begin{cases} NPL & \text{if } LB > 0 \\ 0 & \text{if } LB \leq 0 \end{cases}$$

---

ing of the current account, and a weak banking system with large shares of nonperforming loans.

17. Note that we limit our sample to devaluations in 1997, in the attempt to test whether the devaluations during that year can be explained by fundamentals. During 1998, a number of the crisis countries in Asia (namely Korea, Thailand, and Indonesia) experienced in some degree a currency appreciation. However, such appreciations were the result of macroeconomic adjustment policies and the implementation of structural reforms. Also, while some currencies appreciated relative to their bottom values in early 1998, through 1999 they remained weak relative to their precrisis levels. Note also that some countries in the sample experienced currency and financial crises in 1998 and 1999, outside our sample period. Specifically, Brazil was eventually forced to devalue its currency in January 1999 while Pakistan experienced severe currency and banking distress in 1998. The case of Pakistan fits our model of the crisis very well: Already in 1997 this country had a very fragile banking system with a large stock of nonperforming loans and a large current account deficit. Brazil, instead, did not experience a banking crisis but had an overvalued currency and a large current account deficit, two factors that enter significantly in our empirical analysis. Also note that our sample does not include two countries, Russia and Ecuador, that were hit by currency and banking crises in 1998–99. Adding these two countries to an extended sample would have strengthened the results of our empirical analysis.

18. In the appendix we describe in detail our methodology to estimate the series NPL. As a caveat, NPL measures essentially banking sector nonperforming loans, and may therefore fail to account appropriately for financial distress in countries where the heart of the problems in the initial stage of the crisis was nonperforming loans among nonbank intermediaries (such as Thailand and Korea).

19. These authors argue that such a measure is a proxy for financial fragility as the quality of bank loans is likely to deteriorate significantly—and a large fraction is likely to become nonperforming—when bank lending grows at a rapid pace in a relatively short period of time.

20. The logic of the NPLB variable is straightforward: Nonperforming loans represent a source of severe tension only when observed in tandem with excessive bank lending that enhances the vulnerability of the country to a crisis.

As regards the second indicator, note that according to the theoretical model presented in Corsetti, Pesenti, and Roubini (1999b) the vulnerability of a country to currency and financial crises increases with the implicit fiscal costs of financial bailouts. Under the maintained hypothesis that the time series of NPL provides information about the size of the overall bailout in the event of a crisis, we can obtain a statistical proxy for the associated fiscal costs by taking the ratio of nonperforming loans to GDP in 1996. This series is denoted NPLY and is defined as the product of NPL and commercial bank loans to the private sector as a share of GDP in 1996. This variable allows us properly to assess the performance of those countries with low ratios of bank loans to GDP but relatively large nonperforming loans as a share of banking assets (e.g. India and Pakistan). In those countries, the contingent fiscal liabilities related to bailout costs are smaller relative to countries with a similar NPL, but have a higher ratio of bank lending to GDP.

1.3.3   Indexes of Current Account Imbalances

Table 1.1 reports the average current account balance as a share of GDP in the 1994–1996 period (CA) and the real exchange rate appreciation in the 1990s (RER). There is no simple way to assess when a current account balance is sustainable (e.g., when it is driven by investment in sound projects) and when it is not (e.g., when it reflects a structural loss of competitiveness), or to what extent a real appreciation is due to misalignment as opposed to an appreciation of the fundamental equilibrium real exchange rate. However, the consensus in the empirical literature on crisis episodes is that the *combination* of a sizable current account deficit and a significant real appreciation represents a worrisome signal of external imbalance.

Consistent with this view, we construct an index of current account imbalance, CAI, defined as follows: If the rate of real exchange rate appreciation is above a given threshold T, CAI is equal to the current account balance (as a share of GDP); if the real appreciation is below the threshold (or there is a real depreciation), CAI is set equal to zero.[21]

$$
\text{CAI} = \begin{cases} \text{CA} & \text{if RER appreciates by more than } T \\ & (T = 10\%) \\ 0 & \text{otherwise} \end{cases}
$$

1.3.4   Indexes of Foreign Reserves Adequacy
and Fundamentals Performance

Other things being equal, the vulnerability of a country to a currency crisis is higher when reserves are low relative to some measure of domestic liquid assets or short-term foreign debt. To assess the role played by re-

---

21. In the tables, we present regression results for the 10 percent threshold, but similar results are obtained for the zero threshold.

serves availability, we construct three different measures: the ratio of M1 to foreign exchange reserves (M1/reserves), the ratio of M2 to foreign reserves (M2/reserves), and the ratio of the foreign debt service burden (i.e., short-term foreign debt plus interest payments on foreign debt) to foreign reserves (STD/reserves). The values of these variables are reported in table 1.1.

To test for the joint role of fundamentals and foreign reserves in determining a currency crisis, we classify the countries in our sample as being *strong* or *weak* with regard to these two dimensions using dummy variables. Regarding foreign reserves, we use a broad classification according to which a country is strong if the ratio of M2 to reserves is in the lowest quartile of the sample. The resulting dummy variable for low reserves, $D2^{LR}$, is defined as

$$D2^{LR} = \begin{cases} 1 & \text{if M2/reserves above lowest sample quartile} \\ 0 & \text{otherwise.} \end{cases}$$

Similar dummies are created by replacing M2/reserves with M1/reserves and STD/reserves; such dummy variables are labelled $D1^{LR}$ and $D3^{LR}$.

In regard to fundamentals, we focus on current account imbalances and financial fragility. Countries are classified as being strong or weak according to the scheme

$$D^{WF} = \begin{cases} 1 & \text{if either CAI in highest sample quartile} \\ & \text{or NPLB in lowest sample quartile} \\ 0 & \text{otherwise.} \end{cases}$$

A similar dummy can be obtained by replacing NPLB with NPLY.[22]

1.3.5 Testing for the Role of Fundamentals Imbalances in the Crisis

Financial Fragility and External Imbalances

The results of the regression of IND on CAI and NPLB are shown in column 1 of table 1.2. The coefficients of the two regressors have the expected sign and are statistically significant at the 5 percent level: Both a large current account deficit associated with a real appreciation and a larger rate of nonperforming loans associated with a lending boom worsen the crisis index. In columns 2–4 we interact the two regressors with the dummies for low reserves. The coefficients β_2 and β_3 measure the effects of CAI and NPLB on the crisis index in countries with high reserves ($D^{LR} = 0$); conversely, the sums of the coefficients $\beta_2 + \beta_4$ and $\beta_3 + \beta_5$

22. In this case, the dummy variable would be equal to zero for countries with our index of current account imbalance (CAI) in the highest quartile of the sample, or with a rate of nonperforming loans as a share of GDP, i.e., NPLY, in the lowest quartile of the sample; it would be equal to 1 otherwise.

Table 1.2   Explaining the Crisis Index: Basic Regressions

Estimated Coefficient and Summary Statistic	Independent Variable	Regression with (1)	Regression with M2/reserves (2)	Regression with M1/reserves (3)	Regression with STD2/reserves (4)
β_1	constant	6.877	7.073	7.437	5.324
		(3.755)	(4.094)	(3.956)	(3.552)
β_2	CAI	3.768	0.849	2.210	0.569
		(1.254)	(2.869)	(3.677)	(1.971)
β_3	NPLB	−1.338	−2.888	−2.805	−0.476
		(0.605)	(2.073)	(1.946)	(0.782)
β_4	CAI $\times$ D2^{LR}		3.613		
			(3.191)		
β_5	NPLB $\times$ D2^{LR}		1.761		
			(2.035)		
β_4	CAI $\times$ D1^{LR}			1.467	
				(3.982)	
β_5	NPLB $\times$ D1^{LR}			1.534	
				(1.929)	
β_4	CAI $\times$ D3^{LR}				3.571
					(2.564)
β_5	NPLB $\times$ D3^{LR}				−0.864
					(0.986)
Summary statistic					
$\overline{R}^2$		0.555	0.541	0.536	0.622
R^2		0.594	0.621	0.616	0.688
Addendum: Wald tests					
Null hypothesis		*p*-values	*p*-values	*p*-values	*p*-values
$\beta_2 + \beta_4 = 0$			0.005	0.018	0.023
$\beta_3 + \beta_5 = 0$			0.099	0.057	0.091

Notes: The dependent variable is the crisis index, IND. See appendix for definitions of variables. Standard errors are shown in parentheses.

measure the impact of fundamental imbalances on the crisis index in countries with low reserves ($D^{LR} = 1$).

Looking at the regression results shown in columns 2–4, the coefficients β_2 and β_3 are not significant on their own but only when reserves are low. In fact, for the case in which we use the reserve dummy $D2^{LR}$, based on M2 data, the Wald tests indicate that the hypotheses $\beta_2 + \beta_4 = 0$ and $\beta_3 + \beta_5 = 0$ can be rejected at the 1 percent and 10 percent significance levels.[23] Similar or stronger results are obtained when we use the other two low-reserves dummies, $D1^{LR}$ and $D3^{LR}$. As a whole, these results suggest that structural imbalances (current account deficits/currency appreciation and nonperforming loans/lending boom) play a role in the onset of a crisis to the extent that there is insufficient availability of foreign reserves—that is, in light of both fundamental and nonfundamental models of currency crises, low reserves enhance the vulnerability of the economy to speculative attacks.[24]

In table 1.3 we test whether the effects of current account imbalances CAI on the crisis index depend on weak fundamentals D^{WF} and low reserves $D2^{LR}$. Relative to column 2 of table 1.2, in column 1 of table 1.3 we consider an additional regressor, namely an interaction term equal to CAI times $D2^{LR}$ times D^{WF}. In this case, the sum of the coefficients $\beta_2 + \beta_4 + \beta_6$ captures the effects of current account imbalances on the crisis index in countries with low reserves and weak fundamentals. If $\beta_2 + \beta_4 + \beta_6$ is positive while $\beta_2 + \beta_4$ is not significantly different from zero, the crisis index worsens when a high-deficit country with an appreciated currency meets both weak-fundamentals and low-reserves criteria, but the crisis index does not respond to the reserves indicator if such a country is in the strong-fundamentals region. The results of the Wald tests show that $\beta_2 + \beta_4 + \beta_6$ is indeed significantly positive at the 1 percent significance level, while $\beta_2 + \beta_4$ is not significantly different from zero.[25]

Column 2 of table 1.3 includes a similar test for the role of nonperforming loans. Here we add an additional regressor to those of column 2 in table 1.2, which is an interaction term equal to NPLB times $D2^{LR}$ times D^{WF}. Thus, the sum of the coefficients $\beta_3 + \beta_5 + \beta_7$ captures the effects of nonperforming loans on the crisis index in countries that meet both low-reserves and weak-fundamentals criteria. Our tests show that $\beta_3 + \beta_5 + \beta_7$ is negative at the 5 percent significance level while $\beta_3 + \beta_5$ is not significantly different from zero. The crisis index depends on nonperforming loans in countries with weak fundamentals and weak reserves, but not in

---

23. Their p-values are 0.005 and 0.09, respectively.

24. As a caveat, even when coefficients have the right signs and are statistically significant, the relatively low R^2 of the regressions seems to suggest that the residuals may be large for specific countries; that is, a crisis was predicted but did not materialize, or was not predicted but did occur, according to the sign of the residual.

25. Note also that the coefficient on NPLB (β_3) is still significantly different from zero in this regression.

Table 1.3   Explaining the Crisis Index: The Role of Fundamentals and Reserves

Estimated Coefficient and Summary Statistic	Independent Variable	(1)	(2)	(3)
β_1	constant	−2.861	5.535	5.602
		(2.138)	(3.887)	(4.082)
β_2	CAI	0.841	0.762	0.766
		(2.946)	(2.694)	(2.771)
β_3	NPLB	−1.338	−2.569	−2.583
		(0.605)	(1.954)	(2.017)
β_4	CAI × D2^{LR}	2.851	1.118	1.559
		(6.650)	(3.274)	(6.293)
β_5	NPLB × D2^{LR}	1.769	2.448	2.446
		(2.091)	(1.945)	(2.000)
β_6	CAI × D2^{LR} × D^{WF}	0.834		−0.497
		(6.337)		(6.004)
β_7	NPLB × D2^{LR} × D^{WF}		−2.120	−2.131
			(1.123)	(1.164)
Summary statistic				
$\bar{R}^2$		0.516	0.596	0.572
R^2		0.621	0.684	0.683
Addendum: Wald tests				
Null hypothesis		*p*-values	*p*-values	*p*-values
$\beta_2 + \beta_4 = 0$		0.547	0.337	0.688
$\beta_2 + \beta_4 + \beta_6 = 0$		0.009		0.388
$\beta_3 + \beta_5 = 0$		0.146	0.883	0.875
$\beta_3 + \beta_5 + \beta_7 = 0$			0.017	0.026

Notes: The dependent variable is the crisis index, IND. See appendix for definitions of variables. Standard errors are shown in parentheses.

countries with strong fundamentals and weak reserves. The implication of these results is that a crisis need not be related to current account imbalances or bad loans per se: Such imbalances represent a source of severe tension only when they are observed in parallel with both fundamental *and* reserve weaknesses.[26]

Fiscal Implications of Financial Fragility

Next, in tables 1.4 and 1.5 we perform regressions similar to those in tables 1.2 and 1.3, but now we move our focus away from financial fragility and onto the role of the fiscal implications of financial fragility. We therefore substitute NPLB—the nonperforming loans ratio adjusted to account

26. In column 3 of table 1.3, we consider interactions of both CAI and NPLB with the dummies for weak fundamentals and low reserves. The results for NPLB are similar to those in column 2. For the current account, instead, we fail to reject the hypothesis that both $\beta_2 + \beta_4 + \beta_6$ and $\beta_2 + \beta_4$ are equal to zero. Formal tests such as the variance inflation test suggest that this is due to multicollinearity between the two interaction terms: When they both appear in a regression, the effects of CAI are swamped by those of NPLB.

Table 1.4   Explaining the Crisis Index: Fiscal Implications of Financial Fragility

Estimated Coefficient and Summary Statistic	Independent Variable	(1)	Regression with M2/reserves (2)	Regression with M1/reserves (3)	Regression with STD2/reserves (4)
β_1	constant	6.682	8.142	6.289	5.491
		(3.699)	(3.951)	(3.789)	(3.492)
β_2	CAI	4.156	2.288	−1.402	0.845
		(1.158)	(2.394)	(4.511)	(1.963)
β_3	NPLY	−1.630	−6.579	−4.817	−0.597
		(0.724)	(3.263)	(2.419)	(0.874)
β_4	CAI $\times$ D2^{LR}		2.594		
			(2.657)		
β_5	NPLY $\times$ D2^{LR}		5.133		
			(3.170)		
β_4	CAI $\times$ D1^{LR}			5.760	
				(4.660)	
β_5	NPLY $\times$ D1^{LR}			3.481	
				(2.497)	
β_4	CAI $\times$ D3^{LR}				3.487
					(2.530)
β_5	NPLY $\times$ D3^{LR}				−1.185
					(1.248)
Summary statistic					
$\overline{R}^2$		0.558	0.578	0.634	0.618
R^2		0.596	0.651	0.557	0.684
Addendum: Wald tests					
Null hypothesis		*p*-values	*p*-values	*p*-values	*p*-values
$\beta_2 + \beta_4 = 0$		0.001	0.001	0.002	0.016
$\beta_3 + \beta_5 = 0$		0.074	0.074	0.105	0.107

Notes: The dependent variable is the crisis index, IND. See appendix for definitions of variables. Standard errors are shown in parentheses.

for the lending boom—with NPLY—a more direct proxy for the implicit fiscal costs of banking sector bailouts.

The results are very similar and, if anything, even stronger than those obtained in tables 1.2 and 1.3. First, as table 1.4 column 1 shows, both NPLY and CAI are statistically significant regressors of the crisis index (at the 5 percent and 1 percent levels, respectively). Second, columns 2–4 of table 1.4 confirm that the effects of current account deficits are more relevant when reserves are low.[27] The results of columns 2–3 in table 1.4 are worth emphasizing. Note that the coefficient on NPLY, β_3, maintains the predicted sign and is statistically significant on its own at the 5 percent level. This suggests that nonperforming loans as a share of GDP—that is, as a measure of the intrinsic fiscal burden—affect the crisis index regardless of whether reserves are low or high.

In table 1.5 we present results of regressions equivalent to those in table 1.3, again using NPLY instead of NPLB. Once again, current account deficits and nonperforming loans matter if both reserves and fundamentals are weak.[28] However, observe that the coefficient on NPLY tends to maintain the expected sign and be statistically significant on its own, affecting the crisis index regardless of whether reserves are low or high, as well as regardless of whether fundamentals are weak.[29]

Real and Financial Weaknesses

Finally, we attempt to test whether direct measures of capital productivity have explanatory power as regressors of the crisis index. Conventional wisdom holds that borrowing from abroad is less dangerous for external sustainability if it finances new investment (leading to increased productive capacity and to higher future export receipts) rather than consumption (which implies lower saving). For these reasons, a current account deficit that is accompanied by a fall in savings rates is regarded as more problematic than a deficit accompanied by rising investment rates.

Underlying such conventional conclusions, however, is the implicit as-

---

27. The p-values on the Wald tests for $\beta_2 + \beta_4 = 0$ are 0.001, 0.002, and 0.016 in columns 2, 3, and 4, respectively, under the three different measures of low reserves.

28. These are the implications of the Wald tests on $\beta_2 + \beta_4 + \beta_6 = 0$ in column 1 and $\beta_3 + \beta_5 + \beta_7 = 0$ in columns 2 and 3. The failure to reject $\beta_2 + \beta_4 + \beta_6 = 0$ in column 3 is again due to multicollinearity between CAI times D2^{LR} times D^{WF}, and NPLY times D2^{LR} times D^{WF}.

29. To test for the robustness of our results we perform a number of other tests. First, we use two other indicators of crisis that give more weight to reserve losses relative to exchange rate depreciation; our qualitative results remain the same. As reported in tables 1.2–1.5, the results are also robust to the use of three alternative definitions of low reserves. Next, we test whether the significance of CAI is sensitive to the threshold for the real exchange rate appreciation; instead of a 10 percent trigger, we use a 0 trigger and obtain the same qualitative results. The significance of the two nonperforming loans measures, NPLB and NPLY, is also invariant with respect to modification of the definitions of these variables. All these results are available upon request.

Table 1.5   Explaining the Crisis Index: Bailout Costs, Fundamentals, and Reserves

Estimated Coefficient and Summary Statistic	Independent Variable	(1)	(2)	(3)
β_1	constant	9.060	3.754	3.677
		(4.233)	(2.731)	(3.026
β_2	CAI	2.438	1.570	1.557
		(2.439)	(1.577)	(1.633
β_3	NPLY	−6.912	−4.985	−4.957
		(3.347)	(2.164)	(2.263
β_4	CAI × D2^{LR}	−7.295	−2.753	−2.085
		(14.900)	(2.033)	(9.972
β_5	NPLY × D2^{LR}	5.425	5.287	5.267
		(3.246)	(2.081)	(2.160
β_6	CAI × D2^{LR} × D^{WF}	9.905		−0.685
		(14.676)		(10.005
β_7	NPLY × D2^{LR} × D^{WF}		−5.420	−5.436
			(1.060)	(1.117
Summary statistic				
$\bar{R}^2$		0.566	0.818	0.808
R^2		0.660	0.858	0.858
Addendum: Wald tests				
Null hypothesis		*p*-values	*p*-values	*p*-values
$\beta_2 + \beta_4 = 0$		0.741	0.424	0.957
$\beta_2 + \beta_4 + \beta_6 = 0$		0.001		0.633
$\beta_3 + \beta_5 = 0$		0.073	0.626	0.445
$\beta_3 + \beta_5 + \beta_7 = 0$		0.000		0.000

Notes: The dependent variable is the crisis index, IND1. See appendix for definitions of variables. Standard errors are shown in parentheses.

sumption that the return on investment is at least as high as the cost of the borrowed funds.[30] As evidence on the profitability of the investment projects, one can employ a standard measure of investment efficiency, the ICOR (incremental capital output ratio), defined as the ratio between the investment rate and the output growth rate. In Corsetti, Pesenti, and Roubini (1999c), we document that, for all the Asian countries except Indonesia and the Philippines, the ICOR had increased sharply in the 1993–96 period relative to the previous three years 1987–1992. This evidence suggests that the efficiency of investments in Southeast Asia was already falling in the four years prior to the 1997 crisis.

30. Also implicit is the assumption that high investment rates contribute to the enhancement of productive capacity in the traded sector. If the investment boom is confined to the nontraded sector (commercial and residential construction, as well as inward-oriented services), in terms of sustainability analysis the contribution of such investment projects to future trade surpluses—thus to the ability of the country to repay its external debt obligations—is limited to their indirect impact on the productivity of the traded sector. The two "implicit" assumptions above need not hold in the Asian case.

In Corsetti, Pesenti, and Roubini (1999a) we derive a measure of the ICOR for all the countries in our sample in the period 1993–1996. We then test for its significance in our basic regression model. We find that the ICOR variable is generally not significant; however, a simple transformation of the ICOR is significant in some regressions. We then define a new variable, which is equal to the original ICOR when the lending boom variable is positive, and is equal to zero when the lending boom is negative.[31] When we regress the crisis index on the modified ICOR variable and NPLY we find that both variables have the expected sign and are statistically significant (see Corsetti, Pesenti, and Roubini 1999a).

1.4   Financial Weaknesses and Emerging Market Crises

1.4.1   Banking and Currency Crises in the 1990s

Our interpretation of the Asian crisis focuses on the role played by weaknesses in the financial and banking system in triggering the currency crisis in 1997–98. It is worth stressing that other episodes of currency crises in the 1990s have been associated with banking crises. In the case of Mexico, for instance, recent work shows that the financial system was fragile well before the peso crisis of 1994 (see Krueger and Tornell 1999). Weak regulation and supervision, as well as an inadequate deposit safety net, were all elements leading to moral hazard in the banking system and to a surge in nonperforming loans well before the end of 1994. The weakness of the financial system was exacerbated by a poorly designed privatization program in the early 1990s. This evidence casts doubts on the thesis that the severe Mexican banking crisis emerging after the peso collapse was simply the *result* of the double shock of devaluation and high real interest rates in 1995 on the balance sheets of financial and corporate firms. The 1994 crisis was perhaps the last straw for an already weakened banking system, leading to a meltdown that is estimated to cost about 14–20 percent of GDP.

Currency depreciation was also associated with banking problems in the case of Europe in 1992–93. This is clearly visible in Scandinavian countries such as Sweden and Finland, where a severe banking crisis was emerging since the early 1990s. It is also apparent in Italy, where a fiscal retrenchment and the discontinuation of regional public investment projects made the banking system in the south vulnerable to the consequences

---

31. The idea here is that low capital profitability is not problematic in itself if the corporate and financial sectors are able to assess properly the characteristics of the investment projects, but may significantly contribute to the buildup of tensions in the financial markets if there is a lending boom and excessive credit growth—perhaps driven by moral hazard and implicit guarantees on investment by the public sector.

of changes in the relative price of nontraded goods due to the lira depreciation in 1992 and 1993 (the Italian traded-good sector being comparatively smaller in the south relative to the north).

Some authors, such as Radelet and Sachs (1998) and Chang and Velasco (1998, 2000), have interpreted recent emerging market-crisis episodes as being caused by international runs—the international equivalent of Diamond-Dybvig (1983) bank runs. Such runs are not caused by fundamentals, but rather are triggered by self-fulfilling panics that turn liquidity problems into solvency problems. In support of such interpretation, it is commonly observed that the Asian countries did not suffer from the usual symptoms of fundamental imbalances (high budget deficits, domestic credit expansion, high unemployment, etc.) preceding the currency crises.

In Corsetti, Pesenti, and Roubini (1999a,b,c), we have argued that, along with their many strong economic fundamentals, East Asian crisis countries also featured severe structural distortions and institutional weaknesses. The financial and banking systems in Korea, Thailand, Indonesia, and Malaysia were already in distress before the devaluation in 1997–98. The same can be said for the episodes of currency crises in Ecuador, Pakistan, and Russia following the ones in Asia. While it is likely that these crises were exacerbated by speculative capital flights, it is difficult to argue that such flights hit otherwise healthy economies.

Prior to the crisis in Asia, speculative purchases of assets in fixed supply fed a strong and sustained growth in asset prices. Many observers believe that equity and real estate prices rose well beyond the levels warranted by fundamentals, inflating the value of collateral of households and firms. Moral hazard arose from implicit or explicit government bailout guarantees of financial institutions. Banking regulation and supervision were notably weak. In addition, poor corporate governance and what has now come to be called crony capitalism—widespread corrupt credit practices, as loans were often politically directed to favored firms and sectors—enhanced these distortions and contributed to a lending boom, leading to overinvestment in projects and sectors that were excessively risky and/or of low profitability, such as real estate and other nontraded sectors. In the traded good sectors, these elements led to accumulation of excessive capacity.

Domestic and international capital liberalization may have aggravated the existing distortions by allowing banks and firms to borrow larger funds at lower rates in international capital markets. In Thailand, for instance, liberalization of capital account regulations (e.g., the establishment of the Bangkok International Banking Facility) provided an incentive for Thai banks and firms to borrow heavily in international financial markets in foreign currency and at very short maturities. Moreover, regulations limiting entry into the banking system led to the growth of unregulated, nonbank finance companies, fueling a boom in the real estate sector. Fifty-six of these finance companies were distressed well before the Thai baht crisis and were eventually closed down after the onset of the crisis.

In Korea, excessive investment was concentrated among the chaebols, the large conglomerates dominating the economy. Counting on their control of financial institutions, as well as on government policies of directed lending to favored sectors, Korean *chaebols* undertook large investments in low-profitability sectors such as automobiles, steel, shipbuilding, and semiconductors. By early 1997, seven out of the thirty largest *chaebols* were effectively bankrupt and the Korean economy was mired in a deep recession. Corporate leverage was already high before the crisis. In 1996, the average debt-to-equity ratio of the top thirty *chaebols* was over 300 percent. It then increased dramatically with the devaluation, as this raised the burden of foreign debt.

In Indonesia, a large share of bank credit consisted of directed credit, channeled to politically favored firms and sectors. Although Indonesia had already suffered a banking crisis in the early 1990s, these practices remained prevalent. In this country, however, a significant fraction of foreign banks' lending was directed to the corporate sector, rather than being intermediated through the domestic banking system. Most of the loans were denominated in foreign currency.

An interpretation of the Asian crisis in terms of a pure international bank run must confront the evidence about the shaky financial conditions in the crisis countries preceding the large outflows of capital of the second half of 1997. A large body of literature (see Dziobek and Pazarbasioglu 1997; Honohan 1997; Goldstein and Turner 1996; Demirgüç-Kunt and Detragiache 1997; Caprio 1998) supports the view that banking crises are due not to random runs and panics by depositors, but to weaknesses rooted in excessive lending, distorted incentives, connected and directed lending, a weak macroeconomic environment, poorly designed deposit insurance, and poorly managed liberalization processes. Quite simply, thinking that systemic banking crises occur because of sudden and unjustified depositors' panic appears to be naïve.

Moreover, interpretations of banking crises based on multiple equilibria models are somewhat incomplete, as nothing in those models explains what makes investors shift expectations from a good to a bad equilibrium. Some models rely on exogenous "sunspots" to nail down the probability of a run—this is only a gimmick, with little economic or empirical content. Drawing on the evidence on bank runs, weak banks are what tend to be attacked, not solid and healthy banks. It is therefore plausible that the probability of ending up in the bad equilibrium depends on the state of fundamentals; if fundamentals are weak, the probability that agents attack is higher. If one takes this analogy to a country level, the message is clear.

The countries that come under attack are countries that, in some dimension or the other, have weak fundamentals.[32]

1.4.2   The 1998 Recession in Asia: The Role of Financial Distress and the Need for Systemic Corporate and Bank Restructuring

By the summer of 1998, the combination of sustained high interest rates and illiquidity led to harsh economic contraction and a vast overhang of bad debt throughout Asia. Many corporations were frozen in their production decisions as they had little access to working capital and were severely burdened by a massive stock of debt.

By early 1998, large parts of the banking systems in Korea, Thailand, and Indonesia were effectively bankrupt as the result of high interest rates, a large and increasing amount of nonperforming loans, and the attempts to rapidly recapitalize. The net worth of a large part of the banking system in these countries was negative. Apart from a few domestic banks somehow spared by the crisis, the only viable banks were foreign banks operating in the region. It is also worth mentioning that the actual amount of foreign financing disbursed has been significantly less than the headline amounts announced.

Being under extreme stress, banks essentially stopped making new loans. Because of the combined effect of a liquidity squeeze and the risks of corporate bankruptcies, banks went as far as denying loans for trade credits and working capital. This was an important factor in causing many corporations that would have been solvent under normal credit conditions to go bankrupt. In support of this view, we stress the fact that, by mid-1998, exports of the crisis countries had not significantly increased in spite of massive real depreciation. Firms had so little access to working capital and trade credit that they could not import the intermediate inputs required for producing export goods.

Because of the severe liquidity crunch, for many corporations, liquidity problems were turning into solvency problems. While some firms might have been bankrupt before the crisis, the net worth of many other firms *became* negative per effect of the liquidity crunch; a combination of real depreciation, high real interest rates, collapsing aggregate demand, and liquidity squeeze was leading them to bankruptcy. For these reasons, the net worth turned negative for a large part of the corporate sector. With little alternative source of financing (other than banks), the credit crunch afflicting the crisis economies was giving way to a vicious cycle: retrenchment in credit—further economic downturn—higher nonperforming loans and credit risk—more retrenchment in credit. Contractions in trade

---

32. See, for instance, recent work by Morris and Shin (1998) and Corsetti, Dasgupta, Morris, and Shin (2000).

credit were particularly painful, directly affecting the ability of these economies to acquire foreign currency through exports.

The credit crunch for corporate firms was particularly devastating because, in East Asia, bank loans were the prevailing source of financing for firms. With banks and other financial institutions in severe financial distress, both short-term lending (for working capital purposes) and long-term lending by banks and nonbank financial institutions were drastically reduced.

While a banking crisis was also experienced in Mexico in 1995 following the collapse of the peso, this crisis was different from the Asian crisis in one important respect. Relative to the case of East Asia, corporate bankruptcies in Mexico were much less important in triggering the financial distress of the financial sector. In Mexico, the lending boom preceding the crisis was concentrated in the household sector. Households borrowed heavily from banks (often in foreign currency) to finance their consumption of durable goods and household services. Thus, the peso fell and the ensuing economic recession caused financial distress mainly among heavily leveraged households. The inability of households to service their debt was what led to the collapse of financial institutions.

Over the summer of 1998, interest rates in Asia had significantly fallen relative to the peaks of the crisis, and in Korea they returned to precrisis levels. In spite of this, a credit crunch was still severe in most countries: While the price of credit had been falling, banks that were effectively bankrupt or experiencing financial distress were unwilling to lend to corporations suffering from debt overhang. As loans were still drastically rationed, capital controls leading to lower interest rates would have done little to ease the credit crunch. Moreover, it is far from clear whether they would have helped to remove structural impediments to recovery.

While the need for a more decisive expansionary policy was widely recognized, several observers emphasized the need for an accelerated debt restructuring process as the only effective way to help the Asian countries begin producing and exporting again. Such process consists of the following steps: recapitalize banks, reduce corporate debt overhang, and provide firms with debt moratoria and new priority financing of working capital and trade.

Suggestions for a comprehensive approach to bank and corporate restructuring, including a more active role of governments, were widely debated. An accelerated restructuring of the banking system could be accomplished in a number of alternative ways. Banks that were undercapitalized but still solvent had to be recapitalized, either with capital injections from domestic or foreign investors or through capital injections by the government. In the case of institutions that were clearly insolvent or borderline insolvent, the governments had to intervene directly, eventually deciding among possible alternative actions: Recapitalize them in order to sell them to (domestic or international) private investors, merge them with stronger institutions, or close them down and sell their assets.

Korea, Indonesia, Thailand, and Malaysia tried different approaches to bank capitalization, each with a different mix of private and public participation, including recapitalization (mostly via foreign injections of new equity), closure, and mergers with other financial institutions. Accelerated disposal of bad loans, proper loan classification, and provisioning for bad loans were all elements of an accelerated bank-restructuring strategy.

In these countries the approach to bank and corporate restructuring was modeled on a variant of the "London approach" used by the United Kingdom to achieve out-of-court restructuring. This approach is mostly voluntary, case by case, and market based. Some suggested that the systemic nature of the corporate and bank financial distress in Southeast Asia required a more aggressive approach with coercive elements and greater government involvement. As a matter of fact, the restructuring process has been relatively slow, especially in the corporate area. While the recapitalization of the banking system picked up speed in the second half of 1998, progress on corporate restructuring remained slow through 1999.

1.4.3   The Role of Foreign Ownership of Domestic Banks in Preventing Emerging Market Crises

One key issue raised by recent crises in emerging markets is whether significant ownership of the domestic financial system by foreign banks could help prevent currency and financial crises, or could help reduce the impact of a crisis on the economy. In the case of East Asia, BIS-country banks provided most international lending to Asian local banks, which in turn lent to domestic corporations. Also in the case of Indonesia, where international banks tended to lend directly to corporations, international lending was mostly offshore. It has been argued that direct ownership of a fraction of the domestic financial system by foreign banks may have positive stabilizing effects. The case of Argentina (together with some other Latin American countries) is often mentioned in this respect.

In addition to enhancing competition and efficiency, and to bringing new managerial skills and banking knowledge, international banks may provide specific benefits in periods of crisis. First, if a foreign bank lends only to an emerging market bank, it does not have any stake in the corporate projects financed by the local bank. In anticipation of a crisis it may be rational for a foreign bank not to roll over its loans to the domestic bank, even if, by forcing the domestic bank in turn to call in loans, such decision causes financial distress at corporate level. If, instead, a foreign bank operates locally, it would be more concerned with the health of domestic corporations. It would be less likely to call in loans abruptly and to repatriate liabilities, adding to the risk of a crisis, since this would harm the foreign bank directly.

Second, the presence of foreign banks could mitigate some of the problems that emerge with weak domestic supervision and regulation (an emerging market regulator's ability properly to supervise and regulate domestic banks is often limited for a variety of reasons, and cannot be trusted). International banks may be inclined to follow an arm's-length approach rather than relationship banking; and they may be less exposed to political pressure to provide direct lending. Also, a strict regulation of the foreign bank in its home country (say, the United States) may indirectly affect the activities of the bank's branches in the emerging market economies. Third, foreign ownership of banks operating domestically may reduce the need for central banks in emerging markets to provide a safety net, by performing as lenders of last resort. This is because the foreign-owned local banks can rely on the foreign owners to provide funds in the presence of sudden and rapid deposit withdrawals observed during episodes of panic.

On the basis of these arguments, some have claimed that a fraction of emerging markets' banking systems should indeed be controlled by foreign banks as a way to ensure competition, efficiency, and stability. In favor of such a view, the examples of Hong Kong and Singapore (where a large fraction of the banking system is foreign owned) are often mentioned.

What are the main objections to such a view? One is, of course, a question of sovereignty; but why should countries care about who owns their banks more than they care about who owns their factories? The reason is that banks have traditionally been used for political purposes through direct lending, and as a source of revenue via financial repression. This is why governments are wary of letting go of domestic banks. Note that these elements provide a positive explanation of why governments do not want a foreign ownership of domestic banks; they do not provide, however, a strong normative argument against foreign ownership.

A second objection casts doubts on the presumption that foreign-owned banks would behave properly and avoid excessive risk taking. In the case of Chile in the early 1980s, for instance, the Chilean subsidiaries of foreign banks gambled on very risky projects and engaged in excessive credit creation. A third objection is against the presumption that a financial system owned by a small number of foreign banks would reduce the need for the domestic central bank to intervene in the banking system, acting as lender of last resort. It is far from obvious that these banks would not count on the local central bank as provider of funds, when economic shocks or poor lending decisions lead to financial distress in the banking system. Large foreign banks may have the power to impose ex post liquidity provision and other forms of support, such as a government bailout of bad loans.

Overall, however, these objections do not appear to be strong enough to offset the arguments in favor of foreign ownership of domestic banks in emerging markets—especially in light of the track records of the countries where foreign banks own a large fraction of the domestic banking system. Yet, there are a number of issues that require additional analysis. Do foreign-owned banks in emerging markets need a domestic safety net (lender of last resort and deposit insurance)? Will they expect it, require it, and get it ex post if they experience financial distress? Should the home country rather than the host country provide regulation and lender-of-last-resort support? These are complex questions with no easy answers.

1.5   Conclusions

The results of our empirical analysis provide evidence in support of the thesis that crises are systematically related to the fundamental weaknesses in the real and financial sectors of the economy. The recent turmoil in Asia does not seem to represent an exception in this respect. External imbalances, as measured by the current account deficits associated with real exchange rate appreciation, are significantly correlated with the crisis index. So are measures of financial fragility (nonperforming loans in the presence of a lending boom) and measures of the fiscal costs associated with financial bailouts (nonperforming loans as a share of GDP). The effects of these variables on the crisis index are found to be stronger in countries with low reserves.

The empirical analysis presented in this paper is preliminary, yet it complements other analyses showing the extent of the deterioration of fundamentals in Asia in the years before the crisis. Per se, these results cannot discriminate across alternative explanations of currency crises based on self-fulfilling speculative attacks, as opposed to fundamental factors. They do, however, identify a set of variables that appear to enhance the vulnerability of an economy to a crisis.

The indicator that seems to be most robust in our analysis is the indirect measure of the implicit costs of bailouts in the presence of a financial crisis, i.e., nonperforming loans before the crisis as a share of GDP. In related work (Corsetti, Pesenti, and Roubini 1999b) we have provided a consistent theory of the role that contingent public debt plays in generating twin financial and currency crises. We interpret the empirical evidence presented in this paper as an indication that this is the right direction to pursue in a comprehensive research agenda on the Asian crisis.

The analysis in this paper highlights the role played by the financial distress of banks, other financial institutions, and corporations in the Asian crisis. The fiscal costs of cleaning up the balance sheets of banks is bound to be very high, while the prospects for a rapid and sustained recovery of economic growth in Asia depend on an accelerated process of bank and corporate restructuring in the region. The recent recovery in economic activity in the region may experience a relapse unless bank and corporate restructuring is pursued more aggressively in the near future.

Appendix

In this appendix we describe in detail the construction of the variables used in the empirical analysis.

Crisis Index (IND)

The index is a weighted average of the percentage rate of exchange rate depreciation relative to the U.S. dollar and the percentage rate of change in foreign reserves between the end of December 1996 and the end of December 1997. A large negative value for IND corresponds to a high devaluation rate or a fall in foreign reserves (or both), i.e., a more severe currency crisis. All data are from the *International Financial Statistics* of the International Monetary Fund (*IFS*-IMF).

Real Exchange Rate Appreciation (RER)

This variable measures the percentage rate of change of the real exchange rate between the end of 1996 and an average over the 1988–1990 period. The real exchange rate measure is based on wholesale price indexes, using trade weights of OECD countries (excluding Mexico and Korea). For the three transition economies—Czech Republic, Hungary, and Poland—whose real exchange rates exhibit large fluctuations in the early transition years, the appreciation is calculated between 1996 and 1992. For Argentina, whose real exchange rate experienced large swings in the hyperinflation period, the real exchange rate is computed between 1996 and the end of 1990.

Current Account Deficits (CA) and the CAI Index

The current account deficit as a share of GDP is an average over the 1994–96 period. Data are from *IFS*-IMF. The index of current account imbalances CAI is computed as follows: For countries where the real exchange rate appreciated more than 10 percent over the period defined above, CAI takes the value of the average 1994–96 current account balance (as a share of GDP); for all other countries, CAI is set equal to zero.

Lending Boom (LB)

This variable is the rate of growth between 1990 and 1996 of the ratio between the claims on the private sector of the deposit money banks (line 22d in *IFS*-IMF) and nominal GDP. All data are from *IFS*-IMF. In the case of transition economies, where either data since 1990 are not available or the ratio is very unstable in the early transition years, we take 1992 (rather than 1990) as the starting date.

Nonperforming Loans as a Share of Total Bank Assets (NPL)

As there are no homogeneous series for nonperforming loans, we need to build our data set relying on several sources. For most of the Asian countries in our sample (Korea, Indonesia, Hong Kong, Taiwan, Malaysia, Thailand) there are two available estimates of NPL in 1996: one from the 1997 BIS Annual Report, the other from Jardine Fleming (http://www. jfleming.com). Both estimates are biased; the former underestimates non-performing loans before the onset of the crisis (for instance, the end-of-1996 figure for Korea is 0.8 percent, whereas the latter is based on data from the third quarter of 1997, when nonperforming loans are already reflecting the consequences of the currency crises on the financial conditions of banks and corporate firms (for instance, Korean nonperforming loans are estimated to be 16 percent). We take the average of the two figures as a reasonable estimate of the nonperforming loans before the onset of the crisis, i.e., the end of 1996 through early 1997. For the remaining countries, we proceed as follows: For India, Argentina, Brazil, Chile, Colombia, Mexico, Peru, and Venezuela, we use the estimates for 1996 in the BIS 1997 Annual Report. For China, Singapore, and the Philippines, we use estimates from Jardine Fleming. For the other countries in the sample, we rely on information derived from IMF country reports. It is worth emphasizing that our estimates do not appear to be systematically biased towards the countries that suffered a crisis in 1997. Note, in fact, that noncrisis countries such as Mexico, China, India, and Pakistan all show a very large fraction of nonperforming loans (over 10 percent of total loans).

Fiscal Cost of the Bailout of the Banking System as a Share of GDP (NPLY)

This variable is computed as follows. We take the estimate of the non-performing loans as a share of bank assets (NPL) derived above and multiply it by the ratio of claims on the private sector by deposit money banks at the end of 1996 to GDP. The latter variable is computed from *IFS-IMF* data.

The NPLB Index

In deriving NPLB, we interact the lending boom variable with the non-performing loans variable. For countries where the sign of the lending boom variable is positive, we set NPLB equal to NPL; for countries with a negative lending boom, we set NPLB equal to zero.

Reserve Adequacy Ratios

We compute three ratios for reserve adequacy at the end of 1996. The first is the ratio of M1 to foreign exchange reserves (M1/reserves); the second is the ratio of M2 to foreign reserves (M2/reserves); the third is the ratio of the foreign debt service burden (i.e., short-term foreign debt plus interest payments on foreign debt) to foreign reserves (STD/reserves). Foreign exchange reserve data are from the *IFS*-IMF (line 11d). Data on short-term debt and interest payments on foreign debt are from Datastream (http://www.datastream.com).

Taiwan

Taiwan is not included in the IMF database. Our data for Taiwan are from Datastream and rely on Taiwan national data sources.

References

Alba, Pedro, Amar Bhattacharya, Stijn Claessens, Swati Ghosh, and Leonardo Hernandez. 1999. The role of macroeconomic and financial sector linkages in East Asia's financial crisis. In *The Asian financial crisis: Causes, contagion and consequences,* ed. Pierre Richard Agenor, Marcus Miller, David Vines, and Axel Weber, 9–64. Cambridge: Cambridge University Press.

Berg, Andrew, and Catherine Pattillo. 1999. Are currency crises predictable? A test. *IMF Staff Papers* 46 (2): 107–38.

Buiter, Willem, Giancarlo Corsetti, and Paolo Pesenti. 1998a. *Financial markets and European monetary cooperation: The lessons of the 1992–93 Exchange Rate Mechanism crisis.* Cambridge: Cambridge University Press.

———. 1998b. Interpreting the ERM crisis: Country-specific and systemic issues. *Princeton Studies in International Finance* no. 84.

Burnside, Craig, Martin Eichenbaum, and Sergio Rebelo. 1998. Prospective deficits and the Asian currency crisis. NBER Working Paper no. 6758. Cambridge, Mass.: National Bureau of Economic Research, October.

Calvo, Guillermo. 1998. Varieties of capital market crises. In *The debt burden and its consequences for monetary policy,* ed. G. E. Calvo and M. King 181–202. London: Macmillan.

Calvo, Guillermo, and Carlos Vegh. 1999. Inflation stabilization and balance of payments crises in developing countries. In *Handbook of macroeconomics,* ed. John Taylor and Michael Woodford, 1531–1614. Amsterdam: North-Holland.

Caprio, Gerard, Jr. 1998. Banking on crises: Expensive lessons from recent financial crises. World Bank Working Paper no. 1979. Washington, D.C.: World Bank.

Cavallari, Lilia, and Giancarlo Corsetti. 1996. Policy-making and speculative attacks in models of exchange rate crises: A synthesis. Yale University, Economic Growth Center, Working Paper.

Chang, Roberto, and Andres Velasco. 1998. Financial crises in emerging markets: A canonical model. NBER Working Paper no. 6606. Cambridge, Mass.: National Bureau of Economic Research, June.

———. 2000. Financial fragility and the exchange rate regime. *Journal of Economic Theory* 92 (1): 1–34.

Cole, Harold, and Timothy Kehoe. 1996. A self-fulfilling model of Mexico's 1994–1995 debt crisis. *Journal of International Economics* 41 (3/4): 309–30.

Corsetti, Giancarlo, Stephen Morris, Hyun Song Shin, and Amil Dasgupta. 2000. Does one soros make a difference? The role of a large trader in currency crises. Yale University, Cowles Foundation Discussion Paper no. 1273.

Corsetti, Giancarlo, Paolo Pesenti, and Nouriel Roubini. 1999a. The Asian crisis: An overview of the empirical evidence and policy debate. In *The Asian financial crisis: Causes, contagion and consequences,* ed. Pierre Richard Agenor, Marcus Miller, David Vines, and Axel Weber, 127–63. Cambridge: Cambridge University Press.

———. 1999b. Paper tigers? A model of the Asian crisis. *European Economic Review* 43 (7): 1211–36.

———. 1999c. What caused the Asian currency and financial crisis? *Japan and the World Economy* 11 (3): 305–73.

Demirgüç-Kunt, Asli, and Enrica Detragiache. 1997. The determinants of banking crises in developing and developed countries. *IMF Staff Papers* 45 (1): 81–109.

Diamond, Douglas W., and Philip H. Dybvig. 1983. Bank runs, deposit insurance, and liquidity. *Journal of Political Economy* 91: 401–19.

Diaz-Alejandro, Carlos F. 1985. Good-bye financial repression, hello financial crash. *Journal of Development Economics* 19 (1/2): 1–24. Reprinted in *Trade, development and the world economy: Selected essays of Carlos Diaz-Alejandro,* ed. A. Velasco, 364–86. (Oxford, U.K.: Blackwell, 1988).

Dornbusch, Rudiger. 1998. Asian crisis themes. Cambridge: MIT, Department of Economics. Mimeograph, February.

Dornbusch, Rudiger, Ilan Goldfajn, and Rodrigo O. Valdes. 1995. Currency crises and collapses. *Brookings Papers on Economic Activity,* issue no. 1: 219–70. Washington, D.C.: Brookings Institution.

Dziobek, Claudia, and Ceyla Pazarbasioglu. 1997. Lessons from systemic bank restructuring: A survey of 24 countries. IMF Working Paper no. 97/161. Washington, D.C.: International Monetary Fund.

Eichengreen, Barry, Andrew K. Rose, and Charles Wyplosz. 1996. Contagious currency crises: First tests. *Scandinavian Journal of Economics* 98 (4): 463–84.

Eichengreen, Barry, and Charles Wyplosz. 1993. The unstable EMS. *Brookings Papers on Economic Activity,* issue no. 1: 51–143.

Feldstein, Martin. 1998. Refocusing the IMF. *Foreign Affairs* 77 (2): 20–33.

Fischer, Stanley. 1998. The IMF and the Asian crisis. Forum Funds Lecture, 20 March. Los Angeles: UCLA.

Flood, Robert, and Peter Garber. 1984. Collapsing exchange-rate regimes: Some linear examples. *Journal of International Economics* 17: 1–13.

Flood, Robert, and Nancy Marion. 1999. Perspectives on the recent currency crisis literature. *International Journal of Finance and Economics* 4 (1): 1–26.

Goldfajn, Ilan, and Rodrigo O. Valdes. 1997. Capital flows and the twin crises: The role of liquidity. IMF Working Paper no. 97/87. Washington, D.C.: International Monetary Fund.

Goldstein, Morris. 1998. The Asian financial crisis: Causes, cures, and systemic implications. *Policy Analyses in International Economics* no. 55. Washington, D.C.: Institute for International Economics.

Goldstein, Morris, and Philip Turner. 1996. Banking crises in emerging economies: Origins and policy options. Bank for International Settlements Working Paper no. 46. Basel, Switzerland.

Greenspan, Alan. 1998. Remarks before the 34th Annual Conference on Bank Structure and Competition, 7 May. Chicago: Federal Reserve Bank.

Honohan, Patrick. 2000. Banking system failures in developing and transition countries: Diagnosis and prediction. *Economic Notes* 29 (1): 83–109.

International Monetary Fund. 1998. *World economic outlook.* Washington, D.C.: International Monetary Fund.

Ito, Takatoshi. 1998. The development of the Thailand currency crisis: A chronological review. *Journal of Research Institute for International Investment and Development* 24 (9): 66–93.

Kaminsky, Graciela, Saul Lizondo, and Carmen M. Reinhart. 1998. Leading indicators of currency crises. *IMF Staff Papers* 45 (1): 1–48.

Kaminsky, Graciela, and Carmen M. Reinhart. 1999. The twin crises: The causes of banking and balance-of-payments problems. *American Economic Review* 89 (3): 473–500.

Krueger, Anne, and Aaron Tornell. 1999. The role of bank restructuring in recovering from crises: Mexico 1995–98. NBER Working Paper no. 7042. Cambridge, Mass.: National Bureau of Economic Research, March.

Krugman, Paul. 1979. A model of balance of payments crises. *Journal of Money, Credit, and Banking* 11 (3): 311–25.

———. 1998. What happened to Asia? Cambridge: MIT, Department of Economics, January. Mimeograph.

McKinnon, Ronald, and Huw Pill. 1996. Credible liberalization and international capital flows: The "overborrowing syndrome." In *Financial deregulation and integration in East Asia,* ed. Takatoshi Ito and Anne O. Kruger, 7–50. Chicago: University of Chicago Press.

Milesi-Ferretti, Gian Maria, and Assaf Razin. 1996. Current account sustainability. *Princeton Studies in International Finance* no. 81.

Mishkin, Frederic S. 1997. Understanding financial crises: a developing country perspective. In *Annual World Bank conference on development economics, 1996,* ed. Michael Bruno and Boris Pleskovic, 29–62. Washington, D.C.: World Bank.

Morris, Stephen, and Hyun Song Shin. 1998. Unique equilibrium in a model of self-fulfilling currency attacks. *American Economic Review* 88 (3): 587–97.

Obstfeld, Maurice. 1986. Rational and self-fulfilling balance of payments crises. *American Economic Review* 76 (1): 72–81.

———. 1994. The logic of currency crises. *Cahiers Economiques et Monetaires* 43: 189–213.

Organization for Economic Cooperation and Development (OECD). 1998. *Economic Survey of Korea 1997–98.* Paris: OECD.

Pomerleano, Michael. 1998. The East Asia crisis and corporate finances: The untold micro story. *Emerging Markets Quarterly* Winter: 14–27.

Radelet, Steven, and Jeffrey Sachs. 1998. The East-Asian financial crisis: Diagnosis, remedies, prospects. *Brookings Papers on Economic Activity,* issue no. 1: 1–74.

Roubini, Nouriel, and Paul Wachtel. 1998. Current account sustainability in transition economies. NBER Working Paper no. 6468. Cambridge, Mass.: National Bureau of Economic Research, March.

Sachs, Jeffrey, Aaron Tornell, and Andres Velasco. 1996. Financial crises in emerging markets: The lessons from 1995. *Brookings Papers on Economic Activity,* issue no. 1: 147–215.

Velasco, Andres. 1987. Financial and balance of payments crises: A simple model of the southern cone experience. *Journal of Development Economics* 27 (1/2): 263–283.

Comment   Carmen M. Reinhart

Motivated by the severe Asian crisis of 1997, this paper makes a fine contribution to the growing literature that analyzes the symptoms of a country's vulnerability to currency crises. While the sample of countries covered in the empirical analysis encompasses diverse regions, the discussion in the paper focuses primarily on the Asian crisis. In particular, the authors stress, as they have in their earlier papers, the key role played by weak fundamentals in undermining several of the Asian currencies. Financial sector fundamentals (as in Kaminsky and Reinhart 1999) play an important role, but the authors also devote considerable attention to the countries' capacity to back their "implicit" contingent liabilities, particularly those of the local banking sector (as in Calvo and Mendoza 1996). Furthermore, the analysis by Corsetti, Pesenti, and Roubini (CPR) examines the links between crisis vulnerability and the productivity of investment projects—an important issue, particularly in several of the high-investment Asian countries—that have been largely ignored in this literature.[1]

By focusing on these fundamentals as well as on external imbalances, CPR dismiss a relatively popular explanation of the Asian crisis stressing a liquidity crisis/financial panic story that arises out of self-fulfilling expectations, runs on the banks, and the currency, and that downplays the role of economic fundamentals. Since I happen to concur with most (although not all) of the points made by the authors about the proximate causes of the Asian crisis, I confine my remarks to two areas: First, I focus on issues regarding ways of strengthening the empirical analysis developed in this paper; second, I dwell on some of the features of the antecedents of the Asian crisis that merit attention and are not addressed by the authors.

In the spirit of Sachs, Tornell, and Velasco (1996), the empirical analysis employs a cross-section of countries to examine which variables help explain the extent of depreciation and reserve losses (i.e., a severity index) during the December 1996–97 period. The authors focus primarily on three indicators: the interaction between credit growth and nonperforming loans, to capture the fragility of the banking sector; the interaction between real exchange rate overvaluations and current account imbalances; and the ratio of various monetary aggregates to central bank foreign exchange reserves, to assess the central bank's capacity to back its contingent liabilities. In addition, the authors include the incremental capital-to-output ratio (ICOR) and its interaction with credit growth. The idea is that

Carmen M. Reinhart is professor at the School of Public Affairs and Department of Economics at the University of Maryland, College Park, and a research associate of the National Bureau of Economic Research.

1. CPR is not to be confused with the other CPR—Center for Policy Research.

during lending booms, funds are allocated to increasingly less-productive projects. CPR also experiment with two types of dummy variables that allow for the interaction among the indicators described above. For instance, the current account/real exchange rate variable is allowed to enter directly as well as through an interaction dummy that takes on the value of 1 when the money-to-reserves ratio is in the upper three quartiles.

Both the selection of the variables and the way they are allowed to interact are intuitively appealing and well grounded in theory. I do have, however, some practical reservations about the information content of nonperforming loans for two reasons. First, banks often engage in the "evergreening" of problem loans for extended periods—as a consequence, nonperforming loans often lag rather than lead the crisis, and the authors use 1996 data for nonperforming loans. Secondly, the criteria applied to classify a loan as nonperforming are highly heterogeneous across countries, particularly in emerging markets. My hunch is that most of the information content of this composite term is coming from the lending boom rather than from nonperforming loans.

As to the estimation strategy, my main criticism has to do with the interaction terms introduced through the two dummy variables. While sympathetic to the economic rationale for wanting to include these additional terms in the regression, I find that they introduce serious collinearity problems. The presence of collinearity is evident in the large standard errors reported for most coefficients in tables 1.2–1.5. Most of these terms are not individually statistically significant; the failure to reject the null hypothesis that the sum of several pairs of coefficients (the Wald tests reported at the bottom of tables 1.2–1.5) comes from the actual variable rather than from the secondary interaction term. The absence of the incremental explanatory power of these interaction dummies is also evident in the reported adjusted R^2, which, in the majority of cases, does not increase by much and in some cases actually declines. The introduction of these additional terms also chews up precious degrees of freedom, which in some of the regressions is as low as seventeen.[2]

Apart from the collinearity problem, the results accord well with the priors. External imbalances increase the severity of the currency crisis as does booming credit. The interaction terms, although not statistically significant in almost all cases, also have the anticipated signs.

A second criticism of the paper, albeit one which is easy to remedy, is that the authors downplay some very interesting results on the interaction between the ICOR and lending booms and its role in explaining who is vulnerable to this kind of crisis.[3] As noted earlier, measures of the productivity of new investment projects have been largely overlooked in this liter-

2. Twenty-four observations and seven coefficients to estimate (see table 1.3).
3. The discussion is limited to a couple of paragraphs.

ature. This is a particularly important issue for understanding why the size of the current account may matter—irrespective of whether it arises out of a low saving rate or a high investment rate.[4] In the aftermath of the Mexican crisis, the "received wisdom" of the day was that Mexico's large current account deficit was a problem because it was largely owing to a consumption boom. At the time, there was little concern that Thailand's and Malaysia's large deficits would be problems since—the argument went—the capital inflows were financing record levels of investment. After Asia's crisis it becomes evident that unproductive investments are indistinguishable from consumption, as far as vulnerability is concerned.

Turning to the interpretation of the events and developments leading up to the Asian crisis offered in this paper, I agree with CPR that these crises had their roots in a fragile financial sector and that this vulnerability was manifest well before the crisis erupted.[5] As in so many banking crises, the problems first arose in the asset side of the bank balance sheet. Hence, in the discussion that follows, I will focus mainly on filling some holes in this paper's telling of the proximate causes of the Asian crisis. CPR mention that the liberalization of the capital account and the financial sector was an important factor in explaining the surge in banks' offshore borrowing in the years before the crisis; I would like to mention two additional factors that drove banks in these countries to become ever more dependent on offshore borrowing.

First, while fiscal policy mistakes are usually easy to spot, mistakes in monetary and exchange rate policies are more difficult to single out—unless these produce high inflation. During the capital-inflow phase of the cycle, the most common policy response in the region to the surge in capital inflows was sterilized intervention. Yet, as shown in Montiel and Reinhart (1999), sterilized intervention appears to be a powerful tool in influencing both the volume and the composition of capital inflows, although hardly in the way that policy makers had originally intended it to. By providing a combination of an implicit exchange rate guarantee and high domestic interest rates on short-term assets vis-à-vis comparable international interest rates, sterilization policies are a magnet in attracting short-term flows. These policies are capable of increasing the volume of the flows and skewing their composition away from FDI to short maturities components.

Second, "push" factors were also important in explaining why banks in the region became so dependent on short-term offshore borrowing. In particular, the protracted economic slump in Japan had dried up domestic loan demand and Japanese banks were all too eager to lend increasing amounts to the rapidly growing, capital-importing emerging Asian econo-

---

4. For a different interpretation of why the current account matters in explaining the severity of crises, see Calvo and Reinhart (2000).

5. This pattern of interaction between banking and currency crises is not unique to the Asian cases; see Kaminsky and Reinhart (1999).

mies. Indeed, Japan and emerging Asia in the 1990s appear in many ways to have replayed the roles of U.S. banks and Latin America in the late 1970s and early 1980s.

To sum up, this is an interesting paper which helps us understand the traumatic events of 1997 and 1998 in several Asian economies. Furthermore, the analysis is sufficiently general to provide insights into the more generalized features of financial vulnerability.

References

Calvo, Guillermo A., and Enrique Mendoza. 1996. Mexico's balance-of-payments crisis: A chronicle of a death foretold. *Journal of International Economics* 41 (3/4): 235–64.

Calvo, Guillermo A., and Carmen M. Reinhart. 2000. "When capital inflows come to a sudden stop: Consequences and policy options." In *Key Issues in Reform of the International Monetary and Financial System,* ed. P. Kenen and A. Swoboda. Washington D.C.: International Monetary Fund, 2000: 175–201.

Kaminsky, Graciela, and Carmen M. Reinhart, with G. Kaminsky. 1999. The twin crises: The causes of banking and balance of payments problems. *American Economic Review,* 89 (3): 473–500.

Montiel, Peter, and Carmen M. Reinhart. 1999. Do capital controls influence the volume and composition of capital flows? Evidence from the 1990s. *Journal of International Money and Finance,* 18 (4): 619–35.

Sachs, Jeffrey, Aaron Tornell, and Andres Velasco. 1996. Financial crises in emerging markets: The lessons from 1995. *Brookings Papers on Economic Activity,* issue no. 1: 147–215.

Comment   Aaron Tornell

This very interesting paper belongs to a class of recent papers which show that currency crises do not spread randomly. Although it is not possible to predict the timing of crises, it is possible to explain an important proportion of the cross-country variation in the intensity of the crisis in the event that a generalized crisis hits emerging markets.

This paper focuses on the Asian 1997 crisis and shows that the lending boom and real exchange rate appreciation go a long way in explaining the cross-country variation in the crisis index. These results confirm the findings of earlier papers and provide reinforcing evidence that the behavior of private banks has important macroeconomic effects.

A lending boom is an acceleration of credit from the banking system to private and state-owned firms. During a lending boom, the fast growth of credit might overwhelm both the monitoring capacity of banks and the regulatory capacity of authorities. As a result, a greater share of loans may

Aaron Tornell is professor of economics at the University of California, Los Angeles.

end up in low-return projects or excessively risky activities. Therefore, over the span of a few years, the share of bad loans in the banks' portfolios will increase dramatically. When this occurs, the country becomes an attractive target for a currency attack.

Similarly, a severe real exchange rate appreciation reflects macroeconomic imbalances, and might lead to a greater nominal depreciation in case of an attack. Interestingly, this effect is more pronounced in Latin America than in Southeast Asia.

Unconditionally, a lending boom need not be a bad thing. It might reflect financial deepening, which is important for long-run economic growth. However, as mentioned earlier, it might also reflect overinvestment in low-return projects or excessively risky activities. It is thus important to investigate whether a given lending boom reflects the former situation or the latter. This paper takes a step in this direction by investigating the effects of higher investment on productivity growth. I look forward to further results along these lines in future work by the authors of this paper.

Lending Booms
and Currency Crises
Empirical Link

Aaron Tornell

2.1 Introduction

Imagine a money manager with a crystal ball that predicts the future. This crystal ball tells the manager that a currency crisis will erupt in six months and that it will spread across emerging markets. However, it does not tell the manager anything else. Can he or she use this information to help predict whether a specific country, say Mexico or Indonesia, will fare badly? If this is possible, he or she can then make the right portfolio decision regarding that country.

The answer will depend on the manager's view regarding the manner in which currency crises spread across emerging markets. One view he or she might hold is that that crises spread randomly. In this case the prediction supplied by the crystal ball will help, but not a great deal. A second view the manager might have is that there is a neighborhood effect. That is to say, fads develop and crises spread mainly to countries in the same area. After all, the 1994 Mexican crisis hit Latin American countries hardest, while the 1997 Thai crisis hit mainly Southeast Asian currencies. In this case the crystal ball would not be very valuable, unless the manager knows which neighborhood will be the unlucky one. A third view is that the spread of these crises is determined to a large degree by fundamentals. In this case the manager will be able to exploit the crystal ball's information (a) if there is a set of fundamentals, and a filtering rule that might allow him or her to predict which countries would be hardest hit by the crisis and which would be spared; (b) if it is possible to observe these fundamentals before the onset of the crisis; and (c) if these emerging markets have

Aaron Tornell is professor of economics at the University of California, Los Angeles.

sufficiently free and developed financial markets that permit him to take the right portfolio positions.

In this paper I argue that in light of the Tequila and Asian crises, the third view (c) is the correct one. I find that these crises neither spread across emerging markets randomly, nor were simply driven by fads. Rather, I find that the cross-country variation in the severity of crisis can be largely explained by three fundamentals: the strength of a country's banking system, its real exchange rate appreciation, and the liquidity of its central bank.

I also find that the rule linking fundamentals to the crises' severity is the same in both the Tequila and Asian crises. Hence, if one had estimated such a rule using data from the Tequila crisis, then one could have reasonably attempted to predict how the Asian crisis would spread using data available in late 1996 or early 1997. Thus, the simple knowledge of an upcoming currency crisis is far from useless, and the crystal ball's prophecy is a helpful one.

The idea underlying my analysis is that the eruption of a currency crisis in an emerging market serves as a coordinating device that informs money managers that others will attack certain currencies. The currencies that are attacked are not selected randomly, however. Rather, money managers concentrate their attacks on countries that are most likely to respond with a high depreciation. This view is consistent with balance-of-payments crises models with multiple equilibria, like those of Cole and Kehoe (1996), Obstfeld (1994), and Sachs, Tornell, and Velasco (1996a).

There is a growing empirical literature on the determinants of currency crises. This paper is closely related with a previous paper I wrote with Jeff Sachs and Andres Velasco, in which we tried to explain the spread of the Tequila crisis. Other related papers are those of Frankel and Rose (1996), Kaminsky, Lizondo, and Reinhart (1996), Corsetti, Pesenti, and Roubini (1999), and Radelet and Sachs (1998), to mention just a few.

2.2   Conceptual Framework

In order to determine which countries are more likely to loose reserves or to depreciate during a crisis, I will consider the thought processes of risk-neutral money managers and government officials across emerging markets. Since the short positions involved in a currency attack entail significant interest rate costs, an individual money manager will attack a country only if (a) the manager expects that other money managers will also attack that country; and (b) he or she expects that the country in question will respond with a sizable depreciation.

In order for the first condition to be satisfied it is necessary that money managers coordinate with each other in selecting which currencies should be attacked and the timing of the attack itself. In this respect, the eruption of a crisis in some emerging market acts as a coordinating device that signals money managers that others might attack certain currencies in the near future. Accordingly, the question then becomes, which currencies will be attacked? Money managers will concentrate their attacks on currencies that are expected to react with greater depreciation in response to capital outflow.

The expected response of a country depends on the preferences of the government and on the constraints it faces. A country might respond to an attack by simply loosing reserves, by increasing its interest rate, or by depreciating.

The first alternative may be the least politically costly. At the same time, it is available only to governments with plenty of reserves to cover their liquid liabilities; thus this option is not open to the majority of countries, as their short-run liabilities far exceed their reserves. In these cases, governments are faced with a difficult choice between two unpleasant alternatives. Increasing the interest rate makes speculation against the currency more expensive, and it can help close the external gap by reducing absorption; yet, the effects come at the cost of a recession. In emerging markets, the health of the banking system is a very important determinant of the effect that increasing interest rates have on the economy. When the banking system has a big share of bad loans, a given interest rate increase is more likely to induce a greater recession or even a meltdown of the payments system. Thus, money managers know that the weaker the banking system, the less likely the government to respond to an attack with an interest rate hike.

If a government chooses the third alternative, depreciation, what is the extent of the depreciation the government must engineer in order to close a given external gap? The greater the real appreciation has been during the previous few years, the more likely it is that firms in the tradable sector have shifted to the nontradable sector, and the greater the nominal depreciation necessary to close the external gap.

Summing up, when a currency crisis erupts in an emerging market, money managers will expect others to attack those countries that are more likely to respond to an attack with a big depreciation. Thus, the crisis is not likely to spread to countries with high reserves. Among the low reserves countries, the crisis is more likely to reach those where interest rate increases are likely to generate big recessions (e.g., countries with weak banking systems), and will also affect countries that have experienced a high real appreciation.

2.3 Empirics

There are several ways to measure the three fundamentals discussed in the previous section and the severity of a crisis. In this paper, I have chosen to proxy the three fundamentals with variables that are available in data sources, such as the *International Financial Statistics* (*IFS*), where one might be confident that the same definitions have been applied to all countries. Note that the variables must be available on a timely basis if this exercise is to have some connection with the decision rules used by money managers. In the end, one would like the derived rule to apply to future currency crises in emerging markets. Therefore, the formulas used to construct the indexes will be as simple as possible. By interacting several variables in a nonlinear way, one could produce indexes that eliminate "nasty" observations and insure a fairly good explanation of a specific crisis. The drawback to this approach is that the rule so derived might not explain other crises.

I measure the severity of the crisis in the standard way it is done in the literature.[1] Thus, my crisis index is a weighted average of the loss in reserves and the depreciation against the U.S. dollar. Each of the two components is weighted by its precision over the sum of both precisions, calculated from a monthly series of ten years.

Ideally, one should measure the weakness of the banking system with the "true" share of bad loans. Unfortunately, this information is available neither on a timely basis nor in data sources that insure cross-country comparability. For instance, suppose that country *A* has a smaller true bad-to-total loans ratio than country *B*, but that *A* has adopted U.S. generally accepted accounting procedure (GAAP) rules, while country *B* has not. In this case, it is very likely that *B* might report a smaller bad-loans ratio because it classifies only the debt service that is delinquent as a bad loan. In contrast, country *A* will consider the entire stock of the delinquent debt as a bad loan. A second problem that arises is misreporting, or the so-called "evergreen accounts problem." Banks (and often regulators) have many incentives to disguise the fact that there are nonperforming loans. Hence, banks will simply continue to lend to the nonperforming accounts an amount equivalent to the payments the accounts were supposed to make. This cultivation of evergreen accounts can go on for a long period of time without market participants' noticing the problem. This brings us to the third problem, namely that information on nonperforming loans is not available on a timely basis. For instance, money managers looking at the Mexican bad loans ratio in 1994 saw very decent numbers; the recognition of a sizable share of bad loans did not come until after the crisis had erupted.

For these reasons, I proxy the weakness of the banking system with a lending boom index. This variable is available on a timely basis and is

---

1. This way of measuring crises is used in Frankel and Rose (1996), Kaminsky, Lizondo, and Reinhart (1996), and Sachs, Tornell, and Velasco (1996b).

comparable across countries. I measure the lending boom as the real percent increase in loans provided by the banking system to the private sector and state-owned enterprises over the previous four years. One should expect that the greater the increase of loans provided by the banking system during a short span of time, the greater the share of bad loans in the subsequent period. There are several reasons this is true. First, banks have limited capacity to evaluate projects. Second, regulatory agencies have limited monitoring capacity and resources. Last, there exists only a limited supply of "good" projects with high expected returns relative to their variance.

I then replace the real exchange rate with a weighted average of the bilateral real exchange rates of a given country with respect to the U.S. dollar, the Mark, and the yen. The weights add up to 1 and are proportional to the shares of bilateral trade in the given country with the United States, the European Union, and Japan, respectively. My real depreciation index is the percentage change in this index over the four years prior to the onset of the crisis, i.e., December 1994 relative to December 1990, and December 1996 relative to December 1992.[2] The problems associated with measuring real depreciation in this way are well understood, so I will not discuss them here.

I proxy the government's liquidity by the ratio of M2 to reserves in the month preceding the onset of the crisis (November 1994 or May 1997). If the central bank is not willing to let the exchange rate depreciate, it must be prepared to cover all the liabilities of the banking system with reserves. Thus it is M2, and not simply the monetary base, that must be the relevant proxy of the central bank's contingent liabilities. During a crisis, banks are likely to experience runs. If the central bank does not act as a lender of last resort, generalized bankruptcies are likely to follow. Since, in most circumstances, authorities will not find it optimal to allow the economy to experience generalized bankruptcies, the central bank will have to be prepared to exchange the amount withdrawn by depositors for foreign exchange.

My sample consists of all the developing countries (for which data are available) that have had free convertibility, and financial markets in which foreigners could freely invest during the 1990s. I consider all countries considered as emerging markets by the International Finance Corporation, with the exception of (a) Greece and Portugal, as they belong to the European Union and are not developing countries; (b) China, because there is no free convertibility; and (c) Nigeria, because there is no data availability. Thus, my sample consists of Hong Kong and twenty-two other countries:

---

2. An alternative index is the J. P. Morgan real exchange rate index. I decided to construct my own proxy, since I am unsure how that index is constructed.

Argentina, Brazil, Chile, Colombia, Hungary, India, Indonesia, Korea, Jordan, Malaysia, Mexico, Pakistan, Peru, the Philippines, Poland, South Africa, Sri Lanka, Taiwan, Thailand, Turkey, Venezuela, and Zimbabwe. I discuss the two generalized emerging-market currency crises that have occurred in the 1990s. Previous crises, like the debt crisis of the early 1980s, were of a different nature and are not considered. In those cases, financial markets in emerging markets were not yet liberalized, and the majority of capital inflows took the form of loans to governments by big foreign banks or official agencies. The currency crises of the 1990s have happened under different conditions, and thus one should expect different mechanisms at work.

2.3.1   The Benchmark Regression

As mentioned earlier, I am not trying to determine the timing of a crisis, but rather the manner in which a crisis will spread across emerging markets, given the eruption of a crisis somewhere. As discussed in the previous section, the onset of a crisis in one country serves as a coordinating device for investors. At this point, each money manager knows that others will do the same and will reshuffle his or her portfolio accordingly. If a country has strong fundamentals or high reserves, it is not likely to depreciate significantly in response to an attack. Hence, investors will not find it profitable to attack such a country—they will have to incur the interest costs associated with the attack while the expected capital gains are small. Because of this, one should not expect that variations in the explanatory variables should significantly affect the crisis indexes in this subset of countries. Thus, investors will concentrate their attacks on countries with weak fundamentals and low reserves. Furthermore, within this subset of countries they will allocate more resources to attack countries that are more likely to respond with greater depreciations. Such countries have had a greater lending boom or a greater real appreciation, or both. Countries from the first group have weaker banking systems that induce authorities to resist raising interest rates because of the greater risk of a deep recession or generalized bankruptcies. Countries belonging to the second group will have to engineer a greater nominal depreciation in order to close a given current account deficit.

I implement these ideas empirically by classifying observations into four groups: high- and low-reserves cases, and strong and weak fundamentals cases. In my benchmark regression, I classify most country-years as being the ones with low reserves and weak fundamentals. Then, I consider more and less stringent definitions of the vulnerable region, and see how results change.

In the benchmark case, a country-year has high reserves ($D^{hr} = 1$) if its M2/reserves ratio is below 1.8. A country-year has strong fundamentals ($D^{sf} = 1$) if its lending boom (LB) is below 0 percent and its real exchange rate appreciation is lower than 5 percent. The group with high reserves includes seven country-years while the group with strong fundamentals includes five country-years.

In the benchmark I stack the observations for the 1994 and 1997 crises, and estimate the following regression using ordinary least squares:[3]

$$(1) \quad \text{Crisis}_{it} = \alpha_0 + \alpha_i * LB_{it} + \alpha_2 * RER_{it} + \alpha_3 * D^{hr} * LB_{it} + \alpha_4$$
$$* D^{hr} * RER_{it} + \alpha_5 * D^{sf} * LB_{it} + \alpha_6 * D^{sf} * RER_{it} + \varepsilon_{it},$$

where i indexes the country and t indexes time. Lending boom is represented by LB, and real exchange rate depreciation by RER.

The effects of the lending boom and real depreciation in the case of weak fundamentals and low reserves are captured by α_1 and α_2, respectively. Theory predicts that when there is fragility, the crisis will be greater if the lending boom is large (i.e., $\alpha_1 > 0$) and the real depreciation is low (i.e., $\alpha_2 < 0$). The effects of the lending boom and real depreciation for the case of high reserves are captured by $\alpha_1 + \alpha_3$ and $\alpha_2 + \alpha_4$, respectively. Meanwhile, in the case of strong fundamentals, these effects are captured by $\alpha_1 + \alpha_5$ and $\alpha_2 + \alpha_6$, respectively. According to the theory, if there is no fragility ($D^{hr} = 1$ or $D^{sf} = 1$), neither a greater lending boom nor a greater appreciation will affect the investors' decision to attack. Thus one expects to find that $\alpha_1 + \alpha_3 = \alpha_2 + \alpha_4 = 0$, and $\alpha_1 + \alpha_5 = \alpha_2 + \alpha_6 = 0$.

For the benchmark, I consider the crisis index that corresponds to the five months after the onset of the crisis. In the Mexican crisis, I look at November 1994–April 1995; for the Asian case, I consider May 1997–October 1997. The estimated regression is shown in table 2.1, which shows how the estimates change as the crisis index varies.

The estimates in table 2.1 accord with the theory espoused earlier. First, for countries with weak fundamentals and low reserves, the coefficients corresponding to the lending boom (α_1) and the real depreciation (α_2) are significantly different from zero at the 5 percent level. The point estimates indicate that (a) a unit increase in the LB index for a country with low reserves and weak fundamentals leads to a 0.24 unit increase in the crisis index of that country relative to the average of our emerging markets sample; and (b) a unit increase in the real appreciation index leads to a 0.12 increase in the crisis index relative to the average. Second, as expected, neither the LB index nor the RER enter significantly in countries with high reserves. In these cases, the corresponding point estimates are $\alpha_1 + \alpha_3 = -0.01$ and $\alpha_2 + \alpha_4 = 0.03$. Furthermore, Wald tests indicate that the hypotheses $\alpha_1 + \alpha_3 = 0$ and $\alpha_2 + \alpha_4 = 0$ cannot be rejected (the associated p-values are 0.74 and 0.91, respectively). Similarly, in countries with strong fundamentals, neither LB nor RER affect the severity of the

---

3. Below I test whether there are fixed or random effects.

Table 2.1   Benchmark Regression

Estimated Coefficient and Summary Statistic	Independent Variable	Simple OLS
α_1	LB	0.24
		(0.09)
α_2	RER	−0.12
		(0.05)
α_3	$LB*D^{hr}$	−0.25
		(0.08)
α_4	$RER*D^{hr}$	0.15
		(0.27)
α_5	$LB*D^{sf}$	−0.04
		(0.33)
α_6	$RER*D^{sf}$	0.17
		(0.16)
α_7	constant	−1.27
		(3.63)
Summary statistics		
R^2		0.45
Adjusted R^2		0.37

Note: The dependent variable is the Crisis Index; Newey-West heteroscedasticity–adjusted standard errors in parentheses.

crisis. The p-values associated with Wald tests of the hypotheses that $\alpha_1 + \alpha_5 = 0$ and $\alpha_2 + \alpha_6 = 0$ are 0.51 and 0.74, respectively.

In summary, the regression results support the idea that currency crises do not spread randomly. One can predict—with fair confidence—that a crisis will spread to countries that are vulnerable. A country is vulnerable to an attack if it has had an appreciated real exchange rate for the past few years or if it has experienced a lending boom, increasing the likelihood that its banking system is laden with bad loans. Both effects point in the direction of a higher expected depreciation, unless the country in question has sufficient international reserves relative to its short-term liabilities. In this case, the best response of the government might be to defend the peg.

A few examples illustrate how the combination of these three fundamentals can help one rationalize some puzzling cases. If one looks at Peru, for instance, one sees that over the four years prior to the Tequila crisis Peru had experienced a similar appreciation and a greater lending boom than Mexico. However, Peru's crisis index was only −2.7, while Mexico's was 79.3. This can be explained by the fact that Mexico was illiquid (recall the Tesobonos story), while Peru was not. In fact, in November 1994, the ratio of M2 to reserves was 1.25 for Peru and 9.25 in Mexico.

The results presented here for the two crises are very similar to those obtained by Sachs, Tornell, and Velasco (1996b; henceforth STV) for the Tequila crisis. In order to compare results, one should take note of the following slight differences between the papers. The first difference is that STV multiply the estimated coefficients by ten. Also, STV use a weak fundamentals dummy instead of the strong fundamentals dummy used here. My coefficients α_1 and α_2 correspond to the STV coefficients $\beta_3 + \beta_5 + \beta_7$ and $\beta_2 + \beta_4 + \beta_6$, respectively. Last, due to data availability, the STV sample contains fewer countries than the sample examined here.

2.3.2   Structural Change

At this point in the analysis, a natural question arises as to whether the same model that explains the spread of the crisis in 1995 also explains the cross-country variation in the 1997 crisis, or whether there was, in fact, a structural change. The first column of table 2.2 shows the estimates of the benchmark regression that includes the Tequila and Asian crisis. The second and third columns show the estimates of regression equation (1) for the 1994 and 1997 crises, respectively. The point estimates for the coefficient corresponding to the lending boom (α_1) are very similar (0.24, 0.25, and 0.22, respectively). Those corresponding to the real exchange rate depreciation (α_2) are -0.12, -0.16, and -0.07, respectively.

To test the hypothesis that the coefficients in equation (1) are the same in both periods, I perform a Chow test. The test statistic is

$$F[7, 32] = \frac{\dfrac{[6657 - 3461 - 2985]}{7}}{\dfrac{[3461 + 2985]}{32}} = 0.1496.$$

Since the critical value at the 1 percent level is 3.3, one cannot reject the hypothesis that the sets of coefficients are the same in the two periods.

Next, I check whether the two coefficients that interest me most (α_1 and α_2) are the same in both periods. To do this, I first add the term $\alpha_8 * LB * D^{97}$ to equation (1), where D^{97} takes the value of 1 for observations that correspond to the 1997 crisis. It follows that in countries with weak fundamentals and low reserves, the effect of the lending boom on the crisis index is α_1 for the 1994 crisis and $\alpha_1 + \alpha_8$ for the 1997 crisis. Therefore, the null hypothesis is $\alpha_8 = 0$. As can be seen in column 4 in table 2.2, the estimate of α_8 is not different from zero at the 10 percent significance level. Next, I perform the same test for the real exchange rate depreciation. Column 5 in table 2.2 shows the estimation results for equation (1), adding the extra term $\alpha_9 * RER * D^{97}$. Again, the estimate for α_9 is not significantly different from zero at the 10 percent level.

2.3.3   Predicting the Asian Crisis

Suppose that the crystal ball predicted that a crisis would erupt in mid-1997, and suppose the money manager had estimated the model of equation (1) using data from the 1994 crisis. How well will he or she predict

Table 2.2   **Structural Change**

Estimated Coefficient and Summary Statistic	Independent Variable	Benchmark (1)	Only 1994 Sample (2)	Only 1997 Sample (3)	(4)	(5)
α_1	LB	0.24 (0.09)	0.25 (0.17)	0.22 (0.07)	0.24 (0.11)	0.24 (0.09)
α_2	RER	-0.12 (0.05)	-0.16 (0.08)	-0.07 (0.08)	-0.12 (0.05)	-0.12 (0.08)
α_3	LB * D^{hr}	-0.25 (0.08)	-0.29 (0.19)	-0.23 (0.06)	-0.25 (0.08)	-0.25 (0.08)
α_4	RER * D^{hr}	0.15 (0.27)	-0.39 (0.96)	0.35 (0.24)	0.09 (0.25)	0.15 (0.28)
α_5	LB * D^{sf}	-0.04 (0.33)	-0.63 (0.81)	0.09 (0.24)	-0.05 (0.33)	-0.04 (0.34)
α_6	RER * D^{sf}	0.17 (0.16)	0.07 (0.11)	-0.01 (0.15)	0.17 (0.16)	0.17 (0.16)
α_7	constant	-1.27 (3.63)	-4.12 (6.34)	2.13 (2.83)	-1.51 (3.39)	-1.28 (3.67)
α_8	LB * D^{97}				0.02 (0.07)	
α_9	RER * D^{97}					0.02 (0.12)
R^2		0.45	0.48	0.44	0.45	0.45
Adjusted R^2		0.37	0.29	0.23	0.35	0.35

Note: The dependent variable is the Crisis Index; Newey-West heteroscedasticity-adjusted standard errors in parentheses.

the spread of the crisis across emerging markets? Note that the question is not "When will the next crisis erupt?" Rather, the objective here is simply to make an out-of-sample prediction conditional on the occurrence of a crisis.

Toward this end, I will construct an out-of-sample predicted crisis index by substituting in equation (1) the following: (a) the estimated coefficients of a regression that uses only data from the 1994 crisis; and (b) the explanatory variables that correspond to the 1997 crisis, i.e., the lending boom and the real depreciation over the period 1992–96 and the M2/reserves of May 1997. The resulting predicted crisis indexes are depicted as the dashed line in figure 2.1. The solid line represents the actual crisis indexes, while the dotted lines represent the fitted values of the regression using only the data from 1997. As can be seen in figure 2.1, the predicted crisis indexes using 1994 data are quite similar to the fitted crisis indexes using 1997 data.

To measure how well the out-of-sample prediction fits the actual crisis indexes of 1997, I regressed the actual crisis indexes of 1997 on the predicted crisis indexes

$$97\text{Crisis} = \underset{0.3}{0.88} \times [\text{out-of-sample predicted 97crisis}] + u_i$$

$$R^2 = 0.24.$$

The correlation between the two series is 0.88, and it is significantly different from zero at the 1 percent level. Thus one can see that, by using the 1994 model, a manager would not have fared badly in predicting which countries would have been hard hit in 1997.

2.3.4 The Crisis Index

In order to analyze whether the results are robust to changes in the period over which the crisis index is measured, I estimate the regression equation using six crises indexes. For all indexes, the starting point is the month preceding the onset of the crisis (i.e., November 1994 for the Tequila crisis and May 1997 for the Asian crisis). Then, we vary the terminal month over a period of six months starting in January 1995 or July 1997. As table 2.3 shows, in columns (4)–(6) the point estimates and significance levels are similar to those of the benchmark regression (column [3]). Moreover, the estimate of α_1 (which corresponds to the lending boom) is significantly different from zero at the 5 percent level in all columns, and the point estimates in columns (4)–(6) are very similar to the benchmark estimate of 0.26.

2.3.5 Alternative Definitions of the Dummies

In the benchmark regression, a country year is classified as having high reserves if, at the onset of the crisis, its ratio of M2 to reserves is lower

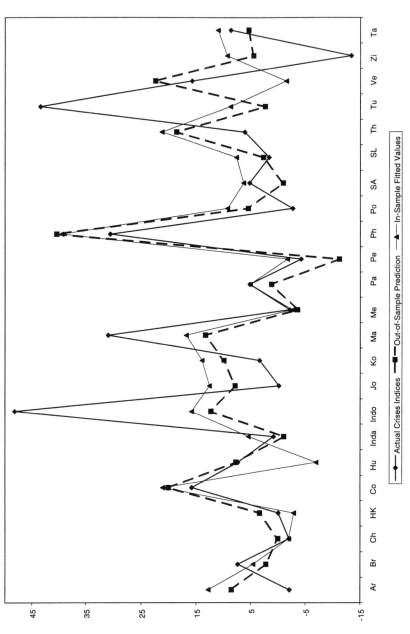

Fig. 2.1 1997 crisis

Table 2.3   Alternative Crisis Indexes

Estimated Coefficient and Summary Statistic	Independent Variable	Interval Used to Calculate Crisis Index[a]					
		Nov.–Jan. May–July	Nov.–Feb. May–Aug.	Nov.–Mar. May–Sept.	Nov.–Apr. May–Oct.	Nov.–May May–Nov.	Nov.–Jun. May–Dec.
α_1	LB	0.13	0.16	0.26	0.24	0.23	0.28
		(0.09)	(0.08)	(0.11)	(0.09)	(0.08)	(0.09)
α_2	RER	−0.04	−0.02	−0.11	−0.12	−0.09	−0.02
		(0.03)	(0.04)	(0.05)	(0.05)	(0.08)	(0.12)
α_3	LB * D^{hr}	−0.14	−0.16	−0.25	−0.25	−0.24	−0.31
		(0.08)	(0.08)	(0.11)	(0.08)	(0.07)	(0.08)
α_4	RER * D^{hr}	−0.12	−0.06	0.02	0.15	0.32	0.33
		(0.18)	(0.22)	(0.28)	(0.27)	(0.30)	(0.41)
α_5	LB * D^{sf}	−0.17	−0.01	−0.12	−0.04	0.09	0.16
		(0.20)	(0.34)	(0.36)	(0.33)	(0.36)	(0.42)
α_6	RER * D^{sf}	0.14	0.12	0.24	0.17	0.20	−0.02
		(0.12)	(0.15)	(0.18)	(0.16)	(0.15)	(0.21)
α_7	constant	−2.40	−1.94	−3.24	−1.27	1.11	4.53
		(2.93)	(2.90)	(4.04)	(3.63)	(3.52)	(4.86)
R^2		0.34	0.40	0.48	0.45	0.43	0.28
Adjusted R^2		0.23	0.30	0.40	0.37	0.35	0.17
Addendum: Wald tests							
Null hypothesis							
$\alpha_1 + \alpha_3 = 0$		0.72	0.94	0.47	0.74	0.42	0.08
$\alpha_2 + \alpha_4 = 0$		0.43	0.71	0.74	0.91	0.45	0.50
$\alpha_1 + \alpha_5 = 0$		0.80	0.65	0.68	0.51	0.36	0.29
$\alpha_2 + \alpha_6 = 0$		0.33	0.50	0.43	0.74	0.46	0.81

Note: The dependent variable is the Crisis Index; Newey-West heteroscedasticity–adjusted standard errors in parentheses.

[a] First row of months for year 1994; second row of months for year 1997.

than 1.8. According to this criterion, seven cases had high reserves. Under the benchmark, a country has strong fundamentals if its lending boom variable is negative and its real appreciation is less than 5 percent (this yields four country years). The second and third columns of table 2.4 show the estimates for different thresholds concerning the high reserves dummy, while keeping the strong fundamentals dummy unchanged. In the second column, the threshold is 1.5 three country years), and, in the third column, 2.0 (ten country years). Column (4) corresponds to the case in which fundamentals are strong if the lending boom is less than 20 percent and the real appreciation is less than 5 percent (nine country years), while in column (5) these thresholds are both zero (two cases).

For countries with low reserves and weak fundamentals, the point estimates corresponding to the lending boom (α_1) and the real depreciation (α_2) are very similar to the benchmark estimates in all cases. Furthermore, they are all significant at the 5 percent and 10 percent levels, respectively. The estimates for the remaining parameters are stable. Lastly, the p-values associated with the Wald tests are greater than 0.10, except in three cases. Since the thresholds we have considered vary over wide ranges, we might conclude that the benchmark results are robust to the way in which I define strong fundamentals and high reserves.

2.3.6   Outliers

To see if the benchmark results are driven by a single outlier, I estimate equation (1) by eliminating, one at the time, the country-years whose residuals are greater than two standard deviations away from the mean. As can be seen in table 2.5, in all cases, the point estimates of α_1 are positive and those of α_2 are negative. Furthermore, both are significantly different from zero at the 5 percent and 10 percent levels, respectively.

2.3.7   Additional Determinants of Currency Crises

High government consumption, excessive capital inflows, and unsustainable current account deficits have been identified as important determinants of currency crises in some well-known episodes. Here, I analyze whether these variables help explain the cross-country variation in the crisis indexes after controlling for the lending boom, the real appreciation, and the reserves adequacy ratio. I measure each concept as the average ratio to GDP over the four years prior to the onset of the crisis (either 1990–94 or 1992–96). In each case I interact the extra variable with the high-reserves dummy and the strong-fundamentals dummy. The estimated coefficients are presented in table 2.6.

My regression estimates indicate that in countries with low reserves and weak fundamentals, government consumption has a positive effect on the crisis index if the lending boom and real depreciation variables are

Table 2.4   Alternative Definitions of the Dummies

Estimated Coefficient and Summary Statistic	Independent Variable	RA < 1.8 RER > −5% LB < 0%	RA < 1.5 RER > −5% LB < 0%	Benchmark RA < 2.0 RER > −5% LB < 0%	RA < 1.8 RER > −5% LB < 20%	RA < 1.8 RER > 0% LB < 0%
α_1	LB	0.24 (0.09)	0.24 (0.09)	0.26 (0.09)	0.24 (0.09)	0.24 (0.09)
α_2	RER	−0.12 (0.05)	−0.11 (0.05)	−0.14 (0.07)	−0.13 (0.07)	−0.12 (0.05)
α_3	LB * D^{hr}	−0.25 (0.08)	−0.23 (0.08)	−0.28 (0.08)	−0.25 (0.08)	−0.25 (0.08)
α_4	RER * D^{hr}	0.15 (0.27)	0.20 (0.19)	−0.27 (0.21)	0.16 (0.27)	0.14 (0.29)
α_5	LB * D^{sf}	−0.04 (0.33)	−0.05 (0.33)	0.10 (0.25)	−0.06 (0.18)	−0.34 (0.34)
α_6	RER * D^{sf}	0.17 (0.16)	0.16 (0.15)	0.26 (0.15)	0.14 (0.16)	0.06 (0.06)
α_7	constant	−1.27 (3.63)	−1.64 (3.57)	−1.63 (3.50)	−1.42 (3.54)	−1.32 (3.39)
R^2		0.45	0.41	0.47	0.45	0.45
Adjusted R^2		0.37	0.32	0.39	0.37	0.37
Addendum: Wald tests Null hypothesis						
$\alpha_1 + \alpha_3 = 0$		0.74	0.93	0.01	0.79	0.72
$\alpha_2 + \alpha_4 = 0$		0.91	0.65	0.05	0.92	0.94
$\alpha_1 + \alpha_5 = 0$		0.51	0.55	0.13	0.30	0.73
$\alpha_2 + \alpha_6 = 0$		0.74	0.71	0.37	0.91	0.00

Note: The dependent variable is the Crisis Index; RA stands for reserves adequacy ratio (M2/reserves); RER stands for real exchange rate depreciation; LB stands for lending boom; Newey-West heteroscedasticity–adjusted standard errors in parentheses.

Table 2.5 **Regression Excluding Some Country-Years**

Estimated Coefficient and Summary Statistic	Independent Variable	All Countries Except								
		Brazil 1994	Hungary 1994	Malaysia 1994	Mexico 1994	Thailand 1994	Hungary 1997	Indonesia 1997	Malaysia 1997	Thailand 1997
α_1	LB	0.25	0.28	0.25	0.15	0.27	0.25	0.23	0.24	0.23
		(0.09)	(0.09)	(0.09)	(0.05)	(0.09)	(0.09)	(0.09)	(0.09)	(0.10)
α_2	RER	−0.10	−0.08	−0.12	−0.10	−0.11	−0.11	−0.12	−0.12	−0.12
		(0.06)	(0.05)	(0.05)	(0.05)	(0.06)	(0.06)	(0.05)	(0.05)	(0.05)
α_3	LB * D^{hr}	−0.25	−0.28	−0.25	−0.16	−0.27	−0.27	−0.24	−0.24	−0.23
		(0.08)	(0.08)	(0.08)	(0.05)	(0.08)	(0.09)	(0.09)	(0.08)	(0.09)
α_4	RER * D^{hr}	0.09	−0.01	0.17	0.28	0.13	−0.01	0.11	0.14	0.15
		(0.27)	(0.26)	(0.26)	(0.23)	(0.27)	(0.26)	(0.27)	(0.27)	(0.27)
α_5	LB * D^{sf}	−0.06	−0.12	−0.03	0.10	−0.05	0.28	−0.05	−0.04	−0.03
		(0.34)	(0.35)	(0.33)	(0.26)	(0.34)	(0.11)	(0.34)	(0.33)	(0.33)
α_6	RER * D^{sf}	0.16	0.18	0.16	0.06	0.17	0.31	0.18	0.17	0.17
		(0.16)	(0.16)	(0.15)	(0.09)	(0.16)	(0.14)	(0.15)	(0.15)	(0.16)
α_7	constant	−1.91	−3.41	−0.96	1.60	−1.52	−1.76	−1.84	−1.49	−1.29
		(3.71)	(3.75)	(3.36)	(1.97)	(3.60)	(3.64)	(3.66)	(3.65)	(3.70)
R^2		0.46	0.50	0.47	0.30	0.51	0.48	0.48	0.45	0.44
Adjusted R^2		0.38	0.42	0.38	0.19	0.43	0.40	0.39	0.36	0.35
Addendum: Wald tests										
Null hypothesis										
$\alpha_1 + \alpha_3 = 0$		0.81	0.99	0.71	0.39	0.78	0.12	0.78	0.75	0.73
$\alpha_2 + \alpha_4 = 0$		0.98	0.74	0.85	0.38	0.94	0.64	0.99	0.95	0.92
$\alpha_1 + \alpha_5 = 0$		0.55	0.62	0.48	0.36	0.51	0.00	0.56	0.53	0.52
$\alpha_2 + \alpha_6 = 0$		0.66	0.50	0.76	0.76	0.69	0.11	0.68	0.72	0.75

Note: The dependent variable is the Crisis Index; Newey-West heteroscedasticity–adjusted standard errors in parentheses.

Table 2.6 Additional Determinants of Crises

Estimated Coefficient and Summary Statistic	Independent Variable	Government Consumption (1)	Government Consumption (2)	Capital Inflows (3)	Capital Inflows (4)	Current Account (5)	Current Account (6)
		Variables Added as the Average Ratio to GDP					
α_1	LB		0.24 (0.10)		0.22 (0.09)		0.22 (0.09)
α_2	RER		-0.14 (0.07)		-0.12 (0.06)		-0.11 (0.06)
α_3	LB * D^{hr}		-0.26 (0.09)		-0.22 (0.08)		-0.21 (0.08)
α_4	RER * D^{hr}		-0.28 (0.28)		0.15 (0.45)		0.07 (0.40)
α_5	LB * D^{sf}		-0.07 (0.32)		-0.003 (0.36)		-0.11 (0.35)
α_6	RER * D^{sf}		0.18 (0.19)		0.16 (0.16)		0.26 (0.18)
α_7	constant	6.54 (2.48)	-0.97 (4.06)	5.75 (2.37)	-0.96 (4.08)	4.98 (2.20)	-3.18 (4.05)
α_8	added variable x	0.14 (0.08)	0.03 (0.06)	0.35 (0.19)	0.11 (0.15)	-0.50 (0.25)	-0.25 (0.22)
α_9	$x * D^{hr}$	-108.97 (49.62)	-68.88 (71.53)	-114.07 (53.53)	-38.66 (64.35)	8.62 (3.56)	-3.15 (8.75)
α_{10}	$x * D^{sf}$	-0.22 (0.08)	-0.04 (0.06)	-0.63 (0.18)	-0.13 (0.15)	0.66 (0.23)	0.31 (0.22)
R^2		0.15	0.47	0.17	0.46	0.20	0.52
Adjusted R^2		0.08	0.33	0.10	0.31	0.14	0.41

Note: The dependent variable is the Crisis Index; Newey-West heteroscedasticity–adjusted standard errors in parentheses.

excluded. As column 1 in table 2.6 shows, the estimated coefficient on government consumption is significantly different from zero at the 10 percent level. However, if the lending boom and real depreciation variables are included, government consumption ceases to be significant (column 2). One can interpret this finding as saying that if excessive government consumption leads to a greater crisis, it does so, not directly, but rather through its effects on the lending boom and the real exchange rate. It is interesting to note that the point estimates and significance levels of the remaining parameters in column 2 are very similar to the ones in benchmark equation (1).

Now I turn the discussion to capital inflows. A popular view is that excessive capital inflows must lead eventually to a currency crisis. The reason for that is because in a short span of time, excessive inflows cannot be efficiently channeled to productive projects. Thus, they end up invested in "white-elephant" or "crony" projects. As a result, the economy is not able to generate, over the medium run, the necessary returns to repay investors. It is at this point that the economy becomes vulnerable to a crisis. Column 3 of table 2.6 presents the estimates of a regression equation that includes only the capital inflows variable. For countries with low reserves and weak fundamentals, capital inflows enter positively and significantly at the 10 percent level. However, if one includes the lending boom and the real depreciation indexes, capital inflows have no effect on the severity of the crisis (column 4). As before, this finding suggests that capital inflows do not have an extra effect on the extent of a crisis beyond the effect they exert on the lending boom and real appreciation.

Last, I consider the ratio of the average current account deficit to gross domestic product (GDP). It is frequently argued that countries cannot run large current account deficits for long periods of time; this view is related to the Feldstein-Horioka finding. Here, I consider the average current account over the four years preceding each crisis. Since four years is hardly the long run, one should not expect to see a positive relation between the current account variable and the crises indexes. Surprisingly, the point estimates of the current account variable are negative. As before, the estimates are significant only when I exclude the lending boom and real depreciation indexes from the regression (see columns 5 and 6).

2.4 Conclusions

These findings suggest that in the recent Tequila and Asian episodes, currency crises did not spread in a purely random way. Rather, a set of fundamentals helps explain the cross-country variation of the severity of those crises. I find that crises did not spread to countries with strong fundamentals or high international reserves; furthermore, within the set of vulnerable countries (those with weak fundamentals and low reserves), I find that the crisis index was increasing in the extent of the lending boom and the severity of the real appreciation experienced by the country.

I also find it untrue that Latin American countries were hardest hit by the crisis in 1995 simply because they were located in Latin America, and that in 1997 Asian countries were the hardest hit simply because they were located in Asia. I find that the same model that explains the spread of the crisis in 1995 also explains the cross-country variation in the 1997 crisis. This finding helps explain why in 1995 the hardest hit countries were Latin American, while in 1997 the Southeast Asian countries were the hardest hit. Prior to the Tequila crisis, Latin American countries, on average, had experienced bigger lending booms and more severe real appreciations than Southeast Asian countries; interestingly, the opposite is true for the period preceding the Asian crisis.

There is an ongoing debate regarding the causes of currency crises. Some researchers argue that crises are caused mainly by fundamentals, while other researchers claim that crises are simply the result of speculative behavior in a world with multiple equilibria. Our findings indicate that both views are in some sense correct. The fundamentalist view is correct in the sense that if fundamentals are strong, it is very unlikely that a country will be attacked. The sunspots view is correct in the sense that if fundamentals are weak, the country enters into a region of multiple equilibria and becomes vulnerable to an attack. Note, however, that the fact that a country is vulnerable does not imply that it must suffer a crisis in the near future. It implies only that if investors' expectations turn pessimistic, a crisis will ensue because the government will be forced to close the external gap through a large depreciation, justifying investors' expectations. To the extent that investors' expectations are unpredictable, the crisis in a particular country is unpredictable.

Appendix

Real Exchange Rate Depreciation

I use the percentage change in the weighted average of the bilateral real exchange rates (using consumer price indexes [CPIs]) with respect to the yen, the U.S. dollar, and the Deutsche mark as a proxy for real exchange depreciation. The weights sum to 1 and are proportional to the bilateral trade shares with Japan, the United States, and the European Union. The extent of depreciation is measured as the percentage increase in the real exchange rate index from 1990 to 1994 for the earlier crisis period and from 1992 to 1996 for the later crisis period. I compute trade shares from the International Monetary Fund's *Direction of Trade Statistics Yearbook,*

1997, for the years 1992 and 1995, and use average nominal exchange rates (line rf from the *IFS* CD-ROM) and CPIs (line 64). Using 1992 weights, J. P. Morgan data are used for Hong Kong and Taiwan.

Lending Boom

I use the percentage change in total domestic credit (line 32 from the *IFS* CD-ROM) minus government claims (line 32an) adjusted for inflation using the December CPIs (line 64). The lending boom is the percentage change from 1990 to 1994 for the earlier crisis and from 1992 to 1996 for the later crisis.

Reserve Adequacy

I use the ratio of M2 to total reserves minus gold (line 1Ld) as a proxy for reserve adequacy; the ratio is calculated as of November 1994 and for June 1997. M2 is calculated using the sum of money (line 34) and quasi-money (line 35). Reserves are converted to national currency using the monthly exchange rate (line rf). Several countries did not have data updated through June 1997, so the most recent measure was used. For Malaysia, Poland, Taiwan, and Hungary the relevant measures are as of November 1996, November 1996, December 1996, and March 1997, respectively. The ratios for these countries are fairly stable over time.

Crisis Index

The crisis index is the depreciation of the exchange rate plus the negative of the percentage change in reserves between November 1994 and a given month in 1995 or May 1997 and various later months. Each of the two components is weighted by its precision over the sum of precision calculated from a monthly series of ten years. For several countries, reserve data were not available monthly for the entire ten-year period and were calculated from the data available in the *IFS.* Precision for Hong Kong is calculated from mixed frequency data (quarterly for several years and then monthly). Precision for Hungary begins September 1989. Taiwan is measured from 1994 through 1997. For Poland, precision calculation begins in 1990 when the currency stabilized after the transition to a free market economy. *IFS* was missing reserve information for many countries for recent data; reserves were filled in using a variety of sources, including *The Economist,* Bloomberg, and the central banks of various countries. In addition, Datastream was used to extend exchange rates. All of these data sources were checked with the previous figures from the *IFS.*

Current Account

I converted (line 78a1) to national currency using annual exchange rates (line rf). This enters into the regression as an average over 1990–94, as a share of GDP over 1992–96, and the percentage change (in U.S. dollars).

Capital Inflows

The sum of capital account (line 78bc), financial account (line 78bj) and net errors and omissions (line 78ca) was converted to national currency using annual exchange rates (line rf). This enters into the regression as average over 1990–94, as share of GDP over 1992–96, and as percent change (in U.S. dollars). Data are missing for Hong Kong and Taiwan.

Government Consumption

This information is taken from line 91f. It enters into the regression as average over 1990–94, as share of GDP over 1992–96, as percent change as share of GDP, and as percent change adjusted for inflation using annual CPIs. Data are missing for Argentina.

Taiwan

Montly reserves and exchange rates were taken from *Bulletin of Statistics* of the Republic of China and supplemented by Datastream and Asian Development Bank (for more recent data).

References

Calvo, Guillermo. 1997. Varieties of capital market crises. Department of Economics. University of Maryland. Mimeograph.

Cole, Harold, and Timothy Kehoe. 1996. A self-fulfilling model of Mexico's 1994–1995 debt crisis. *Journal of International Economics,* 41:309–330.

Corsetti, Giancarlo, Paolo Pesenti, and Nouriel Roubini. 1999. What caused the Asian currency and financial crisis? *Japan and the World Economy* 11 (3): 305–73.

Frankel, Jeffrey A., and Andrew K. Rose. 1996. Currency crashes in emerging markets: An empirical treatment. International Finance Discussion Paper no. 534. Washington, D.C.: Board of Governors of the Federal Reserve System, January.

International Monetary Fund [IMF]. 1997. *Direction of trade statistics yearbook, 1997.* Washington, D.C.: IMF.

Kaminsky, Graciela, Saul Lizondo, and Carmen M. Reinhart. 1998. Leading indicators of currency crises. *IMF Staff Papers* 45 (1): 1–48.

Obstfeld, M. 1994. The Logic of Currency Crises. *Cahiers Economiques et Monetaires* 43:189–213.

Radelet, Steven, and Jeffrey Sachs. 1998. The onset of the East Asian financial crisis," Harvard Institute for International Development. Mimeograph.

Sachs, Jeffrey D., Aaron Tornell, and Andres Velasco. 1996a. Financial crises in emerging markets: The lessons of 1995. *Brookings Papers on Economic Activity* issue no. 1:147–217.

———. 1996b. The Mexican peso crisis: Sudden death or death foretold? *Journal of International Economics* 41 (3–4): 265–83.

Comment   Shinji Takagi

In this paper, Aaron Tornell uses the data from the Tequila and Asian crises to show that the severity of a crisis (defined as a weighted average of the decline in reserves and the extent of currency depreciation) can be explained by three variables: the weakness of the banking system (measured by a lending boom index defined as a real percentage increase in bank loans), real appreciation (measured in effective terms against the U.S. dollar, the Japanese yen, and the Deutsche mark), and central bank liquidity (measured as the ratio of M2 to reserves).

This paper makes an important contribution in showing that fundamentals (as opposed to simple fad or a change in expectations) play a role in explaining the spread of a crisis. The strength of Tornell's approach is that it is simple (consisting of only three explanatory variables) and based only on publicly available, timely information. Simplicity gives power to the prediction model as a policy tool because it allows policy makers to concentrate on a few important fundamental determinants. The use of public and timely information is reasonable because there is no other way that market participants can form expectations that may trigger a crisis.

It is important to keep in mind, however, that the nature of the exercise is conditional, in the sense that prediction is contingent on the occurrence of a crisis. Hence, it does not say anything about whether a certain range of fundamental values will trigger a crisis. In this sense, it is consistent with the so-called second-generation model of currency crises in which there are multiple equilibria. It is not clear, however, to what extent it succeeds in discriminating between first-generation and second-generation models.

There are at least four potential areas of concern. First, the benchmarks of low/high reserves and strong/weak fundamentals seem arbitrary. To the extent that we are interested more in knowing whether a crisis will occur (or spread) than in knowing how severe the crisis will be when one occurs (and spreads), it may be useful to endogenize these benchmarks. Second, in practice, the same benchmarks may have different implications, depending on how the particular outcome is brought about. For example, an increase in reserves may be "bad" if it is caused by an official foreign-exchange market intervention designed to maintain an inappropriate peg. Likewise, real appreciation can be "good" if it reflects the nominal appreciation of the currency in response to capital inflows. Prediction (or fit) may improve if good and bad types of reserve increase or real appreciation is separated out in the data.

Third, control needs to be made for policy responses (e.g., bailout by

Shinji Takagi is visiting professor of economics at Yale University, on leave from his position as professor of economics at Osaka University.

the IMF or capital controls). In other words, the severity of a crisis cannot entirely be captured by the author's variable if the outcome shows up in ways other than declining reserves or depreciation. Finally, there can be a fourth variable, reflecting the real and financial links across countries, which will likely manifest itself as regional links. For example, prediction of a crisis for Latin American and Asian countries may be improved, if it is made conditional on the occurrence of a crisis in Mexico (for 1994–95) and in Thailand (for 1997), respectively. These and other refinements may enhance the usefulness of Tornell's approach to understanding how a crisis may spread across countries.

Comment   Chi-Wa Yuen

Objectives of the Paper

This paper addresses two major issues about the currency crises in 1995 and 1997:

1. What are the "fundamental" determinants of these two crises?
2. Could the Asian crisis have been predicted given the lessons learned from the Tequila crisis and knowledge about the fundamentals above?

Main Findings

Regarding the first issue, the author has constructed a "crisis index" as a weighted average of the loss in reserves and the depreciation against the U.S. dollar, and found that its severity in both the Tequila and Asian crises is determined by three common factors.

1a. Central bank liquidity or foreign-exchange reserve adequacy as proxied by the M2/reserve ratio; the higher the ratio, the more severe the crisis.

1b. Strength of the banking system as proxied by the "lending boom" (LB) index (defined as inflation-adjusted percentage change in total domestic credit less government claims); the higher the LB index, the more severe the crisis.

1c. Extent of real exchange rate (RER) appreciation (where RER is defined as a trade-weighted average of bilateral RER's against the U.S. dollar, the Deutsche mark, and the Japanese yen); the higher the RER (the smaller the appreciation), the less severe the crisis.

Chi-Wa Yuen is associate professor of economics and finance at the University of Hong Kong.

Related to issue number 1 at the beginning of this comment, the author also finds that three other factors usually believed to be important determinants of currency crises—namely, ratios of government consumption, capital inflows, and current account deficits to gross domestic product (GDP)—have significant effects on the crisis index only if the effects from the three common factors (1a, 1b, and 1c) mentioned above are excluded.[1] He then claims that these three alternative factors have only indirect effects on currency crises through their effects on the lending boom and real appreciation.

Regarding issue number 2, the author finds that the "fitted" crisis indexes based on the Asian crisis data are very close to the "predicted" crisis indexes based on parameter estimates from the Tequila crisis data and actual values of the three "fundamental" determinants (1a, 1b, and 1c) from the Asian crisis. In other words, he obtains good out-of-sample forecasts,[2] implying that the Asian crisis could have been predicted given the lessons learned from the Tequila crisis in 1994 and knowledge about the fundamentals in 1997.

Analysis

Let me classify my discussion into three categories: the conceptual framework and definition of variables, "fundamentals" vs. "self-fulfilling expectations" as crisis determinants, and the predictability of the Asian crisis.

Conceptual Framework and Definition of Variables

In analyzing which country will be most prone to currency attacks, the author proposes a conceptual framework that suggests that risk-neutral speculators will pick countries with low reserves and high costs of interest rate adjustment and, among these countries, specifically those which are expected to suffer sizable depreciation when attacked. To most readers, this framework may sound very intuitive and clear. My personal experience with the Hong Kong dollar indicates that countries with high reserves and strong banking systems may nonetheless be subject to speculative attacks even when the speculators do not expect their actions to induce a sizable depreciation. Under the currency board system, any attack on the Hong Kong dollar will drive up the interest rate through an automatic

1. In examining capital inflows as an additional determinant of crisis, one should take into account the composition of these capital flows. In particular, portfolio debt flows can serve as a partial substitute for bank lending. As a result, with both capital inflows and the lending boom as right-hand side variables in the regression equation, there may exist a collinearity problem.

2. Instead of regressing the "97 crisis" on the "out-of-sample predicted 97 crisis" to show that these forecasts are good, the author could have simply reported the mean squared errors from the prediction exercise.

adjustment mechanism. Given the negative correlation between the interest rate and stock prices, this will lead to a drop in the prices of Hong Kong stocks. Anticipating these dynamics, speculators can engineer a "double-market play" to make profits by attacking the Hong Kong dollar in the foreign exchange market and short-selling Hong Kong stocks in the market for stock futures—without actually causing any collapse or depreciation in the Hong Kong dollar. In other words, expectation of a sizable depreciation is not a necessary condition for a currency attack. What is necessary instead is the existence of some sort of expected profits resulting from the attack.

In his conceptual framework, the author lists three possible responses of a country to a currency attack: (a) loss of reserves, (b) depreciation, and (c) rise in interest rate. It is not clear why, in constructing his crisis index, he considers only (a) and (b) and leaves out (c). In addition, there is some inconsistency between the definition of depreciation in his crisis index and that in his RER (the real exchange rate) index. In his crisis index, "depreciation" means depreciation of a country's currency against the U.S. dollar only; whereas in his RER index, it includes depreciation against the Deutsche mark and the Japanese yen in addition to depreciation against the U.S. dollar.

Another important variable in this paper is the weakness of the banking system as proxied by the "lending boom." While it is evident why excessive bank lending may give rise to a crisis, this may not be the case if the total asset value of the banking system as a whole is also growing. I thus think that the lending boom should be redefined to adjust for the values of the banks' loanable assets.

"Fundamentals" vs. "Self-Fulfilling Expectations" as Determinants of the Tequila and Asian Crises

In the speculative attacks literature, there has been a debate on whether fundamentals or self-fulfilling expectations are a more important driving force for currency crises. According to the benchmark regression analysis in section 2.3.1 of the paper, both the Tequila and Asian crises were driven by a common set of fundamentals. This may seem to suggest that the first-generation model of currency crisis (based on fundamentals) better fits the Tequila and Asian stories. A little reflection indicates, however, that the second-generation model (based on self-fulfilling expectations) may fit the stories just as well. This is because the latter has never denied the role of fundamentals in speculative attacks. Instead, it maintains that, in the presence of multiple equilibria, whether self-fulfilling currency attacks will actually occur depends on the range of critical values that the fundamentals fall into.

In fact, the author has gone halfway to addressing this issue by introducing two dummy variables—reserve adequacy (D^{hr} and "fundamentals"

(D^{sf}) reflecting the severity of the lending boom and the extent of RER appreciation—in the interaction terms in his benchmark regression.[3] Some sensitivity analysis is also carried out in table 2.4 by varying the benchmark values of these dummies. Nonetheless, it still cannot resolve the puzzle as to how important fundamentals are relative to self-fulfilling expectations in driving these two crises.

Predictability of the Asian Crisis

Turning to the issue of predictability of the Asian crisis based on the Tequila crisis, I am not sure how useful this exercise really is. This is because the finding that the out-of-sample forecasts are reasonably good is conditional on the absence of structural changes from one crisis to the next (which the author has shown by running a Chow test) and is thus known *after* the fact. However, what is necessary for prediction analysis of the kind examined in this paper (i.e., using reduced-form regression estimates from an earlier crisis to predict the likelihood or severity of a later crisis) is knowledge about the absence of structural changes *before* the fact. Using the same prediction method, can we be sure that we can get accurate forecasts about the crisis index in, say, the year 1999 or 2000 based on the regression estimates from the Tequila and Asian crises? The answer is "no" because there is no way we can know for sure that there will not be any structural change in the year 1999 or 2000. The issue I am raising here is actually well known and general—i.e., the curse of reduced-form regressions and the need to go for structural estimation for prediction purposes when one is uncertain about the possibility of structural change.

In conclusion, the paper has uncovered a common set of fundamentals that drives the Tequila and Asian crises. It remains unclear, however, whether the same will apply to future crises.

3. It is not clear why reserve adequacy is treated separately from lending boom and RER appreciation and not counted as fundamentals as well.

3

Bank Lending and Contagion
Evidence from the Asian Crisis

Graciela L. Kaminsky and Carmen M. Reinhart

3.1 Introduction

There have been several major episodes of "contagious currency crises" during the 1990s. The first of these was the Exchange Rate Mechanism (ERM) crisis of 1992–93. Explanations of why currency instability spread through Europe frequently stressed the interdependence of ERM countries via extensive trade in goods and services (see, e.g., Eichengreen, Rose, and Wyplosz 1996). Yet, the ERM crisis was later followed by the Mexican peso crisis in late 1994, with its "tequila effect" on Argentina and other Latin American countries, and the Russian crisis of 1998, which paralyzed capital flows to emerging markets. There is ample evidence that trade links are not capable of explaining why Argentina was so hard hit by the devaluation of the Mexican peso, as there is minimal bilateral trade between Argentina and Mexico and little scope for competition in a common third market (see Kaminsky and Reinhart 2000 on this issue). Similarly, Russia's importance in world trade is hardly capable of explaining why emerging markets came under such duress following its devaluation and default in August 1998. The absence of obvious trade links in these episodes and the growing importance of financial markets have led academics, policy mak-

Graciela L. Kaminsky is professor of economics and international affairs at the George Washington University.

Carmen M. Reinhart is a professor at the School of Public Affairs and Department of Economics at the University of Maryland, College Park, and a research associate of the National Bureau of Economic Research.

We wish to thank Takatoshi Ito, Anne Krueger, Mahani Zainal-Abidin, Eiji Ogawa, and participants at the tenth annual NBER–East Asia Seminar on Economics for helpful comments and suggestions. We also wish to thank Mark Giancola, Alejandro Guerson, and Rafael Romeu for excellent research assistance.

ers, and the financial press to search for other possible explanations of contagion. Some of these explanations have relied on herding behavior on the part of investors (see Calvo and Mendoza 2000). Other stories have suggested that contagion can arise through exposure to common lenders, be it via hedge funds (as in Calvo 1998) or banks (as in Kaminsky and Reinhart 2000).

The focus of this paper is to analyze how the crisis in Asia spread during the second half of 1997. We cast our net wide and investigate several possible trade and financial linkages among the Asian economies which may help explain why a devaluation in a relatively small country in the region (i.e., Thailand) had such widespread regional consequences. We proceed to construct a series of contagion vulnerability indexes, which capture the various manifestations of exposure through trade and finance to the initial crisis country. We contrast the predictions of this vulnerability index to the actual outcomes during the Asian crisis and compare these results to other recent crisis episodes in emerging markets. We also pay particular attention to the role played by Japanese and European banks, which were lending heavily to emerging Asia on the eve of the crisis.[1] Daily interest rates for Indonesia, Malaysia, the Philippines, South Korea, and Thailand, and exchange rate data are used to assess whether the patterns of causality and interdependence changed as the crisis spread as well as to answer the broader question of whether interdependence among selected Asian economies has changed as the result of the crisis. Our main findings can be summarized as follows.

First, as regards the propagation of shocks across national borders during the Asian crisis, the behavior of foreign banks, particularly Japanese banks that began drastically to curtail their lending to the affected Asian countries following the Thai devaluation, appears to have played a role in spreading the crisis, particularly to Indonesia, Malaysia, and South Korea.[2] The large exposure of European banks to South Korea and their subsequent retrenchment further deepens the regional liquidity crunch.

Second, only Malaysia and South Korea (in that order) appear to have any significant trade links to Thailand. However, these trade links are indirect, through exports to a common third party. Indeed, there is relatively little bilateral trade among these emerging Asian economies. Thus, the spread of crisis to Indonesia and the Philippines cannot be explained through interdependence arising from a substantial volume of trade in goods and services.

Third, the contagion vulnerability indexes do reasonably well in anticipating which countries were most vulnerable to contagion in three recent

---

1. Besides Thailand, the affected countries are taken to include Indonesia, Malaysia, the Philippines, and South Korea.
2. The Philippines had a much lower exposure to Japanese banks.

crises episodes (the Mexican 1994 devaluation, Brazil's crisis in early 1999, and the Asian episode). The indexes, however, are silent as to the severity of these contagion effects. For example, Indonesia, Malaysia, and South Korea are all identified as potential candidates of spillovers from Thailand; yet Indonesia is shown, ex ante, as the one with the least intensive links to Thailand; ex post, it experienced the most severe crisis of the three.[3]

Fourth, the evidence from the daily data suggests that the patterns of causality and interdependence do change during the course of the crisis, as turbulence in affected countries such as Indonesia begins to have additional feedback effects on the other countries, including the initial crisis country, Thailand. Furthermore, there is a marked difference in pre- 'and post-crisis interest rates and exchange rate linkages among the countries in our sample. Prior to the crisis, there is little evidence of systematic causality or interdependence among these five countries; the post-crisis patterns are markedly different, particularly for Indonesia, the Philippines, and Thailand, all of which show a much greater degree of dependence on external shocks.

Lastly, Malaysia's interest rates remain uninfluenced by shocks to other interest rates in the region in the post-crisis sample. This result may be due to the presence of extensive capital controls—an issue which merits further scrutiny.

The paper is organized as follows. Section 3.2 discusses the patterns in Japanese, European, and U.S. bank lending to emerging Asia and analyzes the behavior of foreign bank lending as the crisis unfolds. Section 3.3 discuses trade linkages and other financial channels of contagion. In this section, contagion vulnerability indexes are developed and used to analyze and compare recent crisis episodes. In section 3.4, we study the issue of cross-country interdependence between daily interest rate and exchange rate shocks and how international linkages may have changed during the post-crisis period. The last section presents some brief concluding remarks.

3.2   Bank Lending and Contagion in Asia: Stylized Evidence

Much of the recent literature on contagion has suggested that trade links are a vehicle for the transmission of currency crises across national borders (see, e.g., Gerlach and Smets 1994 and Glick and Rose 1998). Other recent papers on the subject have focused on the role that capital markets play in spreading turbulence internationally (see, e.g., Frankel and Schmukler 1998 and Calvo 1998). Yet nearly all of this literature has ignored the role that banks can play in transmitting disturbances across countries. This

---

3. Obviously, differences across countries in how the crisis is managed by policy makers can go a long way toward differences in the severity and duration of the crisis.

channel of transmission is straightforward. Through its loan portfolio, a bank may be exposed to a country that has a financial crisis. If the crisis occurs, it impacts the bank's balance sheet and the bank is faced with the need to rebalance its portfolio. To make up for the deterioration in the quality of its loans, the bank may shift away from lending and increase its holdings of government bonds. Other countries which were borrowing from the affected bank will be vulnerable to cutbacks in their lines of credit. Furthermore, if these countries' loan contracts were of short maturity and the bank's rebalancing needs are significant, the initial crisis could trigger large capital outflows from the other borrowers. That is, not only may the bank be unwilling to extend new credits to the other borrowers, it may also refuse to roll over their existing loans—hence, the capital outflow. If the capital flow reversal is sufficiently large and abrupt, it could spark a financial crisis in one or more of the other borrowers. This type of problem is particularly acute if the borrowers were heavily dependent on that bank and do not have immediate recourse to alternative sources of financing. The bank's inability or unwillingness to lend may be compounded by the requirement that banks must provision for bad loans.

In an earlier paper, we examined the potential for contagion through exposure to a common lender (see Kaminsky and Reinhart 2000). We found evidence that common bank lenders have played a significant role in the spread of currency crises—indeed, the bank-lending channel outperforms trade channels in explaining the vulnerability of a country to contagion.

Contagion during the ERM crises of 1992 and 1993 in Europe and in Argentina and Brazil following the devaluation of the Mexican peso in 1994 appear to have little to do with the withdrawal of a common bank creditor. High and rising international interest rates and poor economic fundamentals have been blamed for the wave of currency and banking crises that swept developing countries (particularly in Latin America) in the early 1980s. Yet, badly burned by Mexico's default in August of 1982, U.S. banks were rapidly retrenching from the emerging world. The drive to reduce loan exposure was most acute for Latin America, which depended almost exclusively on U.S. banks. A more recent example of the role of banks in propagating disturbances internationally can be found in the Asian crisis of 1997; the remainder of this section is devoted to this issue.

3.2.1 Banks and Contagion in Asia

International capital had been pouring into much of Asia, most notably Indonesia, Malaysia, and Thailand, throughout most of the 1990s. Other emerging markets, particularly the largest countries in Latin America, experienced a similar surge in capital inflows (see Calvo, Leiderman, and Reinhart 1996). A key difference between the two regions, however, was that an important share of capital inflows to Latin America came through

Table 3.1   Bank Lending to Emerging Asia, June 1997–June 1998

	June 1997	December 1997	June 1998
European banks			
US$ billions	85,338	87,846	76,820
Percent change since June 1997	n.a.	2.9	−10.0
Japanese banks			
US$ billions	97,232	86,651	74,297
Percent change since 1997	n.a.	−10.9	−23.6
U.S. banks			
US$ billions	23,738	21,974	16,566
Percent chance since June 1997	n.a.	−7.4	−30.2

Notes: Emerging Asia comprises Indonesia, Malaysia, the Philippines, South Korea, and Thailand. n.a. = not applicable.

portfolio bond and equity flows, while in Asia, bank lending loomed large, particularly in the two years preceding the crisis. As shown in Table 3.1, lending to emerging Asia expanded markedly.[4] There were two factors behind this sharp growth in bank credit. Part of the rise in lending was owing to the European banks' goal to achieve a higher profile in emerging markets, particularly in South Korea. Much of the lending boom, however, especially in the case of Thailand, Indonesia, and South Korea, was owing to a rapid expansion in credit from Japanese banks. Faced with a slumping economy and little domestic loan demand, Japanese banks increasingly looked overseas to the rapidly growing economies of Southeast Asia as potential borrowers.

Table 3.2 presents the distribution of lending of U.S., Japanese, and European banks to emerging Asia. Three features are worth noting. First, U.S. bank exposure to Asia was modest on the eve of the crisis; emerging Asia amounted to about US$24 billion (table 3.1) and accounted for only 20 percent of all U.S. bank lending to developing countries (table 3.2). Second, and by way of contrast, Japanese banks were lending four times as much as U.S. banks (i.e., US$97 billion) to emerging Asia; the five crisis countries listed in table 3.2 accounted for two-thirds of all loans to emerging markets.[5] Third, Japanese banks were most exposed to Thailand— which is the first country to experience a crisis. Indeed, the extent of their exposure is similar to that of U.S. banks to Mexico in 1982.[6] Fourth, European bank lending to emerging Asia was also significant and accounted for about a half of all their lending to emerging markets; South Korea alone accounted for 40 percent of their lending to the developing world.

4. Emerging Asia comprises Indonesia, Malaysia, the Philippines, South Korea, and Thailand.
5. Most of the remaining one-third was going to China.
6. See Kaminsky and Reinhart (2000) for a comparison of these episodes.

Table 3.2   Banks: Liabilities as a Percent of Borrower's Total Liabilities, 1994–98

	December 1994	June 1995	December 1995	June 1996	December 1996	June 1997	December 1997	June 1998
			Liabilities to the United States					
Indonesia	7.020	5.680	6.240	7.200	9.510	7.820	8.390	6.420
Malaysia	10.176	7.288	9.076	9.433	10.511	8.264	6.487	4.990
The Philippines	37.408	35.830	35.379	31.042	29.363	19.450	16.336	16.992
South Korea	9.695	9.971	9.790	10.885	9.359	9.564	10.119	10.227
Thailand	6.131	5.791	6.522	6.387	7.198	5.761	4.304	3.754
			Liabilities to Japan					
Indonesia	52.476	50.758	47.103	43.853	39.686	39.421	37.712	37.857
Malaysia	43.215	41.373	43.627	40.453	36.925	36.420	31.057	34.343
The Philippines	13.939	15.591	11.817	12.987	11.724	14.603	13.296	12.964
South Korea	30.792	29.223	27.673	25.574	24.335	22.787	21.525	26.136
Thailand	60.284	60.869	58.654	54.102	53.495	54.413	56.377	55.811
			Liabilities to Europe					
Indonesia	31.253	33.476	33.777	36.661	37.842	38.277	39.862	43.704
Malaysia	40.495	44.057	36.947	39.164	41.446	44.000	50.863	47.429
The Philippines	41.376	40.275	42.020	43.520	47.618	49.363	53.088	60.203
South Korea	33.729	34.306	30.455	30.512	33.835	35.568	35.747	38.813
Thailand	24.187	24.853	23.730	26.066	27.283	28.546	29.182	32.809

Source: Bank for International Settlements (BIS), various issues.

Notes: Each entry is the amount owed by that country to the lender, divided by that country's total debt (grand total). Europe total includes Spain, the United Kingdom, Sweden, Norway, the Netherlands, Luxembourg, Italy, Ireland, Germany, France, Finland, Denmark, Belgium, and Austria.

Fifth, Japanese banks were quick to pull out of emerging Asia. Between June and December of 1997, lending by Japanese banks fell by 10 percent, while lending by European banks actually rose slightly. This is not surprising in light of the previous discussion. Japanese banks were most exposed to Thailand; European and U.S. banks were most exposed to South Korea. The Thai devaluation occurred in early July, while South Korea abandoned its defense of the won in mid-November. By June 1998, however, the reduction in lending to emerging Asia was across the board. United States bank lending fell by a cumulative 30 percent, representing a decline of about US$5 billion. The 24 percent decline in Japanese bank lending in June 1997–98, however, translates into a reduction of about US$26 billion.

The previous observations suggest that, even if the banks were not the immediate trigger of financial contagion, their actions certainly made the spillovers, first from Thailand and later from South Korea, far more severe than they would be otherwise. In the following section, we construct a composite contagion vulnerability index; exposure to a common bank creditor figures prominently in this index.

3.3 A Contagion Vulnerability Index

In this section, we provide a brief review of the "signals" approach that we will use to assess the probability of a "contagious" currency crisis. This methodology was first used to analyze the performance of a variety of macroeconomic and financial indicators around "twin crises" (i.e., the joint occurrences of currency and banking crises) in Kaminsky and Reinhart (1999).[7]

In the analysis that follows, we focus on a sample of twenty countries over the period 1970 to 1998. The countries in our sample are Argentina, Bolivia, Brazil, Chile, Colombia, Denmark, Finland, Indonesia, Israel, Malaysia, Mexico, Norway, Peru, the Philippines, Spain, Sweden, Thailand, Turkey, Uruguay, and Venezuela. As an out-of-sample exercise, we apply this approach to analyze South Korea's vulnerability to contagion during recent episodes of global financial turmoil.

While the preceding section stressed the key role played by foreign banks in spreading the crises throughout Asia during 1997, this section will develop a contagion vulnerability index that also allows for other types of links across countries. Specifically, we consider both bilateral and third-party trade links as well as contagion arising from other financial channels.

In order to implement the signals approach to analyze contagion, however, we need to clarify a minimum number of concepts which will be used throughout the analysis.

---

7. This methodology is described in some detail in Kaminsky, Lizondo, and Reinhart (1998), Kaminsky (1998), and Goldstein, Kaminsky, and Reinhart (2000).

3.3.1 Defining Currency Crises

A currency crisis is defined as a situation in which an attack on the currency leads to substantial reserve losses or a sharp depreciation of the currency—if the speculative attack is ultimately successful. This definition of currency crisis has the advantage that it is comprehensive enough to capture not only speculative attacks on fixed exchange rates (e.g., Thailand's experience prior to 2 July 1997) but also attacks that force a large devaluation beyond the established rules of a crawling-peg regime or an exchange rate band (e.g., Indonesia's widening of the band prior to its flotation of the rupiah on 14 August 1997.) Since reserve losses also count, the index also captures unsuccessful speculative attacks.

We constructed an index of currency-market turbulence as a weighted average of exchange rate changes and reserve changes. Interest rates were excluded as many emerging markets in our sample had interest rate controls through much of the sample.

The index, I, is a weighted average of the rate of change of the exchange rate, $\Delta e/e$, and of reserves, $\Delta R/R$, with weights such that the two components of the index have equal sample volatilities

$$(1) \qquad I = \left(\frac{\Delta e}{e}\right) - \left(\frac{\sigma_e}{\sigma_R}\right) \cdot \left(\frac{\Delta R}{R}\right),$$

where σ_e is the standard deviation of the rate of change of the exchange rate and σ_R is the standard deviation of the rate of change of reserves. Since changes in the exchange rate enter with a positive weight and changes in reserves have a negative weight attached, readings of this index that were three standard deviations or more above the mean were cataloged as crises. For countries in the sample that had hyperinflation, the construction of the index was modified.[8] As noted in earlier studies which use the signals approach, the dates of the crises map well onto the dates obtained if one were to rely exclusively on events, such as the closing of the exchange markets or a change in the exchange rate regime, to define crises.

3.3.2 Defining Contagion

As noted earlier, the term "contagion" has been used to mean different things across studies. In this paper, contagion refers to the case in which knowing that there is a currency crisis elsewhere increases the probability

---

8. While a 100 percent devaluation may be traumatic for a country with low to moderate inflation, a devaluation of that magnitude is commonplace during hyperinflation. A single index for the countries that had hyperinflation episodes would miss sizable devaluations and reserve losses in the moderate inflation periods, since the historic mean is distorted by the high-inflation episode. To avoid this, we divided the sample according to whether inflation in the previous six months was higher than 150 percent, then constructed an index for each subsample.

of a crisis at home.[9] We are interested in understanding the channels of transmission of what we call "fundamentals-based contagion," which arises when countries are linked via trade or finance.

Since what we are interested in explaining is how turbulence is transmitted across countries which are connected by trade or finance and in assessing which of these links are most important, it matters greatly how we define "elsewhere." As in Kaminsky and Reinhart (2000), we define "elsewhere" by grouping the countries in our sample into various clusters. As noted in section 3.2, an important source of fundamentals-based contagion in the Asian crisis was countries' exposure to a common bank lender. We identify two distinct bank clusters in our sample; one of these clusters is made up of countries that borrow primarily from U.S. banks, while a second bank cluster consists of countries where an important share of their borrowing is concentrated among Japanese banks.

The growing practice of cross-market hedging in recent years also suggests that countries which have (for whatever reason) exhibited a moderately positive correlation of asset returns (with the crisis country) and have relatively liquid markets may be vulnerable to contagion via cross-market hedges. We identify two high-correlation clusters in our sample in Asia and Latin America.

A competitive devaluation story, as in Gerlach and Smets (1994), suggests that a currency crisis in one country may lead to a devaluation in a second country if the two countries engage in a significant amount of bilateral trade. In a similar vein, Corsetti et al. (1998) stress that competitive devaluation pressures may arise even if two countries do not trade directly with one another. Such pressures may be present if the two countries are competing in a common third market.

The countries in each of these clusters are listed in table 3.4.[10] On the basis of the information in tables 3.3 and 3.4, we can construct a rough index of vulnerability to fundamentals-based contagion for each country in the sample at each point in time. Consider the case of the Asian crisis, which began on 2 July 1997 with the devaluation of the Thai baht. To assess how the Thai devaluation could affect other countries, one could simply count the number of common clusters through which a country is exposed to Thailand. For example, Malaysia is in the same bank cluster as Thailand, as well as in the same high-correlation and third-party trade clusters—a total of three. The Philippines are also part of the same third-party trade and Asian high-correlation cluster, but not a part of the Japanese bank cluster—a total of two. Indonesia shares the same high-correlation and Japanese bank clusters with Thailand—a total of two.

---

9. This is the definition used in Eichengreen, Rose, and Wyplosz (1996) and Kaminsky and Reinhart (2000).

10. Details on the criteria used to define the clusters are given in Kaminsky and Reinhart (2000).

Table 3.3   **Banks: Liabilities as a Percent of Lender's Total Liabilities, 1994–98**

	December 1994	June 1995	December 1995	June 1996	December 1996	June 1997	December 1997	June 1998
Liabilities to the United States								
Indonesia	2.82	2.63	2.94	3.45	5.59	4.04	4.32	2.95
Malaysia	1.58	1.23	1.61	1.84	2.47	2.09	1.58	1.05
The Philippines	2.95	3.02	3.12	3.26	4.13	2.47	2.84	2.77
South Korea	6.33	8.15	8.03	9.32	9.90	8.75	8.41	6.78
Thailand	3.10	3.55	4.34	4.31	5.34	3.51	2.23	1.61
Liabilities to Japan								
Indonesia	15.23	15.09	15.14	15.43	15.91	15.58	15.75	15.49
Malaysia	4.84	4.48	5.29	5.80	5.93	7.06	6.12	6.44
The Philippines	0.79	0.84	0.71	1.00	1.13	1.42	1.88	1.88
South Korea	14.47	15.36	15.49	16.06	17.56	15.97	14.51	15.42
Thailand	21.96	24.01	26.60	26.79	27.09	25.40	23.74	21.27
Liabilities to Europe								
Indonesia	3.22	3.67	4.21	4.79	5.89	5.15	4.65	4.28
Malaysia	1.61	1.75	1.74	2.09	2.58	2.90	2.80	2.13
The Philippines	0.83	0.80	0.98	1.24	1.77	1.63	2.09	2.09
South Korea	25.39	28.14	30.12	31.71	43.15	38.77	30.86	22.98
Thailand	3.12	3.60	4.18	4.79	5.36	4.53	3.43	2.99

Source: Bank for International Settlements (BIS), various issues.

Notes: Each entry is the amount owed by that country to the lender, divided by the lender's total outstanding claims to developing countries, as reported to BIS. The total claims of the lenders on developing countries is calculated as their total outstanding claims less the total claims to developed countries. European data include Spain, the United Kingdom, Sweden, Norway, the Netherlands, Luxembourg, Italy, Ireland, Germany, France, Finland, Denmark, Belgium, and Austria.

Table 3.4   **Trade and Financial Clusters**

	Bank Cluster		High-Correlation Cluster		Third-Party Trade Cluster		Bilateral Trade Cluster
	Japan	United States	Asia	Latin America	Asia	Latin America	Latin America
Argentina	1			1			1
Bolivia							
Brazil	1			1		1	1
Chile	1						1
Colombia	1					1	
Denmark							
Finland							
Indonesia	1		1				
Israel							
Malaysia	1		1		1		
Mexico	1			1		1	
Norway							
Peru			1				
The Philippines	1	1	1		1		
South Korea[a]	1				1		
Spain							
Sweden							
Thailand	1		1		1		
Turkey							
Uruguay		1					1
Venezuela		1				1	

Note: See text for detailed explanation.

[a]Not part of our sample.

South Korea borrows from Japanese banks; it is part of the Asian third-party trade cluster, but asset returns correlation with Thailand is low— also a total of two. Argentina (for example) is not exposed to Thailand via any of the financial or trade links analyzed here.[11] On the basis of this simple tally, one would conclude that Malaysia is the most vulnerable to fundamentals-based contagion from Thailand and Argentina the least; but this simple tally does not allow us to rank the relative vulnerabilities of Indonesia, the Philippines, and South Korea, as they all share two (although different) clusters with Thailand. In the remainder of this section, we describe an approach that allows us to assign different weights in a contagion vulnerability index to the different trade and financial links; the

11. It is important to note that this is not an exhaustive analysis of all possible financial sector links. For instance, Brazil and Russia were directly impacted by the Korean crisis, as Korean financial intermediaries sold their holdings of Brazilian and Russian debt (see Calvo and Reinhart, 1996 for examples and discussion of other potential links).

weights will depend on the accuracy of these links in predicting the incidence of contagious crises.

3.3.3   Signals, Noise, and Crises Probabilities

A crisis elsewhere may or may not be a reliable signal of a future crisis at home. A summary of the possible outcomes is presented in the following 2 × 2 matrix.

	Crisis Occurs in the Following 24 Months	No Crisis Occurs in the Following 24 Months
Signal = 1, if there is a crisis elsewhere	A	B
No signal = 0, if no crisis elsewhere	C	D

A perfect indicator would have entries only in cells A and D. Hence, with this matrix we can define several useful concepts which we will use to evaluate the predictive ability of each of the clusters.

We begin by calculating, for a given sample, the unconditional probability of crisis,

$$(2) \qquad P(C) = \frac{A + C}{A + B + C + D}.$$

If knowing that there is a crisis elsewhere helps predict a crisis at home, then it can be expected that the probability a of crisis, conditional on a signal, $P(C|S)$, is greater than the unconditional probability. Where

$$(3) \qquad P(C|S) = \frac{A}{A + B}.$$

Formally,

$$(4) \qquad P(C|S) - P(C) > 0.$$

If crisis elsewhere is not a "noisy" indicator (prone to sending false alarms), then there are relatively few entries in cell B and $P(C|S) \approx 1$. However, since "elsewhere" is defined differently for each of the clusters, their forecasting track records will differ.

We can also define the noise-to-signal ratio, N/S as,

$$(5) \qquad \frac{N}{S} = \frac{B/(B + D)}{\dfrac{A}{A + C}}.$$

In the remainder of this section, we employ these concepts to provide evidence on the relative merits in anticipating crises of the trade and finance clusters.

Table 3.5 **Conditional Probabilities and Noise-to-Signal Ratios for Trade and Financial Clusters**

Noise-to-Signal Ratio	Bank Cluster	High-Correlation Cluster	Third-Party Trade Cluster	Bilateral Trade Cluster
25 to 50	0.90	0.58	1.54	2.34
50 and above	0.07	0.39	0.57	0.08
		Weight in Vulnerability Index		
25 to 50	1.10	1.73	0.64	0.42
50 and above	14.08	2.57	1.75	12.5
		$P(C\|CE) - P(C)$		
25 to 50	−3.1	20.8	−6.3	−21.8
50 and above	52.0	47.1	30.7	47.3

Source: Based on Kaminsky and Reinhart (2000).

Table 3.5 presents the results from this exercise for each of the clusters. As noted in Kaminsky and Reinhart (2000), contagion appears to be a highly nonlinear process, irrespective of which country grouping scheme is used. If one-quarter to one-half of the countries in a given cluster have a crisis, the probability of a crisis at home does not increase by much; this is shown under the rows labeled 25 to 50 percent. Yet, if more than one-half of the countries in the cluster have a crisis, the probability of a crisis at home increases dramatically. This nonlinearity is evident in the marked declines in the noise-to-signal ratios as the proportion of countries affected by crises increases. The decline in the noise-to-signal ratio is most dramatic for the Latin American bilateral trade cluster, which falls from 2.34 to 0.08. This sharp improvement in forecasting accuracy is also evident in its marginal predictive ability, $P(C\|S) - P(C)$. The common bank lender cluster has the lowest noise-to-signal ratio while the third-party trade cluster has the highest. While assessing the predictive ability of the individual clusters is a useful exercise to discriminate among competing explanations of contagion, countries which are linked in trade are also often linked in finance. This implies that multiple channels of contagion may be operating at once. To examine exposure to contagion via a variety of channels, we now turn to the construction of a composite vulnerability index.

3.3.4 Trade and Financial Clusters, and a Composite Contagion Index

Kaminsky (1998) and Goldstein, Kaminsky, and Reinhart (2000) show how to construct a composite index to gauge the probability of a crisis conditioned on multiple signals from various indicators (i.e., economic fundamentals); the more reliable indicators receive a higher weight in this composite index. This methodology can be readily applied to construct a composite contagion vulnerability index.

In weighing individual indicators, a good argument can be made for eliminating from our list of potential leading indicators those variables which had a noise-to-signal ratio above unity; this is tantamount to stating that their marginal forecasting ability $P(C|S)$ is zero or less. Applying this criterion to our results, we would focus on the case where more than 50 percent of the countries in the cluster are experiencing a crisis. As shown in table 3.5, the highest noise-to-signal ratio is 0.57, well below unity— but the track record of the signals in each of the clusters is far from uniform. Thus, we weigh the signals by the inverse of the noise-to-signal ratios reported in table 3.5.

Formally, we construct the following composite indicator,

$$(6) \qquad I_t = \sum_{j=1}^{n} \frac{S_t^j}{\omega^j}.$$

In equation (6) it is assumed that there are n different indicators (i.e., clusters). Each cluster has a differentiated ability to forecast crises and, as before, this ability can be summarized by the noise-to-signal ratio, here denoted by ω^j, S_t^j is a dummy variable that is equal to 1 if the univariate indicator, S^j, crosses its critical threshold and is thus signaling a crisis and zero otherwise. As before, the noise-to-signal ratio is calculated under the assumption that an indicator issues a correct signal if a crisis occurs within the following twenty-four months. All other signals are considered false alarms.

The maximum value that this composite vulnerability index could score is 30.9 if a country belonged to the same four clusters as the crisis country. This score is a simple sum of the inverse of the noise-to-signal ratio.

3.3.5   Evidence from Three Recent Crisis Episodes

We now consider, on the basis of the trade and financial sector linkages discussed here, which countries would have been classified as vulnerable to contagion during three recent episodes of currency crises in emerging markets. The first of these episodes begins with the devaluation of the Mexican peso in December 1994.

On the heels of the Mexican devaluation, Argentina and Brazil were the countries to come under the greatest speculative pressure. In a matter of a few weeks in early 1995, the central bank of Argentina lost about 20 percent of its foreign exchange reserves, and bank deposits fell by about 18 percent as capital fled the country. Such a severe outcome could hardly be attributed to trade linkages and competitive devaluation pressures, as Argentina does not trade with Mexico on a bilateral basis and does not compete with Mexican exports in a common third market.[12] In the case of Brazil, the speculative attack was more brief, although the equity mar-

---

12. See Kaminsky and Reinhart (2000) for details on the pattern of trade.

ket sustained sharp losses. Both of these countries record high readings in their vulnerability indexes following the Mexican devaluation. While the effects on Asia of the Mexican crisis were relatively mild, the country which encountered the most turbulence in the region was the Philippines, which also registers a relatively high vulnerability score.

In the case of the Thai crisis, Malaysia shares both trade and finance links with Thailand. For the other Asian countries the potential channels of transmission are fewer. As noted earlier, the Philippines are part of the same third-party trade cluster as Thailand, which receives a weight of 1.75 (i.e., 1/0.57) in the composite index; it is also part of the Asian high-correlation cluster, which receives a weight of 2.57 (i.e., 1/0.39) in the index. Indonesia shares the same high-correlation cluster with Thailand and is a part of the Japanese bank cluster, which receives a weight of 14.08 (i.e., 1/0.07). Hence, as shown in table 3.6, Indonesia's and the Philippines' contagion vulnerability indexes score 16.65 and 4.32, respectively. South Korea, as noted in section 3.2, also borrowed heavily from Japanese banks. Accordingly, its exposure to Thailand came more from having a common lender than from conventional competitive trade pressures.

Table 3.6   **A Contagion Vulnerability Index**

	Contagion Vulnerability Index		
	December 1994: Mexican Crisis	July 1997: Thai Crisis	January 1999: Brazilian Crisis
Argentina	16.65	0	29.15
Bolivia	0	0	0
Brazil	18.4	0	n.a.
Chile	0	0	26.58
Colombia	12.5	0	15.83
Denmark	0	0	0
Finland	0	0	0
Indonesia	0	16.65	0
Israel	0	0	0
Malaysia	0	28.33	0
Mexico	n.a.	0	18.4
Norway	0	0	0
Peru	2.57	0	2.57
The Philippines	14.08	4.32	14.08
South Korea	0	26.58	0
Spain	0	0	0
Sweden	0	0	0
Thailand	0	n.a.	0
Turkey	0	0	0
Uruguay	0	0	26.58
Venezuela	12.5	0	15.83

Note: n.a. = not applicable.

The most recent of these emerging market crises was Brazil's devaluation of the real in early 1999. Not surprisingly, Argentina, which has both trade (Mercosur) and financial linkages with Brazil, shows the highest vulnerability; other Mercosur countries come close in suit.

3.4   Contagion and Interdependence: Interest Rates and Exchange Rates

The preceding discussion has suggested that, even in the absence of any shifts in market sentiment or herding behavior on the part of investors, there are multiple reasons that a crisis in one country may have important repercussions on other countries which are exposed to the crisis through financial or trade arrangements. Yet these fundamental channels of crisis transmission are not likely to emerge or disappear quickly. Developing mutually satisfactory trade arrangements or building close ties with possible creditors may take time and is not likely to change dramatically from one moment to the next. For example, as shown in table 3.2, countries which were in the Japanese-bank cluster before the crisis remain so after the crisis; a similar statement can be made about the U.S. borrower group.

A proximate way to explore whether vulnerability to "true contagion"— that is, interdependence that cannot be accounted for by the kinds of conventional trade or finance links that we have focused on thus far—may be to examine causal patterns (or interdependence) among the affected countries in market-determined variables such as interest rates, exchange rates, and stock returns. One possible explanation of contagion has to do with the "wake-up call hypothesis" (see Goldstein, Kaminsky, and Reinhart 2000), which suggests that the initial crisis serves as a wake-up call, leading investors to reassess the risks of other countries which share some of the vulnerabilities with the crisis country—irrespective of whether they have a common bank lender or are linked in trade. Alternatively, herding may arise even when investors are rational if verifying rumors (or information in general) is costly (see Calvo and Mendoza 2000). If rumors become more frequent in the aftermath of a crisis, this may impart greater interdependence or increased comovement among financial indicators across countries.

3.4.1   Methodology Issues

To examine whether there is greater interdependence or unidirectional causal links among five of the affected Asian countries following the financial crisis that began with the 2 July 1997 devaluation of the Thai baht, we assembled daily data on domestic interest rates and exchange rates for Indonesia, Malaysia, the Philippines, South Korea, and Thailand. The data begin on 1 January 1996 and run through July 1999. Hence, there is a roughly comparable number of observations prior to the crisis (392 observations) and following the crises (334 observations.) We employ a simple vector autoregression (VAR) framework, which treats all variables as potentially endogenous, and include ten lags of each of the variables in the system. Omitting time subscripts, a representative equation for domestic interest rates (r) in Indonesia (denoted by the subscript i) in this five-equation system is given by

$$(7) \quad r_i = \alpha_i + A_1(L)r_i + A_2(L)r_m + A_3(L)r_p + A_4(L)r_{sk} + A_5(L)r_t + \varepsilon_i.$$

The subscripts m, p, sk, and t refer to Malaysia, the Philippines, South Korea, and Thailand, respectively. The lag operators are the A's and ε's denote the random shocks. A comparable system was estimated for daily changes in the exchange rate (in percent). For each block of regressors we conducted F- and log-likelihood ratio tests that tested the null hypothesis of no causal relationship.

3.4.2   Interest Rate and Exchange Rate Links: Evidence from Asia

Table 3.7 reports the results for interest rates; the detailed test statistics and their associated probability values are presented in appendix tables 3A.1–3A.4. The columns "cause" the rows; an N denotes that the null hypothesis of no causality was not rejected while a Y indicates rejection of the null hypothesis at a 5 percent level of significance or higher. For example, the top row, which summarizes the results for Indonesia for the 1 January 1996–1 July 1997 period, shows four N entries, indicating that interest rates in the four remaining countries in the system had no systematic influence on Indonesian interest rates. The last column of table 3.7 tallies the number of significant entries. Table 3.8 summarizes in comparable manner the results for the daily exchange rate changes.

Several features of the pre- and post-crisis results for interest rate patterns are worth noting. First, for the precrisis sample, none of the regressors (other than lags of the dependent variable) are statistically significant at standard confidence levels. Second, the post-crisis period is quite different in that regard with a greater degree of interdependence among the countries. Fluctuation in Thai and Philippine interest rates significantly influences interest rates in Indonesia. Likewise, interest rates in Indonesia influence the Philippines and Thailand. Third, interdependence was most intense during the period immediately following the Thai devaluation and the subsequent devaluation of the Korean won on 17 November 1997.

Fourth, Malaysian interest rates are not significantly affected by interest rate developments in the other four countries in the full post-crisis period. One could speculate that this insulation may be due to the introduction of exchange controls in September 1998. Indeed, prior to the imposition of exchange restrictions, Malaysian interest rates were influenced by other countries' interest rates during the height of the crisis in July 1997–April 1998.

Fifth, no clean unidirectional causality pattern from Thailand to the

Table 3.7   Daily Interest Rates: Causality Tests

	Indonesia	Malaysia	The Philippines	South Korea	Thailand	Numbers That Are Significant
Indonesia						
1 January 1996–1 July 1997		N	N	N	N	0
2 July 1997–1 July 1999		N	Y	N	Y	2
2 July 1997–16 November 1997		Y	N	N	Y	2
17 November 1997–30 April 1998		N	Y	Y	Y	3
Malaysia						
1 January 1996–1 July 1997	N		N	N	N	0
2 July 1997–1 July 1999	N		N	N	N	0
2 July 1997–16 November 1997	Y		Y	Y	N	3
17 November 1997–30 April 1998	N		N	Y	Y	2
The Philippines						
1 January 1996–1 July 1997	N	N		N	N	0
2 July 1997–1 July 1999	N	N		N	Y	1
2 July 1997–16 November 1997	N	Y		N	N	1
17 November 1997–30 April 1998	Y	Y		N	N	2
South Korea						
1 January 1996–1 July 1997	N	N	N		N	0
2 July 1997–1 July 1999	N	N	N		N	0
2 July 1997–16 November 1997	Y	Y	Y		Y	4
17 November 1997–30 April 1998	Y	Y	N		Y	3
Thailand						
1 January 1996–1 July 1997	N	N	N	N		0
2 July 1997–1 July 1999	Y	N	Y	N		2
2 July 1997–16 November 1997	N	N	Y	Y		2
17 November 1997–30 April 1998	Y	N	Y	N		2

Note: N = null hypothesis (no causality) was not rejected. Y = rejection of null hypothesis at the 5 percent level of significance.

Table 3.8   Daily Exchange Rate Changes: Causality Tests

	Indonesia	Malaysia	The Philippines	South Korea	Thailand	Numbers That Are Significant
Indonesia						
1 January 1996–1 July 1997		N	N	N	N	0
2 July 1997–1 July 1999		Y	N	Y	N	2
2 July 1997–16 November 1997		Y	N	Y	N	2
17 November 1997–30 April 1998		N	Y	Y	N	2
Malaysia						
1 January 1996–1 July 1997	N		N	N	N	0
2 July 1997–1 July 1999	N		N	Y	N	1
2 July 1997–16 November 1997	N		N	N	N	0
17 November 1997–30 April 1998	N		N	N	Y	1
The Philippines						
1 January 1996–1 July 1997	N	N		N	N	0
2 July 1997–1 July 1999	Y	Y		Y	Y	4
2 July 1997–16 November 1997	Y	Y		N	Y	3
17 November 1997–30 April 1998	Y	Y		Y	Y	4
South Korea						
1 January 1996–1 July 1997	N	N	N		N	0
2 July 1997–1 July 1999	Y	N	N		Y	2
2 July 1997–16 November 1997	Y	Y	N		N	2
17 November 1997–30 April 1998	Y	Y	Y		Y	4
Thailand						
1 January 1996–1 July 1997	N	N	N	N		0
2 July 1997–1 July 1999	Y	Y	N	Y		3
2 July 1997–16 November 1997	Y	Y	Y	Y		4
17 November 1997–30 April 1998	Y	N	N	Y		2

Note: See table 3.7 note for explanation of N and Y.

other countries emerges from this exercise—not even in the earlier stages of the crisis. For the period 2 July 1997–16 November 1997, there is causality from Thailand to Indonesia and South Korea but not to the Philippines or Malaysia. Indeed, as the crisis progresses causal relationships among the countries most often go both ways.

Turning to the patterns that emerge from performing the same exercise on daily exchange rate changes, there are important similarities with the results for interest rates. First, for the precrisis sample none of the regressors (other than lags of the dependent variable) are statistically significant at standard confidence levels—as was the case for interest rates. Second, during the post-crisis period there is a much greater degree of interdependence among the exchange rates of the five countries—even greater than that exhibited by interest rates.

Third, exchange rates in the two smaller countries in the group, the Philippines and Thailand, are the most influenced by exchange rate developments elsewhere in the region. In the case of the Philippines, all four exchange rates (baht, ringgit, rupiah, and won) are statistically significant in the regressions; for Thailand, nearly all. This may be consistent with evidence of "large neighbor effects" on capital flow movements.[13] Fourth, changes in the Korean won (South Korea is the largest country of this group) significantly influence the remaining four currencies in the post-crisis period.

Taken together, these results suggest that interdependence among currencies and interest rates among these five Asian economies has increased in the wake of the financial crisis. Given that trade and financial linkages have not changed markedly during this recent period, one interpretation for this greater interdependence is that, in the aftermath of the crisis, financial market participants are more likely to lump these economies into one group than they were previously.

3.5 Thoughts on Further Research

This paper has suggested that financial sector links have played an increasingly important role in the 1990s in transmitting disturbances across national boundaries. Many of the channels of transmission (i.e., cross-market hedges) and many of the agents (i.e., hedge funds and mutual funds) are still relatively novel, particularly in the context of emerging market finance. As such, these potential channels of interdependence merit much closer scrutiny at both the theoretical and empirical dimensions. Microeconomic data at the institutional level are certainly bound to increase our understanding of the role played by capital markets and their new instruments in an increasingly globalized environment.

---

13. See Calvo and Reinhart (1998) for applications to Latin America.

In addition, while banks in financial centers have a long history of lending to the developing world and booms and busts in such lending are not a new phenomenon, banks' lending strategies and decisions are still not well understood. Foreign banks' lending practices may be a source of instability to emerging markets when the shock originates at the center, as it did with the sharp rise in U.S. interest rates in October 1979, or when the shock originates in the difficulties faced by a relatively small borrower (i.e., Thailand) to whom the banks have substantial exposure. To gain insights into this phenomenon, it is necessary to go beyond the aggregate macroeconomic data and analyze the response of individual bank balance sheets and lending decisions to the kinds of shocks discussed in this paper. This analysis is not only useful for better understanding past booms and busts in foreign lending—it is of increasing relevance in anticipating future ones. Indeed, given the trend in many emerging markets toward greater openness in their financial sectors and a rising presence of foreign or "truly international" banks, the issue of what role these banks play in transmitting disturbances across borders is of increasing relevance.

Appendix
Causality Tests

Table 3A.1   Daily Interest Rates, 1 January 1996–1 July 1997

	Indonesia	Malaysia	The Philippines	South Korea	Thailand
Indonesia					
f-statistic		0.82	0.15	0.51	0.09
		(0.61)	(0.99)	(0.88)	(0.99)
Log-likelihood		9.33	1.77	5.79	1.03
		(0.50)	(0.99)	(0.83)	(0.99)
Malaysia					
f-statistic	1.02		0.45	1.25	0.78
	(0.43)		(0.92)	(0.26)	(0.64)
Log-likelihood	11.54		5.13	14.10	8.92
	(0.32)		(0.88)	(0.17)	(0.54)
The Philippines					
f-statistic	1.31	0.45		0.70	0.55
	(0.22)	(0.92)		(0.73)	(0.85)
Log-likelihood	14.73	5.18		7.96	6.30
	(0.14)	(0.88)		(0.63)	(0.79)
South Korea					
f-statistic	0.69	1.15	1.23		0.43
	(0.73)	(0.32)	(0.26)		(0.93)
Log-likelihood	7.87	13.04	13.90		4.90
	(0.64)	(0.22)	(0.18)		(0.90)

(*continued*)

Table 3A.1 (continued)

	Indonesia	Malaysia	The Philippines	South Korea	Thailand
Thailand					
f-statistic	0.18	0.57	0.46	1.09	
	(0.99)	(0.84)	(0.92)	(0.37)	
Log-likelihood	2.02	6.49	5.20	12.31	
	(0.99)	(0.77)	(0.88)	(0.26)	

Notes: Number of observations = 392. Probability numbers in parentheses.

Table 3A.2   **Daily Interest Rates, 2 July 1997–1 July 1999**

	Indonesia	Malaysia	The Philippines	South Korea	Thailand
Indonesia					
f-statistic		0.37	2.44	0.38	2.34
		(0.95)	(0.01)**	(0.95)	(0.01)**
Log-likelihood		4.36	27.64	4.47	26.49
		(0.93)	(0.00)**	(0.92)	(0.00)**
Malaysia					
f-statistic	0.48		0.68	0.23	0.82
	(0.90)		(0.74)	(0.99)	(0.61)
Log-likelihood	5.65		7.97	2.74	9.52
	(0.84)		(0.63)	(0.99)	(0.48)
The Philippines					
f-statistic	1.49	1.24		0.71	1.61
	(0.14)	(0.26)		(0.71)	(0.10)**
Log-likelihood	17.09	14.36		8.29	18.46
	(0.07)*	(0.16)		(0.60)	(0.05)**
South Korea					
f-statistic	0.38	0.30	0.22		0.30
	(0.95)	(0.98)	(0.99)		(0.98)
Log-likelihood	4.49	3.57	2.63		3.51
	(0.92)	(0.96)	(0.98)		(0.97)
Thailand					
f-statistic	3.12	0.58	2.19	0.43	
	(0.00)**	(0.83)	(0.02)**	(0.93)	
Log-likelihood	34.93	6.80	24.91	5.09	
	(0.00)**	(0.74)	(0.01)**	(0.88)	

Notes: Number of observations = 334. Probability numbers in parentheses.
**Significant at 5 percent confidence level.
*Significant at 10 percent confidence level.

Table 3A.3   Daily Interest Rates, 2 July 1997–16 November 1997

	Indonesia	Malaysia	The Philippines	South Korea	Thailand
Indonesia					
f-statistic		1.06	0.72	0.48	1.66
		(0.41)	(0.70)	(0.90)	(0.12)
Log-likelihood		19.71	13.90	9.39	29.42
		(0.03)**	(0.18)	(0.50)	(0.00)**
Malaysia					
f-statistic	1.11		1.37	1.17	0.41
	(0.37)		(0.22)	(0.33)	(0.93)
Log-likelihood	20.68		24.78	21.28	8.19
	(0.02)**		(0.01)**	(0.02)**	(0.48)
The Philippines					
f-statistic	0.61	1.52		0.46	0.77
	(0.80)	(0.16)		(0.91)	(0.66)
Log-likelihood	11.79	27.27		9.11	14.66
	(0.30)	(0.00)**		(0.52)	(0.15)
South Korea					
f-statistic	1.49	1.59	1.40		1.10
	(0.17)	(0.14)	(0.21)		(0.38)
Log-likelihood	29.69	28.30	25.37		20.36
	(0.00)**	(0.00)**	(0.01)**		(0.03)**
Thailand					
f-statistic	0.79	0.64	1.68	1.73	
	(0.64)	(0.77)	(0.11)	(0.10)*	
Log-likelihood	15.02	12.35	29.78	30.44	
	(0.13)	(0.26)	(0.00)**	(0.00)**	

Notes: Number of observations = 99. Probability numbers in parentheses.
**Significant at 5 percent confidence level.
*Significant at 10 percent confidence level.

Table 3A.4   Daily Interest Rates, 17 November 1997–30 April 1998

	Indonesia	Malaysia	The Philippines	South Korea	Thailand
Indonesia					
f-statistic		0.47	1.71	1.31	1.84
		(0.90)	(0.10)*	(0.24)	(0.07)*
Log-likelihood		8.01	26.65	20.95	28.55
		(0.63)	(0.00)**	(0.02)**	(0.00)**
Malaysia					
f-statistic	0.47		0.19	1.19	1.18
	(0.90)		(0.99)	(0.32)	(0.32)
Log-likelihood	7.93		3.23	19.12	18.99
	(0.64)		(0.97)	(0.04)**	(0.04)**

(*continued*)

Table 3A.4 (continued)

	Indonesia	Malaysia	The Philippines	South Korea	Thailand
The Philippines					
f-statistic	1.17	1.34		1.08	1.04
	(0.33)	(0.22)		(0.39)	(0.42)
Log-likelihood	18.92	21.34		17.62	17.00
	(0.04)**	(0.02)**		(0.06)*	(0.07)*
South Korea					
f-statistic	3.72	1.17	1.06		1.58
	(0.00)**	(0.33)	(0.41)		(0.13)
Log-likelihood	51.99	18.89	17.20		24.84
	(0.00)**	(0.04)**	(0.07)*		(0.01)**
Thailand					
f-statistic	2.49	0.57	1.52	1.13	
	(0.01)**	(0.83)	(0.15)	(0.35)	
Log-likelihood	37.11	9.65	23.94	18.281	
	(0.00)**	(0.47)	(0.01)**	(0.05)**	

Notes: Number of observations = 119. Probability numbers in parentheses.
**Significant at 5 percent confidence level.
*Significant at 10 percent confidence level.

Table 3A.5 **Daily Exchange Rate Changes, 1 January 1996–1 July 1997**

	Indonesia	Malaysia	The Philippines	South Korea	Thailand
Indonesia					
f-statistic		0.71	0.50	0.51	0.71
		(0.71)	(0.89)	(0.88)	(0.71)
Log-likelihood		8.03	5.71	5.83	8.13
		(0.63)	(0.84)	(0.83)	(0.62)
Malaysia					
f-statistic	1.38		0.58	0.83	0.68
	(0.19)		(0.83)	(0.60)	(0.74)
Log-likelihood	15.54		6.65	9.38	7.74
	(0.11)		(0.76)	(0.50)	(0.65)
The Philippines					
f-statistic	1.11	0.93		0.89	1.54
	(0.35)	(0.50)		(0.54)	(0.12)
Log-likelihood	12.58	10.55		10.11	17.36
	(0.25)	(0.39)		(0.43)	(0.07)*
South Korea					
f-statistic	0.48	0.78	0.97		0.45
	(0.90)	(0.64)	(0.46)		(0.92)
Log-likelihood	5.52	8.90	11.01		5.16
	(0.85)	(0.54)	(0.36)		(0.88)
Thailand					
f-statistic	0.17	0.73	1.41	0.93	
	(0.99)	(0.70)	(0.17)	(0.51)	
Log-likelihood	1.91	8.29	15.86	10.47	
	(0.99)	(0.60)	(0.10)*	(0.40)	

Notes: Number of observations = 392. Probability numbers in parentheses.
*Significant at 10 percent confidence level.

Table 3A.6   Daily Exchange Rate Changes, 2 July 1997–1 July 1999

	Indonesia	Malaysia	The Philippines	South Korea	Thailand
Indonesia					
f-statistic		1.95	1.07	3.19	0.85
		(0.04)**	(0.39)	(0.00)**	(0.59)
Log-likelihood		21.22	11.67	34.17	9.29
		(0.02)**	(0.31)	(0.00)**	(0.51)
Malaysia					
f-statistic	1.09		1.08	1.89	1.27
	(0.37)		(0.38)	(0.04)**	(0.25)
Log-likelihood	11.98		11.83	20.57	13.85
	(0.29)		(0.30)	(0.02)**	(0.18)
The Philippines					
f-statistic	1.74	2.79		4.07	3.18
	(0.07)*	(0.00)**		(0.00)**	(0.00)**
Log-likelihood	18.94	30.00		43.22	34.08
	(0.04)**	(0.00)**		(0.00)**	(0.00)**
South Korea					
f-statistic	1.87	1.36	0.97		0.45
	(0.05)**	(0.19)	(0.47)		(0.92)
Log-likelihood	20.28	14.85	11.01		5.16
	(0.03)**	(0.14)	(0.36)		(0.88)
Thailand					
f-statistic	3.58	3.03	1.41	3.62	
	(0.00)**	(0.00)**	(0.17)	(0.00)**	
Log-likelihood	38.24	32.57	15.42	38.68	
	(0.00)**	(0.00)**	(0.12)	(0.00)**	

Notes: Number of observations = 334. Probability numbers in parentheses.
**Significant at 5 percent confidence level.
*Significant at 10 percent confidence level.

Table 3A.7   Daily Exchange Rate Changes, 2 July 1997–16 November 1997

	Indonesia	Malaysia	The Philippines	South Korea	Thailand
Indonesia					
f-statistic		1.11	0.76	1.67	0.83
		(0.38)	(0.66)	(0.12)	(0.61)
Log-likelihood		20.53	14.61	29.56	15.71
		(0.02)**	(0.15)	(0.01)**	(0.11)
Malaysia					
f-statistic	0.49		0.25	0.57	0.53
	(0.89)		(0.99)	(0.83)	(0.86)
Log-likelihood	9.64		5.00	11.06	10.34
	(0.47)		(0.89)	(0.35)	(0.41)
The Philippines					
f-statistic	1.13	1.66		0.66	4.06
	(0.35)	(0.12)		(0.75)	(0.00)**
Log-likelihood	20.99	29.47		12.80	60.63
	(0.02)**	(0.00)**		(0.23)	(0.00)**

(continued)

Table 3A.7 (continued)

	Indonesia	Malaysia	The Philippines	South Korea	Thailand
South Korea					
f-statistic	2.15	1.93	0.97		0.62
	(0.04)**	(0.06)	(0.49)		(0.79)
Log-likelihood	36.67	33.51	18.14		12.00
	(0.00)**	(0.00)**	(0.05)**		(0.29)
Thailand					
f-statistic	1.87	1.59	1.29	2.17	
	(0.07)*	(0.14)	(0.26)	(0.04)**	
Log-likelihood	32.5	28.31	23.63	36.96	
	(0.00)**	(0.02)**	(0.01)**	(0.00)**	

Notes: Number of observations = 99. Probability numbers in parentheses.
**Significant at 5 percent confidence level.
*Significant at 10 percent confidence level.

Table 3A.8 **Daily Exchange Rate Changes, 17 November 1997–30 April 1998**

	Indonesia	Malaysia	The Philippines	South Korea	Thailand
Indonesia					
f-statistic		0.77	1.28	1.44	0.53
		(0.66)	(0.26)	(0.18)	(0.87)
Log-likelihood		12.71	20.51	22.84	8.88
		(0.24)	(0.02)**	(0.01)**	(0.54)
Malaysia					
f-statistic	0.75		0.38	0.57	1.24
	(0.68)		(0.95)	(0.83)	(0.28)
Log-likelihood	12.45		6.54	9.62	19.88
	(0.26)		(0.77)	(0.47)	(0.03)**
The Philippines					
f-statistic	2.58	2.62		2.19	1.24
	(0.01)**	(0.01)**		(0.03)**	(0.28)
Log-likelihood	38.22	38.82		33.16	19.90
	(0.00)**	(0.00)**		(0.00)**	(0.03)**
South Korea					
f-statistic	1.99	1.43	1.94		2.93
	(0.05)**	(0.19)	(0.05)**		(0.00)**
Log-likelihood	30.48	22.65	29.90		42.67
	(0.00)**	(0.01)**	(0.00)**		(0.00)**
Thailand					
f-statistic	1.40	0.82	0.75	1.36	
	(0.20)	(0.61)	(0.68)	(0.22)	
Log-likelihood	22.25	13.57	12.42	21.68	
	(0.01)**	(0.19)	(0.26)	(0.02)**	

Notes: Number of observations = 119. Probability numbers in parentheses.
**Significant at 5 percent confidence level.

References

Bank for International Settlements. Various issues. Annual report.

Calvo, G. A. 1998. Capital market contagion and recession: An explanation of the Russian virus. College Park, Md.: University of Maryland.

Calvo, G. A., and E. Mendoza. 2000. Rational contagion and the globalization of securities markets. *Journal of International Economics* 51 (1): 79–113.

Calvo, G. A., L. Leiderman, and C. Reinhart. 1996. Capital flows to developing countries in the 1990s: Causes and effects. *Journal of Economic Perspectives* 10 (Spring): 123–37.

Calvo, S., and C. M. Reinhart. 1998. Capital flows to Latin America: Is there evidence of contagion effects? In *Private capital flows to emerging markets,* ed. G. A. Calvo, M. Goldstein, and E. Hochreitter, 151–71. Washington, D.C.: Institute for International Economics.

Corsetti, G., P. Pesenti, N. Roubini, and C. Tille. 1998. Structural links and contagion effects in the Asian crisis: A welfare based approach. New York, N.Y.: New York University.

Eichengreen, B., A. Rose, and C. Wyplosz. 1996. Contagious currency crises. NBER Working Paper no. 5681. Cambridge, Mass.: National Bureau of Economic Research.

Frankel, J. A., and S. Schmukler. 1998. Crisis, contagion, and country funds. In *Managing capital flows and exchange rates,* ed. R. Glick, 232–66. Cambridge: Cambridge University Press.

Gerlach, S., and F. Smets. 1994. Contagious speculative attacks. CEPR Discussion Paper no. 1055. London: Center for Economic Policy Research.

Glick, R., and A. Rose. 1998. Contagion and trade: Why are currency crises regional? Berkeley: University of California.

Goldstein, M., G. L. Kaminsky, and C. M. Reinhart. 2000. Assessing financial vulnerability: Developing an early warning system for emerging markets. Washington, D.C.: Institute for International Economies.

Kaminsky, G. L. 1998. Currency and banking crises: The early warnings of distress. International Finance Discussion Paper no. 629, October. Washington, D.C.: Board of Governors of the Federal Reserve System.

Kaminsky, G. L., S. Lizondo, and C. M. Reinhart. 1998. Leading indicators of currency crises. *IMF Staff Papers* 45 (March): 1–48.

Kaminsky, G. L., and C. M. Reinhart. 1999. The twin crises: The causes of banking and balance of payments problems, *American Economic Review* 89 (3): 473–500.

———. 2000. On crises, contagion, and confusion. *Journal of International Economics* 51 (1): 145–68.

Kaminsky, G. L., and S. Schmukler. 1999. What triggers market jitters? A chronicle of the Asian crisis. *Journal of International Money and Finance* 18 (4): 537–60.

Comment   Eiji Ogawa

Kaminsky and Reinhart's paper empirically analyzes whether financial sector links via common bank lenders form a powerful channel for funda-

Eiji Ogawa is professor of commerce at Hitotsubashi University.

mentals-based contagion. They achieve an interesting result, that the performance of bank links better explained the contagion effects than did third-party trade links, bilateral links, high-correlation cluster, or a global crisis elsewhere. They conclude that foreign banks' behavior exacerbated the original crisis by calling in loans in countries where the banks had exposure. They also point out that Japanese banks played an important role in the Asian crisis of 1997.

I have three comments on their paper, placing a focus on the use of bank links to explain the contagion effects.

First, if we focus on foreign banks' presence in Asian loan markets, we should also watch European banks' behavior in those countries. Figure 3C.1 shows stocks of bank loans to the Asian countries. European banks have a relatively larger share in the loan markets of those countries (except for Thailand), although Japanese banks have a relatively larger share in Thailand's loan market.

Second, banks do not always call in loans from countries where they have exposure. We should observe banks' loan-calling behavior by looking at the decrease in bank loans rather than at stocks of bank loans. It is certain that Japanese banks had a relatively large share in the stocks of bank loans to the Asian countries except for the Philippines. Figure 3C.2 shows flows of bank loans to these countries. Japanese banks have had a relatively large share in decreases in bank loans to Thailand since the second half of 1997. However, Japanese banks had a small share in decreases in bank loans to Korea and the Philippines, and not a very large share in decreases in bank loans to Indonesia and Malaysia. Thus, Japanese banks did not seem substantially to draw back loans from the Asian countries (except for Thailand) after the currency crisis.

Third, we should watch the capital inflows to these countries *before* the currency crises because it has been pointed out that excess capital inflows to countries with fragile banking systems brought about the severe currency and banking crises. In the Asian countries, the asset price bubbles ended by early 1994; consequently, Asian banks seemed to have built up nonperforming loans since 1994. Part of the cause of the crises was that foreign banks gave excess loans to Asian banks that had too many nonperforming loans during the 1994–97 period. Figure 3C.2 shows that European banks made relatively larger contributions to increases in bank loans to these countries (except for Thailand) during the precrisis period.

Reference

Bank for International Settlements (BIS). Various issues. *Consolidated International Banking Statistics.* [http://www.bis.org].

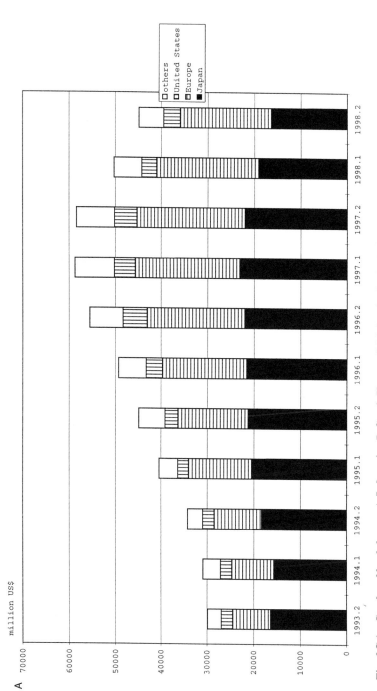

Fig. 3C.1   Stocks of bank loans: *A*, **Indonesia;** *B*, **South Korea;** *C*, **Malaysia;** *D*, **the Philippines;** *E*, **Thailand**
Source: Bank for International Settlements (BIS), various issues.

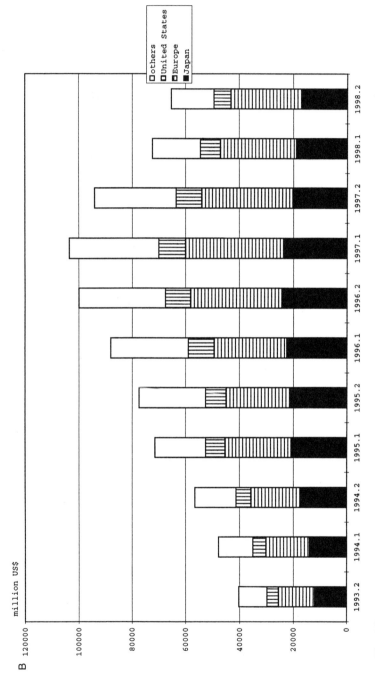

Fig. 3C.1 (cont.)

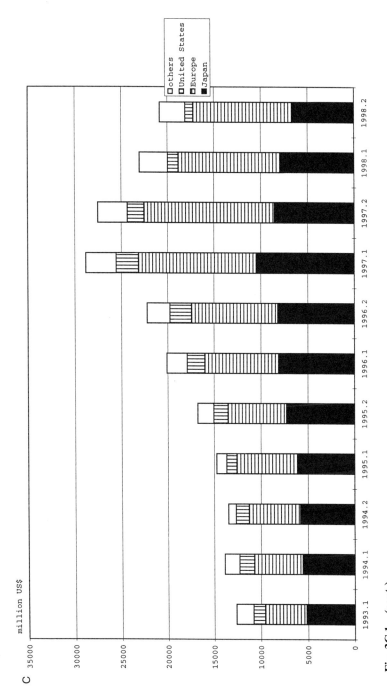

Fig. 3C.1 (cont.)

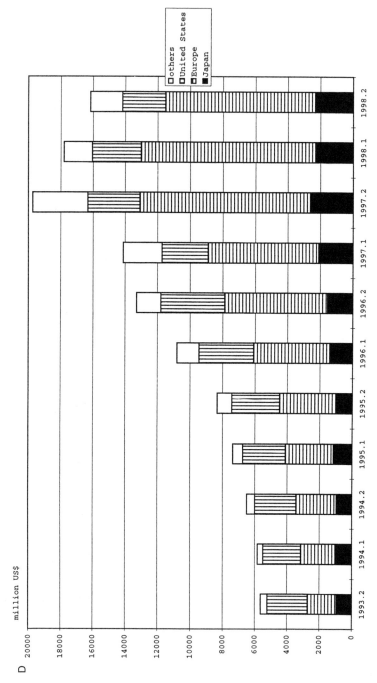

Fig. 3C.1 (cont.)

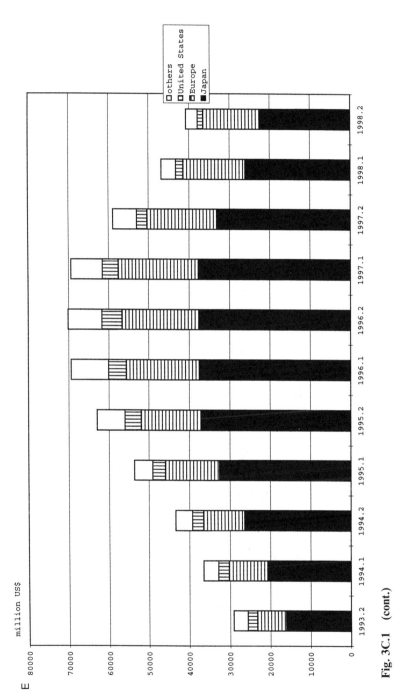

Fig. 3C.1 (cont.)

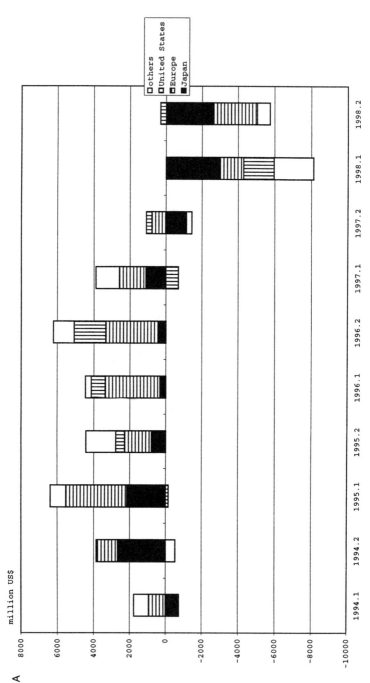

Fig. 3C.2 Flows of bank loans: *A*, Indonesia; *B*, South Korea; *C*, Malaysia; *D*, the Philippines; *E*, Thailand
Source: BIS, various issues.

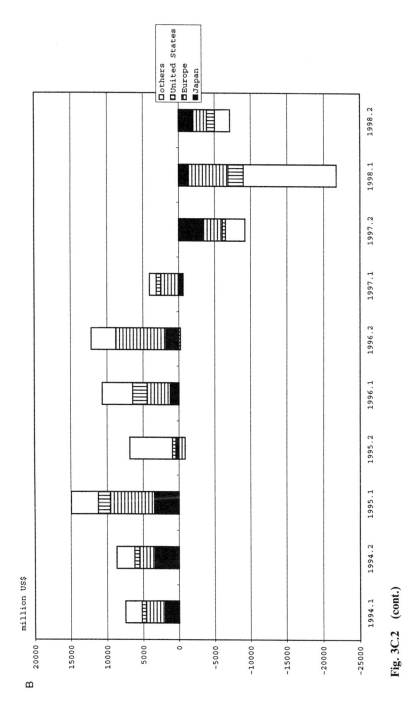

B   million US$

Legend:
□ Others
□ United States
◪ Europe
■ Japan

20000
15000
10000
5000
0
-5000
-10000
-15000
-20000
-25000

1994.1   1994.2   1995.1   1995.2   1996.1   1996.2   1997.1   1997.2   1998.1   1998.2

Fig. 3C.2 (cont.)

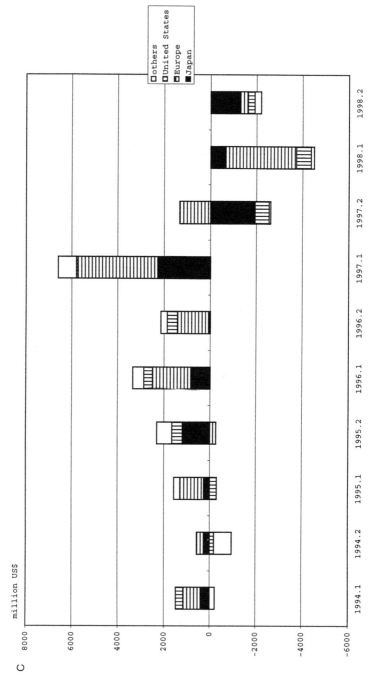

Fig. 3C.2 (cont.)

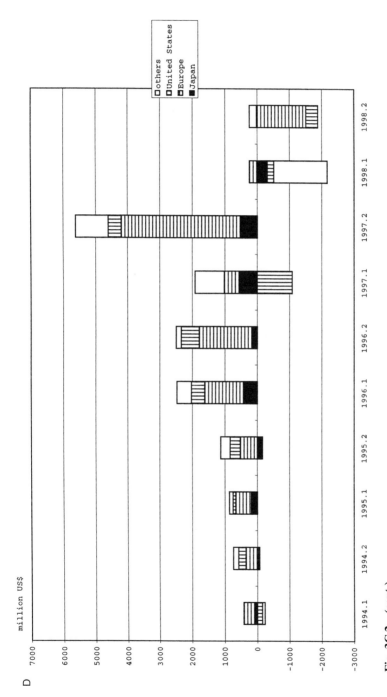

Fig. 3C.2 (cont.)

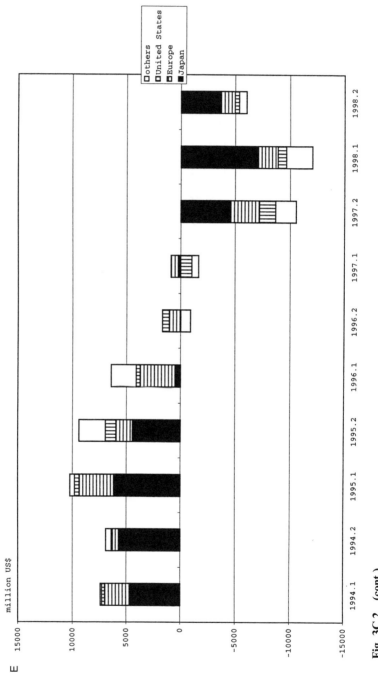

million US$

Fig. 3C.2 (cont.)

Comment   Mahani Zainal-Abidin

This paper is another contribution to the growing literature on contagion from economic and financial crises. Previous studies on the East Asian crisis have examined the causes of the crisis, but this paper has opened a new horizon—namely, a vulnerability index. This identifies the links that give rise to vulnerability and thus contagion. Exposure to a common bank is one of the channels in which the disturbances arising from a crisis are transmitted; other channels of transmission are trade and financial links. The role of a common bank lender was painfully clear in the Latin American crises, where U.S. banks' presence was almost omnipotent. Subsequent stabilization hinged on rescheduling these loans. The presence of a common lender in East Asian economies is a more recent phenomenon and this paper defines how much or how little foreign banks have to do with contagion. Another aspect of contagion that the paper examines is the interdependence or pattern of causality among the affected countries. It refers to the daily pattern of interest and exchange rates among the affected East Asian countries and confirms that there was a strong interdependence among most of these countries in the full post-crisis period.

The vulnerability index developed by this paper shows that (in descending probability) Malaysia, South Korea, Indonesia, and the Philippines are exposed to Thailand, the "initiator" of the crisis. This index is an improvement on earlier indicators of linkages, which were based mainly on trade and financial relationships, because it captures the third transmission channel and ranks each country's vulnerability. However, as acknowledged by the authors, this index is unable to predict the severity of the contagion effects. Moreover, the vulnerability ranking does not follow the actual sequence in which the countries were affected last time. For example, although Malaysia's ranking is higher than Indonesia's (meaning that Malaysia is more vulnerable to a crisis in Thailand), in actuality, Malaysia experienced a deep economic contraction much later than did Indonesia, namely in the first quarter of 1998.

The efficacy of the vulnerability index in explaining the transmission outcome and the role of a common bank lender can perhaps be improved by taking into account the following.

Ratio of Foreign Borrowing to Total Loan Exposure

In identifying whether a country belongs to a common bank cluster, the paper classifies the foreign liability of Indonesia, Malaysia, the Philippines, South Korea, and Thailand according to its source—Japan, Europe, or the United States. However, the impact of recall of loans by foreign

Mahani Zainal-Abidin is professor in the department of applied economics at the University of Malaya, Kuala Lumpur.

banks depends in the first instance on the relative exposure of each country to foreign bank loans. Among the affected East Asian countries, Malaysia has the smallest percentage of foreign borrowings. For example, as at end of June 1997, Malaysia's short-term external debt was 11.2 percent of its total borrowing, while for South Korea it was 67.5 percent, for Thailand, 45.7 percent, and for Indonesia, 34.2 percent (Raghavan 1998). This was because of the Malaysian policy that only companies with foreign income capability can borrow overseas. Thus, the recall of funds by foreign banks in Malaysia had relatively little effect.

The Role of Foreign Bank Withdrawals in Transmitting the Effects of the Crisis

Bank loan recalls are arguably less damaging than the other two effects in finance and trade because banks are unlikely to trigger a massive capital outflow from borrowing countries. The crisis usually unfolds in stages. During the first stage, there is interaction among portfolio investment, local equity market, and domestic banks. An event triggers portfolio outflows and causes a sharp decline in the equity market. Then local banks become vulnerable either because they have extended financing to purchase overvalued shares or because shares have been used as collateral for loans. Interest rates are raised to support the exchange rate and banks begin to trim their loans. In the second stage, the domestic financial system faces a liquidity crunch and this massively hits all other parts of the national economy. Foreign banks reduce their exposure to such a troubled economy, which exacerbates the matter.

Foreign banks are not leaders in contagion because, as shown above, they are not in the first stage. Furthermore, they may not be able to liquidate their positions easily. To recall a loan is more difficult than to repatriate short-term capital or trade flows. Bank loans are very frequently invested in tangible assets such as buildings, machinery, and equipment. In East Asian countries, the proceeds from foreign loans during their high growth period (1990–97) were directed mainly to roads, energy plants, and property development. The only immediately available action is to revoke those few loans not yet disbursed. Thus, in view of these different sequences and speeds of transmission among the three channels, the index would be useful as a predicative tool, provided that appropriate weights were assigned to the three channels.

Exposure to European Banks as a Common Lender

The paper has shown that East Asian economies borrowed heavily from both Japanese and European banks. In Indonesia, Malaysia, the Philippines, and South Korea, the exposure to European banks in June 1998 was much larger than for Japanese banks. Thailand was the exception. The withdrawal pattern of the two bank blocs was also different—the Japanese withdrew first, from the middle of 1997, whereas Europeans did not begin until the first half of 1998 and their percentage of withdrawal was larger. Thus, Europe should be considered a separate cluster.

Investment Component of the Index

The index consists of trade and financial links and exposure to a common lender. Perhaps the analysis on regional economic links can be extended to investment relationships as a channel for contagion. The development experience of the Southeast Asian region demonstrates the role of foreign direct investment (FDI) in linking these economies through an integrated production chain. For example Japanese multinational companies have strings of production units in different countries of the Association of Southeast Asian Nations (ASEAN), each producing one part of the production chain. Nonmultinational regional investment is also substantial; for example, Singapore has significant investments in Malaysia and Indonesia. With close investment links, a crisis in one country may quickly affect production in another, the most obvious reasons being shortage of fresh capital and lower demand. In an integrated FDI production network, an external factor, say, low demand as a result of any unrelated event outside the region, can reduce the production of the entire network. Since the early 1990s, South Korea has been a major investor in ASEAN, and when the latter's economy contracted, a number of Korean companies in the region scaled down their operations.

Interdependence Test Results

The results of the interdependence test prompt a question: Why was the interdependence, as instanced by similarities in trends in interest rates and exchange rates, seen during the crisis and not before? An explanation is that the crisis forced the affected countries to adopt similar monetary and exchange rate policies. Countries floated their exchange rates and since their economies were already closely linked, a similar impact across the border was not unexpected. A more convincing explanation is that Thailand, South Korea, and Indonesia followed closely a set of conditionalities when they received assistance from the International Monetary Fund (IMF). Another explanation is that investors viewed the affected region as a single entity. Delay in times of crisis can be costly and investors used information about one country as a surrogate for all countries in the region.

The finding from the interdependence test that causality extended from Thailand to Indonesia and South Korea but not to the Philippines or Malaysia (during the period 2 July 1997 to 16 November 1997) should be compared with earlier estimates of the vulnerability index. According to that index, Malaysia is the most vulnerable to a crisis originating from Thailand, followed by South Korea, Indonesia, and the Philippines. Thus a relationship defined solely on financial channels (the causality result using interest and exchange rates) can give a different picture from one constructed using broader criteria (the vulnerability index estimated from trade and financial links and exposure to a common bank lender). This supports the earlier assertion that it is essential to understand the order of events in the transmission channel. As shown by these two indicators, the financial and trade channels depict the immediate impact while the banking perspective takes place at a later stage. Nevertheless, the impact of all channels can be equally strong.

Another finding of the interdependence test is that Malaysia's interest rate was not significantly affected in the full post-crisis period, and the paper speculates that this insulation came from the introduction of selective exchange control in September 1998. Malaysia, like other affected countries, adopted a restrictive monetary policy in order to support the exchange rate during the early period of the crisis (2 July–16 November 1997). However, this was reversed to a looser monetary stance in the first quarter of 1998, and the other affected countries took a similar approach (albeit a bit later). The lowering of the interest rate did not have much effect at first, as there was still a big liquidity crunch. Thus, the policy to lower the interest rate was introduced much earlier than the selective capital control initiative.

To sum up, this paper notes that many emerging economies are moving toward greater financial sector liberalization and that foreign banks have an increasing presence. This had serious implications, as seen during the East Asian crisis. Financial liberalization has woven regional economies together irrevocably. No member of the group or cluster can be fully immune from the afflictions of its neighbors. The financial sector liberalization has increased the emerging economies' capability to attract capital to finance growth. During the crisis, the two most obvious clusters were those based on equity markets (portfolio flows) and monetary policy (interest rates). Another indicator of the existence of a cluster is the interest rate spread of bonds, which are the closest surrogate for a state's sovereign risk. As shown by this paper, a country is more vulnerable to the problems of other members of the same cluster and is less exposed to crises in other clusters. Financial liberalization may well encourage the widening of a cluster as more economies become integrated. Eventually, will all clusters combine to form a single global group? If so, does financial liberalization lead to frequent crises and less immunity from contagious events?

As they recover from their respective crises, the affected East Asian countries are under pressure to open their doors to foreign banks. Among the reasons given are that domestic banks are too close to some selected customers, that they are not prudently managed, and that they need fresh injections of funds to replenish their depleted capital. These criticisms are not totally incorrect, but foreign banks are not blameless, either. They lent aggressively during the boom, especially in overinvested sectors such as property and infrastructure. There have been calls to "bail-in" (that is, to share the burden of the crisis) foreign banks to encourage them to be more prudent in the future. Another concern about a large presence of foreign banks is that in times of a crisis, a government or central bank is likely to have more persuasive power over domestic banks than foreign banks. The evidence provided by this paper on the role of foreign banks in a crisis is a vital lesson for emerging economies to bear in mind when facing the challenges posed by financial liberalization.

Reference

Raghavan, C. 1998. BIS banks kept shovelling funds to Asia despite warnings. *Third World Economics* 177.

4

The Impacts of Bank Loans on Economic Development
An Implication for East Asia from an Equilibrium Contract Theory

Shin-ichi Fukuda

4.1 Introduction

In the 1990s, financial liberalization expanded the volume of private capital flows to developing countries. In particular, the miraculous economic success of East Asia attracted a large share of industrialized countries' private capital to the region. As a result, the East Asian economies (e.g., Thailand, Indonesia, and Korea) accumulated significant amounts of unhedged short-term external liabilities before 1997. It is now widely recognized that a large fraction of short-term external liabilities was one of the main reasons why the East Asian countries experienced the serious crisis. A large number of studies have suggested that otherwise solvent East Asian countries might have suffered from a short-run liquidity problem because the available stock of reserves was low relative to the overall burden of external debt service (interest payments plus the renewal of loans coming to maturity).[1] This implies that if a large fraction of external liabilities had longer maturities, the East Asian crisis might not have taken place in the form of a liquidity shortage.

Interestingly, time series evidence suggests that the degree of postcrisis capital mobility in East Asia was quite different in four forms of capital inflows: direct investment, portfolio investment, bank loans, and other investments. For example, table 4.1 reports the quarterly and annual data

Shin-ichi Fukuda is associate professor of economics at the University of Tokyo.

I would like to thank Takatoshi Ito, Yukiko Fukagawa, and other participants, particularly Nouriel Roubini and Carmen Reinhart, for their helpful comments. This research is part of a project supported by Japan Bank for International Cooperation (formerly the Export-Import Bank of Japan).

1. See, for example, Corsetti, Pesenti, and Roubini (1998); Radelet and Sachs (1998); Furman and Stiglitz (1998); and Ito (1999).

Table 4.1 Capital Inflows to the East Asian Economies Before and After the East Asian Crisis, Quarterly Data

	95.1	95.2	95.3	95.4	96.1	96.2	96.3	96.4	97.1	97.2	97.3	97.4	98.1	98.2	98.3	98.4	99.1
A. Direct Investment (IMF Code = 78bed)																	
Thailand	539	588	304	637	810	453	456	617	645	842	1222	1037	1870	2608	1431	1031	1025
Indonesia	978	765	1344	1259	1990	1024	1640	1540	2342	1267	1392	−324	−502	367	−144	−77	−32
Korea	260	503	414	599	405	680	256	985	624	791	611	819	505	1168	2162	1582	1407
The Philippines	316	293	260	609	531	295	551	140	565	214	295	148	251	198	222	1042	373
B. Portfolio Investment (IMF Code = 78bgd)																	
Thailand	773	1283	1412	615	1407	786	856	537	169	1630	2533	466	210	−92	−307	348	297
Indonesia	375	819	1586	1320	1327	919	630	2129	1009	1103	646	−5390	−3548	1840	−17	−277	−536
Korea	1740	3235	5521	3379	3048	6574	5163	6398	2903	6107	5364	−2086	2592	1734	−3793	−824	1080
The Philippines	292	649	1046	632	424	1612	1205	1885	1205	514	−442	−677	−177	335	−666	232	1996
C. Bank Loans (IMF Code = 78bud)																	
Thailand	3378	5149	2235	2455	456	3016	−1722	1159	2543	245	−3022	−3288	−2216	−1710	−3362	−4094	−2539
Indonesia	854	71	−225	1253	−1133	155	126	94	−244	−99	709	−642	−840	−1064	−204	−362	−1445
Korea	4120	2714	3526	1030	2104	2158	2764	2925	1220	1664	−1179	−11490	−3378	−445	−2230	−181	947
The Philippines	−649	1293	89	915	965	2097	1236	738	1323	2243	−359	−1539	−24	681	−693	−369	−1207
D. Other Investment excluding Bank Loans (IMF Code = 78bid−78bud)																	
Thailand	−2089	2886	2250	3119	4923	2170	512	1362	−820	−6216	−5867	−5757	−5146	−1522	65	−1309	−590
Indonesia	−783	882	−34	398	233	21	593	159	880	−20	−940	−2114	−1308	−927	−1931		2329
Korea	3125	2525	1777	2633	5461	4544	76	4539	2279	2321	−908	−2224	−4711	−1910	−1353	339	−683
The Philippines	670	7	597	118	570	41	709	14	224	285	1317	902	−30	654	273	−636	619

Source: IMF (1997) for data from 95.1 to 95.4; IMF (2000) for data from 96.1 to 99.1.

Note: Unit = millions of U.S. dollars.

Table 4.2   **Capital Inflows to the East Asian Economies Before and After the East Asian Crisis, Annual Data**

	92	93	94	95	96	97	98
A. Direct Investment (IMF Code = 78bed)							
Thailand	2113	1804	1366	2068	2336	3746	6941
Indonesia	1777	2004	2109	4346	6194	4677	−356
Korea	728	589	810	1776	2326	2844	5415
Malaysia	5183	5006	4342	4178	5078	5106	n.a.
The Philippines	228	1238	1591	1478	1517	1222	1713
China	11156	27515	33787	35849	40180	44236	43751
Singapore	2204	4686	8550	7206	7883	9710	7218
B. Portfolio Investment (IMF Code = 78bgd)							
Thailand	924	5455	2486	4083	3585	4798	159
Indonesia	−88	1805	3877	4100	5005	−2632	−2002
Korea	4953	10553	8149	13875	21183	12287	−292
Malaysia	−1122	−709	−1649	−436	−268	−248	n.a.
The Philippines	155	897	901	2619	5126	600	−276
China	393	3646	3923	710	2372	7703	97
Singapore	1398	2867	114	410	1672	590	1258
C. Bank Loans (IMF Code = 78bud)							
Thailand	1758	6589	14295	13218	2909	−3522	−11382
Indonesia	n.a.	1357	527	1953	−758	−276	−2470
Korea	1820	720	7368	11389	9952	−9785	−6233
Malaysia	3150	6282	−3789	468	2974	807	n.a.
The Philippines	1921	−229	1694	1648	5036	1668	−405
China	−786	−415	−5222	−4045	−5959	n.a.	−3151
Singapore	5146	1949	5409	4423	8032	18687	−12787
D. Other Investment excluding Bank Loans (IMF Code = 78bid−78bud)							
Thailand	4721	150	−4456	6165	8967	−18659	−6017
Indonesia	n.a.	822	−2065	463	1006	−2194	−5475
Korea	3104	−2175	6264	10061	14619	1468	−7635
Malaysia	33	1159	1880	4211	1633	−1933	n.a.
The Philippines	1019	2684	1868	1392	1334	2728	261
China	−3296	−161	3726	9161	7241	n.a.	−5469
Singapore	−45	6375	502	7558	7814	17405	−3076

Source: IMF (1997, 2000).
Note: Unit = millions of U.S. dollars.

series of *International Financial Statistics (IFS)* to show how capital inflows to the East Asian economies changed before and after the crisis. Both quarterly and annual data (i.e., tables 4.1 and 4.2) show that before 1997 all forms of net private capital inflows tended to increase among the East Asian countries, including Thailand, Indonesia, and Korea. However, the quarterly data in table 4.1 also indicate that inflows of both bank loans and portfolio investments turned out to be negative after the crisis in these East Asian countries.[2] In particular, except for in the Philippines, bank loans turned from inflows to large outflows after the crisis and remained until the end of the sample period. This implies that the crisis was accompanied by a significant amount of bank loan withdrawal from the East Asian countries. In contrast, except for Indonesia, inflows of direct investment never declined in the East Asian countries, even after the crisis in table 4.1. Instead, inflows of direct investment steadily increased in Thailand and were quite stable in Korea after the crisis.

The evidence implies that if a large fraction of external liabilities had been financed by direct investment, the East Asian crisis might not have taken place in the form of a liquidity shortage. In other words, a liquidity shortage in the East Asian crisis was attributable to highly mobile forms of capital inflows, particularly by commercial bank debt. It is probably true that liquidity problems emerged in several Asian countries when panicking external creditors became unwilling to roll over existing short-term bank loans in 1997. However, a pure liquidity shortage could have taken place for any short-term forms of external liabilities. Thus, it is not necessarily clear why commercial bank loans played a leading role in causing a liquidity shortage in the East Asian economies.

In domestic financial markets, banks are known as one of the most prominent means of channeling savings to investments with highest return.[3] Through providing liquidity and permitting the efficient pooling of risk, their activities alter the composition of capital in a way that is potentially favorable to enhanced capital accumulation. As banks have monitoring power delegated by their depositors, they also specialize in gathering information about firms and reduce corporate myopia by overcoming the problems associated with informational asymmetry (e.g., Leland and Pyle 1977 and Diamond 1984). In particular, several previous studies emphasized the special role of banks not only in selecting borrowers but also in monitoring their ex post performance (see, among others, Aoki 1994 and Hoshi, Kashyap, and Scharfstein 1991). If banks could prevent unnecessary liquidation, these monitoring activities would have a positive impact on economic growth. However, efficient ex post monitoring activities also mean that the debt maturity composition becomes shorter. Thus, they could increase the probability of a liquidity shortage in the sense of Diamond and Dybvig (1983) if panicking external creditors became unwilling to roll over existing short-term credits.[4] In particular, without prudential

2. The only exception is portfolio investment in Thailand, which remained positive after the crisis. However, other investments in Thailand took large negative values after the crisis.
3. Noting these roles of banks, classical studies by Patrick (1966), Cameron (1967), Goldsmith (1969), McKinnon (1973), and Shaw (1973) asserted that the extent of financial intermediation in an economy affects rates of economic growth. See also World Bank (1989) and Fry (1995) for their surveys.
4. See also Sachs, Tornell, and Velasco (1996) and Chang and Velasco (1998) in the international market.

regulation or a safety net, the liquidity problems of private bank loans may be intensified in the international capital market.

The purpose of this paper is to present a simple theoretical explanation of why efficient monitoring activities by banks may increase the probability of a liquidity shortage in the competitive international bank loan market.[5] The theoretical model of this paper extends Diamond (1991, 1993), who formulated the choice of a loan's term structure by private firms under asymmetric information.[6] The model contains a liquidity risk because internal funds are not sufficient. When a liquidity shortage develops, borrowers lose the control right, and the project will be liquidated. This indicates that when the manager's control rent is large, long-term debt will be preferred by the firm to eliminate the liquidity risk.[7] However, when asymmetric information exists between lenders and borrowers, short-term debt lowers a good borrower's expected financing costs because of a possible arrival of good information. Thus, when an arrival of new credit information is imminent, borrowers tend to prefer short-term debt (see Flannery 1986).

Note that monitoring activities will be enhanced when an arrival of new information is used. The theory then predicts that efficient monitoring activities by banks tend to make the debt maturity shorter. Unless unnecessary liquidation took place, short-term loans with efficient monitoring would have a positive effect on economic growth. However, when neither prudential regulation nor a safety net is well established, panicky capital outflows may occur with some probability. In such a case, efficient monitoring activities by banks can increase the possibility of having catastrophic liquidity problems by shortening the maturities of bank loans.

The paper proceeds as follows. Before presenting a theoretical model, section 4.2 will show that middle-term and long-term commercial bank loans are less mobile forms of capital flows. It will also show that a large fraction of external bank debt had been financed by short-term loans not only in the East Asian countries but also in a large number of other countries. Section 4.3 will then focus on the role of monitoring in explaining these findings. Section 4.4 will explain a basic structure of our theoretical model, and section 4.5 will define long-term and short-term debt contracts. Section 4.6 will investigate the maturity choices by all borrowers and show that the vulnerable financial structures in developing countries might emerge as a result of efficient monitoring activities by banks. Sections 4.7 and 4.8 will discuss how the main results will change when I alter one of the key assumptions in the model. Section 4.9 will summarize our results and refer to their policy implications.

---

5. In previous studies, Rodrik and Velasco (1999) made an exceptional attempt to analyze the choice of short-term debt in the international market. However, they did not assume the asymmetric information, which is crucial in this paper.

6. See also Fukuda, Ji, and Nakamura (1998).

7. Another case in which long-term debt may be preferred by borrowers is when borrowers have moral hazard problem. See Rajan (1992).

4.2   Maturity Distribution of Bank Loans Before and After the Crisis

4.2.1   Growth Rates of Bank Loans to East Asia

As we discussed in the introduction, a large fraction of liabilities in highly mobile forms of capital was one of the main reasons for the East Asian crisis in 1997. In particular, the East Asian crisis occurred when foreign lenders suddenly refused to roll over their bank loans in 1997. However, when I look at the time series data of international bank loans based on the Bank for International Settlements (BIS) data, I find that the degree of capital mobility was quite different in different terms to maturity. For example, table 4.3 shows the semiannual growth rates of international bank loans to the East Asian economies before and after the crisis in three different types of maturities: maturities up to one year (short-term loans), maturities over one year and up to two years (medium-term loans), and maturities over two years (long-term loans).[8]

It suggests that until 1997, bank loans to the East Asian economies had steadily increased in almost all terms to maturity. In Thailand from 1994 to 1995, the average semiannual growth rate of short-term loans was close to 20 percent, and those of middle-term and long-term loans were slightly higher than 20 percent. Similarly, both short-term and long-term loans grew on average about 10 percent in Indonesia and about 15 percent in Korea from 1994 to 1996.

In contrast, after the crisis, bank loans declined sharply only for short-term loans. For example, in Korea the semiannual growth rate of short-term loans was -16.12 percent in December 1997 and -44.23 percent in June 1998 (see fig. 4.1). During the same period, however, the semiannual growth rates of middle-term and long-term loans were still significantly positive in Korea (see fig. 4.2 and fig. 4.3). Similarly, almost all of the other East Asian economies experienced significant declines of short-term loans from December 1997 to June 1998. However, except for Thailand in December 1997, they experienced no serious decline in middle-term and long-term loans for the same period. Instead, several East Asian economies experienced significant increases in middle-term and long-term loans during this period (see fig. 4.2 and fig. 4.3).

4.2.2   Shares of Short-Term Loans in East Asia

In general, liquidity problems emerge when panicking external creditors become unwilling to roll over existing credits. Thus, if panicking external creditors could cancel their long-term contracts, liquidity problems might have occurred even when external liabilities were financed by long-term

---

8. The data sources are BIS (1996) for the data from 94.6 to 95.12, BIS (1998b) for the data from 96.12 to 97.12; and BIS (1998a) for 98.6 data.

Table 4.3   Semi-Annual Growth Rates of International Bank Loans to the East Asian Economies for Different Terms to Maturity (%)

	Thailand	Indonesia	Korea	Malaysia	The Philippines	Taiwan	China	Hong Kong	Singapore
A. Maturities Up To and Including One Year									
94.6	27.03	0.14	18.95	10.94	12.17	7.34	−5.84	10.83	6.51
94.12	14.06	13.12	15.00	−19.80	19.84	11.90	25.13	8.58	1.46
95.6	23.21	18.69	28.14	10.58	7.44	23.87	−4.87	7.16	23.65
95.12	14.29	9.13	5.51	8.52	19.37	−16.72	33.18	−8.13	−12.34
96.6	9.70	7.28	14.84	26.55	46.25	−1.25	6.25	−13.76	−1.96
96.12	−4.46	15.75	8.30	11.88	30.08	−2.76	9.85	−5.05	−0.48
97.6	−0.31	1.22	5.02	45.37	11.41	16.41	12.12	7.19	11.88
97.12	−14.86	2.07	−16.12	−10.06	38.34	−2.57	12.15	−8.32	−8.65
98.6	−28.42	−21.83	−44.23	−23.37	−14.72	−13.14	−8.77	−20.90	−31.64
B. Maturities Over One Year, Up To and Including Two Years									
94.6	−3.21	8.05	13.96	−20.03	21.46	53.74	4.98	13.39	−39.26
94.12	18.39	16.41	9.43	77.05	−15.55	3.15	5.26	1.11	122.22
95.6	38.91	−9.88	−6.63	61.71	0.00	13.06	8.63	−7.97	40.13
95.12	20.93	2.43	−6.11	−15.66	44.35	59.71	14.94	6.33	−0.93
96.6	15.47	10.01	34.67	−27.29	53.91	−10.00	15.19	4.77	26.61
96.12	18.27	3.34	19.46	−13.55	6.40	−17.44	1.23	2.52	−33.54
97.6	−4.91	−1.31	0.78	−14.70	−42.30	−51.14	−10.74	−15.83	−4.45
97.12	−9.30	4.46	26.17	48.94	31.29	23.31	2.88	32.15	8.90
98.6	2.64	0.68	77.40	7.31	92.29	33.33	0.60	17.23	73.34
C. Maturities Over Two Years									
94.6	17.51	2.39	−6.13	6.90	−2.21	−1.70	8.40	10.10	21.23
94.12	42.20	12.35	21.95	13.30	12.66	73.73	7.79	11.90	25.52
95.6	13.13	18.53	32.35	−2.81	5.55	−7.49	10.95	5.17	10.17
95.12	25.84	11.97	11.35	21.59	5.26	44.16	−2.47	0.04	11.73
96.6	9.79	14.97	11.70	29.65	7.82	13.33	2.53	−0.58	−11.04
96.12	9.46	8.14	18.24	−1.33	10.81	14.09	9.95	9.72	21.76
97.6	0.89	10.94	3.03	12.57	−2.68	−0.08	−0.62	9.71	4.27
97.12	−16.16	1.77	0.45	14.14	57.34	42.65	7.24	12.00	10.32
98.6	−7.49	−0.41	15.08	−8.75	−7.83	−6.48	−3.96	−6.91	2.33

Sources: BIS (1996) for data from 94.6 to 95.12; BIS (1998b) for data from 96.12 to 97.12; BIS (1998a) for 98.6 data.

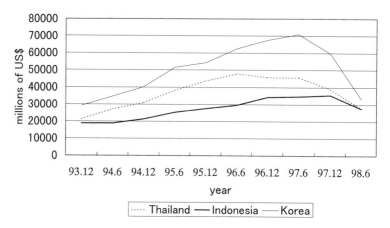

Fig. 4.1   Short-term loans before and after the East Asian crisis

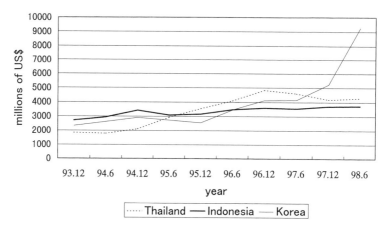

Fig. 4.2   Medium-term loans before and after the East Asian crisis

loans. However, the evidence in the East Asian economies suggests that like direct investment, long-term commercial loans were less mobile forms of capital flows. This may imply that if a large fraction of international commercial bank debt took the form of long-term loans, the East Asian crisis might not have taken place—at least not as a liquidity shortage.

In reality, a large fraction of international commercial bank debt was financed by short-term loans in the East Asian economies. Table 4.4, based on the BIS data, shows how the maturity of international bank loans was distributed before and after the crisis for three different types of maturities. Among the East Asian economies, Taiwan, Hong Kong, and Singapore had remarkably high shares of short-term loans. Needless to say, these data are not enough to capture general situations in East Asia before

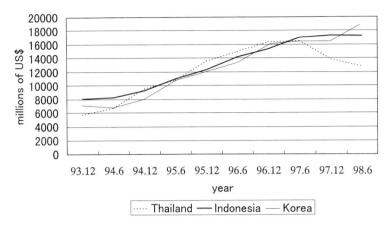

Fig. 4.3   Long-term loans before and after the East Asian crisis

the crisis because Taiwan has been a net creditor, whereas Hong Kong and Singapore are large international financial and intermediation centers. However, even in the other East Asian economies, shares of short-term loans were relatively high in the early 1990s (e.g., 72.0 percent in Thailand, 70.6 percent in Korea in December 1993, etc.).

Because bank loans steadily expanded in almost all terms to maturity, the shares of short-term loans in these East Asian economies slightly declined before the crisis. However, even just before the crisis, these East Asian economies still had relatively high shares of short-term loans, which made their financial structure vulnerable to a liquidity shortage. The crisis in 1997 caused a significant decline only in short-term loans. As a result, the shares of short-term loans in these East Asian economies dropped to nearly 50 percent in 1998.

4.2.3   Shares of Short-Term Loans in the International Market

BIS provides detailed data on the maturity distribution of cross-border loans from BIS reporting banks. Based on this data set, table 4.5 decomposes the cross-border bank loans by region and generates average shares of short-term loans for many emerging countries as well as developed countries. It indicates that even the world average share of short-term loans was above 50 percent throughout the 1990s. Among the different regions, Eastern Europe had lower shares of short-term loans, whereas offshore banking centers had very large shares of short-term loans in general. Compared to developed countries, developing countries had relatively larger shares of short-term loans. Because liquidity problems emerge when external creditors become unwilling to roll over existing short-term credits, the evidence implies that many developing countries could have had liquidity problems.

Table 4.4   The Percentage Distribution of International Bank Loans to the East Asian Economies

	Thailand	Indonesia	Korea	Malaysia	The Philippines	Taiwan	China	Hong Kong	Singapore
A. Maturities Up To and Including One Year									
93.12	72.0	61.7	70.6	56.8	40.4	92.9	45.5	88.0	96.0
94.6	74.3	60.9	72.5	59.1	44.2	92.7	41.1	88.1	95.9
94.12	70.6	60.9	70.9	48.8	46.4	90.4	44.0	87.6	94.5
95.6	71.2	62.5	72.0	49.4	46.3	92.3	40.2	88.1	94.9
95.12	69.4	61.9	70.0	47.0	48.8	87.2	47.6	86.6	93.3
96.6	68.9	60.0	70.8	49.7	55.1	86.4	48.4	85.1	93.1
96.12	65.2	61.7	67.5	50.3	58.2	84.4	48.9	82.5	92.6
97.6	65.7	59.0	68.1	56.4	59.7	87.3	52.0	82.4	93.1
97.12	65.9	60.6	63.1	53.1	60.4	81.7	53.5	79.2	91.9
98.6	59.3	55.0	45.8	48.6	57.1	80.1	52.0	76.0	87.6
B. Maturities Over One Year Up To Two Years									
93.12	6.2	8.9	5.6	4.6	4.0	1.3	7.7	2.2	0.7
94.6	4.9	9.5	5.5	3.4	4.7	1.9	7.7	2.2	0.4
94.12	4.8	9.8	5.1	6.2	3.5	1.7	7.0	2.1	0.9
95.6	5.5	7.6	3.8	9.2	3.2	1.6	7.3	1.8	1.0

95.12	5.6	7.1	3.3	6.8	4.1	2.9	7.4	2.0	1.1
96.6	5.9	7.0	3.9	4.1	4.9	2.6	8.2	2.4	1.4
96.12	6.9	6.5	4.1	3.2	4.3	2.2	7.6	2.5	1.0
97.6	6.6	6.0	4.0	2.1	2.3	0.9	6.5	2.0	0.8
97.12	7.1	6.3	5.5	3.3	2.2	1.1	6.1	2.8	1.0
98.6	9.1	7.4	12.8	4.3	4.6	1.7	6.5	3.9	2.3
				C. Maturities Over Two Years					
93.12	19.3	26.5	17.2	30.7	48.1	5.2	40.5	8.1	2.9
94.6	18.4	26.8	13.9	30.8	45.9	4.7	42.1	8.0	3.3
94.12	21.8	26.6	14.4	35.9	45.3	7.2	38.8	8.2	4.0
95.6	20.2	27.3	15.1	32.0	44.4	5.5	41.3	8.1	3.6
95.12	21.6	27.7	15.5	34.1	41.3	8.9	35.8	8.7	4.5
96.6	21.5	28.8	15.3	36.9	34.4	10.1	35.1	9.8	4.1
96.12	23.3	27.6	15.9	32.9	30.9	11.6	35.5	11.0	5.0
97.6	23.8	29.0	15.7	28.6	27.7	10.3	33.5	11.2	4.7
97.12	23.5	29.6	17.5	34.2	31.9	14.1	32.9	13.2	5.6
98.6	27.3	34.3	26.1	37.3	32.6	14.9	33.7	14.9	7.9

Sources: **BIS** (1995) for 93.12 data; **BIS** (1996) for data from 94.6 to 95.12; **BIS** (1998b) for data from 96.12 to 97.12; **BIS** (1998a) for 98.6 data.

Table 4.5   Percentages of Short-Term Loans Whose Maturities are Less Than or Equal to One Year

	93.12	94.6	94.12	95.6	95.12	96.6	96.12	97.6	97.12
All countries	53.04	53.67	53.59	55.53	55.29	55.53	55.1	56.28	54.88
Developed countries	53.21	53.62	52.79	55.98	53.6	52.21	53.22	53.98	53.51
Eastern Europe	37.15	36.45	35.19	39.65	39.08	41.85	44.19	50.68	43.4
Developing countries	55.93	56.69	57.05	58.69	58.41	58.8	57.66	58.18	58.1
Latin America	48.83	50.07	51.27	52.86	52.25	53.08	53.67	52.51	54.76
Middle East	66.6	62.16	59.61	58.7	59.13	60.15	56.71	62.14	59.94
Africa	45.82	47.57	50.24	52.52	53.11	52.12	49.75	50.93	56.26
Asia	63.02	63.82	62.86	64.07	63.45	63.32	61.5	62.31	60.6
East Asia excluding Hong Kong and Singapore									
Thailand	72.03	74.29	70.58	71.18	69.42	68.92	65.15	65.67	65.91
Indonesia	61.65	60.91	60.88	62.53	61.93	60.01	61.68	59.02	60.6
Korea	70.63	72.53	70.93	72.01	70.01	70.81	67.54	68.07	63.12
Malaysia	56.76	59.12	48.76	49.42	47.05	49.71	50.27	56.42	53.08
The Philippines	40.38	44.17	46.43	46.31	48.84	55.1	58.22	59.69	60.43
Taiwan	92.91	92.71	90.41	92.33	87.2	86.36	84.38	87.29	81.71
China	45.53	41.09	43.97	40.2	47.59	48.37	48.87	52.03	53.45
Offshore banking centers	82.29	82.41	81.9	81.68	80.41	75.54	74.26	73.84	72.05
Hong Kong	88.01	88.15	87.59	88.08	86.59	85.11	82.45	82.37	79.2
Singapore	96.01	95.87	94.51	94.91	93.3	93.07	92.6	93.07	91.86
Bahamas	85.80	82.76	84.11	83.79	84.11	87.08	87.08	86.64	85.97
Bahrain	83.04	82.49	77.81	79.57	77.81	71.19	71.19	73.91	73.77

Notes: Asia does not include banking centers such as Hong Kong and Singapore. Unallocated loans are included in total loans.

In the table, average shares of short-term loans in Asia were above 60 percent throughout the periods.[9] This implies that a typical country in the East Asian region had a more vulnerable composition of external debt than did other developing countries. However, even compared to the world standard, shares of short-term loans in the East Asian economies were not necessarily outliers except for Taiwan, Hong Kong, and Singapore. Figure 4.4 is a histogram of short-term loan shares in 180 countries that received the BIS reporting banks' loans in December 1996. It shows that short-term loan shares are greater than 70 percent in a large number of countries in the world. Among the East Asian economies, Taiwan, Hong Kong, and Singapore are three of the outliers that are included in the range over 80 percent. However, except for these economies, Korea is the only East Asian economy included in the range over 70 percent. This implies that shares of short-term loans in the East Asian economies before the crisis were not remarkable outliers even in the world standard.

4.3   Previous Discussions on the Role of Monitoring

In the last section, I showed that middle-term and long-term commercial bank loans were less mobile capital flows in the sense that they never declined, even when panicking external creditors became unwilling to roll over existing short-term credits. However, we also showed that a large fraction of external bank debt had been financed by short-term loans not only in the East Asian countries but also in a large number of countries, which might have made several developing countries vulnerable to liquidity problems. The result may partly be influenced by regulatory factors such as domestic government regulations, the BIS risk-weighted capital adequacy regulation, and so on. However, the world-wide evidence cannot be explained solely by the regulatory factors.

The purpose of the following sections is to present a simple theoretical model in which financial structures in developing countries may become vulnerable as a result of efficient monitoring by competitive foreign banks. In general, it is important for the suppliers of funds (or their agents) to monitor borrowers in order to ensure that funds are used appropriately. In particular, in order to reduce information costs and the costs of duplicate monitoring, the monitoring is usually delegated to financial intermediaries rather than performed by individual investors. In the literature, banks are typical financial intermediaries of such delegated monitors (see Diamond 1984).

In many cases, outside investors are not as well informed beforehand regarding the profitability and risk potential of proposed projects. The monitoring is thus considered economically valuable because it can reduce

---

9. For example, in December 1996, the share of short-term loans in Bangladesh was 70.4 percent, whereas those of Cambodia, Fiji, and Laos were 86.7 percent.

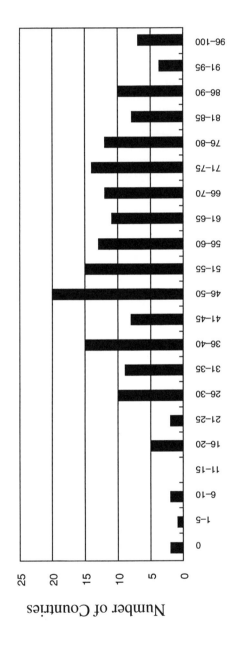

Fig. 4.4 A histogram of short-term loan shares

the degree of the adverse selection problem. It may also be a necessary response to the problem of moral hazard arising from informational asymmetry. In some cases, ex ante monitoring may be performed by investment banks acting as underwriters, by venture capital firms, and so on. Interim monitoring may also be provided by rating companies in that they keep track of the changing financial state of the firm. However, directly placed debt (commercial paper) is usually a contract with terms (covenants). Thus, investors need to base their decisions only on public information, including the borrower's track record. In contrast, the contract of a bank loan uses not only public information but also information from costly monitoring of borrower's actions. Consequently, monitoring of private information can be delegated to banks more efficiently than it can be collected by other financial institutions or many individual investors.

In the following model, we consider the choice of bank loan maturity in an international financial market. In particular, we investigate how the efficiency of banks' monitoring can affect the choice of bank loan maturity. Without the possibility of liquidity shortage due to herd behavior, the choice of bank loan maturity in the international market is similar to that in the domestic market. However, because neither prudential regulation nor a safety net (e.g., deposit insurance) tends to be established well in the emerging market, a liquidity shortage is more likely to occur in the competitive international financial market as the bank loan maturity becomes shorter.

4.4 The Model

We consider a small open economy model that modifies Diamond's (1991, 1993) closed-economy model. In the small open economy, domestic borrowers (that is, domestic firms or domestic financial institutions) need to fund their indivisible investment projects from foreign banks. As in McKinnon and Pill (1996) and Krugman (1998), I assume that domestic borrowers directly own capital and engage in investment projects. Strictly speaking, the assumption may be too restrictive for domestic financial institutions because they generally lend money instead of buying capital assets outright. However, lending to a very highly leveraged firm that engages in risky projects is very much like buying the capital directly. Thus, the assumption holds approximately true for a large number of domestic financial institutions in developing countries.[10]

10. In fact, the data seem to show that the maturity distributions of international loans indicate no significant difference depending on the fact that most domestic borrowers are domestic firms or domestic financial institutions. For example, in Indonesia a large number of domestic firms directly borrowed from foreign banks before the crisis. However, I could not find evidence that the maturity distributions in Indonesia were significantly different from those of other East Asian countries in table 4.4.

In the model are three dates: 0, 1, and 2. All projects require the fixed amount of K in capital at date 0 and produce cash flows only at date 2 (none at date 1). At date 0, each borrower has no internal (domestic) fund or outside equity. Thus, at date 0, a borrower needs to fund external debt of K from foreign banks for the project.

Both domestic borrowers and foreign lenders (that is, foreign banks) are risk neutral. Foreign banks consume only at date 2 and have a constant returns-to-scale investment technology that returns R per unit invested per period. One unit invested at date 0 produces returns of R units at date 1; and if this is invested until date 2, the terminal value will be R^2. There are many potential foreign banks that all observe the same information. Thus, borrowers face a competitive international loan market at each date and can borrow as long as lenders receive an expected return of R per period per unit loaned.

Borrowers' technological environments are summarized in figure 4.5. When successful, each borrower's project yields a cash flow of X. It also produces a nonassignable control rent of C if the management has control right at date 2. Examples of the nonassignable control rent might be the

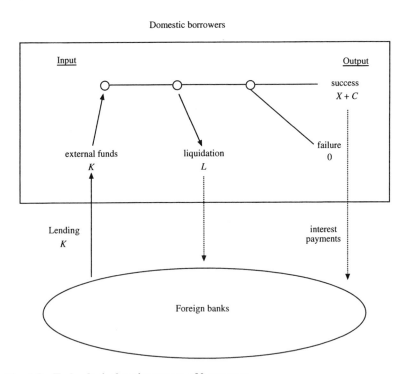

Fig. 4.5   Technological environments of borrowers

manager's desire to keep his business going, the manager's consumption of perquisites, or the manager's disutility from dismissing long-standing employees. I assume that $X > R^2K$ and $C > 0$.

The project can be liquidated at date 1 for a liquidation value of L. Because $C > 0$, no borrowers have an incentive to liquidate their projects by themselves. However, foreign banks liquidate their borrower's project at date 1 either when its expected present value is less than L or when a financial panic occurs against the borrower. If a project is liquidated, it produces no cash flows nor control rents at date 2. In addition, the liquidation value of L is assumed to be less than RK. This implies that a successful project always yields a higher cash flow when not liquidated.

There are two types of borrowers. The two types of borrowers differ only in the probability that their projects are successful at date 2. The types of borrowers are characterized as follows.

Type G borrower: The project succeeds for sure at date 2.
Type B borrower: The project returns succeed with probability q but fail with probability $1 - q$, where $qX < R^2K$.

Because the control rent of C is positive, borrowers never liquidate their projects when they have the control right to force the liquidation. However, since $X > R^2K > qX$, the type B borrower's project has a negative net present value in terms of cash flows. Thus, when foreign banks find out that the borrower is type B, the type B borrower cannot raise funds.

The key assumption in this model is that a project's ex ante prospects are private information observed only by the domestic borrower. No one but the borrower knows his own type. Each foreign bank's information set on borrowers' type, which is summarized in figure 4.6, is as follows.

At date 0 (the initial period), a foreign bank only knows that its domestic borrower is type G with probability f and type B with probability $1 - f$. I assume that

(1) $$R^2K \leq [f + (1 - f)q]X.$$

This assumption implies that on average the project has a positive net present value in terms of cash flows. The assumption is realistic for developing countries with high growth rates such as the East Asian economies before the crisis. It is, however, restrictive for stagnated developing countries or countries in crisis because the average project has low net present value in these countries. In section 4.8 I will discuss how the main results change when the assumption does not hold.

At date 1, each foreign bank's monitoring partially reveals types of domestic borrowers. That is, the monitoring identifies some type G and type B borrowers, but it cannot identify all type G and type B borrowers. Define e as the probability that the monitoring identifies the type among type G borrowers at date 1 and m as the probability that the monitoring identifies the type among type B borrowers at date 1. Then, given the previous

date 0   date 1   date 2

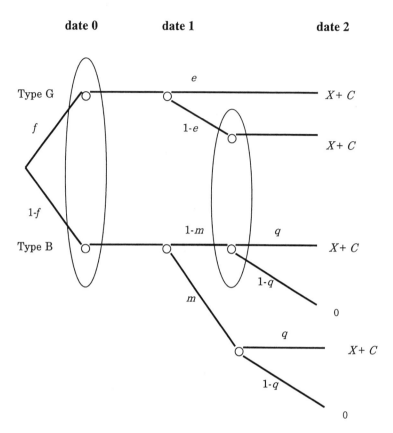

Fig. 4.6   Information structure of foreign banks

assumptions, Bayes law implies that a borrower whose type was not identified at date 1 is type G with probability $(1 - e)f/[(1 - e)f + (1 - m)(1 - f)]$ and type B with probability $(1 - m)(1 - f)/[(1 - e)f + (1 - m)(1 - f)]$.

It is easy to see that the larger e and m are, the more efficient the foreign bank's monitoring is. However, the revealed information at date 1 is not verifiable, so contracts contingent on it are not enforceable in the international capital market. Thus, only when a short-term loan is chosen, refinancing at date 1 will depend on what foreign banks can find out about types of borrowers.

4.5   Loan Contracts

4.5.1   Long-Term Loan

A *long-term loan* is bank debt floated at date 0 that matures at date 2, with no refinancing at date 1. The face value r^L of this debt is set so that foreign banks can obtain the expected return of R^2 per unit invested. Under the assumption that $qX < R^2K \leq [f + (1 - f)q]X$, we can verify that the equilibrium with long-term loans is a pooling equilibrium, realizing that debt is repaid with probability $f + (1 - f)q$. Thus, as long as $r^L \leq X$, the face value of a long-term loan is given by[11]

(2) $r^L = R^2K/[f + (1 - f)q].$

The lower f is, the higher is the promised interest r^L, owing to the higher default rate of type B borrowers. In other words, reflecting a risk premium, the long-term interest rate becomes higher as the proportion of type B borrowers becomes larger.

Recall that at date 1, each foreign bank's monitoring might reveal information about some type G and type B borrowers. However, the information does not influence the face value of long-term loan and does not lead to liquidation because long-term lenders have no such rights.[12] Therefore, the payoff of a type G borrower with a long-term loan is equal to

(3) $\Pi_g^L = X + C - r^L$

             $= X + C - R^2K/[f + (1 - f)q],$

which is independent of e and m (i.e., the degree of foreign banks' monitoring efficiency).

On the other hand, the expected payoff of a type B borrower with long-term loan is equal to

(4) $\Pi_b^L = q(X + C - r^L)$

             $= q(X + C) - qR^2K/[f + (1 - f)q].$

Because $[f + (1 - f)q]X > qR^2K$ and $C > 0$, it always holds that $\Pi_g^L > \Pi_b^L > 0$.

4.5.2   Short-Term Loan

A *short-term loan* is bank debt financed at date 0, maturing at date 1 with face value r^1. At date 1, the short-term loan can be either refinanced or repaid, at least partially, by liquidation of the project. If the short-term loan is rolled over at date 1, the refinanced short-term loan matures at date 2. The refinanced short-term loan at date 1 has different face values depending on the realization of date 1 information. Each face value of the short-term loan issued at date 1 is set so that foreign banks at date 1 get

---

11. If $r^L > X$, borrowers cannot issue long-term debt because they cannot provide lenders with an expected return of R^2K. Because $R^2K \leq [f + (1 - f)q]X$, we can rule out this possibility in the following analysis.

12. When C is small, renegotiation between lenders and borrowers may be possible. However, assuming that C is large enough rules out this possibility.

an expected return of R per unit invested, given the information about a borrower at that date.

Short-term borrowers who were identified as type G at date 1 will succeed the project with a probability of 1. Thus, unless a financial panic occurs, each of them can always refinance to pay the full face value of the debt r^1 at date 0. Noting that a new short-term loan maturing at date 2 is repaid with probability 1, the face value of this short-term loan issued at date 1, which is denoted by r^B, satisfies

(5) $$r^B = r^1 R.$$

However, the determination of the face value of a short-term loan issued at date 1 is more complicated for borrowers whose type was not identified, because even if no financial panic occurs, the borrowers might not be able to refinance to pay the full face value of their date 0 debt. In the following sections (up to section 4.8), I consider the case in which foreign banks always choose liquidation when their monitoring cannot identify the type of borrowers at date 1.[13] In this case, foreign banks liquidate their borrower's project at date 1 either when their monitoring cannot identify the borrower's type, when their monitoring identifies the borrower as type B, or when a financial panic occurs in this lending market. I assume that even if the borrower was identified as type G, a financial panic occurs for him with probability $1 - \theta$.

Because lenders can identify type G borrowers out of all borrowers with the probability fe at date 1, the expected rate return for a date 0 short-term lender is $\theta fe\, r^1 + (1 - \theta fe)L$, where L is a liquidation value of the project. Equating this to the one-period riskless return RK leads to

(6) $$r^1 = [RK - (1 - \theta fe)L]/(\theta fe),$$

so that equations (5) and (6) lead to

(7) $$r^B = [RK - (1 - \theta fe)L]R/(\theta fe).$$

Because $RK \geq L$, both r^1 and r^B are decreasing in f. Thus, the short-term interest rates also become higher as the proportion of type B borrowers becomes larger, due to a risk premium.[14]

The payoff of a type G borrower with a short-term loan is

(8a) $X + C - r^B$ when the project is not liquidated at date 1,

13. This case is more likely when the bank's monitoring reveals more type G borrowers than type B borrowers. I think that the case is realistic because type G borrowers have an incentive to reveal their type, but type B borrowers do not.

14. Because X is the maximum amount that type G borrowers can repay for the banks, r^B needs to be less than X for the short-term loans to be supplied. In the following analysis, I implicitly guarantee this condition assuming that $R^2K \leq (1 - \theta fe)RL + \theta feX$.

and

(8b)   0   when the project is liquidated at date 1.

Because the ex ante probability that the project is liquidated at date 1 is θe at date 0, the expected payoff of a type G borrower with a short-term loan S at date 0 is

$$(9) \qquad \Pi_g^S = \theta e(X + C - r^B)$$

$$= \theta e(X + C - RL) - (1/f)R(RK - L).$$

Because all type G borrowers are identical at date 0, Π_g^S is common for all type G borrowers. It is easy to see that Π_g^S is increasing in e (i.e., the degree of foreign banks' efficiency to sort out type G borrowers). However, it is independent of m (i.e., the degree of foreign banks' efficiency to sort out type B borrowers).

4.6   The Maturity Choice by Borrowers

In our model, domestic borrowers choose the maturity of their external loans at date 0 in order to maximize their expected payoffs. However, because $qX < R^2K$, choosing a maturity that only type B borrowers would prefer would reveal that the borrower was type B, and no loan would be made to him. Therefore, as long as the expected payoff rate of a type B borrower is positive, the maturity of a bank loan that is chosen by type G borrowers is also chosen by type B borrowers. Assuming the existence of such a pooling equilibrium, this indicates that all borrowers choose short-term loans if $\Pi_g^L < \Pi_g^S$ but choose long-term loans otherwise.

Subtracting equation (9) from equation (3) leads to

$$(10) \qquad \Pi_g^L = \Pi_g^S = (1 - \theta e)(X + C) - (1/f)R(1 - \theta f e)L$$

$$+ \frac{(1 - f)q}{[f + (1 - f)q]f} R^2K.$$

Thus, in this international financial market all domestic borrowers choose short-term loans if and only if

$$(11) \quad (1 - \theta e)(X + C - RL) + \frac{(1 - f)q}{[f + (1 - f)q]f} R^2K < \left[\frac{(1 - f)}{f}\right]RL.$$

Equation (11) has two noteworthy implications for the terms to maturity in international bank loans. The first is that given other parameters, an increase in θ makes equation (11) more probable. Because θ denotes the probability that a financial panic will not occur, this implies that foreign banks tend to choose short-term loans when they are optimistic about the borrowers' financial conditions. The intuition behind this result is that when lenders perceive that liquidity risk is small, long-term contracts appear less attractive for lenders.

Because foreign lenders were optimistic about the precrisis East Asian economies, the result can explain why the East Asian economies had comparatively higher shares of short-term loans in the world standard before the crisis.[15] It may also imply that some optimistic confidence made the precrisis East Asian economies vulnerable to the crisis not only through increasing the total amount of external liabilities but also through making their terms to maturity shorter.

The second noteworthy implication is that given other parameters, an increase in e makes equation (11) more probable. Because the value of e is a proxy for the degree of monitoring efficiency, this implies that borrowers tend to choose short-term loans when monitoring can make use of new information arrival efficiently. In general, short-term debt can lower a good borrower's expected financing cost because of a possible arrival of good information. Thus, when lenders can make use of additional credit information arrival more efficiently by ex post monitoring, short-term debt will be preferred in debt contracts.

The latter implication is important in considering the choice of bank loan maturity because banks usually have better monitoring abilities than do other financial intermediaries. The result generally predicts that efficient monitoring activities by banks tend to make the debt maturity composition shorter. Without the possibility of unnecessary liquidation, the efficient monitoring might have a positive effect on economic welfare. However, without prudential regulation or a safety net in the international financial market, the efficiency of banks' monitoring can increase the possibility that an otherwise solvent country may suffer a short-run liquidity problem. The negative consequence is particularly likely when the available stock of reserves is low relative to the overall burden of external debt service.

This theoretical result is consistent with the empirical fact that a large fraction of external bank debt had been financed by short-term loans in a large number of countries, which might make several developing countries vulnerable to liquidity problems. In particular, because the East Asian crisis took the form of a pure liquidity shortage in private bank loans, the experience of several Asian countries in 1997 may provide striking examples of such negative consequences of efficient bank monitoring.

---

15. In table 4.4, one finds remarkably high shares of short-term loans in Taiwan. This finding may be consistent with our result because large amounts of foreign reserves made a financial panic least likely in Taiwan.

4.7 Discussions

I have discussed how the maturity of bank loans is determined in the competitive international financial market. The results are, however, based on several assumptions that may not be relevant for some developing countries. For example, my simple theoretical model did not take into account several regulatory factors in the international loan market. In reality, the maturity structure of international bank loans may have been influenced not only by the government policy to regulate long-term capital inflows but also by the regulations on foreign banks such as the BIS risk-weighted capital regulation, which favors short-term loans. In terms of this theoretical analysis, these regulatory factors can be modeled as taxes on long-term loans. Thus, if these factors exist, short-term loans would be chosen even under relatively milder conditions in our model.

In addition, this model assumed that borrowers face a competitive international loan market. The assumption may be justified when a large number of potential foreign lenders are in the international loan market. In particular, the assumption may be realistic for the East Asian economies before the crisis, during which time many foreign banks competed with others in the loan market under the lending boom. However, in several developing countries, private loans from foreign banks took the form of syndicated loans. Under such circumstances, borrowers in developing countries did not necessarily face a competitive international loan market.

Without rigorous analyses, it is not clear how the main results will change when foreign banks have some monopolistic power in the international loan market. However, even when the international loan market is not competitive, it is always true that efficient monitoring activities can make use of new information arrival more efficiently under asymmetric information between lenders and borrowers. Thus, I conjecture that under some mild conditions, monopolistic foreign banks can still have an incentive to choose short-term loans when they have better monitoring abilities.

Finally, our model assumed equation (1), under which the average project in the economy has a positive net present value. In general, however, we cannot rule out the case in which equation (1) does not hold. In fact, equation (1) does not hold when the average project in the economy has a negative net present value in terms of cash flows, i.e., when $R^2 K > [f + (1 - f)q]X$. I think that the case is unrealistic for the East Asian economies before the crisis because their expected growth rates were very high. However, it may hold true for several stagnant developing countries where the percentage of bad quality borrowers in the economy is large.

When $R^2 K > [f + (1 - f)q]X$ holds in the model, a long-term loan is never supplied by foreign banks at date 0 because foreign banks cannot get the expected rate return of R^2. However, as long as $R^2 K \leq (1 - \theta fe)RL$

$+ \theta feX$ holds, short-term loan can be supplied by foreign banks at date 0. This implies that when the average project in the economy has a negative net present value, foreign banks provide only short-term loans to the economy.

Although the analysis focused on international bank lending, the result may be extended to explain several noteworthy events in the international bond market for some stagnant developing countries.[16] For example, in 1994 foreign investors refused to purchase long-term Mexican government bonds because of the likelihood of a devaluation of the Mexican peso. As a result, in Mexico the term structure of government bonds shifted to the shortend before the eventual crisis in December 1994.[17] Similarly, in 1998 foreign investors became skeptical about the sustainability of fiscal deficits in Russia. As a result, they shifted their investment to short-term Russian bonds before the eventual devaluation of the ruble.[18] Although these events happened in the bond market rather than in the loan market, they are consistent with the previous discussions, which allowed for the case that $R^2K > [f + (1 - f)q]X$ in our model.

4.8   Some Extensions

In previous sections, I have considered the case in which foreign banks always choose liquidation when their monitoring cannot identify the type of borrowers at date 1. However, when the bank's monitoring reveals more type B borrowers than it does type G borrowers, this case becomes less likely because the percentage of type G borrowers becomes larger among unidentified borrowers. In this section, I discuss how our main results would change if foreign banks never liquidate the projects of unidentified borrowers at date 1.[19]

For analytical simplicity, we assume that the probability of a financial panic is 0 (i.e., $\theta = 1$). Then, when the projects of unidentified borrowers are never liquidated, foreign banks liquidate the borrower's project at date 1 if and only if the monitoring identifies the borrower as type B. Because the percentage of identified type B borrowers among all borrowers is $m(1 - f)$ at date 1, this implies that the expected rate of return for a date 0 short-term lender is equal to $[1 - m(1 - f)]r^1 + m(1 - f)L$, where r^1 is the face value of short-term loan issued at date at date 0, maturing at date 1. Equating this to the one-period riskless return RK leads to

16. The following arguments were suggested by Takatoshi Ito.
17. The Mexican government also had to issue dollar-linked government bonds.
18. However, investors were to be surprised at eventual de facto default of the bonds.
19. However, I do not think that the case where the bank's monitoring reveals type B borrowers more than it does type G borrowers is realistic in many countries because type G borrowers have an incentive to reveal their type, but type B borrowers do not.

(12) $r^1 = [RK - m(1 - f)L]/[1 - m(1 - f)]$.

Recall that at date 1 unidentified borrowers are type G with probability $(1 - e)f/[(1 - e)f + (1 - m)(1 - f)]$ and type B with probability $(1 - m)(1 - f)/[(1 - e)f + (1 - m)(1 - f)]$. Recall also that type G borrowers succeed for sure and that type B borrowers succeed with probability q at date 2. Then, when a new short-term loan is supplied to them at date 1, the new short-term loan maturing at date 2 is repaid with probability $[(1 - e)f + (1 - m)(1 - f)q]/[(1 - e)f + (1 - m)(1 - f)]$. This implies that the face value of a short-term loan issued for unidentified borrowers at date 1, which is denoted by r^c, needs to satisfy

(13) $$\frac{(1 - e)f + (1 - m)(1 - f)q}{(1 - e)f + (1 - m)(1 - f)} r^C = r^1 R.$$

For borrowers who were identified as type G, the face value of a short-term loan issued at date 1, r^B, is determined by equation (5), that is, $r^B = r^1 R$. Therefore, equations (5), (12), and (13) lead to

(14) $$r^B = \frac{RK - m(1 - f)LR}{1 - m(1 - f)},$$

(15) $$r^C = r^B \frac{(1 - e)f + (1 - m)(1 - f)}{(1 - e)f + (1 - m)(1 - f)q} > r^B.$$

When the project of unidentified borrowers is never liquidated, the payoff of a type G borrower with short-term loan is written as

(16a) $X + C - r^B$ when the type is identified at date 1,

and

(16b) $X + C - r^C$ when the type is not identified at date 1.

Because a type G borrower is identified at date 1 with probability e, the expected payoff of a type G borrower with a short-term loan at date 0 can be calculated as

(17) $\Pi_g^S = e(X + C - r^B) + (1 - e)(X + C - r^C)$

$$= X + C - r^B \frac{(1 - e)f + (1 - m)(1 - f)[1 - (1 - q)e]}{(1 - e)f + (1 - m)(1 - f)q}.$$

As was Π_g^S in equation (9), Π_g^S in equation (17) depends on the parameter e. However, contrary to Π_g^S in equation (9), Π_g^S in equation (17) also depends on the parameter m, i.e., the degree of foreign banks' efficiency to sort out type B borrowers.

Subtracting equation (17) from equation (3) leads to

(18) $\Pi_g^L - \Pi_g^S = -r^L + er^B + (1 - e)r^C$

$$= r^B \frac{(1 - e)f + (1 - m)(1 - f)[1 - (1 - q)e]}{(1 - e)f + (1 - m)(1 - f)q}$$

$$- \frac{R^2 K}{f + (1 - f)}.$$

That all borrowers choose short-term loans if and only if $\Pi_g^L < \Pi_g^S$ implies that all domestic borrowers choose short-term loans if and only if $r^L > e$ $r^B + (1 - e)r^C$, or equivalently,

(19) $r^B \dfrac{(1 - e)f + (1 - m)(1 - f)[1 - (1 - q)e]}{(1 - e)f + (1 - m)(1 - f)q} < \dfrac{R^2 K}{f + (1 - f)}.$

After some tedious calculation, I can verify that given other parameters, an increase in e makes the inequality in equation (19) more probable. Thus, even in cases in which unidentified borrowers are never liquidated, foreign banks that have the better monitoring ability to sort out type G borrowers will tend to choose short-term loans.

In contrast, the effect of the parameter m on equation (19) is not clear in general. In particular, when L is small enough, an increase in m makes the inequality in equation (19) less probable. Thus, under some circumstances foreign banks with better monitoring ability to sort out type B borrowers may choose long-term loans. However, when L is close to RK, an increase in m makes the inequality in equation (19) more probable. Thus, at least when a liquidation value is large, foreign banks with better monitoring ability to sort out type B borrowers can tend to choose short-term loans even when unidentified borrowers are never liquidated.

4.9   Concluding Remarks

In this paper, I first demonstrated that middle-term and long-term commercial bank loans are less mobile forms of external liabilities. I also showed that a large fraction of external bank debt had been financed by short-term loans not only in the East Asian countries but also in a large number of other countries. I then presented a simple theoretical model in which the financial structure may become vulnerable as a result of banks' efficient monitoring activities.

In the literature of corporate finance, a large number of studies stressed the positive role of banks as delegated monitors that specialize in gathering information about borrowers. It is probably true that when government regulations are established well in the financial market, the efficient role of banks as delegated monitors unambiguously improves economic welfare. For example, in Japan during the 1950s and 1960s, nearly 90 percent of loans supplied by the city and local banks were short-term funds whose

Table 4.6   **Percentage Distribution of Outstanding Loans and Discounts by Maturity: The Case of Japan during High Growth Period**

End of Year	3 months and less	3 months– 1 year	More than 1 year	Overdrafts
City banks				
1955	76.2	17.7	5.1	0.9
1960	70.0	22.4	6.4	1.2
1965	53.7	35.2	10.0	1.1
1970	53.0	32.2	13.7	1.1
1975	40.4	28.8	29.3	1.5
Local banks				
1955	78.5	12.7	7.6	1.2
1960	68.6	22.2	8.4	0.8
1965	53.5	34.8	11.1	0.6
1970	45.6	35.3	18.5	0.5
1975	36.3	31.2	31.7	0.8

Sources: Bank of Japan, Economic Statistics Annual, various issues.

terms to maturity was less than one year (see table 4.6). If a financial panic was likely, the financial structure in Japan would have been vulnerable to a liquidity shortage. However, under strict administrative regulations, a financial panic never occurred in Japan during the 1950s and 1960s. As a result, short-term loans made a significant contribution for remarkable economic growth in postwar Japan under the regulated financial market.

Unfortunately, we can expect neither satisfactory government regulation nor a safety net (say, deposit insurance) in the current international financial market. Given the circumstances, efficient monitoring activities by competitive banks are not necessarily desirable. In other words, international bank lending may have an ironic consequence that an improvement of bank's monitoring ability can increase the possibility of an unnecessary liquidity shortage and may have a negative effect on economic growth.

References

Aoki, M. 1994. Monitoring characteristics of the main bank system: An analytical and developmental view. In *The Japanese main bank system,* ed. M. Aoki and H. Patrick, 109–41. Oxford: Oxford University Press.

Bank for International Settlements (BIS). 1995. *The maturity, sectoral and nationality distribution of international bank lending.* Basel, Switzerland: BIS.

———. 1996. *The maturity, sectoral and nationality distribution of international bank lending.* Basel, Switzerland: BIS.

———. 1998a. *International banking and financial market development.* Basel, Switzerland: BIS.

———. 1998b. *The maturity, sectoral and nationality distribution of international bank lending.* Basel, Switzerland: BIS.

Cameron, R. 1967. *Banking in the early stages of industrialization.* New York: Oxford University Press.

Chang, R., and A. Velasco. 1998. Financial crises in emerging markets: A canonical model. NBER Working Paper no. 6606. Cambridge, Mass.: National Bureau of Economic Research.

Corsetti, G., P. Pesenti, and N. Roubini. 1999. What caused the Asian currency and financial crises? *Japan and the World Economy* 11 (3): 305–454.

Diamond, D. W. 1984. Financial intermediation and delegated monitoring. *Review of Economic Studies* 5 (3): 393–414.

———. 1991. Debt maturity structure and liquidity risk. *Quarterly Journal of Economics* 106 (3): 709–37.

———. 1993. Bank loan maturity and priority when borrowers can refinance. In *Capital markets and financial intermediation,* ed. C. Mayer and X. Vives, 46–68. Cambridge: Cambridge University Press.

Diamond, D. W., and P. H. Dybvig. 1983. Bank runs, deposit insurance, and liquidity. *Journal of Political Economy* 91 (3): 401–19.

Flannery, M. J. 1986. Asymmetric information and risky debt maturity choice. *Journal of Finance* 41 (1): 19–38.

Fry, M. J. 1995. *Money interest and banking in economic development.* 2nd ed. Baltimore, Md.: John Hopkins University Press.

Fukuda, S., C. Ji, and A. Nakamura. 1998. Determinants of long-term loans: A theory and empirical evidence in Japan. *Journal of Multinational Financial Management* 8 (2/3): 113–36.

Furman, J., and J. E. Stiglitz. 1998. Economic crises: Evidence and insights from East Asia. *Brookings Papers on Economic Activity,* issue no. 2: 1–135. Washington, D.C.: Brookings Institution.

Goldsmith, R. W. 1969. *Financial structure and development.* New Haven, Conn.: Yale University Press.

Hoshi, T., A. Kashyap, and D. Scharfstein. 1991. Corporate structure, liquidity and investment: Evidence from Japanese industrial groups. *Quarterly Journal of Economics* 106 (1): 33–60.

International Monetary Fund (IMF). 1997. *International financial statistics, December.* Washington, D.C.: IMF.

———. 2000. *International financial statistics, January.* Washington, D.C.: IMF.

Ito, T. 1999. Capital flows in Asia. NBER Working Paper no. 7134. Cambridge, Mass.: National Bureau of Economic Research.

Krugman, P. 1998. What happened to Asia? MIT Department of Economics. Mimeograph.

Leland, H. E., and D. H. Pyle. 1977. Informational asymmetries, financial structure and financial intermediation. *Journal of Finance* 32 (2): 371–87.

McKinnon, R. I. 1973. *Money and capital in economic development.* Washington, D.C.: Brookings Institution.

McKinnon, R. I., and H. Pill. 1996. Credible liberalizations and international capital flows: The "Overborrowing Syndrome." In *Financial deregulation and integration in East Asia,* ed. T. Ito and A. O. Krueger, 7–48. Chicago: University of Chicago Press.

Patrick, H. T. 1966. Financial development and economic growth in underdeveloped countries. *Economic Development and Cultural Change* 14 (2): 174–89.

Radelet, S., and J. Sachs. 1998. The onset of the East Asian financial crisis. NBER Working Paper no. 6680. Cambridge, Mass.: National Bureau of Economic Research.

Rajan, R. G. 1992. Insiders and outsiders: The choice between informed and arm's-length debt. *Journal of Finance* 47 (4): 1367–1401.

Rodrik, D., and A. Velasco. 1999. Short-term capital flows. NBER Working Paper no. 7364. Cambridge, Mass.: National Bureau of Economic Research.

Sachs, J. D., A. Tornell, and A. Velasco. 1996. Financial crises in emerging markets: The lessons from 1995. *Brookings Papers on Economic Activity,* issue no. 1: 147–215.

Shaw, E. S. 1973. *Financial deepening in economic development.* New York: Oxford University Press.

World Bank. 1989. *World development report.* New York: Oxford University Press.

Comment   Takatoshi Ito

I have two kinds of comments on Fukuda's paper. First, I will examine the plausibility of the basic assumptions on information asymmetry and their implications; second, I will comment on the data interpretation.

Basic Assumptions

This paper sets up a theoretical model of asymmetric information on bank lending, motivated by recent problems in international bank lending to Asian countries (as shown by the author, citing statistics collected by the Bank for International Settlements [BIS]). Given how important international bank lending has been in Asian economies, both positively (before the crisis) and negatively (during the crisis), a contribution on understanding banks' lending behavior is welcome.

In Fukuda's model, borrowers know that they are of either good type (higher probability to succeed) or bad type (lower probability to succeed). Lenders cannot distinguish between them when making bank loans, unless they behave differently. Lending can be made for either one period or two periods; bank monitoring reveals some of the good borrowers after one period. Knowing this monitoring activity, good-type borrowers have incentive to borrow short (one-period loans) in the hope that they may be identified as being of good type. The tradeoff for going short is that, after one period, there may be a bank run, and even good-type borrowers would not have a rollover of bank loans. Without a rollover, only a fraction of a project is recovered in the process of liquidation. If good-type borrowers choose to borrow short, then bad-type borrowers must also borrow short in order to avoid being identified as bad. Comparative statics shows that if the proportion of the good-type borrower is higher, then good-type borrowers tend to borrow short. If monitoring to identify good-type borrowers after one period becomes more accurate, good-borrowers tend to borrow short.

Takatoshi Ito is professor at the Institute of Economic Research at Hitotsubashi University, Tokyo, and a research associate of the National Bureau of Economic Research.

This conclusion is counterintuitive. In the real world, my intuition says, a good borrower tends to favor a long-term loan, not a short-term loan, because the good borrower would not like to be caught by liquidity shortage in the middle of the project. My intuition also says that a lender, not a borrower, prefers short-term loans if it suspects that there are more bad borrowers than before, or if the monitoring technique is enhanced to pick bad borrowers after one period. If Fukuda's model is right, we should expect to find that bank lending to Asia has a higher short-term lending ratio in good times (1993–95), while the long-term lending ratio would rise as the crisis nears (1996–97). This is hard to be confirmed in table 4.3 of the paper. So, empirically, theoretical prediction is somewhat inconclusive.

In 1994, the maturity structure of Mexican government bonds shifted to short-term (and dollar indexed) before the eventual crisis in December. Investors refused to purchase long-term bonds, fearing a devaluation. Similarly, short-term Russian bonds (GKOs) in 1998 soared, with investors becoming increasingly skeptical about the sustainability of fiscal deficits and the level of the ruble. Of course, these are bonds, not bank lending, which is the focus of the study in the Fukuda paper; but these examples would suggest the lender's preference and behavior.

So, the rest of my comments explore why my intuitions are not predicted by his theory. Basically, I will argue that assumptions of the model are responsible for these counterintuitive results.

First, monitoring is assumed to distinguish a portion of only good-type borrowers after one period, but none of the bad-type borrowers. This is analogous to a situation in which there is only upside risk and no downside risk in lending. If there is a possibility that bad-type borrowers can be identified, then lenders—not borrowers—may want to keep loans in the short term. Second, in Fukuda's model, decisions are made only by borrowers; but in the real world, lenders may be more influential in determining the maturity structure. Taking the first and second comments seriously, I conjecture the following comparative statistics result. The higher the proportion of bad-type borrowers, the more likely the loans will be of short term.

Third, there is no interest rate as a market-clearing price. I wonder whether it is possible to extend the Fukuda model so that the loan demand function is derived from the borrower's choice, while the loan supply function is derived from the lender's choice. The interest rate is then determined in equilibrium. Once this is done, then the yield curve (the difference between the short-term and the long-term interest rates) may be derived. The slope of the yield curve reflects, among other things, the degree of risk to be revealed later (the future short-term interest rate and the exchange rate fluctuation, for example).

Fourth, in deriving the yield curve as an equilibrium of lender's and borrower's choices, it may be worthwhile to introduce uncertainties about public information, such as the world interest rate, the exchange rate changes, and general economic conditions of the country where borrowers reside.

Integrating these comments would make the paper much more relevant to the real-world problem of international bank lending.

Data Interpretation

Medium-term and long-term loans (that is, those with maturity of one to two years, and beyond two years, respectively) did not decrease as much as short-term loans (with maturity of less than one year). From this, Professor Fukuda concludes that longer-term loans are less mobile. He tries to explain the proportion of short- to medium- and long-term loans by asymmetry of information. However, in reality, these two types of loans may represent different kinds of customers and loan conditions. For example, medium- and long-term loans from Japanese banks are directed to subsidiaries of Japanese companies and may be guaranteed by Japanese parent companies. Short-term loans may be directed to local banks. Local banks direct the loans to corporations. What lenders have to do is to monitor local banks' performance, but not the companies' performance directly. If this inference is right, then there is a good reason for the way loan maturity is chosen and for the mobility of longer-term loans. The ratio between short-term loans and long-term loans is determined by such factors as how banks are financing foreign direct investment and how banks obtain parent companies' guarantees—which are reasons other than monitoring technology and the ratio of good and bad companies. The BIS statistics do not tell us information with regard to guarantees, currency risk exposure, and hedge ratio; it would be difficult to derive policy implication. Hence, one should be cautious in interpreting the BIS statistics and the implications of the model.

In summary, this paper raises interesting issues on how a maturity structure of bank loans is determined. The model highlights the roles of monitoring ability and choice by borrowers. It will be interesting to extend the Fukuda model to include other important factors in loan decisions.

Comment   Yukiko Fukagawa

The crisis in East Asia prompted academic and practical interests on the role of short-term loans in bringing about the crisis. The paper undertakes

Yukiko Fukagawa is associate professor of development economics at Aoyama Gakuin University and a research associate of Research Institute of Economy, Trade and Industry (RIETI).

a theoretical analysis of how efficient monitoring by foreign commercial banks can increase (as opposed to decrease) the possibility of a liquidity crisis and credit crunch. The result has significant implications for an international financial crisis.

Despite the theoretical contribution of the paper, some important factors seem to have been ignored. As the paper acknowledges, regulatory or institutional factors such as Bank for International Settlements (BIS) regulations were not considered in the lenders' decision-making process. Several regulations influenced the maturity choice for both lenders and borrowers, such as controls on offshore banking and direct controls on the operation of foreign banks. In some cases, short-term loans were inevitable simply because there was no market for long-term lending, as in the case of Thailand. On the lenders' side, a choice of maturity may be affected not only by regulations, but also by the lending scheme itself. Even in East Asia—a region of relatively successful economies—syndicated loans were still a common form of lending, especially in large-scale projects. Here maturity choice may depend on a liquidation value at date 1 (L in equation [19] in the paper), plus cost of negotiation with other lenders. The factors of risk include the existence (or lack) of the host government's guarantees. In syndicate loans, therefore, L (for one bank) could be small, and foreign banks may perform monitoring and sort out type B; then the bank may prefer long-term loans, as was mentioned in the extension section of the paper.

The paper also examines the possibility of alternative assumptions, such as an uncompetitive loan market for less developed countries, lender monopoly, and the case of negative present value of the project. In addition to these, however, there might have been several other factors. For instance, assumptions about the degree of information asymmetry between domestic and international monitoring can be modeled. The cost of monitoring in domestic lending is intuitively smaller compared to that in international lending. Therefore, in practice, instead of incurring the monitoring cost, foreign banks often opt to rely on secondhand information from major rating firms in deciding the credit lines, or simply follow the leading bank's decision in a case of herd behavior. When Korean banks started to suffer from spillovers of the Thai crisis, many leaders decided not to roll-over long-term loans to Korean banks. Foreign banks cut the credit line until the liquidity completely dried up. This may be the case for efficient monitoring, as the model suggests; but if this were to occur in the domestic market, the information asymmetry might not have been as serious, and lenders could have accessed firsthand information on the borrowers easily taking a differentiated strategy instead of blind herding.

My third critique concerns the paper's remark that unless satisfactory prudential regulations or a safety net is established in the international financial market, improvement of bank monitoring may increase the possibility of an unnecessary liquidity shortfall. This was different from Japan's experience in the 1950s–80s, where there was intensive short-term lending monitored by banks, yet the finance was sustained for good firms. However, even if the institutional environment must be different in international finance, domestic finance in the troubled economies could have been the same way with Japan to prevent the turmoil. So, what was the crucial difference? Probably, it was not only international short-term capital allocation that mattered, but also the combination of long-term investments and borrowed capital in the domestic capital market. This was the case in Thailand and Indonesia. The maturity mismatch could have been adjusted in the domestic capital market if only minimal financial supervision had been maintained. Here, the problem in Korea was more serious in that the borrowing and substantial lending were done in the overseas market. How supervision could have checked this aspect remains in question.

The model also does not specify the nature of the borrowers—whether banks, firms, or both. If foreign banks lend directly to firms, the model holds; but if they lend to local banks, the borrowers' risk is partially up to domestic intermediaries as well as to foreign lenders to domestic banks. Domestic banking problems can be alleviated by domestic regulations and a safety net. Indeed, Malaysia as well as Korea had maintained relatively strict domestic regulations, and borrowing had been concentrated on local banks, unlike in Indonesia, where many firms borrowed directly from foreign banks. The restructuring process has been relatively rapid in Korea and Malaysia, thanks to the regulations on domestic finance. Therefore, the probability of liquidity shortfall may be greater with better monitoring by banks if domestic monitoring remains poor—but this does not deny the importance of reforms in the domestic market.

Finally, the model assumes that the average project has a positive net present value, which may not be the case in stagnant economies. As the paper argues, long-term loans are never supplied by foreign banks at time 0 if the percentage of type B borrowers is substantially large, because when $R^2K > [f + (1 - f)q]X$, R^2 cannot be expected. On the other hand, as long as $R^2K \leq (1 - \theta fe)RL + \theta feX$ holds, only short-term loans can be supplied at time 0, even if the net present value is negative. In fact, in a very competitive environment banks often try to take the risk of type B with potentially negative present value by extending short term loans. Nowadays, with the sophistication of the modern asset liability management (ALM) system and complicated risk-hedging techniques, including various kinds of derivatives, foreign banks may even be willing to continue short-term lending regardless of the present net value. Therefore, regarding the massive capital flows to emerging markets as a reflection of technological development in international finance, the choice of maturity may be more complex. The choice of maturity may not depend solely on the type of borrowers; instead, it may be decided based on an independent project value (both at present and in the future in project finance), or it could be influenced by other external valuables such as the risk hedging environment. However, these suggested challenges to the model do not deny its original contribution on the subject of the role of foreign banks' monitoring in short-term lending.

5

How Were Capital Inflows Stimulated under the Dollar Peg System?

Eiji Ogawa and Lijian Sun

5.1 Introduction

The Asian currency crisis that started in Thailand in July 1997 had spread rapidly to other Association of Southeast Asian Nations (ASEAN) countries and the Newly Industrializing Economies (NIES) in Asia. Among the affected nations, Thailand, Indonesia, and Korea faced the most severe currency crises. Their governments requested financial support from the International Monetary Fund (IMF).

It is commonly stated that the Asian currency crisis had the following features (IMF 1997c, 1998; Ito 1999). First, the monetary authorities of the affected countries adopted an exchange rate policy of pegging the domestic currency to the U.S. dollar with an extremely large weight. The de facto dollar peg system influenced both the nation's current and capital accounts. An appreciation of the U.S. dollar had worsened the current accounts under the de facto dollar peg system since May 1995.[1] De facto dollar pegging also made domestic borrowers and foreign lenders ignore the risk of foreign exchange.

Second, macroeconomic variables, except for large current account deficits in Thailand, Malaysia, and Korea, were in sustainable condition before the crisis. Neither budget deficits nor decreases in foreign reserves

Eiji Ogawa is professor of commerce at Hitotsubashi University. Lijian Sun is associate professor of international finance at Fudan University, Shanghai.

We appreciate Takatoshi Ito, Francis T. Lui, Pranee Tinakorn, Carmen Reinhart, Toshiki Jinushi, and a referee for their useful comments and suggestions. We also appreciate the help of Yukiko Takase (Economic Planning Agency) for providing us the statistical data. Ogawa received a grant from the Japan Securities Scholarship Foundation.

1. Ito, Ogawa, and Sasaki (1998) calculated an optimal weight of currency basket for stabilizing trade balances.

were found—especially as compared to the past currency crises in Latin America. Although growth rates of export revenues had abruptly gone down in these countries since 1996, the large amounts of capital inflows made the governments complacent about their current account deficits.

Lastly, the currency crisis occurred simultaneously with a financial crisis which made some financial intermediaries go bankrupt. The IMF (1997c, 1998) pointed out that in the background of the financial crisis, there was a fragile financial sector. In an effort to prevent further deterioration, the IMF required the governments of the various countries to restructure their financial sectors as conditionality for receiving financial support. Large capital inflows to the countries with inadequate financial institutions brought about the financial crisis.

According to Kaminsky, Lizondo, and Reinhart (1997), there seems to be a consistent relationship between financial and currency crises in emerging market countries. Indeed, in the past, currency crisis often occurred along with financial crisis. The literature on financial and currency crises has been classified into three groups. The first group (Velasco 1987; Dooley 1997; Calvo and Mendoza 1996) explains that a financial crisis brings about a currency crisis, whereas the second group (IMF 1997b; Miller 1996) explains that a currency crisis causes a financial crisis. The third group (Calvo, Leiderman, and Reinhart 1993; Goldfajn and Valdes 1997) accounts for the possibility of a common external factor that brings about both the financial and currency crises at the same time—e.g., fluctuations of the world interest rate that influenced the flow of international capital to and from the domestic financial markets triggered the Mexico crisis in 1994.

This paper places emphasis on external factors as the cause of currency and financial crises. It focuses on fluctuations of the exchange rate under the de facto dollar peg system. In the 1990s, there were large swings of the yen against the U.S. dollar; the yen rapidly appreciated during the early 1990s and depreciated after 1995. If the monetary authorities of a country were to adopt a dollar peg system, the fluctuations in the exchange rate of the yen against the U.S. dollar would have caused the same fluctuations in the exchange rate of the yen against the relevant currencies.

This paper empirically analyzes how the de facto dollar peg system adversely influenced capital inflows to the countries in crisis by studying the relationship between the de facto dollar peg system and the capital inflows to these countries. Focus is placed on countries that requested IMF financial support during the Asian crisis, namely, Thailand, Korea, and Indonesia. We regress capital flows on explanatory variables such as interest rates, foreign exchange risks, export growth rate, and rate of change in stock prices. We then use an instrumental variable method to take into account how the instrumental variables are influenced by other variables.

The estimated regression equations are then used to conduct a simulation analysis of how the capital inflows would have behaved had the monetary authorities of these countries adopted a currency basket peg system instead of the de facto dollar peg system. The currency basket peg system would have increased fluctuations in the exchange rate of the domestic currency against the U.S. dollar, whereas it would have decreased the fluctuations of the exchange rate against the yen. Accordingly, a currency basket peg system would have changed the actual and the expected changes in exchange rates, and led to a change in foreign exchange risks.

The simulation analysis generates the following results: A currency basket peg system would have had a depressing effect on capital inflows to Thailand and Korea during the analyzed period 1985–96. It would also have had a slightly depressing effect on capital inflows to Indonesia. Increases in foreign exchange risk against the U.S. dollar under a currency basket peg system would have contributed most to the depressing effect. This is because the estimated foreign exchange risk variable against the U.S. dollar is the most significant variable among the explanatory variables in the capital flow equation.

This paper is organized as follows. Section 5.2 gives an overview of how different variables influence capital inflows to the Asian countries before the crisis. In section 5.3, a simple model of capital inflows that consists of a capital flow equation with instrumental variables is set up. An instrumental variable method is then used to estimate the capital flow equation. We drop the instrumental variables that have a coefficient with the wrong sign and proceed to estimate the regression equations. In section 5.4, the estimated regression equations are used to conduct a simulation analysis of the capital inflows under the currency basket peg system. Simulated values under the currency basket peg system are compared with estimated values under the actual de facto dollar peg system. The simulation shows how the dollar peg system influenced the capital inflows to these countries and how a currency basket peg system would have influenced them. Finally, we summarize analytical results and conclude in section 5.5.

5.2   Capital Inflows before the Asian Currency Crisis

According to the classification by the IMF (1997a), before the crisis, the Asian countries with currencies attacked by speculation in 1997 had in fact adopted exchange rate arrangements other than the dollar peg system. The exchange rate arrangements in Indonesia, Malaysia, and Korea were classified as the *managed float system*. The exchange rate arrangement in the Philippines was classified as an *independent float system*. The exchange rate system in Thailand was described as a *basket peg system*. Hong Kong was the only one under the dollar peg system in the IMF's classification.

However, research by Frankel and Wei (1994), Kawai and Akiyama (1998), and Kawai (1997) on the currency to which the monetary authori-

Table 5.1   Weights on the Dollar and the Yen in Exchange Rate Policies of
                 Asian Countries

	Sample Period 1979–92		Sample Period 1990–96	
	Coefficient on the Dollar	Coefficient on the Yen	Coefficient on the Dollar	Coefficient on the Yen
Singapore	0.75	0.13	0.420[a]	0.021
Hong Kong	0.92	−0.00	1.002	−0.002
Korea	0.96	−0.10	0.941	0.088
Malaysia	0.78	0.07	0.589	0.044
Thailand	0.91	0.05	0.789	0.104
The Philippines	1.07	−0.01	1.087	−0.094
Indonesia	0.95	0.16	0.966	0.014

Sources: Frankel and Wei (1994); Kawai (1997).
[a]Coefficient on the SDR is 0.600.

ties of the Asian countries pegged their currencies suggests otherwise. Frankel and Wei (1994) estimated the weights placed on major foreign currencies in their exchange rate policy during the period 1979–92. Kawai (1997) also estimated them during the period 1990–96 using the same method as Frankel and Wei. The result of estimation is summarized in table 5.1. For example, the weight on the U.S. dollar is 0.91 (Frankel and Wei 1994) and 0.789 (Kawai 1997) for Thailand. The weight placed on the U.S. dollar is nearly equal to one for Korea and Indonesia. Thus, the estimation indicates that these three countries have indeed adopted the de facto dollar peg system.

Next, we examine fluctuation of the exchange rates of these currencies against the U.S. dollar and the yen under the de facto dollar peg system. Figure 5.1 shows movements in the exchange rates of the Asian currencies against the U.S. dollar in the 1990s. The exchange rates in terms of the U.S. dollar were relatively stable until July 1997. The Thai baht and the Hong Kong dollar had been kept almost stable since 1990. The Malaysian ringgit had been kept relatively stable although it had been perfectly pegged to the U.S. dollar. The Korean won also had been kept relatively stable. The Indonesian rupiah had been changing at a predictable and constant rate because the monetary authorities had adopted a crawling peg to the U.S. dollar.

Figure 5.2 shows movements in the exchange rates of these currencies in terms of the yen. The exchange rates in terms of the yen underwent more substantial fluctuations compared to those against the U.S. dollar. Although they had a tendency to depreciate against the yen from 1990 to 1995, all of the currencies have been appreciating against it since May 1995. The joint movements of the exchange rates in terms of the yen were attributed to the de facto dollar peg system.

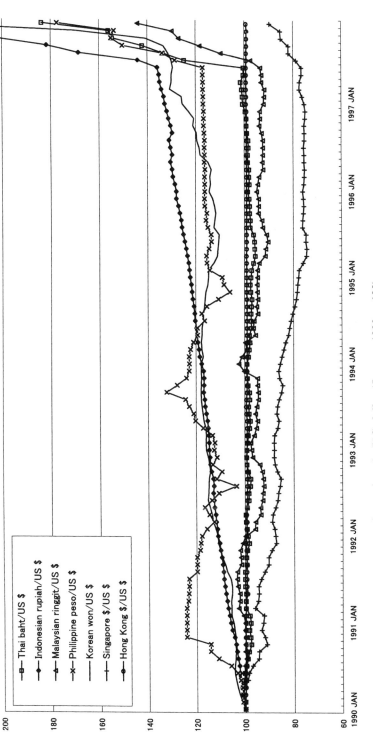

Fig. 5.1 Exchange rates of Asian currencies against the U.S. dollar (January 1990 = 100)

Source: International Monetary Fund (IMF) (2000).

Legend:
- Thai baht/US $
- Indonesian rupiah/US $
- Malaysian ringgit/US $
- Philippine peso/US $
- Korean won/US $
- Singapore $/US $
- Hong Kong $/US $

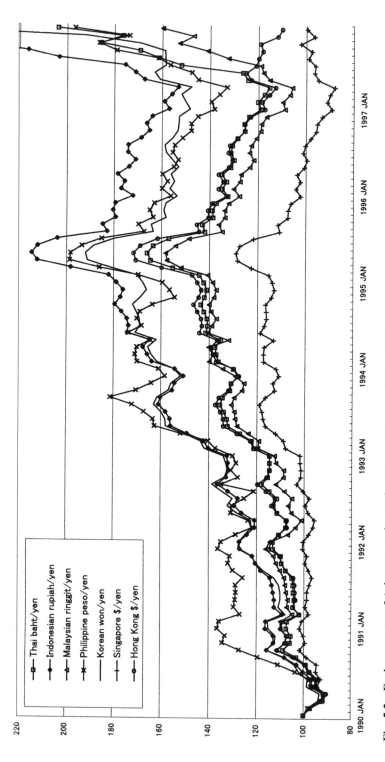

Fig. 5.2 Exchange rates of Asian currencies against the yen (January 1990 = 100)
Source: IMF (2000).

The vacillations in the exchange rates have had negative effects on the international trade competitiveness of these countries. Figure 5.3 shows movements of the real effective exchange rates of these countries. The real effective exchange rates of the Thai baht, the Malaysian ringgit, and the Indonesian rupiah fluctuated without any appreciating trends in the early 1990s. However, they began appreciating after May 1995. The Korean won was the only one to be fluctuating without any appreciating trend throughout the period 1992–97. Thus, the real effective exchange rates of the currencies except for the Korean won began appreciating since 1995. The de facto dollar peg system and the depreciation of the yen against the U.S. dollar influenced these movements in the real effective exchange rates.

In the early 1990s, depreciation of the U.S. dollar against the yen depreciated the countries' currencies against the yen under the de facto dollar peg system. Although these countries had trade deficits due to increases in imports of capital goods—which is a sign of good economic growth— exports in these countries had been steadily increasing due to the depreciation of their currencies against the yen. Nevertheless, the depreciating trend of the yen against the U.S. dollar after 1995 decreased the competitiveness of these countries against Japan, and in turn, decreased growth rates of export revenues. The movements of the export growth rates of Thailand, Korea, and Indonesia are shown in figure 5.4.

It is not so important whether or not a country has trade deficits as long as its imported capital goods continue to increase its future production capacities and export revenues.[2] However, if the export growth rate is decreasing at the present time and is expected to continue to decrease in the future, the present trade deficits will not be sustainable. The expectation could trigger speculative attacks against the currency even if these countries are increasing their foreign reserves.

Private capital inflows to Thailand, Indonesia, and Korea increased in the 1990s as shown in figures 5.5 to 5.7. The figures show that there was an oversurge of capital inflows to all three countries in 1995 and 1996. The oversurge of capital inflows to Thailand was mainly caused by other investments, such as international bank loans. Figure 5.6 shows that portfolio investments to Korea were larger than international bank loans in 1993 but that the opposite was true after 1994. Because private capital inflows had reached their peak in 1996, the international bank loans prevailed in the capital inflows to these Asian countries. This is the opposite of the situation in Latin American countries, where the portfolio investments prevailed in the capital inflows.

Movements in flows of international bank loans categorized by countries are shown in figures 5.8 through 5.10. In the case of Thailand, the share of Japanese banks was relatively high in 1994 and 1995. European

2. Frankel and Rose (1996) obtained a result that current account deficits are insignificant as a cause of currency crisis, as they were for the past currency crisis.

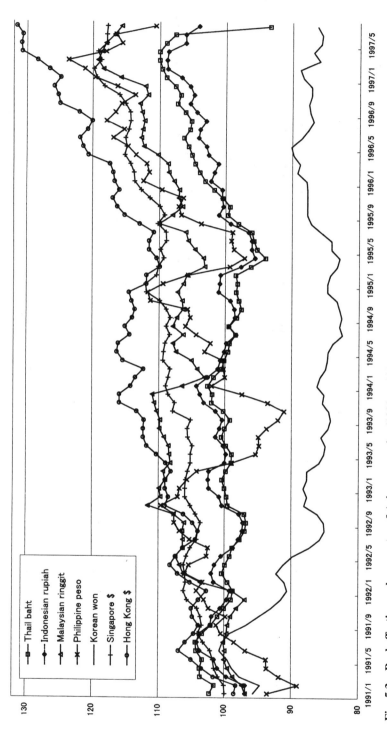

Fig. 5.3   Real effective exchange rates of Asian currencies (1990 = 100)
Source: J. P. Morgan index.

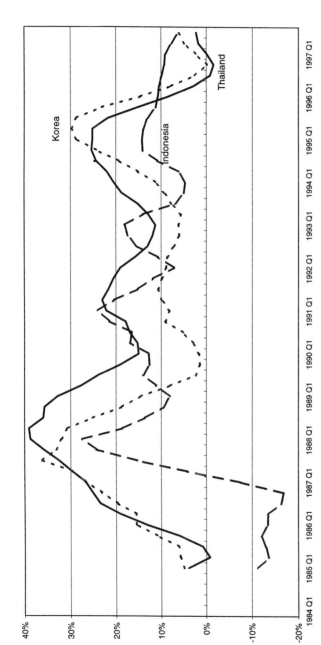

Fig. 5.4 Growth rate of export revenues (change from a year ago; five quarterly moving average)
Source: IMF (2000).

billion US$

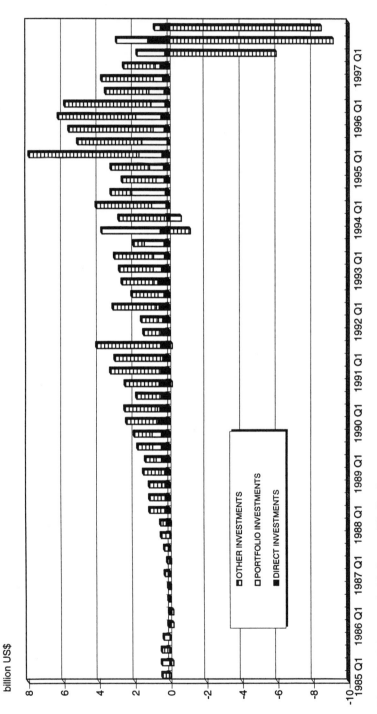

Fig. 5.5   Private capital inflows to Thailand
Source: IMF (2000).

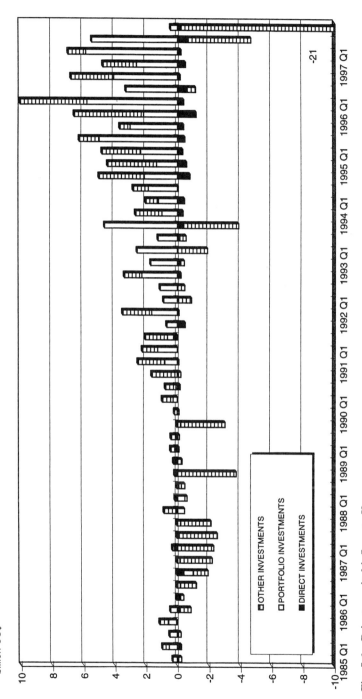

Fig. 5.6 Private capital inflows to Korea

Source: IMF (2000).

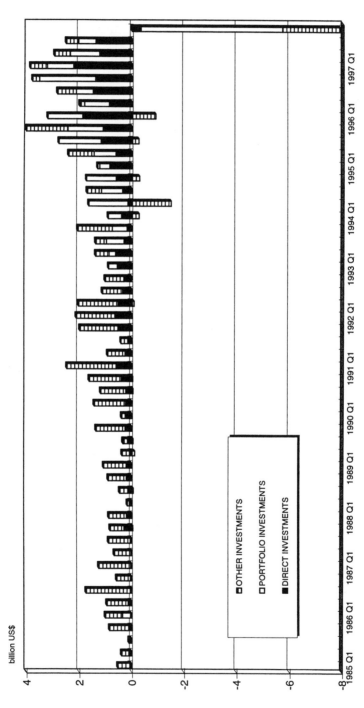

Fig. 5.7 Private capital inflows to Indonesia
Source: IMF (2000).

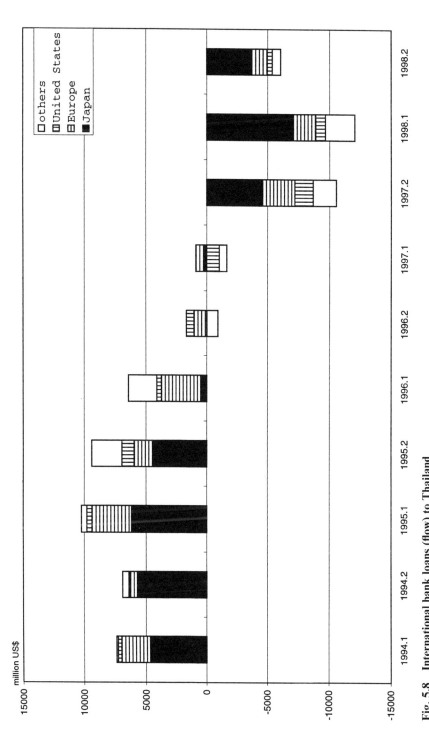

Fig. 5.8   International bank loans (flow) to Thailand
Source: Bank for International Settlements (BIS), Consolidated International Banking Statistics.

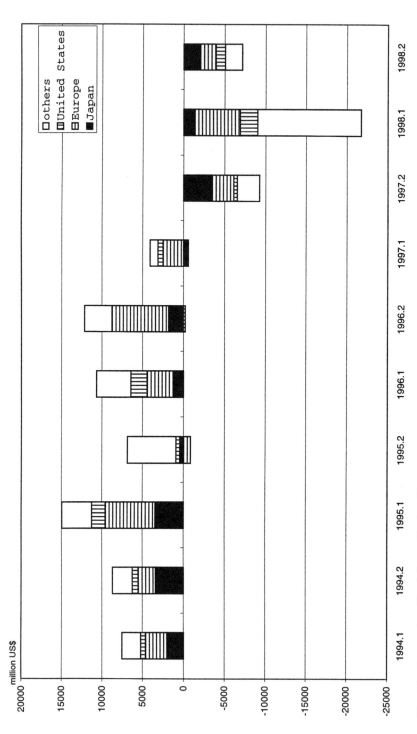

Fig. 5.9 International bank loans (flow) to Korea
Source: BIS, Consolidated International Banking Statistics.

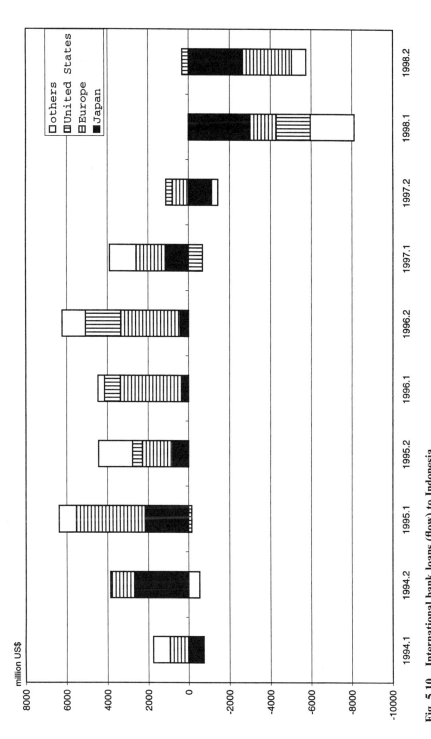

Fig. 5.10 International bank loans (flow) to Indonesia
Source: BIS, Consolidated International Banking Statistics.

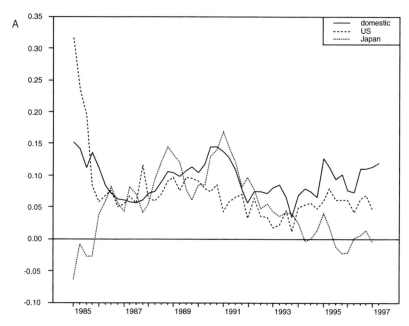

Fig. 5.11   Interest rates: *A*, Thailand; *B*, Korea; *C*, Indonesia

banks also increased their loans to Thailand in 1996. Although flows of international bank loans to Korea and Indonesia by European banks seemed to be higher than Japanese banks, Kaminsky and Reinhart (chapter 3, this volume) pointed out that Japanese banks had larger shares in stocks of international bank loans in these three countries.

The impact of both the de facto dollar peg system and depreciation or appreciation of the U.S. dollar against the yen on interest rates is examined. We calculate exchange rate adjusted foreign interest rates by adding expected depreciation rates of the domestic currency to the relevant foreign interest rate.[3]

Figure 5.11 shows movements of exchange rate adjusted foreign interest rates and domestic interest rates.[4] The movements of the interest rates had some common characteristics. Both the U.S. and the Japanese interest rates tended to be lower than the domestic interest rates in the 1990s.

3. The expected depreciation rates of the home currency at each period are calculated by assuming that economic agents use data on rates from the last five years to forecast exchange rates as explained in the next section. Specifically, we use a time series model of the ARIMA (1,1,1) process to forecast a value of the next period based on historical data of the last five years for the relevant exchange rate.
4. Values in figure 5.11 are seasonally adjusted data of the exchange rate–adjusted interest rate in terms of the U.S. dollar and the yen that are used in a regression analysis in section 5.3.

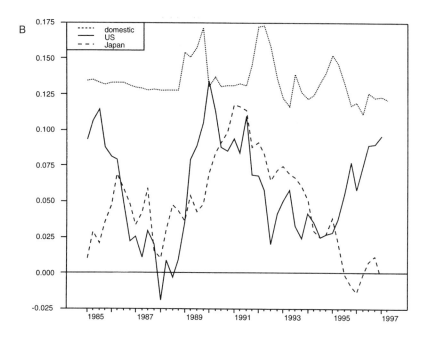

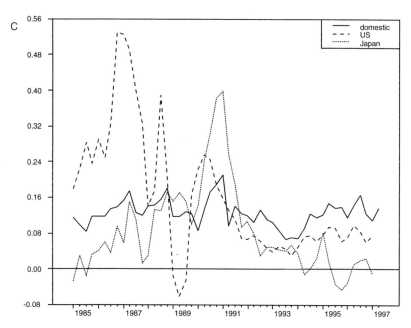

Fig. 5.11 (cont.)

Moreover, the Japanese interest rates have been consistently lower than the U.S. interest rates since 1995.

Before turning to regression analysis of the capital inflows, let's look at the timing between the surge of capital inflows and the asset bubbles in these countries. The countries in crisis experienced asset bubbles in the 1990s during different time periods as shown in figure 5.12. Thailand and Indonesia experienced a bubble of stock prices in 1993. They had a peak of stock prices in the latter half of 1993. The stock prices in Korea also increased from 1993 through 1994. The stock prices in Thailand and Korea were kept at high levels during 1995. However, they started to drop sharply after early 1996. In Indonesia, the stock prices continued to increase until early 1997, but they also dropped sharply afterward. As shown, the bubble and the peak of stock prices preceded the surge of capital inflows in 1995 and 1996. Thus, we can conclude that no bubbles in stock prices seemed to stimulate capital inflows to these countries.

5.3   Capital Inflows under the Dollar Peg System

5.3.1   A Simple Model of Capital Inflows

We first conduct a regression analysis of capital inflows to the countries under the de facto dollar peg system in order to analyze empirically how the de facto dollar peg system influenced capital inflows to these countries. We then set up a model of capital inflows to be estimated in a regression analysis. The model consists of a capital flow equation and equations that explain some of the instrumental variables in the capital flow equation.

In many developing countries including those in East Asia, monetary authorities impose measures to control international capital flows. Therefore, capital flows are caused by partial adjustments of capital asset stocks to changing optimal levels. According to a portfolio-balance approach, the risk-averse investors should attempt to hold optimal portfolio balances of foreign assets denominated in terms of foreign currencies relative to domestic assets denominated in terms of the home currency. The optimal portfolio balances are determined by both relative expected return rates and foreign exchange risks.

Thus, capital flows are influenced by factors such as domestic interest rate, exchange rate–adjusted foreign interest rates, and foreign exchange risks. Positive exchange rate–adjusted interest rate differentials stimulate capital inflows to these countries from the viewpoint of foreign lenders and domestic borrowers. Signs of coefficients of the domestic interest rates are expected to be positive, and exchange rate–adjusted foreign interest rates to be negative. Coefficients of foreign exchange risks are also expected to be negative. Thus, foreign exchange risks depress economic agents' foreign lending and borrowing if they are risk averse.

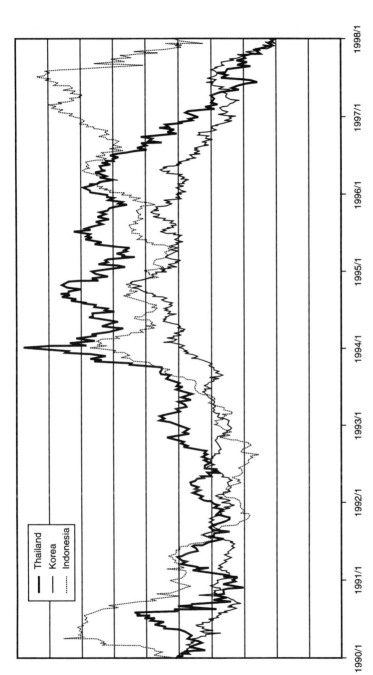

Fig. 5.12 Stock prices (3 January 1990 = 100)
Source: Datastream (http://www.datastream.com).

We also take into account the possible effects that a rate of change in domestic stock prices has on capital flows. Increases in domestic stock prices also stimulate foreign investors to invest in domestic stocks. Also, they might encourage both domestic borrowers to borrow from abroad and foreign lenders to lend to the domestic economy. Thus, coefficients on the variables should be positive.

Moreover, a higher export growth rate might give domestic borrowers easier access to international capital because they are regarded to have a higher capacity to repay their debt. Economies with higher economic growth should have more sustainable levels of foreign debts according to intertemporal macroeconomic models. In small developing countries, economic growth tends to depend a lot on export growth. Thus, a higher export growth rate might have positive effects on capital inflows.

We regress capital flows on the explanatory variables with a time lag to take into account the causality between the explanatory variables and the capital flows. A ratio of capital flow to nominal GDP is used in order to eliminate an increasing trend in capital flows. A capital flow equation is formalized below:

$$(1) \quad cf_t = a_1 + a_2 i_{t-1} + a_3 di_{t-1} + a_4 yi_{t-1} + a_5 d\text{risk}_{t-1} + a_6 y\text{risk}_{t-1}$$
$$+ a_7 \Delta \log X_{t-1} + a_8 \pi_{t-1}^{\text{stock}} + \varepsilon_t$$

$$di_t \equiv i_t^{\text{usd}} + \{\log[E_t(s_{t+1}^{\text{hc/usd}})] - \log(s_t^{\text{hc/usd}})\}$$

$$yi_t \equiv i_t^{\text{yen}} + \{\log[E_t(s_{t+1}^{\text{hc/yen}})] - \log(s_t^{\text{hc/yen}})\},$$

where cf is the ratio of capital flows to nominal GDP, i is the domestic interest rate, di is the exchange rate–adjusted U.S. interest rate, yi is the exchange rate–adjusted Japanese interest rate, $d$risk is the foreign exchange risk of exchange rate of domestic currency in terms of the U.S. dollar, $y$risk is the foreign exchange risk of exchange rate of domestic currency in terms of the yen, $\Delta \log X$ is the export growth rate, π^{stock} is the rate of change in domestic stock prices, ε is the error term, i^{usd} is the U.S. dollar–denominated interest rate, i^{yen} is the yen-denominated interest rate, $s^{\text{hc/usd}}$ is the exchange rate of domestic currency in terms of the U.S. dollar, $s^{\text{hc/yen}}$ is the exchange rate of domestic currency in terms of the yen, and E is the expectation operator.

We regard the domestic interest rate, export growth rate, and rate of change in stock prices to be the explanatory variables in the capital flow equation (1). We also assume that the variables are endogenous and influenced by exogenous variables.

A domestic interest rate is influenced by the above determinants of capital flows in a small economy with international capital mobility.

(2) $i_t = b_1 + b_2 di_t + b_3 yi_t + b_4 d\text{risk}_t + b_5 y\text{risk}_t + \varepsilon_t$

Interest rate arbitrage tend to make domestic interest rates move with foreign interest rates in the same direction. Under perfect capital mobility, coefficients of exchange rate–adjusted foreign interest rates would be one. However, it is not necessarily true under imperfect capital mobility. Foreign exchange risks tend to make foreign lenders prefer domestic currency–denominated assets to other currency–denominated assets. In contrast, they tend to make domestic borrowers prefer domestic currency–denominated liabilities to other currency-denominated liabilities. The preferences of both foreign lenders and domestic borrowers make the domestic interest rates of the crisis countries higher than the foreign interest rates by a risk premium. Thus, coefficients of the foreign interest rates and foreign exchange risks are expected to be positive.

Exports are regarded as a function of real exchange rates and foreign incomes. Export growth rate is influenced by the depreciation rate of domestic currency against the U.S. dollar and the yen, domestic inflation rate, foreign inflation rate, and growth rate of foreign GDP. It is expected that coefficients of the depreciation rate of domestic currency and the foreign inflation rate will be negative while those of domestic inflation rates and growth rates of foreign GDP will be positive:

(3) $\Delta \log X_t = c_1 + c_2 \Delta \log s_{t-1}^{hc/usd} + c_3 \Delta \log s_{t-1}^{hc/yen} + c_4 \pi_{t-1} + c_5 \pi_{t-1}^*$

$$+ c_6 \Delta \log \text{GDP}_t^* + \varepsilon_t,$$

where π is the domestic inflation rate, π^* is the foreign inflation rate, and $\Delta \log \text{GDP}^*$ is the growth rate of foreign GDP.

In addition, the domestic inflation rate is influenced by changes in exchange rates and foreign inflation rates through a pass-through effect. It is not necessary that coefficients on depreciation rates of domestic currency and foreign inflation rates will be one if there is imperfect pass-through.[5]

(4) $\pi_t = d_1 + d_2 \Delta \log s_{t-1}^{hc/usd} + d_3 \Delta \log s_{t-1}^{hc/yen} + d_4 \pi_{t-1}^* + \varepsilon_t$

Capital inflows might have stimulated domestic investors to invest in domestic stocks. As a result, domestic stock prices might have increased. However, stock prices would not have been influenced if the monetary authorities sterilized increases in foreign reserves. We formulate the following stock price equation to take into account the effect on stock prices.

(5) $\pi_t^{stock} = e_1 + e_2 \text{cf}_t + \varepsilon_t$

---

5. Krugman (1987) and Marston (1990) explained that imperfect pass-through effects were caused by exporting firms' pricing to market.

5.3.2   An Analytical Method and Data

At first, we use an instrumental variable method to estimate all of the five equations. In our case, endogenous variables are the domestic interest rate, export growth rate, domestic inflation rate, and rate of change in stock prices. Economic variables in the foreign countries are exogenous under the assumption of a small open economy. We further assume that the monetary authorities can intervene in foreign exchange markets to control exchange rates. Accordingly, we assume that not only actual and expected depreciation rates of domestic currency, but foreign exchange risks are also controlled by the monetary authorities although both the expected depreciation rates and foreign exchange risks are perceived by investors and might be forward-looking variables. Both are regarded as exogenous policy variables.

Next, after we check the signs of coefficients on export growth rate and rate of change in stock prices in the capital flow equations, we drop variables whose coefficients have an incorrect sign. The instrumental variable method is again used to estimate all of the equations for the selected instrumental variables. Interest rates and foreign exchange risks are kept as explanatory variables in the second round of estimation because we want to focus on the basic determinant variables of capital flows.

It is difficult but nevertheless important to generate a time series of expected exchange rates for countries where data on expected exchange rates is unavailable. Here, we assume that both foreign lenders and domestic borrowers act on the basis of expectations, and that foreign exchange risks are calculated by using historical data on exchange rates, although we cannot forecast the effects that expected future events such as a peso problem have on exchange rates. Data of the past five years from each period are used to forecast exchange rates in the next period according to a time series model (autoregressive integrated moving-average [ARIMA] 1,1,1). The forecasted values are used as the expected exchange rate.

We use the forecasted values of exchange rates to calculate foreign exchange risks. We further assume that both foreign lenders and domestic borrowers regard standard deviations of actual exchange rates from the forecasted values as foreign exchange risks.[6] Figure 5.13 shows movements of foreign exchange risks in Thailand, Indonesia, and Korea. The foreign exchange risks against the U.S. dollar were lower than those against the yen over the analyzed period in all of these countries. All foreign exchange

---

6. We have another option to calculate foreign exchange risks. The foreign exchange risks can be assumed to be standard errors of the time series model, i.e., deviations of actual exchange rates from the estimated values. However, standard errors are almost unchanged once a large devaluation of exchange rate occurs. We do not choose this calculation because it is not natural for foreign exchange risks to remain unchanged for a period of time after the large devaluation.

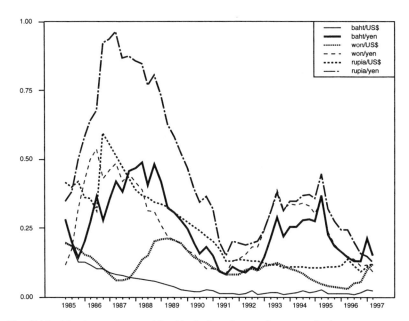

Fig. 5.13   Foreign exchange risks (deviations from a forecast value)

risks were lower during the 1990s than during the 1980s. The foreign exchange risks against the yen jumped in 1993 and kept increasing from 1993 to 1995 in all three countries.

Quarterly data are used in all of the regression analyses due to data constraints. Monthly data on the exchange rates are used in order to secure a sample size for making an autoregression of the exchange rates according to the ARIMA model. Monthly data are then converted to quarterly data by simply averaging the data over a three-month period. We chose to analyze the period between the Plaza Agreements of September 1985 and the Thai baht crisis of July 1997. Accordingly, the period lasts from the first quarter of 1986 to the first quarter of 1997 for all three countries.

"Other investments" in the financial account of the balance of payments is used as the major proxy on capital inflows, because international bank loans prevail in capital inflows to these countries. "Portfolio and other investments" is also present in Thailand and Korea. Data on portfolio investments are not available due to missing values in the data.

We add dummy variables that show a representative deregulation of international capital transactions that are statistically significant in explaining variables when estimating the capital flow equations. In Thailand, the Bangkok International Banking Facility opened in March 1993. In Indonesia, regulations on foreign borrowings of financial institutions were removed in March 1989. Korea also had regulations on foreign borrowings of financial institution removed in 1989. Accordingly, a dummy variable is added from the second quarter of 1993 for Thailand, from the first quarter of 1989 for Korea, and from the second quarter of 1989 for Indonesia.

We select the United States and Japan as foreign influences for these three countries because they trade heavily with the United States and Japan. As for both the foreign inflation rate and the growth rate of foreign GDP, simple averages of the U.S. and Japanese data are calculated.

As for data on interest rates, we use money market interest rates such as the call rates for Thailand and Indonesia because deposit interest rates and loan interest rates are kept unchanged. A three-month commercial paper (CP) interest rate is used for Korea, and a three-month London Interbank Offered Rate (LIBOR) is used for both Japan and the United States. As for inflation rates, wholesale price indexes are used for Thailand, Indonesia, and Japan, whereas producer price indexes are used for Korea and United States.

All data except for stock prices are available from the *International Financial Statistics* IMF CD-ROM. Data on stock price can be found in Datastream (http://www.datastream.com). When conducting the regression analysis, seasonal adjustments were made for the data that require it. Regressions are estimated by correcting for first-order serially correlated errors when necessary.

5.3.3 Results of the Regression Analysis

Capital Flow Equations

We use equation (1) to regress all capital inflows on interest rates, foreign exchange risks, export growth rate, rates of changes in stock prices, and a deregulation dummy for each country.

As for the other investments of Thailand, coefficients on both the domestic interest rate and foreign exchange risk against the U.S. dollar are statistically significant and in the correct signs, as shown in equation (1), specification (a) (henceforth equation [1a]; likewise equations [1b]–[1k], etc.). Coefficients on the U.S. interest rate, foreign exchange risk against the yen, and rate of change in stock prices are also in the correct signs, although they are statistically insignificant. The coefficient on the export growth rate is in the wrong sign, and the deregulation dummy is statistically insignificant. As a result, both the export growth rate and deregulation dummy are dropped from the capital flow equation in the next round of estimation.

In the second regression, we obtain the results shown in equation (1b) in table 5.2. The results are almost the same as those of equation (1a). *P*-value of both the domestic interest rate and the foreign exchange risk against the U.S. dollar are lower than those in equation (1a). It is noteworthy that a responsiveness of capital flows to the foreign exchange risk

Table 5.2   Estimation of Capital Flow Equations for Thailand

Capital flows	Eq. 1, Specification (a) Other	Eq. 1, Specification (b) Other	Eq. 1, Specification (c) Portfolio and Other	Eq. 1, Specification (d) Portfolio and Other	Eq. 1, Specification (e) Portfolio and Other
Constant	0.0913**	0.0498***	0.1025***	0.0620***	0.0620***
	(2.7159)	(3.1029)	(3.3941)	(4.0393)	(4.1079)
	[0.0101]	[0.0036]	[0.0017]	[0.0002]	[0.0002]
$i(t-1)$	0.3425**	0.3704**	0.3833***	0.4427***	0.4422***
	(2.2492)	(2.4588)	(2.7676)	(3.0530)	(3.1184)
	[0.0308]	[0.0187]	[0.0089]	[0.0041]	[0.0034]
$di(t-1)$	-0.0180	-0.0554	-0.0071	-0.1219	-0.1196
	(-0.0862)	(-0.3179)	(-0.0376)	(-0.7239)	(-0.7234)
	[0.9317]	[0.7522]	[0.9702]	[0.4736]	[0.4738]
$yi(t-1)$	0.1365	0.0977	0.0678	-0.0218	-0.0223
	(1.2302)	(1.1552)	(0.6744)	(-0.2703)	(-0.2950)
	[0.2267]	[0.2553]	[0.5044]	[0.7883]	[0.7696]
$drisk(t-1)$	-0.5182*	-0.8961***	-0.4779*	-1.0018***	-1.0025***
	(-1.9156)	(-5.5032)	(-1.95159)	(-6.5340)	(-6.5958)
	[0.0636]	[0.0000]	[0.0590]	[0.0000]	[0.000]
$yrisk\,(t-1)$	-0.0441	-0.0046	-0.0327	0.0363	0.0353
	(-0.6969)	(-0.0944)	(-0.5726)	(0.7672)	(0.8017)
	[0.4904]	[0.9252]	[0.5705]	[0.7672]	[0.8017]
$\Delta \log X(t-1)$	-1.3144*		-1.5076**		
	(-1.7912)		(-2.2750)		
	[0.0819]		[0.0291]		

(continued)

Table 5.2   (continued)

	Eq. 1, Specification (a) Other	Eq. 1, Specification (b) Other	Eq. 1, Specification (c) Portfolio and Other	Eq. 1, Specification (d) Portfolio and Other	Eq. 1, Specification (e) Portfolio and Other
Capital flows					
$\pi^{stock}(t-1)$	0.1233 (1.1107) [0.2742]	0.0358 (0.3786) [0.7071]	0.1275 (1.2674) [0.2133]	-0.0055 (-0.0608) [0.9518]	
Deregulation dummy	0.0046 (0.2777) [0.7828]		0.0145 (0.9711) [0.3381]		
ρ	0.3709 (1.6346) [0.1110]	0.3918** (2.2585) [0.0298]	0.3678** (2.1288) [0.0403]	0.3811** (2.672) [0.0111]	0.3836*** (2.7377) [0.0093]
R^2	0.8021	0.7911	0.8480	0.8193	0.8241
Durbin-Watson	1.5175	1.3602	1.4934	1.2963	1.2962

Notes: Numbers in parentheses are *t*-values. Numbers in brackets are *p*-values.

***Significant at the 1 percent level.

**Significant at the 5 percent level.

*Significant at the 10 percent level.

against the U.S. dollar is much larger compared to the foreign exchange risk against the yen. It is expected that this asymmetry will induce capital inflows to decrease under the currency basket peg system where the standard deviation for the U.S. dollar increases and the standard deviation for the yen decreases.

As for the "portfolio and other investments" of Thailand, a result similar to "other investments" is obtained. Equation (1c) in table 5.2 shows that coefficients on both the domestic interest rate and the foreign exchange risk against the U.S. dollar are statistically significant and of the correct signs. The coefficient on the export growth rate is significant but of the wrong sign, while the deregulation dummy is statistically insignificant.

Equation (1d) documents the results of regressing "portfolio and other investments" without the export growth rate and deregulation dummy. The coefficient of the rate of change in stock prices becomes negative. This variable is dropped from the capital flow equation because its coefficient has an incorrect sign, and we obtain new results shown in equation (1e). Coefficients on both the domestic interest rate and the foreign exchange risk against the U.S. dollar are statistically significant and of the correct sign.

As for both the "other investments" and the "portfolio and other investments" of Korea, coefficients on the foreign exchange risk against the U.S. dollar are statistically significant and negative as expected. The deregulation dummy is statistically significant and positive, and the coefficients on the export growth rate and the rate of change in stock prices are of the wrong sign.

As shown in table 5.3, we obtain capital flow equations (1g) and (1i) when we drop the export growth rate and the rate of change in stock prices from equations (1f) and (1h). Coefficients on the foreign exchange risk against the U.S. dollar are negative while their p-values are lower than those in equation (1f) and (1g). Coefficients on the domestic interest rates turn positive although the variable is statistically insignificant. A responsiveness of the capital flows to the foreign exchange risk against the U.S. dollar is greater than that against the yen.

In the case of Indonesia, a satisfactory capital flow equation cannot be obtained—especially, the variable of the export growth rate is statistically significant but of the wrong sign. A capital flow equation is reestimated after dropping both the export growth rate and the deregulation dummy in equation (1j), but the result is the same.

The rate of change in stock price variables is statistically insignificant regardless of the sign in the capital flows equation for all three countries. It implies that the rate of change in stock prices did not influence the capital inflows to the countries. The result of the regression analysis is consistent with our hypothesis that stock price bubbles did not stimulate capital inflows to the countries.

Table 5.3 Estimation of Capital Flow Equations for Korea and Indonesia

Capital Flows	Eq. 1, Specification(f) Other	Eq. 1, Specification (g) Other	Eq. 1, Specification (h) Portfolio and Other	Eq. 1, Specification (i) Portfolio and Other	Eq. 1, Specification(j) Other	Eq. 1, Specification (k) Other
Constant	0.0028	-0.0032	0.0441	0.0276	-0.0333	-0.0100
	(0.0889)	(-0.1081)	(1.1465)	(0.7447)	(-0.7397)	(-0.2757)
	[0.0296]	[0.9144]	[0.2593]	[0.4611]	[0.4643]	[0.7842]
$i(t-1)$	-0.0043	0.0426	-0.0866	0.0058	-0.0233	-0.0095
	(-0.0232)	(0.2311)	(-0.3825)	(0.0256)	(-0.7281)	(-0.2836)
	[0.9815]	[0.8184]	[0.7043]	[0.9796]	[0.4713]	[0.7782]
$di(t-1)$	0.1010	0.0953	0.0491	0.0560	0.0078	-0.0007
	(0.8567)	(0.9074)	(0.3417)	(0.4344)	(0.5721)	(-0.0687)
	[0.3974]	[0.3700]	[0.7345]	[0.6665]	[0.5708]	[0.9455]
$yi(t-1)$	-0.0921	-0.0839	-0.1957	-0.1881	0.0231	0.0238
	(-0.8073)	(-0.7258)	(-1.3713)	(-1.2604)	(1.4154)	(1.2656)
	[0.4249]	[0.4724]	[0.1790]	[0.2153]	[0.1657]	[0.2135]
$drisk(t-1)$	-0.1506*	-0.1813**	-0.2786**	-0.3231***	0.0149	0.0034
	(-1.6981)	(-2.1324)	(-2.3979)	(-2.7784)	(0.6733)	(0.1574)
	[0.0983]	[0.0396]	[0.0219]	[0.0085]	[0.5051]	[0.8757]

	(1)	(2)	(3)	(4)	(5)	(6)
yrisk(t − 1)	−0.0139	−0.0312	−0.0077	−0.0399	0.0110	0.0145
	(−0.3439)	(−0.8327)	(−0.1639)	(−0.8837)	(0.8434)	(1.0813)
	[0.7329]	[0.4103]	[0.8706]	[0.3825]	[0.4047]	[0.2865]
$\Delta \log X (t − 1)$	−0.0124		−0.0812		1.2043	0.7999
	(−0.0941)		(−0.5368)		(0.8822)	(0.5502)
	[0.9255]		[0.5947]		[0.3836]	[0.5854]
$\pi^{stock}(t − 1)$	−0.0700		−0.1214		−0.0808**	
	(−1.0636)		(−1.5504)		(−2.2174)	
	[0.2947]		[0.1300]		[0.0331]	
Deregulation dummy	0.0231*	0.0280**	0.0349**	0.0436***	0.0027	
	(1.8562)	(2.4211)	(2.1949)	(2.8676)	(0.3657)	
	[0.0718]	[0.0204]	[0.03489]	[0.0067]	[0.7167]	
ρ	0.5953***	0.6134***	0.6743***	0.7007***	0.9737***	0.9210***
	(3.7554)	(4.3802)	(5.0256)	(5.9352)	(11.744)	(11.529)
	[0.0006]	[0.0000]	[0.0000]	[0.0000]	[0.0000]	[0.0000]
R^2	0.7966	0.7981	0.8826	0.8778	0.8748	0.8685
Durbin-Watson	1.5036	1.5307	1.7154	1.6555	2.0224	1.8679

Notes: Numbers in parentheses are t-values. Numbers in brackets are p-values.

***Significant at the 1 percent level.

**Significant at the 5 percent level.

*Significant at the 10 percent level.

Other Estimation Equations

Results of estimating the equations relevant to the selected instrumental variables are shown in table 5.4. The domestic interest rate and the rate of change in stock prices are selected as instrumental variables in the case of the "other investments" for Thailand, and only the domestic interest rate is selected as an instrumental variable in the case of the "portfolio and other investments" for Thailand. In equation (2a) with domestic interest rate as the dependent variable, both variables of exchange rate–adjusted foreign interest rates are statistically significant and have a positive coefficient, although they are not significantly one. Equation (5a) with the rate of change in stock prices as the dependent variable has no statistically significant variables, indicating that no external factors influenced the stock prices.

In the case of Korea, only the domestic interest rate is selected as an instrumental variable. In equation (2b), the exchange rate–adjusted Japanese interest rate variable is statistically significant. The exchange rate–adjusted U.S. interest rates and the foreign exchange risk against the yen are also relatively significant (with p-value of approximately 0.11).

Domestic interest rate, export growth rate, and domestic inflation rate are selected as instrumental variables in the case of Indonesia. The exchange rate of the Indonesian rupiah in terms of the U.S. dollar is statistically significant in both equation (3a), with export growth rate as the dependent variable, and (4a), with domestic inflation rate as the dependent variable. None of the three selected explaining variables have an effect on the change of domestic interest rate, as shown in equation (2c).

5.4   Capital Inflows under a Basket Peg System

5.4.1   A Simulation Method

In this section, a simulation analysis of capital inflows is used to analyze how a currency basket peg system would have influenced the capital inflows. We then compare the capital inflows under the actual de facto dollar peg system with results of the simulation. A currency basket peg system means that the monetary authorities increase the weight on the yen and decrease the weight on the U.S. dollar in the currency basket to which the domestic currency is pegged. A currency basket peg system is likely to change the fluctuations in exchange rates against the U.S. dollar and the yen.

We assume that coefficients on the explanatory variables in the regression equations estimated in the previous section are unchanged even if the monetary authorities change their exchange rate policy.[7] If the currency

---

7. The Lucas critique tells us that the change in the exchange rate policy might change the coefficients in the estimated equations.

Table 5.4 Estimation of Other Equations for Thailand, Korea, and Indonesia

	Thailand		Korea		Indonesia	
	Eq. 2, Specification (a)[b]	Eq. 5, Specification (a)[b]	Eq. 2, Specification (b)[a]	Eq. 2, Specification (c)[a]	Eq. 3, Specification (a)[c]	Eq. 4, Specification (a)[d]
Constant	0.0738*** (5.5387) [0.0000]	−0.0344 (−0.3102) [0.7579]	0.0979*** (7.2117) [0.0000]	0.1274*** (8.9582) [0.0000]	0.0244*** (168.124) [0.0000]	0.0103** (2.3976) [0.0212]
di	0.3800** (2.6522) [0.1115]		0.0856 (1.6306) [0.1110]	−0.1075 (−1.1311) [0.2649]		
yi	0.1961** (2.0684) [0.0452]		0.1913*** (3.2655) [0.0022]	0.0527 (0.5121) [0.6114]		
$drisk$	−0.1977 (−0.7386) [0.4645]		−0.1835 (−1.6008) [0.1174]	0.1185 (1.5269) [0.1348]		
$yrisk$	−0.0527 (−0.9866) [0.3298]		0.0882 (1.6128) [0.1148]	−0.0064 (−0.2047) [0.8388]		
cf		−0.1095 (−0.4768) [0.6359]				
$\Delta \log s^{hc/\$}\,(t-1)$					0.0071** (2.2829) [0.0281]	0.3935*** (3.1158) [0.0033]
$\Delta \log s^{hc/yen}\,(t-1)$					−0.0057** (−2.2218) [0.0323]	0.0272 (0.3339) [0.7401]

(continued)

Table 5.4 (continued)

	Thailand		Korea		Indonesia	
	Eq. 2, Specification (a)[a]	Eq. 5, Specification (a)[b]	Eq. 2, Specification (b)[a]	Eq. 2, Specification (c)[a]	Eq. 3, Specification (a)[c]	Eq. 4, Specification (a)[d]
$\pi^*(t-1)$					−0.0112 (−1.2677) [0.2125]	0.6220 (1.2784) [0.2084]
$\pi(t-1)$					0.0021 (1.0101) [0.3188]	
$\Delta \log \text{GDP}^*(t-1)$					0.0065 (1.675) [0.1019]	
ρ	0.6114*** (5.1314) [0.0000]	0.9676*** (10.4894) [0.0000]	0.4805** (3.3346) [0.0018]	0.6394*** (4.8989) [0.0000]	0.4431*** (2.7750) [0.0085]	−0.4111*** (−1.9674) [0.0560]
R^2	0.6146	0.7590	0.4179	0.4147	0.2840	0.2691
Durbin-Watson	1.6423	1.5875	1.9955	1.6772	1.8404	2.3549

Notes: Numbers in parentheses are *t*-values. Numbers in brackets are *p*-values.

[a] Dependent variable = *i*.

[b] Dependent variable = π^{stock}.

[c] Dependent variable = $\Delta \log X$.

[d] Dependent variable = π.

***Significant at the 1 percent level.

**Significant at the 5 percent level.

*Significant at the 10 percent level.

basket peg system influences fluctuation in exchange rates, it will certainly change actual and expected change in exchange rates and the standard deviations of exchange rates (foreign exchange risk) from the forecast. The currency basket peg system should have a direct impact on exchange rate–adjusted foreign interest rates via the expected changes in exchange rates. Thus, it has direct effects on capital inflows via the foreign interest rates and the foreign exchange risk variables. Since we use an instrumental variable method to estimate the regression equations, we can analyze not only the direct effects but also the indirect effects that minor instrumental variables, such as the domestic interest rate and export growth rate, have on capital inflows.

If the monetary authorities adopted the currency basket peg system instead of the de facto dollar peg system, the weight on the U.S. dollar in a currency basket would be lowered, and the weight on the yen would be increased. Consequently, the exchange rate of the domestic currency against the U.S. dollar would fluctuate more, and the exchange rate of the domestic currency against the yen would fluctuate less.

Assuming that the monetary authorities stabilize the exchange rate of domestic currency against a currency basket consisting of only the U.S. dollar and the yen, we come up with the following equation:

$$(6) \qquad 0 = \omega\Delta s^{hc/usd} + (1 - \omega)\Delta s^{hc/yen}$$

where $\Delta s^{hc/usd}$ is the rate of change in the exchange rate of the domestic currency against the U.S. dollar, $\Delta s^{hd/yen}$ is the rate of change in the exchange rate of the domestic currency against the yen, and ω is a weight on the U.S. dollar in a currency basket.

From equation (6), we can obtain the following equation:

$$(7) \qquad \frac{1 - \omega}{\omega} = -\frac{\Delta s^{hc/usd}}{\Delta s^{hc/yen}}.$$

Supposing that the actual weight on the U.S. dollar is 0.8 ($\omega = 0.8$), the ratio of the fluctuations in the exchange rates of the domestic currency against the U.S. dollar to the exchange rate of domestic currency against the yen would be 1:4. If the monetary authorities decreased the weight on the U.S. dollar in a currency basket to 0.5, the ratio of fluctuations in exchange rate would be 1.

Assuming that the changes in exchange rate fluctuations are equally divided into both the changes in exchange rate fluctuations against the U.S. dollar and against the yen, we take a square root of the change in the fluctuation ratio to calculate the changes in exchange rate fluctuations. Under the currency basket peg system, fluctuations of the exchange rate of the domestic currency against the U.S. dollar would be doubled, whereas fluctuations of the exchange rate against the yen would be halved.

In addition, we assume that the foreign exchange risks, which are supposed to be deviations from the forecast value, would be changed in the same direction as fluctuation of the exchange rate. Therefore, foreign exchange risks of the domestic currency against the U.S. dollar would be doubled, whereas foreign exchange risks of domestic currency against the yen would be halved under the currency basket peg system.

5.4.2   Results of the Simulation Analysis

Figures 5.14 through 5.18 show results of the simulation analysis for the capital inflows to each of the three countries. Movements in simulated values as well as actual values and estimated values of capital inflows are depicted in these figures. Estimated values are calculated by using the regression equations (1b), (1e), (1g), (1i), and (1k). Simulated values under the currency basket peg system are compared with estimated values under the de facto dollar peg system.

Simulated values for the "other investments" of Thailand are calculated by substituting supposed values of the fluctuations and deviations of the exchange rates into the regression equations (1b), (2a), and (5a). Equations (1e) and (2a) are used to calculate simulated values for the "portfolio and other investments" of Thailand. Equations (1g), (1i), and (2b) are used for Korea. Equations (1k), (2c), (3a), and (4a) are used for Indonesia.

In the cases of the "other investments" and the "portfolio and other investments" of Thailand, the simulated values of capital inflows are

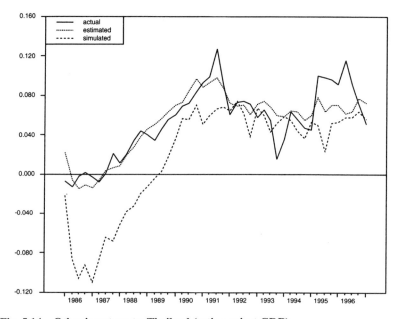

Fig. 5.14   Other investments: Thailand (ratio against GDP)

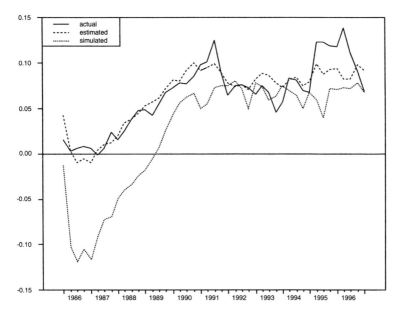

Fig. 5.15   Portfolio and other investments: Thailand (ratio against GDP)

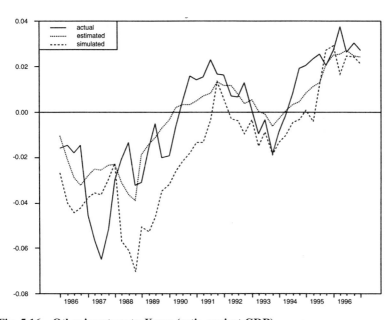

Fig. 5.16   Other investments: Korea (ratio against GDP)

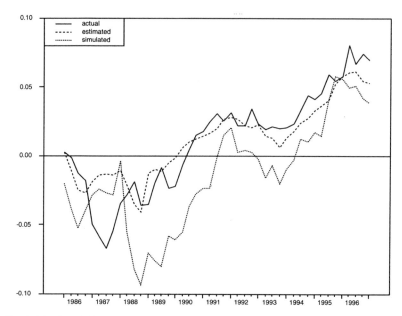

Fig. 5.17   Portfolio and other investments: Korea (ratio against GDP)

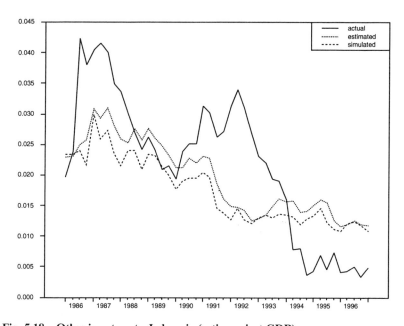

Fig. 5.18   Other investments: Indonesia (ratio against GDP)

Table 5.5   **Means and Standard Errors of Estimated and Simulated Values for Thailand, Korea, and Indonesia**

	Thailand		Korea		Indonesia
Capital Flows	Other Investments	Portfolio and Other Investments	Other Investments	Portfolio and Other Investments	Other Investments
1986Q1–1997Q1					
estimated	0.0528	0.0646	−0.0025	0.0116	0.0195
	(0.0318)	(0.0332)	(0.0182)	(0.0264)	(0.0060)
simulated	0.0178	0.0237	−0.0164	0.0140	0.0175
	(0.0558)	(0.0633)	(0.0251)	(0.0393)	(0.0053)
1990Q1–1997Q1					
estimated	0.0720	0.0856	0.0089	0.0272	0.0158
	(0.0118)	(0.0086)	(0.0095)	(0.0178)	(0.0036)
simulated	0.0544	0.0653	−0.0017	0.0050	0.0141
	(0.0113)	(0.0109)	(0.0166)	(0.0316)	(0.0028)

Note: Numbers in parentheses are standard errors. Q1 = first quarter.

smaller than the estimated values during the analyzed period as shown in figures 5.14 and 5.15. Moreover, when we focus on the capital inflows in the 1990s, gaps between simulated and estimated values are large in 1991 and 1995 when surges of capital inflows to Thailand occurred.

Table 5.5 shows that means of simulated values are smaller than those of estimated values—especially, the simulated values of the "portfolio and other investments" are significantly smaller than the estimated values. Thus, it can be concluded that the currency basket peg system would have had a depressing effect on capital inflows to Thailand.

Figures 5.16 and 5.17 show the case of the "other investments" and the "portfolio and other investments" of Korea, respectively. The simulated values of capital inflows are smaller than the estimated ones during the analyzed period, except for some quarters in 1995. Table 5.5 also shows that means of simulated values are smaller than means of estimated values in Korea. Although the gaps are not as large as the gaps in Thailand, it still proves that the currency basket peg system would have had a depressing effect on capital inflows to Korea.

The actual capital inflows to Thailand were larger than the estimated values in both 1991 and 1995. The actual capital inflows were also larger than the estimated values during the period in 1996 for Korea. This fact implies that factors other than interest rates and foreign exchange risks had substantial effects on a surge of capital inflows during the mentioned period.

In the case of Indonesia, the simulated values of capital inflows were smaller than the estimated values during the analyzed period, although differences between them are small. Table 5.5 shows that means of simulated values are smaller than those of estimated values also in Indonesia, although they are not significantly different. Thus, the currency basket peg system would only have had a slightly depressing effect on capital inflows to Indonesia.

The results of the simulation imply that the currency basket peg system would have had a depressing effect on capital inflows to both Thailand and Korea and only a slightly depressing effect on capital inflows to Indonesia during the analyzed period.

5.5   Conclusion

East Asian countries that suffered the currency and financial crises had adopted a de facto dollar peg system. The de facto dollar peg system tended to extend fluctuations in trade balances of the countries as pointed out by Ito, Ogawa, and Sasaki (1998). In this paper, special attention is paid to the effect that the dollar peg system has on capital accounts. We empirically analyzed how the de facto dollar peg system stimulated capital inflows to Thailand, Korea, and Indonesia before the crises.

We conducted a simulation analysis of the impact on capital inflows to the countries under a currency basket peg system. From the regression analysis of the actual capital inflows, we found that responsiveness of capital flows to the foreign exchange risk against the U.S. dollar is much larger than responsiveness of capital flows to the foreign exchange risk against the yen in the case of Thailand and Korea. From the simulation analysis, we obtained the result that the currency basket peg system would have had a depressing effect on capital inflows to Thailand and Korea.

The asymmetry in the responsiveness to foreign exchange risks against the U.S. dollar and against the yen would have decreased capital inflows under the currency basket peg system. In other words, capital inflows were stimulated more through stable exchange rates against the U.S. dollar under the dollar peg system. Thus, we conclude that capital inflows would have been more stable under the currency basket peg system.

The following questions remains as an agenda for the future: What other factors explained the oversurges of the capital inflows? We tried to explain the oversurges of capital inflows using several explanatory variables, including export growth rate, stock prices, and the interest rates as well as the foreign exchange risks. Further attempts need to be made to discover other possible factors. Deregulation of capital inflows by the domestic monetary authorities is an important factor; we set it up as a deregulation dummy variable when estimating the capital flow equations. Other external factors such as speculative pressures from abroad may also be good candidates.

Another question is whether the coefficients in the capital flow equation could in fact be kept constant if the monetary authorities were to switch their exchange rate regime. In this paper, we assumed that they would be kept constant if the currency basket peg system were the one to be adopted in these countries. In addition, historical data and time series models were used to estimate the expected exchange rates and the foreign exchange risks. It implies that investors did not take into account the possibility of a future switch of regime when forming their expectations.

References

Bank for International Settlements (BIS). 1998a. *Annual report*. Basel, Switzerland: BIS.
———. 1998b. *International banking and financial market developments*. Basel, Switzerland: BIS.
Calvo, Guillermo A., Leonardo Leiderman, and Carmen M. Reinhart. 1993. Capital inflows and real exchange rate appreciation in Latin America. *IMF Staff Papers* 40 (1): 108–51.
Calvo, Guillermo A., and Enrique G. Mendoza. 1996. Mexico's balance-of-payments crisis: A chronicle of a death foretold. *Journal of International Economics* 41 (3/4): 235–64.
Dooley, Michael P. 1997. A model of crises in emerging markets. NBER Working Paper no. 6300. Cambridge, Mass.: National Bureau of Economic Research.
Demirgüç-Kunt, Asli, and Enrica Detragiache. 1997. The determinants of banking crises: Evidence from developing and developed countries. IMF Working Paper no. WP/97/106. Washington, D.C.: International Monetary Fund.
———. 1998. Financial liberalization and financial fragility. IMF Working Paper no. WP/98/83. Washington, D.C.: International Monetary Fund.
Eichengreen, Barry, and Andrew K. Rose. 1998. Staying afloat when the wind shifts: External factors and emerging-market banking crises. NBER Working Paper no. 6370. Cambridge, Mass.: National Bureau of Economic Research.
Frankel, Jeffrey A., and Andrew K. Rose. 1996. Currency crashes in emerging markets: An empirical treatment. *Journal of International Economics* 41 (3/4): 351–66.
Frankel, Jeffrey A., and Shang-Jin Wei. 1994. Yen bloc or dollar bloc? Exchange rate policies of the east Asian economies. In *Macroeconomic linkage: Savings, exchange rates, and capital flows*, ed. Takatoshi Ito and Anne O. Krueger, 295–392. Chicago: University of Chicago Press.
Goldfajn, Ilan, and Rodrigo O. Valdes. 1997. Capital flows and the twin crises: The role of liquidity. IMF Working Paper no. WP/97/87. Washington, D.C.: International Monetary Fund.
International Monetary Fund (IMF). 1997a. *Exchange arrangements and exchange restrictions: Annual report*. Washington, D.C.: IMF.
———. 1997b. *International capital markets: Developments, prospects, and policy issues*. Washington, D.C.: IMF.
———. 1997c. *World economic outlook: Interim assessment, Dec. 1997*. Washington, D.C.: IMF.
———. 1998. *World economic outlook, May 1998*. Washington, D.C.: IMF.
———. 2000. *International Financial Statistics* CD-ROM. Washington, D.C.: IMF Publication Services.

Ito, Takatoshi. 1999. Capital flows in Asia. NBER Working Paper no. 7134. Cambridge, Mass.: National Bureau of Economic Research.
Ito, Takatoshi, Eiji Ogawa, and Yuri N. Sasaki. 1998. How did the dollar peg fail in Asia? *Journal of the Japanese and International Economies* 12 (4): 256–304.
Kaminsky, Graciela, Saul Lizondo, and Carmen M. Reinhart. 1997. Leading indicators of currency crises. IMF Working Paper no. WP/97/79. Washington, D.C.: International Monetary Fund.
Kawai, Masahiro. 1997. East Asia currency turbulence: Implications of financial system fragility. A paper prepared for a seminar at the World Bank, Washington, D.C., November.
Kawai, Masahiro, and Shigeru Akiyama. 1998. The roles of the world's major currencies in exchange rate arrangements. *Journal of the Japanese and International Economies* 12 (4): 334–87.
Krugman, Paul. 1987. Pricing to market when the exchange rate changes. In *Real-financial linkages among open economies,* ed. Sven W. Arndt and J. David Richardson, 49–70. Cambridge: MIT Press.
Marston, Richard C. 1990. Pricing to market in Japanese manufacturing. *Journal of International Economics* 29 (3/4): 217–36.
Miller, Victoria. 1996. Speculative currency attacks with endogenously induced commercial bank crises. *Journal of International Money and Finance* 15 (3): 383–403.
Velasco, Andres. 1987. Financial crises and balance of payments crises: A simple model of the southern cone experience. *Journal of Development Economics* 27 (1/2): 263–83.

Comments   Francis T. Lui

The main issue raised by Ogawa and Sun is what would have happened to capital inflows in Thailand, Indonesia, and Korea had they adopted a basket peg system. These countries had adopted a de facto dollar peg during the sample period, but Japanese bank loans to them were significantly higher than those from the United States. It seems to make sense if their currencies were at least partially pegged to the yen. From the policy perspective, it is therefore of interest to measure the effects on capital inflows if the Japanese yen had a larger weight in determining the exchange rates in these countries.

The authors have proceeded in two steps to answer this question: one step based on regression analysis, the other on counterfactual simulations. There are therefore two sets of results that need to be discussed.

The authors first attempt to measure the effects of several determinants of capital inflows (as a share of GDP). These include, among others, the home country's interest rate, exchange rate–adjusted U.S. interest rate, exchange rate–adjusted Japanese interest rate, and foreign exchange risks of

Francis T. Lui is professor of economics at the Hong Kong University of Science and Technology.

the domestic currency against both the dollar and the yen. Significant t-values have only been found for the domestic interest rate variable for Thailand, and exchange rate risks against the dollar for Thailand and Korea. In an earlier version of the paper, the authors tried to use interest rate differentials between domestic currencies and the two foreign currencies. The latter method yielded even less significant results.

One may want to understand why the seemingly disappointing t-values are obtained for Korea and Indonesia. There may be two problems. The regressions have controlled for interest rates in the United States and Japan. An increase in the domestic interest rate, holding other interest rates constant, is similar to a rise in interest rate differential. In principle, when there is free flow of capital, the possibility of interest rate arbitrage implies that the interest rate differential between two countries reflects the relative risk premium of holding one of their currencies. The risk premium may reflect various types of risks, e.g., devaluation risks, default risk of banks in the home country, sovereign risk, or even the loosely labeled "Asian risk premium" popularized in the media. In Ogawa and Sun's paper, there is an attempt to make adjustment for the devaluation risk. Such adjustment is necessary. Otherwise, an increase in the domestic interest rate could simply be due to a rise in risk premium. This would not cause capital to flow in, and the t-value of the domestic interest rate variable would not be significant. However, is the adjustment in the paper big enough or too small?

Adjustment for exchange risks is based on the forecasted values of exchange rates, which are estimated by an ARIMA (1,1,1) model using historical data of the exchange rates for the past five years. Although this method is a reasonable one, figure 5.13 seems to indicate that the performance of the ARIMA model in making forecasts is not impressive. (The baht:U.S. dollar rate is a notable exception.) Has enough information been captured in historical data of the exchange rates? Do practitioners in these markets pay more attention to risks from sources other than exchange rate fluctuations? The paper has not explicitly adjusted for some of the risks listed above, such as default risks of banks. This may be a reason why significant results have not been obtained in some cases.

There are also other possible explanations for the low t-values. Suppose that there is an exogenous technological shock in the home country causing the interest rate to go up. Because of various types of institutional rigidities, it may take time for capital to come in. Capital flows at time t may depend on interest rates of the home and foreign countries at time $t - i, i = 1, 2, \ldots, n$. The regression equation has lag terms of only one period. It is not clear that this is good enough to capture reality.

The data used include those up to the second quarter of 1997, when the Asian financial crisis had not taken place. If postcrisis data were also included, forecast exchange risks would likely be bigger. Data of the financial turmoil period should also show that there were large capital out-flows. Perhaps regressions using updated data will show stronger results than those reported in the paper.

Simulations based on estimated parameters in the regressions constitute the second set of results. The main one is that capital inflows in Korea and Thailand would have decreased if a basket peg had been adopted. It would be advisable to have a more detailed theoretical discussion on why these results are obtained. There are two issues that may be of concern here.

First, the estimated parameters used in the simulations may not be robust, in view of the low *t*-values for some parameters. Second, moving to the basket peg means that U.S. investors have to face more exchange rate volatility, whereas Japanese investors are less affected by exchange rate fluctuations. These cause opposite effects on capital inflows. The net outcome depends on a lot of institutional and historical factors not discussed in the paper.

Finally, the paper has gone some distance in assessing the impact of moving to a basket peg. However, further improvements in the estimation method and a longer data series are still desirable.

Comments   Pranee Tinakorn

As a native of Thailand, I started reading this paper with great interest. This is because among the many factors alleged to have caused the crisis in Thailand, capital account liberalization under a fixed exchange rate has been seen as one of the main causes. Although, in my view, the crisis in Thailand was a result of both real sector and financial sector problems, the capital inflow and its reversal have been in the limelight.

First, I would like to summarize my reading of the paper and then offer my comments. In this paper, the authors tried to examine how the exchange rate, which was tied to the U.S. dollar, affected capital inflows to the three crisis-hit Asian countries: Thailand, Korea, and Indonesia (all of which had sought IMF financial support).

I agree with the authors' point that although these countries may be said to adopt the managed float system, as in Indonesia and Korea, or the basket peg system, as in Thailand, they all, as a matter of fact, were pegging to the U.S. dollar.

As can be seen from the movement of local currency to the dollar in figures 5.1–5.2 of the paper, this is more true in the case of Thailand than in the other two countries included in the study. The nominal baht value

Pranee Tinakorn is associate professor of economics at Thammasat University and a research specialist at the Thailand Development Research Institute.

during the 1990s hardly moved away from its par value with the U.S. dollar until July 1997, when the Bank of Thailand could no longer defend the value of the baht. A majority of Thai economists tended to believe that the weight of the dollar in the Thai basket was over 90 percent prior to the crisis.

If these crisis-hit countries were in fact pegging their currencies to the dollar, what was the consequence on their capital inflows? And if they had in fact used the basket system, would the pattern of capital inflows have been different? These were the two main questions posed by the authors, and they tried to answer these questions by postulating that capital inflows are influenced by the following factors: domestic interest rate, exchange rate–adjusted foreign interest rates, and foreign exchange risks. A positive exchange rate–adjusted interest rate differential is expected to have a positive impact on the country's capital inflows, and the foreign exchange risk is expected to have a negative impact on capital inflows.

Although I admire Ogawa and Sun's effort in trying to understand these important issues, I have some concerns about their estimation results based on two major grounds. The first reason has to do with how one interprets the diagnostic statistics from the estimation, and the second with how one should treat different types of capital inflows. As we know, capital inflows can be either long-term or short-term depending on the nature of their movement.

Let me first address the estimation results. In the section reporting the results of the regression analysis, one finds many instances of statistically insignificant effects of the independent variables on capital flows. One can clearly see this in the estimation results reported in table 5.2 for all the countries under study. It is also a little disturbing to have most of the coefficients on interest variables (especially di and yi) not significant. Given the statistical reliability of the estimates, I am afraid I should not proceed to discuss the simulation results, which are based on these estimated coefficients.

Let me turn now to the second issue: whether we should treat all kinds of capital inflows as being determined by the same set of variables. It is true that in macroeconomic analysis, we use the interest parity reasoning to explain capital flows. When it comes to the behavioral estimation, however, I think there are some types of capital flows that respond not only to the interest rate differentials and foreign exchange risks but also to other economic factors, depending on the nature of the flow.

Therefore, lumping all types of flows together or separating them into only two categories as Ogawa and Sun did may overlook some other important determinants of capital flows, resulting in possible specification error.

For example, when I look into the balance of payments of Thailand, I can distinguish between five different types of capital flows:

1. Foreign direct investment (FDI)
2. Portfolio investment
3. Private loans
4. Nonresident baht account (currency and deposits)
5. Other loans, such as trade credits and borrowing in the banking sector.

Among these, FDI can be regarded as long-term. Although we may generally consider portfolio investment as short-term like the other categories, the determinants of portfolio investment could also be different from those of private loans and other short-term flows.

Whereas long-term inflows are based on economic fundamentals and are reversed only when fundamentals change, short-term inflows, even though they are also influenced by economic fundamentals, tend to be speculative and easily reversible. Therefore it is more difficult to estimate a behavioral equation for them unless we take other factors into account.

For example, in the case of FDI, interest rate differentials may not be as important a determinant as much as the other pull factors in the host country, such as real GDP growth rate (reflecting return to investment), real wages (reflecting cost), and real exchange rate (reflecting competitiveness). Some push factor from the investing country may also be important.

In contrast to FDI, the flow of nonresident baht account is obviously short-term. This is foreign-owned money deposited in local commercial banks to do many activities, such as to gain from interest differentials, speculate in the foreign exchange market, and wait for other trade and investment opportunities.

In the 1980s, the net capital flow of nonresident baht account was about 7 percent of the total private nonbank flows. In 1991, Thailand's foreign exchange control was greatly relaxed, and in 1993 the capital account was liberalized and enhanced by the establishment of the Bangkok International Banking Facility (BIBF). As a consequence, the share of nonresident baht account increased to 40 percent of the total net flows in 1993 and swung down to 22 percent in 1996. However, if we look at the total inflow, and not net flow, the nonresident baht account share in the total private nonbank inflow was over 90 percent. The same is true for the total private nonbank outflow.

I think we should model the behavior of the nonresident baht account quite differently from that of FDI. I raise these two items as examples to suggest that if we don't differentiate for their behavioral differences, it may be difficult to obtain reliable estimates for the capital flows. I understand that one cannot be so detailed in working with international data across countries because the International Financial Statistics produced by the IMF do not show these details, but I think they should release the data upon request because they obtain these detailed data from their member countries.

I would also like the study to separate out the estimates of interest differentials and exchange risks on each type of capital flows by controlling for other important factors in each category so that the estimates will not suffer from the bias arising from exclusion error.

Finally, I thank both authors for initiating our interest in this area, and I hope that they continue to expand on this study.

6

Sterilization and the Capital Inflow Problem in East Asia, 1987–97

Shinji Takagi and Taro Esaka

6.1 Introduction

At the end of the 1980s, a large volume of capital began to flow into the emerging market economies of East Asia, owing to both external (or "push") and internal (or "pull") factors.[1] Among other things, the factors that were external to the recipient countries included the lower interest rates, recessions, and regulatory changes favoring international portfolio diversification, all taking place in the industrialized world. The factors that were internal to the recipients included their sound economic policies (supported, for instance, by trade and capital market liberalization), exchange rate stability and deposit guarantees, and strong economic fundamentals. Roughly, the beginning of the surge in capital inflows can be identified as 1988 for Thailand, 1989 for Malaysia and the Philippines, 1990 for Indonesia, and 1990–91 for Korea (Calvo, Leiderman, and Reinhart 1996; Bartolini and Drazen 1997; Chuhan, Claessens, and Mamingi 1998; Montiel 1998; Villanueva and Seng 1999).

East Asia led the developing world in attracting private capital flows in the late 1980s, and became the most important destination for private capital flows in the early 1990s, with its share in total global capital flows to developing countries rising from around 10 percent in the early 1980s to

Shinji Takagi is visiting professor of economics at Yale University, on leave from his position as professor of economics at Osaka University. Taro Esaka is a doctoral candidate in economics at Osaka University.

The authors thank Leonard Cheng, Takatoshi Ito, Ryuzo Miyao, Carmen Reinhart, Hiroshi Shibuya, Kazuo Yokokawa, Mahani Zainal-Abidin, and an anonymous referee for useful comments. Needless to say, the authors alone assume responsibility for any remaining errors.

1. Latin America (particularly Argentina, Brazil, Mexico, and Venezuela) was another region that attracted a large volume of capital from the late 1980s into the 1990s.

over 40 percent in the 1990s. While the largest portion (about one-half) of capital inflows was initially foreign direct investment (FDI), an increasing amount of inflows took the form of short-term borrowing in later years (Chen and Khan 1997; Alba et al. 1998). In fact, for the period as a whole, the bulk of the capital inflows was in the form of offshore borrowing by banks and private corporations, except for Malaysia, where FDI inflows remained larger than bank and private sector borrowing (Radelet and Sachs 1998).

On an individual level, the capital inflows were massive indeed. In terms of GDP, the volume of cumulative capital inflows from 1988 to 1995 amounted to 51.5 percent in Thailand, 45.8 percent in Malaysia, 23.1 percent in the Philippines, 9.3 percent in Korea, and 8.3 percent in Indonesia. Of the two largest recipients, Malaysia received surges of massive capital inflows in 1992 and 1993, amounting to 15.3 and 23.2 percent of GDP, respectively, while Thailand received consistent flows averaging about 10 percent of GDP annually (Villanueva and Seng 1999). At the end of 1996, the balance of claims held by foreign banks against these countries stood at $261.2 billion; of this total, $100 billion was accounted for by Korea, $69.4 billion by Thailand, $58.7 billion by Indonesia, $28.8 billion by Malaysia, and $14.1 billion by the Philippines. Except in Korea, more than a half of these claims were the obligations of the nonbank private sector (Radelet and Sachs 1998).

Undoubtedly, capital inflows have both benefits and costs. As benefits, they promote investment and economic growth in the recipient countries, allow intertemporal smoothing in consumption, and thus raise welfare across countries. At the same time, as costs, they may lead to a rapid monetary expansion, an excessive rise in domestic demand and inflationary pressures, an appreciation of the real exchange rate, and widening current account deficits. They may even increase the vulnerability of recipients to a sudden reversal in capital flows. For these reasons, and perhaps in the light of the earlier international debt crisis, the surge in capital inflows was, almost from the inception, perceived by the recipient countries as posing a challenge for domestic macroeconomic management, and soon began to be referred to as the "capital inflow problem" in the literature on open-economy macroeconomics (Isard 1995; Montiel 1998).

This paper will examine the extent to which a part of this capital inflow problem was policy induced in the East Asian countries of Indonesia, Korea, Malaysia, the Philippines, and Thailand during the decade preceding the outbreak of the currency crisis in July 1997. The motivation for this investigation comes from the large accumulation of official foreign exchange reserves in the recipient countries that was associated with the capital inflows. This indicated that the volume of capital inflows was in excess of the current account deficits; during this period, the reserve accumulation in each country amounted to 25–35 percent of the total capital flows (see section 6.2 for details). The accumulation of reserves might have been an offsetting response to the tight stance of monetary policy, which was supported by various measures to limit the expansionary impact of reserve inflows in the first place. The paper will indirectly test whether such tight monetary policy measures—described broadly in the paper as "sterilization"—promoted additional capital inflows through keeping the level of interest rates high, by examining the effectiveness of sterilization in limiting the impact of reserve inflows on the growth of monetary aggregates.[2]

The rest of the paper is organized as follows. Section 6.2 presents an overview of the capital inflow episode in the context of Indonesia, Korea, Malaysia, the Philippines, and Thailand, by emphasizing the relationship between the capital inflows and the growth of monetary aggregates. Section 6.3 summarizes the policy responses, collectively called "sterilization," taken by the East Asian monetary authorities to limit the expansionary impact of reserve inflows on the growth of monetary aggregates. Section 6.4 tests for the effectiveness of sterilization in limiting the growth of monetary aggregates, by using both time series and structural approaches. Finally, Section 6.5 presents concluding remarks.

6.2 An Overview of the Capital Inflow Episode in East Asia

During the capital inflow episode, the volume of capital inflows (as measured by the surplus in the capital and financial account) exceeded the deficit in the current account in all of the countries concerned, hence resulting in increases in the foreign-asset source component of the monetary base. In Indonesia, for example, there was a capital inflow of $4,495 million against the current account deficit of $2,988 million in 1990 (the year in which the surge of inflows began), with an increase in the foreign exchange reserve of $2,088 million (or about 46 percent of the net capital inflows).[3] For the period 1989–96, about 26 percent of the net capital inflows were accumulated as foreign exchange reserves in Indonesia.

A similar story can be told for the other countries. In Korea, the proportion of the net capital inflows which were accumulated as foreign exchange reserves was about 32 percent for the period 1992–96. It was particularly high in 1992 (when there was a net capital inflow of $6,994 million against the current account deficit of $3,944 million) and in 1993 (when there was a net capital inflow of $3,217 million against the current account surplus of $990 million). In Malaysia, almost 80 percent of the net capital inflows was accumulated as foreign exchange reserves from 1989 (when the surge

2. The exclusive emphasis of this paper is on the domestic monetary system of the recipient country, as our primary interest lies in the effectiveness of sterilization as a monetary policy measure. On the other hand, Montiel and Reinhart (1999) directly test the effect of sterilization on the volume and composition of capital inflows.

3. These balance-of-payments figures do not necessarily add up to zero because of errors and omissions. The figures are all from the IMF, *International Financial Statistics.*

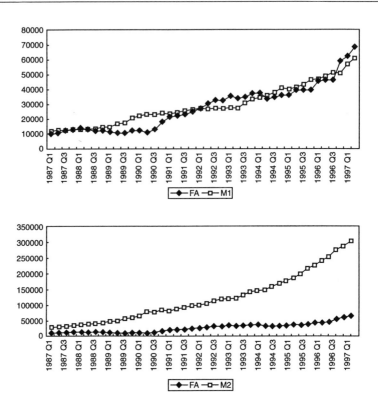

Fig. 6.1   Indonesia: Foreign assets and monetary aggregates, 1987–97 (in billions of rupiah)
Source: IMF (various months).

of inflows began) to 1993. However, it lost reserves in 1994 and 1995 before moderately gaining them again in 1996. About one-third of the net capital inflows were accumulated as foreign exchange reserves in both the Philippines and Thailand during the inflow period.

Reflecting the accumulation of foreign exchange reserves, the foreign assets (FA) source component of the monetary base rapidly expanded in these countries.[4] At the same time, all the countries saw a rapid growth in both narrow and broad money (M1 and M2). In Indonesia, for example, FA rose about 5.0 times from 1989 to 1996, with M1 rising 2.5 times and M2 4.7 times during the same period; over the entire sample period, however, there seems to be a closer correspondence between FA and M1 (fig. 6.1). In Korea, FA, M1, and M2 all increased by roughly the same percent-

4. There is not necessarily a perfect correspondence between changes in the value of foreign assets held by the monetary authorities and the official settlement accounts in the balance of payments, owing to valuation and other accounting differences.

age (i.e., 2.6 times, 1.8 times, and 2.1 times, respectively, from 1991 to 1996); one can observe volatile changes in the growth of M1 (fig. 6.2). In Malaysia, FA rose 3.2 times from 1989 to 1996, with M1 and M2 both rising 3.6 times. Corresponding to the surge of capital inflows, there was a rapid growth in FA from 1992 to early 1994; M1 then contracted through the first part of 1995 (fig. 6.3). In the Philippines, FA rose 5.8 times from 1989 to 1996, with M1 rising 2.9 times and M2 about 4.0 times. There were volatile fluctuations in the growth of FA; similar but more subdued fluctuations were observed for the growth of M1, sometimes displaying negative correlations between the two (fig. 6.4). Finally, in Thailand, FA rose 5.5 times from 1988 to 1996, with M1 rising 2.9 times and M2 3.9 times (fig. 6.5).

In each country, there was a sustained growth in FA, which was associated with the sustained growth in M1 and M2, hence giving rise to the common view that the surge in FA associated with the capital inflows somehow caused the rapid growth of monetary aggregates during the capital

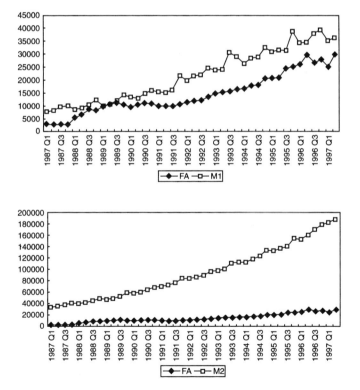

Fig. 6.2   Korea: Foreign assets and monetary aggregates, 1987–97 (in billions of won)
Source: IMF (various months).

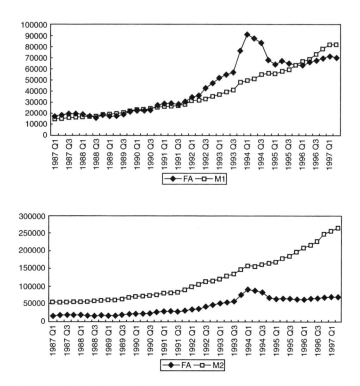

Fig. 6.3 Malaysia: Foreign assets and monetary aggregates, 1987–97 (in millions of ringgit)
Source: IMF (various months).

inflow episode. The validity of this view will be the subject of our investigation in the sections to follow.

6.3 Policy Responses to the Capital Inflows

As stated earlier, it was feared from the very beginning that the capital inflows might lead to a rapid monetary expansion, an excessive rise in aggregate demand and inflationary pressures, an appreciation of the real exchange rate, and widening current account deficits. For this reason, the monetary authorities of East Asian countries resorted to various policy measures to mitigate that possibility, including capital controls, trade liberalization, greater exchange rate flexibility, fiscal contraction, and a variety of monetary measures (Montiel 1998; Reinhart and Reinhart 1998; Villanueva and Seng 1999). The monetary measures, the focus of the present paper, included the conventional form of sterilized intervention (designed to offset the effect of reserve inflows on the monetary base by open market

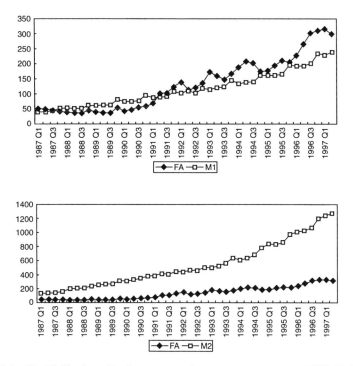

Fig. 6.4   The Philippines: Foreign assets and monetary aggregates, 1987–97 (in billions of pesos)
Source: IMF (various months).

sales of domestic securities), increases in reserve requirements (designed to limit the impact of reserve inflows on the growth of monetary aggregates by reducing the money multiplier), shifting government deposits from commercial banks to the central bank, an increase in the discount rate or otherwise a greater limit on the discount window, moral suasion, and credit controls. Of these and other monetary measures, sterilized intervention and the tightening of reserve requirements were the most common and were employed at one time or another by all of the central banks concerned.

By far, the most common and extensive was sterilized intervention, at least initially. Often lacking the depth of markets in government securities, the East Asian central banks supplemented operations in government securities by issuing their own debt instruments (Villanueva and Seng 1999). For example, in 1987, the Bank of Thailand (BOT) began to issue short-term BOT bonds with maturities of six months to one year. Monetary Stabilization Bonds (MSBs) and Bank Indonesia Certificates (SBIs) were the principal tools of open market operations used by the Bank of

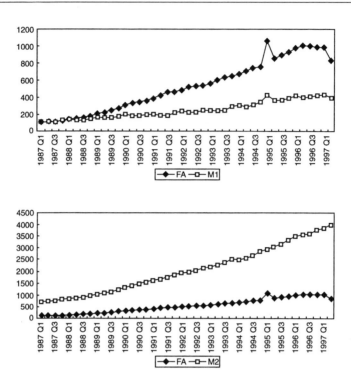

Fig. 6.5   Thailand: Foreign assets and monetary aggregates, 1987–97 (in billions of baht)
Source: IMF (various months).

Korea and Bank Indonesia, respectively.[5] The Central Bank of the Philippines had routinely used Central Bank Certificates of Indebtedness (CBCIs), at least until 1994, when open market operations in government securities gained prominence. Even in Malaysia where the market for government securities is fairly well developed by East Asian standards, Bank Negara issued series of Bank Negara Bills and Malaysian Savings Bonds during the peak inflow period of 1993.[6]

After the initial period, however, most of the central banks began to rely much less on conventional sterilized intervention, in part owing to the quasi-fiscal costs of such operations. The quasi-fiscal cost arises because, in sterilized intervention, the central bank typically exchanges high-yielding domestic assets for low-yielding foreign assets (Calvo 1991; Kletzer and Spiegel 1998). In the consolidated government and central bank

5. In Korea, the first auction in MSBs was conducted in April 1993, although they had been issued earlier. In Indonesia, SBIs were first issued in 1984.
6. In Malaysia, central bank securities were first issued in 1987.

portfolio, the public sector ends up paying more on its liabilities than it receives on its assets, as more government debt is held outside the central bank. Villanueva and Seng (1999) identify the period of active sterilized intervention as 1988–95 for Thailand, 1989 and 1992–93 for Korea, 1990–93 and 1996 for Indonesia, 1990–93 for the Philippines, and 1992–93 for Malaysia. Thus, it was only in Thailand that sterilized intervention was used consistently throughout much of the capital inflow episode.

In addition to sterilized intervention, other measures were also used to control either the monetary base or the growth of monetary aggregates. Measures to control base money included central bank borrowing from commercial banks, and the shifting of government deposits from commercial banks to the central bank. The latter tool was frequently used in Malaysia, Thailand, and Indonesia. In Malaysia, the most important funds to be so shifted were deposits of the Employee Provident Fund (EPF). It is said that more than US$2.6 billion in EPF funds were shifted from commercial banks to Bank Negara in 1992 (Villanueva and Seng 1999). In the Philippines, the government borrowed from the private sector to make deposits at the central bank. Access to the discount window was reduced in Korea during 1986–88, in Thailand during 1989–90, and in Malaysia during 1995–96. In Indonesia, moral suasion and various reporting requirements were imposed on commercial banks during 1994–96. Some control measures acted almost like cross-border capital controls, such as the ceiling on the external liabilities of domestic banks and the prohibition of sales of short-term financial instruments to foreigners, both imposed by Malaysia for several months during 1994.

The most common tool for containing the growth of monetary aggregates (while accepting the increase in base money itself) was to effect a rise in reserve requirements. Malaysia frequently raised reserve requirements and expanded the coverage of institutions and deposits subject to the requirements. Indonesia and Thailand, although initially reluctant to raise reserve requirements, became more active users of this tool in later years. Villanueva and Seng (1999) identify the period during which the reserve requirements were raised as 1989–92, 1994, and 1996 for Malaysia, 1990 for Korea and the Philippines, 1995–96 for Thailand, and 1996 for Indonesia.

In this paper, as elsewhere in the recent literature on this subject, what we call sterilization includes not only the conventional form of sterilized intervention (in which domestic and foreign securities are exchanged in an open market transaction), which may be termed "sterilization in the narrower sense," but also any form of transaction which is designed to limit the impact of reserve inflows on the growth of monetary aggregates, which may be termed "sterilization in the broader sense." Whether it is defined narrowly or broadly, sterilization tends to raise the level of domestic interest rates, provided that foreign and domestic assets are imperfect substitutes and sterilization is thus effective.[7]

In the case of narrowly defined sterilization, domestic interest rates rise so as to induce the market participants to hold the greater amount of domestic assets willingly. In the case of broadly defined sterilization, domestic interest rates rise so as to clear the money market, given the restricted money supply. In either case, a rise in foreign assets would be prevented from increasing the volume of monetary aggregates at least one to one, and the resulting rise in interest rate differentials favoring the domestic assets would promote additional capital inflows, given flexible but stable nominal exchange rates (Takagi 1999). Of course, no additional capital inflows would result if the market participants correctly perceived that the higher interest rates only reflected the higher risk premium of domestic assets and the nonzero probability of currency depreciation. However, it is said that many market participants tried to exploit the interest rate differentials that existed between U.S. dollar–denominated and East Asian currency–denominated assets by taking unhedged short-term positions for supposed financial gains, believing that the markets were imperfect (Furman and Stiglitz 1998, particularly n. 34).

6.4   Estimating the Effectiveness of Sterilization

The foregoing discussion makes it clear that, in testing for the effectiveness of sterilization, the conventional method of estimating the offset coefficient of the capital flow equation along with the monetary policy reaction function would be inappropriate in the context of the East Asian experience (for an example of the conventional method applied to developing countries, see Takagi 1986). In East Asia, various monetary measures were used at various times in various intensities in order to sterilize the effect of capital inflows on the growth of monetary aggregates. For this reason, in what follows, we will test for the effectiveness of sterilization by estimating the extent to which foreign assets (FA) in the monetary base explains or predicts monetary aggregates, setting aside the question of how sterilization is actually effected.

We will use quarterly data for the ten-year period from the first quarter of 1987 through the second quarter of 1997, immediately preceding the outbreak of the Thai crisis in July 1997. Both narrow money (M1) and broad money (M2) are used as measures of monetary aggregates, and consumer price indexes are used as the price level (P). For Korea and the Philippines, real GDP is used for output (Y), whereas industrial production is used for the other three countries. For the interest rate (i), the money

7. It should be noted that, in practice, sterilization was generally supported by tight fiscal policy, which reinforced the upward pressure on the level of interest rates.

market rate is used (see the appendix for the sources and descriptions of the data). Table 6.1 summarizes the time series properties of the variables, where all but the interest rate are expressed in natural logarithm. The table overwhelmingly suggests that the variables are integrated of order one, that is, $I(1)$. The only exceptions are nominal and real FA, and Y in Thailand. Although not formally reported in the table, all the variables are found to become stationary when they are differenced once.

6.4.1 Cointegration Tests

Before proceeding further, we test for the presence of cointegration between money and foreign assets by using Johansen's (1988) trace tests, with lag length chosen by Schwarz' Bayesian information criterion (SBIC). In a bivariate system (expressed in natural logarithm), we find that neither M1 nor M2 is found to be cointegrated with FA, except for M2 in Indonesia (table 6.2). In a multivariate system (consisting of real M1 or M2, real FA, i, and Y, where all but i are expressed in natural logarithm), a cointegrating relationship is found only for M1 in the Philippines. In what follows, given the overwhelming evidence that all variables are $I(1)$ and the general absence of cointegration, we will estimate regression equations in first difference form without an error correction term.

6.4.2 Granger Causality Tests

First, we will test for Granger causality between money and foreign assets. A stationary time series x (e.g., FA) is said to Granger-cause a stationary time series z (e.g., M1 or M2), if the hypothesis that the coefficients c_j are collectively zero can be rejected at a given level of significance.

$$(1) \qquad z_t = a + \sum b_j z_{t-j} + \sum c_j x_{t-j} + sw + e_t,$$

where t is a time subscript, a is a constant, Σ is a summation from 1 to k (where lag length [k] is chosen by SBIC), b_j's are the coefficients of the lagged dependent variables, w is a vector of other variables, including seasonal dummies (and, in a multivariate system, the lagged values of other variables, such as output and the interest rate), s is a vector of coefficients associated with w, and e is a random error term. Both causality from FA to M1 or M2 and causality from M1 or M2 to FA are tested, although only the first type of causality, which is the focus of this paper, is discussed in the text below.[8]

In a bivariate system with FA and M1 or M2 (in logarithmic differ-

---

8. As we are considering the impact of a change in FA on monetary aggregates (which must be effected through the banking sector and presumably takes some time), we believe that the use of quarterly data is appropriate. If the adjustment of monetary aggregates in response to a change in FA is completed quickly within a quarter, however, Granger causality is not revealed in quarterly data.

Table 6.1   Augmented Dickey-Fuller Statistics, 1987–97

Variables	Seasonal Dummies	Time Trend
Indonesia		
ln M1	−0.320 (4) [0.922]	−2.904 (4) [0.160]
ln M2	−0.920 (3) [0.781]	−2.009 (3) [0.596]
ln FA	−0.112 (3) [0.948]	−2.666 (4) [0.250]
ln (M1/P)	−0.741 (2) [0.835]	−2.642 (2) [0.260]
ln (M2/P)	−1.009 (3) [0.749]	−2.090 (3) [0.552]
ln (FA/P)	−0.154 (3) [0.943]	−2.554 (4) [0.301]
ln Y	−0.312 (4) [0.923]	−2.544 (4) [0.306]
i	−2.603 (2) [0.278]	−2.603 (2) [0.278]
Korea		
ln M1	−1.686 (3) [0.438]	0.171 (4) [0.995]
ln M2	−2.240 (4) [0.191]	−1.269 (4) [0.895]
ln FA	−0.289 (4) [0.926]	−3.087 (4) [0.110]
ln (M1/P)	−1.367 (4) [0.597]	−0.516 (4) [0.982]
ln (M2/P)	0.038 (4) [0.961]	−2.725 (4) [0.225]
ln (FA/P)	−0.544 (4) [0.883]	−2.986 (4) [0.144]
ln Y	−0.661 (4) [0.856]	−2.697 (3) [0.237]
i	−2.079 (2) [0.557]	−2.079 (2) [0.557]
Malaysia		
ln M1	0.499 (2) [0.984]	−2.396 (2) [0.381]
ln M2	1.155 (2) [0.995]	−2.992 (2) [0.134]
ln FA	−0.957 (3) [0.768]	−1.583 (3) [0.798]
ln (M1/P)	0.220 (4) [0.973]	−2.376 (2) [0.392]
ln (M2/P)	1.014 (2) [0.994]	−2.778 (2) [0.204]
ln (FA/P)	−1.043 (3) [0.736]	−1.597 (3) [0.793]
ln Y	0.520 (4) [0.985]	−2.191 (4) [0.494]
i	−1.918 (3) [0.644]	−1.918 (3) [0.644]
The Philippines		
ln M1	0.070 (4) [0.964]	−1.617 (4) [0.785]
ln M2	−1.643 (2) [0.460]	−2.071 (4) [0.562]
ln FA	−0.217 (2) [0.936]	−2.280 (2) [0.444]
ln (M1/P)	1.839 (4) [0.998]	0.169 (4) [0.995]
ln (M2/P)	−0.842 (2) [0.806]	−1.491 (4) [0.831]
ln (FA/P)	−0.261 (2) [0.930]	−2.679 (2) [0.244]
ln Y	0.651 (4) [0.988]	−2.131 (4) [0.528]
i	−2.008 (2) [0.596]	−2.008 (2) [0.596]
Thailand		
ln M1	−0.981 (2) [0.760]	−2.197 (4) [0.491]
ln M2	−2.413 (3) [0.137]	−1.708 (4) [0.747]
ln FA	−2.917 (3) [0.043]**	0.324 (3) [0.996]
ln (M1/P)	−1.112 (2) [0.709]	−2.135 (4) [0.526]
ln (M2/P)	−2.309 (2) [0.168]	−1.071 (4) [0.933]
ln (FA/P)	−2.948 (3) [0.039]**	0.441 (3) [0.990]
ln Y	−2.056 (4) [0.262]	−3.736 (4) [0.022]**
i	−2.069 (2) [0.563]	−2.069 (2) [0.563]

Notes: The figures are augmented Dickey-Fuller statistics obtained from running a regression with a constant term and seasonal dummies (left column) or with a constant term and time trend (right column); for the interest rate only, neither seasonal dummy nor time trend is included (hence, the same statistics are reported in both columns). Lag length was chosen on the basis of Schwarz's Bayesian information criterion (SBIC). Numbers in parentheses denote lag length; those in brackets are p-values.

**Significant at the 5 percent level.

Table 6.2   Tests of Cointegration between Money and Foreign Assets, 1987–97

Cointegrating Vectors (r)	Null		
	$r = 0$	$r \leq 1$	
Bivariate: M1 and FA (first row); M2 and FA (second row)			
Indonesia			
VAR (1)	11.90 [0.286]	0.337 [0.770]	$r = 0$
VAR (1)	22.99 [0.012]**	1.705 [0.603]	$r = 1$
Korea			
VAR (3)	8.017 [0.622]	2.955 [0.424]	$r = 0$
VAR (3)	6.574 [0.735]	1.976 [0.565]	$r = 0$
Malaysia			
VAR (1)	5.096 [0.826]	0.019 [0.801]	$r = 0$
VAR (1)	6.369 [0.749]	1.246 [0.665]	$r = 0$
The Philippines			
VAR (1)	6.036 [0.771]	0.005 [0.803]	$r = 0$
VAR (1)	6.958 [0.707]	0.006 [0.803]	$r = 0$
Thailand			
VAR (1)	13.59 [0.180]	1.539 [0.626]	$r = 0$
VAR (1)	11.12 [0.347]	0.555 [0.747]	$r = 0$
Multivariate: real M1, real FA, output and interest rate (first row); real M2, real FA, output and interest rate (second row)			
Indonesia			
VAR (1)	39.38 [0.284]	19.43 [0.544]	$r = 0$
VAR (1)	44.32 [0.119]	25.80 [0.184]	$r = 0$
Korea			
VAR (1)	36.23 [0.432]	10.25 [0.930]	$r = 0$
VAR (1)	41.13 [0.217]	14.29 [0.821]	$r = 0$
Malaysia			
VAR (1)	38.60 [0.318]	18.52 [0.602]	$r = 0$
VAR (1)	39.20 [0.292]	19.82 [0.518]	$r = 0$
The Philippines			
VAR (1)	55.73 [0.009]***	19.85 [0.516]	$r = 1$
VAR (1)	38.87 [0.400]	18.95 [0.575]	$r = 0$
Thailand			
VAR (1)	39.87 [0.264]	21.27 [0.424]	$r = 0$
VAR (1)	45.10 [0.102]	21.65 [0.399]	$r = 0$

Notes: Johansen's trace tests on a vector autoregression (VAR) system with a constant term and seasonal dummies. Lag length (in parentheses) is chosen on the basis of Schwarz's Bayesian information criterion (SBIC). r denotes the number of cointegrating vectors. Numbers in brackets are p-values.

***Significant at the 1 percent level.

**Significant at the 5 percent level.

Table 6.3   Granger Tests of Causality between Money and Foreign Assets,
                   1987–97 (bivariate VAR)

	FA causes M	M causes FA
	M1 and FA (first row); M2 and FA (second row)	
Indonesia		
VAR (1)	$F(1,34)$ 0.388 [0.537]	$F(1,34)$ 0.337 [0.565]
VAR (1)	$F(1,34)$ 1.132 [0.295]	$F(1,34)$ 0.022 [0.882]
Korea		
VAR (1)	$F(1,34)$ 1.421 [0.241]	$F(1,34)$ 0.474 [0.496]
VAR (1)	$F(1,34)$ 1.638 [0.209]	$F(1,34)$ 0.231 [0.634]
Malaysia		
VAR (1)	$F(1,34)$ 4.035 [0.053]*	$F(1,34)$ 1.455 [0.236]
VAR (1)	$F(1,34)$ 0.000 [0.991]	$F(1,34)$ 0.480 [0.493]
The Philippines		
VAR (1)	$F(1,34)$ 0.324 [0.573]	$F(1,34)$ 4.622 [0.039]**
VAR (1)	$F(1,34)$ 3.146 [0.085]*	$F(1,34)$ 1.349 [0.254]
Thailand		
VAR (1)	$F(1,34)$ 0.039 [0.845]	$F(1,34)$ 0.673 [0.418]
VAR (1)	$F(1,34)$ 1.077 [0.307]	$F(1,34)$ 4.315 [0.045]**

Notes: F-statistics in a bivariate VAR of money (M1 or M2) and foreign assets (FA) with a constant term and seasonal dummies. Lag length (in parentheses following VAR) was chosen on the basis of Schwarz's Bayesian information criterion (SBIC). Numbers in brackets are p-statistics.
**Significant at the 5 percent level.
*Significant at the 10 percent level.

ences), FA is found to Granger-cause M only in Malaysia when M1 is used and in the Philippines when M2 is used, both at the 10 percent level of significance (table 6.3). At the 5 percent level of significance, however, no Granger causality is found from FA to either M1 or M2.[9] In a multivariate system with real FA, real M1 or M2, Y, and i (in logarithmic differences, except for i which is expressed in simple first difference), no Granger causality is found at the 10 percent level of significance or lower (table 6.4). To the extent that the multivariate system can generally be considered more appropriate,[10] we conclude that no Granger causality was found from foreign assets to monetary aggregates during 1987–97 in any of the countries.[11]

9. We have also followed the procedure of Toda and Yamamoto (1995) to apply Granger causality tests in the levels of integrated or cointegrated variables. In a bivariate system, the only evidence of causality from FA to money is found in the case of Malaysia (at the 5 percent level of significance) when M1 is used.
10. If the true model includes more variables, the bivariate system of foreign assets and money may show a spurious relationship.
11. As an additional test, we have also applied Granger causality tests in Johansen's error correction model (ECM) framework, given the possible presence of cointegration between FA and M2 in Indonesia and between real M1, real FA, Y, and i in the Philippines (see table

Table 6.4   **Granger Tests of Causality between Money and Foreign Assets, 1987–97 (multivariate VAR)**

	FA causes M	M causes FA
M1, Y, i, and FA (first row); M2, Y, i, and FA (second row)		
Indonesia		
VAR (1)	$F(1,28)$ 0.000 [0.975]	$F(1,28)$ 0.073 [0.788]
VAR (1)	$F(1,28)$ 0.002 [0.963]	$F(1,28)$ 0.038 [0.845]
Korea		
VAR (1)	$F(1,28)$ 1.235 [0.275]	$F(1,28)$ 0.641 [0.429]
VAR (1)	$F(1,28)$ 1.191 [0.256]	$F(1,28)$ 0.432 [0.515]
Malaysia		
VAR (1)	$F(1,28)$ 1.520 [0.227]	$F(1,28)$ 1.407 [0.245]
VAR (1)	$F(1,28)$ 0.093 [0.762]	$F(1,28)$ 0.005 [0.942]
The Philippines		
VAR (1)	$F(1,28)$ 0.531 [0.472]	$F(1,28)$ 6.674 [0.015]**
VAR (1)	$F(1,28)$ 2.048 [0.163]	$F(1,28)$ 1.242 [0.274]
Thailand		
VAR (1)	$F(1,28)$ 1.298 [0.264]	$F(1,28)$ 2.351 [0.136]
VAR (1)	$F(1,28)$ 0.303 [0.586]	$F(1,28)$ 0.918 [0.346]

Notes: F-statistics in a multivariate VAR of real money (M1 or M2), real foreign assets (FA), output, and the interest rate, with a constant term and seasonal dummies. Lag length (in parentheses following VAR) was chosen on the basis of Schwarz's Bayesian information criterion (SBIC). Numbers in brackets are p-statistics.
**Significant at the 5 percent level.

Another important channel of influence concerns how a change in FA might have affected the level of interest rates. Our earlier discussion suggested that effective sterilization would limit the growth of monetary aggregates and raise the level of interest rates at the same time. So far, the causality tests (along the lines of equation [1]) have suggested the possibility that sterilization was effective in limiting the growth of monetary aggregates. How then was the level of interest rates affected by sterilization, given a change in FA? Table 6.5 reports the results of multivariate causality tests in logarithmic differences (except for i, which is expressed in simple differences). The tests suggest, rather surprisingly, that no Granger causality was found from FA to the money market rate during 1987–97 for any of the countries, except for the Philippines, where causality was found at the 1 percent significance level regardless of whether M1 or M2 was used. This may mean that sterilization was effective, not necessarily in raising the level of interest rates, but in keeping it from falling toward the world interest rates. More will be said on this point in the concluding section.

6.2). On the basis of the procedure of Toda and Phillips (1993), the only evidence of causality (from FA to M1) was found for the Philippines at the 10 percent level of significance. Hence, our conclusion based on tables 6.3 and 6.4 does not change.

Table 6.5   Granger Tests of Causality between Foreign Assets and the Interest Rate, 1987–97 (multivariate VAR)

	FA causes i	i causes FA
M1, Y, i, and FA (first row); M2, Y, i, and FA (second row)		
Indonesia		
VAR (1)	$F(1,28)$ 2.251 [0.144]	$F(1,28)$ 2.009 [0.167]
VAR (1)	$F(1,28)$ 1.791 [0.191]	$F(1,28)$ 1.933 [0.175]
Korea		
VAR (1)	$F(1,28)$ 0.251 [0.619]	$F(1,28)$ 0.011 [0.913]
VAR (1)	$F(1,28)$ 0.134 [0.716]	$F(1,28)$ 0.011 [0.915]
Malaysia		
VAR (1)	$F(1,28)$ 0.239 [0.628]	$F(1,28)$ 0.428 [0.517]
VAR (1)	$F(1,28)$ 0.775 [0.386]	$F(1,28)$ 0.234 [0.631]
The Philippines		
VAR (1)	$F(1,28)$ 12.27 [0.002]***	$F(1,28)$ 2.217 [0.145]
VAR (1)	$F(1,28)$ 8.765 [0.006]***	$F(1,28)$ 1.569 [0.220]
Thailand		
VAR (1)	$F(1,28)$ 0.268 [0.608]	$F(1,28)$ 2.692 [0.112]
VAR (1)	$F(1,28)$ 0.546 [0.465]	$F(1,28)$ 0.327 [0.571]

Notes: F-statistics in a multivariate VAR of real money (M1 or M2), real foreign assets (FA), output, and the interest rate, with a constant term and seasonal dummies. Lag length (in parentheses following VAR) was chosen on the basis of Schwarz's Bayesian information criterion (SBIC). Numbers in brackets are p-statistics.
***Significant at the 1 percent level.

6.4.3   Tests of Structural Equations

Second, as an additional test of the effect of foreign assets on the growth of monetary aggregates, we will estimate the following structural equation.

$$(2) \qquad \Delta \ln\left(\frac{M_t}{P_t}\right) = d + h\,\Delta \ln\left(\frac{FA_{t-1}}{P_{t-1}}\right) + qv + u_t$$

where Δ is a first-difference operator, M is either M1 or M2, d is a constant, h is the coefficient of lagged foreign assets, q is a vector of coefficients, v is a vector of other explanatory variables, including seasonal dummies, $\Delta \ln Y$, and Δi, and u is a random error term.

Equation (2) includes lagged FA, and not current FA, because a change in FA is believed to affect M1 or M2 over time through the banking sector. Use of lagged FA also has an additional advantage in that it alleviates the potential difficulty with M1 or M2 affecting FA contemporaneously. Moreover, in the light of the earlier causality test that, except for the Philippines, there was no causality between FA and i in either direction, there is no need to worry about correlation between lagged FA and i, either (except for the Philippines, of course). However, equation (2) is estimated both with and without i in order to check robustness. We are particularly interested in the estimated value of h.

Table 6.6 through table 6.10 (first two columns under each heading M1 or M2) report the results of estimating equation (2) by ordinary least squares (OLS) for Indonesia, Korea, Malaysia, the Philippines, and Thailand. The F-statistics are generally significant (except for Indonesia and Malaysia when M2 is used); considering that the regression equation is estimated in first-difference form, the R^2 is remarkably high, especially when M1 is used. The coefficient of output is positive when it is significant, while the coefficient of the interest rate is negative when it is significant. Many of the coefficients of the seasonal dummies (not formally reported in the tables) are significant.

From these tables, we find that regardless of whether M1 or M2 is used or whether i is included, the coefficient of lagged FA (h) is not significantly different from zero. The only exception is found for the Philippines when M2 is used and i is included. Because of the potential simultaneity problem, not too much confidence can be placed in the present result at this time. So far as this result is concerned, however, the coefficient (h) is negative, suggesting that a rise in foreign assets reduces M2 in the next period. All in all, the overall weight of the evidence seems to suggest that sterilization was effective in limiting the growth of monetary aggregates during 1987–97 in all countries, affirming the results of the Granger causality tests.

Finally, the tables (last two columns under each heading) also report the results of estimating equation (2) by including a slope dummy for the coefficient of $\Delta \ln(FA_{t-1}/P_{t-1})$, with the dummy indicating the intensity of sterilization

$$(3) \quad \Delta \ln\left(\frac{M_t}{P_t}\right) = d + h_1 \Delta \ln\left(\frac{FA_{t-1}}{P_{t-1}}\right) + DUM_t h_2 \Delta \ln\left(\frac{FA_{t-1}}{P_{t-1}}\right) + qv + u_t,$$

where DUM is the dummy variable which takes the value of unity when sterilization is considered to be particularly intense, and h_1 and h_2 (replacing h) are the coefficients of lagged real foreign assets under normal conditions and under intense sterilization, respectively. The annual series of dummy variables were constructed on the basis of information provided by Villanueva and Seng (1999) and a similar construction of the sterilization index presented by Reinhart and Reinhart (1998) and Montiel and Reinhart (1999). The quarterly series are created by simply assuming that, during a given calendar year, they take the same value as the annual series. Here, sterilization was considered to be intense if open market operations were large in scale and accompanied by increased reserve requirements or transfers of government deposits from commercial banks to the central bank (see the annual series in table 6.11).

Table 6.6   Indonesia: Money Supply Adjustment, 1987–97

	Real Narrow Money (M1)				Real Broad Money (M2)			
	(1)	(2)	(3)	(4)	(1)	(2)	(3)	(4)
Constant	0.046***	0.045***	0.078*	0.044***	0.054***	0.052***	0.060	0.051***
	(3.249)	(3.180)	(1.930)	(3.135)	(3.661)	(3.506)	(1.425)	(3.498)
Output	0.284**	0.285**	0.270**	0.297**	0.028	0.029	0.040	0.047
	(2.284)	(2.290)	(2.103)	(2.384)	(0.224)	(0.225)	(0.296)	(0.364)
Interest rate	−0.003		−0.003		−0.005		−0.001	
	(−0.936)		(−0.884)		(−1.349)		(−0.222)	
Lagged real foreign assets	−0.068	−0.049	0.021	0.021	−0.036	−0.009	0.093	0.093
	(−0.783)	(−0.586)	(0.198)	(0.198)	(−0.403)	(−0.097)	(0.825)	(0.839)
DUM * lagged real foreign assets			−0.104	−0.166			−0.222	−0.238
			(−0.615)	(−1.078)			(−1.250)	(−1.494)
F-statistic	1.912*	2.136*	1.800	1.983*	0.909	0.711	0.828	0.986
R^2	0.259	0.239	0.282	0.265	0.142	0.094	0.154	0.152
Durbin-Watson	1.764	1.717	1.715	1.703	2.666	2.714	2.696	2.720

Notes: Coefficients are estimated in first difference form by ordinary least squares (OLS). Coefficients for the seasonal dummies are not reported. Except for Korea, DUM is a slope dummy for intense sterilization. *t*-values are in parentheses.

***Significant at the 1 percent level.

**Significant at the 5 percent level.

*Significant at the 10 percent level.

Table 6.7   Korea: Money Supply Adjustment, 1987–97

	Real Narrow Money (M1)		Real Broad Money (M2)	
	(1)	(2)	(1)	(2)
Constant	0.064	0.064	0.053***	0.054***
	(1.203)	(1.226)	(3.394)	(3.459)
Output	0.280	0.278	0.064	0.062
	(0.879)	(0.897)	(0.681)	(0.679)
Interest rate	0.0003		0.0003	
	(0.033)		(0.134)	
Lagged real foreign assets	0.120	0.120	0.040	0.040
	(1.303)	(1.322)	(1.466)	(1.484)
F-statistic	10.97***	16.13***	16.13***	19.93***
R^2	0.666	0.746	0.746	0.746
Durbin-Watson	2.680	2.738	2.738	2.743

Notes: See table 6.6.
***Significant at the 1 percent level.

We consider equation (3) in order to see whether the relationship between FA and monetary aggregates was invariant through time. If the policy of intense sterilization was particularly effective in limiting the impact of an increase in FA on the growth of M1 or M2, we should expect the value of h_2 to be negative, so that the coefficient of (FA_{t-1}/P_{t-1}) under intense sterilization (i.e., $h_1 + h_2$) is algebraically smaller than that under normal conditions (h_1). Because no sterilization was considered intense in Korea, the results are reported for the other four countries only. The last two columns under each heading show that the coefficient h_2 is not statistically significant in any of the countries regardless of whether M1 or M2 is chosen (confirming the earlier results obtained without the slope dummies), although it is indeed negative in Indonesia, the Philippines, and Thailand. We can thus reaffirm our earlier conclusion that sterilization was effective in limiting the growth of monetary aggregates during 1987–97, with the additional insight that the effectiveness of sterilization was indeed greater (albeit marginally) when it was intense.

6.5   Conclusion

The East Asian countries of Indonesia, Korea, Malaysia, the Philippines, and Thailand received large volumes of capital inflows from the end of the 1980s through early 1997. The cumulative inflows were massive indeed, amounting to 50 percent of GDP in Malaysia and Thailand, more than 20 percent in the Philippines, and about 10 percent in Indonesia and Korea. Although a large portion of the inflows initially took the form of FDI, they increasingly took the form of offshore borrowing by banks and

Table 6.8 Malaysia: Money Supply Adjustment, 1987–97

	Real Narrow Money (M1)				Real Broad Money (M2)			
	(1)	(2)	(3)	(4)	(1)	(2)	(3)	(4)
Constant	0.068***	0.066***	0.067***	0.064***	0.049***	0.048***	0.048***	0.047***
	(6.067)	(6.094)	(5.651)	(5.666)	(4.070)	(4.128)	(3.813)	(3.862)
Output	−0.100	−0.127	−0.054	−0.080	−0.053	−0.070	−0.033	−0.049
	(−0.421)	(−0.542)	(−0.216)	(−0.323)	(−0.208)	(−0.283)	(−0.123)	(−0.188)
Interest rate	−0.009		−0.009		−0.006		−0.006	
	(−0.807)		(−0.788)		(−0.487)		(−0.475)	
Lagged real foreign assets	0.025	0.046	0.008	0.028	0.022	0.035	0.014	0.027
	(0.424)	(0.844)	(0.115)	(0.447)	(0.338)	(0.603)	(0.195)	(0.408)
DUM * lagged real foreign assets			0.086	0.088			0.038	0.039
			(0.663)	(0.680)			(0.269)	(0.281)
F-statistic	2.921**	3.41**	2.524**	2.874**	1.314	1.564	1.105	1.282
R^2	0.347	0.334	0.356	0.343	0.192	0.187	0.195	0.189
Durbin-Watson	2.514	2.434	2.433	2.356	1.882	1.862	1.892	1.872

Notes: See table 6.6.

***Significant at the 1 percent level.

**Significant at the 5 percent level.

Table 6.9   The Philippines: Money Supply Adjustment, 1987–97

	Real Narrow Money (M1)				Real Broad Money (M2)			
	(1)	(2)	(3)	(4)	(1)	(2)	(3)	(4)
Constant	0.069	0.071	0.070	0.071	0.004	0.012	0.004	0.012
	(1.109)	(1.147)	(1.129)	(1.161)	(0.063)	(0.175)	(0.063)	(0.171)
Output	0.620	0.600	0.626	0.615	0.643*	0.536	0.645	0.543
	(1.589)	(1.569)	(1.628)	(1.633)	(1.639)	(1.294)	(1.610)	(1.302)
Interest rate	−0.001		−0.001		−0.008**		−0.008**	
	(−0.412)		(−0.251)		(−2.175)		(−2.079)	
Lagged real foreign assets	0.028	0.037	0.071	0.077	−0.108**	−0.059	−0.093	−0.038
	(0.542)	(0.810)	(1.206)	(1.475)	(−2.090)	(−1.201)	(−1.509)	(−0.652)
DUM * lagged real foreign assets			−0.134	−0.137			−0.048	−0.071
			(−1.411)	(−1.471)			(−0.481)	(−0.694)
F-statistic	34.60***	42.52**	30.83***	37.01***	7.836***	7.621***	6.593***	6.334***
R^2	0.863	0.862	0.871	0.871	0.588	0.528	0.591	0.535
Durbin-Watson	2.534	2.563	2.442	2.466	2.139	2.180	2.109	2.168

Notes: See table 6.6.
***Significant at the 1 percent level.
**Significant at the 5 percent level.
*Significant at the 10 percent level.

Table 6.10   Thailand: Money Supply Adjustment, 1987–97

	Real Narrow Money (M1)				Real Broad Money (M2)			
	(1)	(2)	(3)	(4)	(1)	(2)	(3)	(4)
Constant	0.094***	0.093***	0.090***	0.090***	0.048***	0.048***	0.047***	0.047***
	(4.917)	(4.949)	(4.681)	(4.713)	(7.805)	(7.585)	(7.522)	(7.307)
Output	0.078	0.071	0.076	0.070	0.072	0.080	0.072	0.080
	(0.378)	(0.352)	(0.372)	(0.345)	(1.108)	(1.176)	(1.098)	(1.164)
Interest rate	−0.002		0.002		−0.003**		−0.003**	
	(−0.532)		(0.527)		(−2.002)		(−2.000)	
Lagged real foreign assets	−0.086	−0.090	0.131	0.126	0.038	0.045	0.092	0.097
	(−0.728)	(−0.784)	(0.575)	(0.562)	(1.021)	(1.145)	(1.255)	(1.275)
DUM * lagged real foreign assets			−0.262	−0.263			−0.064	−0.064
			(−1.110)	(−1.126)			(−0.853)	(−0.804)
F-statistic	12.71***	15.52**	11.14***	13.25***	6.000***	5.879***	5.205***	4.956***
R^2	0.698	0.695	0.709	0.707	0.522	0.464	0.532	0.474
Durbin-Watson	2.254	2.276	2.375	2.402	1.729	1.852	1.745	1.854

Notes: See table 6.6.
***Significant at the 1 percent level.
**Significant at the 5 percent level.

Table 6.11   The "Intense Sterilization" Dummy

	Indonesia	Korea	Malaysia	The Philippines	Thailand
1987	0	0	0	0	0
1988	0	0	0	0	0
1989	0	0	0	0	0
1990	0	0	0	1	1
1991	1	0	1	0	1
1992	1	0	1	0	0
1993	0	0	1	0	0
1994	0	0	0	0	0
1995	0	0	0	0	1
1996	1	0	1	0	0
1997	0	0	0	0	0

Sources: The authors' judgment based on Reinhart and Reinhart (1998), Montiel and Reinhart (1999), and Villanueva and Seng (1999).
Notes: Sterilization is considered intense (i.e., a value of unity is assigned) if open market operations were large in scale and accompanied by increased reserve requirements or transfers of government deposits from commercial banks to the central bank. The quarterly series for a given year are assumed to have the same value as the annual series.

nonbank private corporations in later years. Because of the potential risks they entail, these capital inflows were, almost from the inception, considered as posing a serious challenge for macroeconomic management, leading the profession to coin the expression "the capital inflow problem."

An important aspect of the capital inflow episode was that the volume of inflows far exceeded the current account deficits, such that the increases in foreign exchange reserves amounted to 25–35 percent of the net capital inflows. Needless to say, the accumulation of reserves was the result of foreign exchange market intervention to maintain the level of nominal exchange rates. Short of allowing the exchange rate to appreciate, the East Asian monetary authorities responded decisively to the massive reserve inflows, first by the conventional form of sterilization and then by taking a wide range of measures to limit the effect of the reserve inflows on the growth of monetary aggregates, the measures which are called "broadly defined sterilization" in this paper.

We began the paper by noting that, whether narrowly or broadly defined, effective sterilization should not only limit the growth of monetary aggregates in response to an increase in foreign assets, but also raise the level of domestic interest rates. The resulting tight monetary condition (often supported by tight fiscal policy) and higher domestic interest rates should then promote additional capital inflows. The Granger causality tests and OLS estimates of structural parameters, however, gave the somewhat perplexing results indicating that, while sterilization was apparently effective in fully limiting the growth of monetary aggregates arising from an increase in foreign assets, it was not causing the level of interest rates to rise.

At this point, a word of reservation might be expressed about the nature of the methodologies used. We noted at the outset that, given the variety of tools used to mitigate the impact of reserve inflows on the growth of monetary aggregates in these countries, the conventional method of estimating the offset coefficient of the capital flow equation along with the monetary-policy reaction function would be inappropriate as a test of the effectiveness of sterilization. Instead, what we decided to do was to use a "black box" way of measuring the effectiveness of sterilization, by essentially estimating the statistical significance of FA in the equation describing the growth of M1 or M2, without explicitly considering how sterilization is actually effected. While we believe that this is an intuitively appealing procedure, given the ultimate objective of sterilization, we also recognize that it may be subject to potential problems. For instance, the lack of statistical significance may reflect, not the effectiveness of sterilization, but the much smaller magnitude of FA relative to that of either M1 or M2; the results may also be sensitive to the choice of lag length, particularly when the methodologies are applied in first-difference form. In the future, it will be useful to check the robustness of our methodologies against alternative specifications or alternative sample countries.[12]

Subject to these and other limitations, our results (suggesting the effectiveness of sterilization, while indicating little evidence of an interest rate rise) are capable of yielding two possible interpretations. First and most likely, the lack of evidence linking a rise in foreign assets to a rise in interest rates may simply suggest that sterilization was effective, not necessarily in raising the level of interest rates, but in keeping it from falling toward the lower world-interest rates. To support this claim, the moving average representations of the estimated vector autoregression (VAR) system (reported earlier) suggest that interest rates do rise in response to an innovation in foreign assets in all countries except Korea (fig. 6.6). It is also possible that a more systematic relationship between foreign assets and interest rates might have been evident for a more appropriate interest rate or interest rate differential. In Indonesia, for example, it is said that the interest rate on SBIs rose sharply from 11.6 percent in 1988 to 18.8 percent in 1990 and 21.5 percent in 1991; Furman and Stiglitz (1998) note that interest rate differentials did widen in East Asian countries over the period of sterilization.[13]

12. In this context, as a robustness check, the referee has suggested the usefulness of applying our methodologies to countries under currency boards. Data limitations, however, have prevented us from pursuing this course.

13. According to Furman and Stiglitz (1998), in Thailand, short-term money market rates rose 400 basis points above comparable U.S. interest rates in 1996, and similar spreads were observed for other East Asian countries.

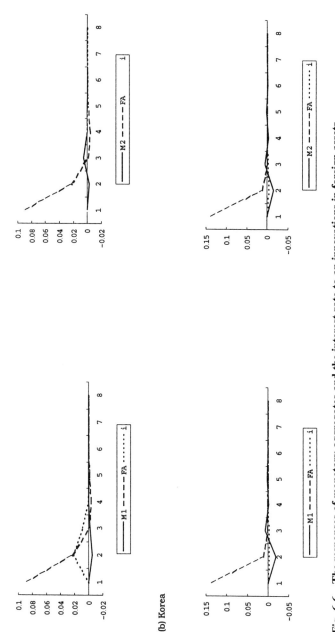

Fig. 6.6   The responses of monetary aggregates and the interest rate to an innovations in foreign assets

Notes: The impulse responses of real money (M1 or M2) and the interest rate (i) to a 1–standard deviation innovation in real foreign assets (FA) in a multivariate VAR system consisting of real M1 or M2, real FA, Y, and i, with a constant term and seasonal dummies. In the case of M1 for the Philippines, a vector error correction model (VECM) was applied, given the possible presence of cointegration.

(c) Malaysia

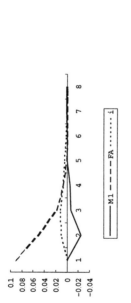

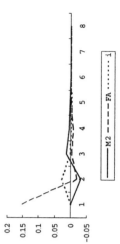

(d) The Philippines

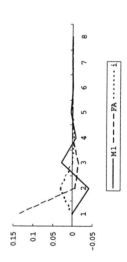

Fig. 6.6 (cont.)

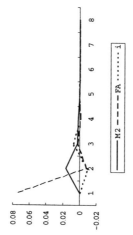

(e) Thailand

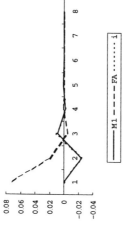

Fig. 6.6 (cont.)

Second, as another possible interpretation of the seeming lack of evidence on the interest rate channel, it is possible that sterilization was not so effective in limiting the growth of overall monetary assets, although it was effective in limiting the growth of M1 or M2 which is under the supervised banking sector. Although broadly defined sterilization measures (such as changes in reserve requirements, credit controls, and moral suasion) may be effective against the supervised banking sector, they may result in disintermediation in an environment where there is a viable nonbank financial sector. In the case of Korea, for example, Spiegel (1995) documents that the share of assets controlled by the banking sector declined over the period 1986–93, although no such evidence was found for the Philippines and Malaysia, where the nonbank financial sector is not well developed. It should be noted that this disintermediation interpretation is not necessarily incompatible with the story that sterilization kept the level of interest rates high.

In either case, the policy of sterilization pursued by the monetary authorities of East Asia during the capital inflow episode was effective in fully limiting the growth of M1 or M2, and possibly magnified the risk of capital inflows by keeping the level of interest rates high (hence promoting additional capital inflows), by channelling resources to the relatively unsupervised nonbank financial sector, or both. In this context, the work of Montiel and Reinhart (1999) suggests that the sterilization policy of the Asian monetary authorities not only magnified the volume of capital inflows but also skewed the composition of capital flows towards short-term maturities. Both through additional capital inflows with a short-term bias and through possible disintermediation, it is likely that the capital inflow problem of East Asia leading up to the crisis of 1997 was made more serious by the active and persistent policy of sterilization.

Appendix

Sources of Data

Except for industrial production in Indonesia and Thailand (which were obtained from the Bank of Japan's economic database), all data were obtained from the International Monetary Fund, *International Financial Statistics,* as follows. Foreign Assets (FA) were obtained from line 11. Narrow money (M1) and quasi-money were obtained from lines 34 and 35, respectively; M1 and quasi-money constitute broad money (M2). Interest rates were obtained from the money market rate (line 60b) for Indonesia, Korea, Malaysia, and Thailand, and from the Treasury bill rate (line 60c) for the Philippines.

References

Alba, Pedro, Amar Bhattacharya, Stijn Claessens, Swati Ghosh, and Leonard Hernandez. 1998. The role of macroeconomic and financial sector linkages in East Asia's financial crisis. unpublished, World Bank. 1998. Mimeograph.

Bartolini, Leonardo, and Allan Drazen. 1997. Capital-account liberalization as a signal. *American Economic Review* 87 (March): 138–54.

Calvo, Guillermo A. 1991. The perils of sterilization. *IMF Staff Papers* 38 (December): 921–26. Washington, D.C.: International Monetary Fund.

Calvo, Guillermo A., Leonard Leiderman, and Carman M. Reinhart. 1996. Inflows of capital to developing countries in the 1990s. *Journal of Economic Perspectives* 10 (Spring): 123–39.

Chen, Zhaohui, and Mohsin S. Khan. 1997. Patterns of capital flows to emerging markets: A theoretical perspective. IMF Working Paper no. 97/13. Washington, D.C.: International Monetary Fund, January.

Chuhan, Punam, Stijn Claessens, and Nlandu Mamingi. 1998. Equity and bond flows to Latin America and Asia: The role of global and country factors. *Journal of Development Economics* 55 (April): 439–63.

Furman, Jason, and Joseph E. Stiglitz. 1998. Economic crises: Evidence and insights from East Asia. *Brookings Papers on Economic Activity,* issue no. 2:1–135. Washington, D.C.: Brookings Institution.

International Monetary Fund (IMF). Various months. *International financial statistics.* Washington, D.C.: International Monetary Fund.

Isard, Peter. 1995. *Exchange rate economics.* Cambridge: Cambridge University Press.

Johansen, Soren. 1988. Statistical analysis of cointegration vectors. *Journal of Economic Dynamics and Control* 12 (June/September): 231–54.

Kletzer, Kenneth, and Mark M. Spiegel. 1998. Speculative capital inflows and exchange rate targeting in the Pacific basin: Theory and evidence. In *Managing capital flows and exchange rates: Perspectives from the Pacific Basin,* ed. Reuven Glick, 409–35. Cambridge: Cambridge University Press.

Montiel, Peter J. 1998. The capital inflow problem. World Bank Institute Working Paper no. 37135. World Bank, Economic Development Institute, January.

Montiel, Peter J., and Carmen M. Reinhart. 1999. Do capital controls and macroeconomic policies influence the volume and composition of capital flows? Evidence from the 1990s. *Journal of International Money and Finance,* 18 (August): 619–35.

Radelet, Steven, and Jeffrey Sachs. 1998. The onset of the East Asian financial crisis. NBER Working Paper no. 6680. Cambridge, Mass.: National Bureau of Economic Research.

Reinhart, Carmen M., and Vincent Raymond Reinhart. 1998. Some lessons for policy makers: Dealing with the mixed blessing of capital inflows. In *Capital flows and financial crises,* ed. M. Kahler, 93–127. New York: Council on Foreign Relations.

Spiegel, Mark M. 1995. Raising reserve requirements in response to Asian capital inflow surges. Federal Reserve Bank of San Francisco, Weekly Newsletter no. 95–41, 1 December.

Takagi, Shinji. 1986. Rediscount policy and official capital flows: A study of monetary control in Central America in the 1950s. *Journal of Money, Credit, and Banking* 18 (May): 200–10.

———. 1999. The yen and its East Asian neighbors, 1980–1995: Cooperation or competition? In *Changes in exchange rates in rapidly developing countries: The-*

ory, practice, and policy issues, ed. Takatoshi Ito and Anne O. Krueger, 185–210. Chicago: University of Chicago Press.

Toda, Hiro T., and Peter C. B. Phillips. 1993. Vector autoregressions and causality. *Econometrica* 61 (November): 1367–93.

Toda, Hiro T., and Taku Yamamoto. 1995. Statistical inference in vector autoregressions with possibly integrated processes. *Journal of Econometrics* 66 (March/April): 225–50.

Villanueva, Delano, and Lim Choon Seng. 1999. Managing capital flows in SEACEN countries: A policy agenda. Southeast Asian Central Banks Research and Training Centre, February. Mimeograph.

Comment   Leonard K. Cheng

A factor widely considered critical to the East Asian financial crisis in 1997–98 is its enormous short-term foreign debt. This paper examines the extent to which the "capital inflow" problem was induced by the "sterilization" policy or equivalently tight monetary policy pursued by the East Asian governments. It goes on to test whether sterilization was effective in limiting the growth of monetary aggregates during the decade before the East Asian financial crisis. The questions raised in this paper are both interesting and timely.

An inflow of capital (as measured by the foreign asset in the monetary base, abbreviated as FA) will put downward pressure on the domestic interest rate, other things being equal. The effect of any sterilization policy is to keep the domestic interest rates in the East Asian economies higher than otherwise, thus inducing an additional amount of capital inflow. I agree with this logic, but I also think the time dimension should be explicitly recognized.

In one example, capital flows in, the interest rate falls in response, sterilization policy kicks in, and the aggregate money supply drops, thus pushing up the interest rate. In another example, sterilization policy kicks in as soon as capital flows in, and the movement of the interest rate depends on the extent of sterilization. The interest rate will fall by an amount that is smaller than that without sterilization if sterilization serves to offset the capital inflow only partially. In contrast, if sterilization serves to more than offset the capital inflow, then the interest rate will rise. Which of these examples fits the quarterly data better? Do the responses of the monetary aggregates and interest rates to an innovation in FA as summarized in figure 6.6 of the paper imply that sterilization was more than offsetting the capital inflow? Or were both responses the results of an increase in demand

Leonard K. Cheng is professor of economics at the Hong Kong University of Science and Technology.

for money that was met by partial sterilization of the induced capital inflow and an increase in the domestic interest rate? From the point of view of the East Asian economies faced with the potential of a speculative boom, is it desirable to let the domestic interest rate fall farther to the world level? Is capital control an appropriate response? The authors did not set out to answer these questions, but the theory of distortions may be able to shed some light on them.

The authors point out that a central bank "typically exchanges high-yielding domestic assets for low-yielding foreign assets" in the open-market operations. Given the financial costs involved, central banks often turn to other policy tools to control the growth of monetary aggregates, the most common of which was raising the commercial banks' reserve requirements. While both of these measures make domestic bank lending more costly, they do not make direct foreign borrowing more expensive, thus causing a diversion to foreign borrowing and additional capital inflow.

If excessive capital inflow is considered undesirable, then the optimal policy suggested by the theory of distortions is one that acts directly on the inflow (such as a capital inflow tax as levied by some Latin American countries). Measures such as open market operations and reserve requirements are necessarily suboptimal because they deal with the symptoms rather than tackling the root problem directly. In this sense, perhaps one can even say that the capital inflow problem empirically ascertained in this paper was the result of inappropriate policy responses.

Comment   Mahani Zainal-Abidin

This paper provided a succinct and perceptive summary of the pattern of capital inflow into East Asia during the 1986–97 period and of the policy responses undertaken to minimize its adverse effects, such as an excessive rise in aggregate demand, a rapid monetary expansion, and rising inflationary pressures. The measures employed to manage large capital inflows include capital controls, trade liberalization, greater monetary flexibility, fiscal contraction, and monetary instruments. The frequently used monetary measures comprise open market sales of domestic securities (a conventional form of sterilized intervention), increase in reserve requirements, shifting of government deposits from commercial banks to central banks, increase in discount rates, moral suasion, and credit controls.

The paper set out the hypothesis that effective sterilization not only limits the growth of monetary aggregates but also raises the level of domestic

Mahani Zainal-Abidin is professor in the Department of Applied Economics at the University of Malaya, Kuala Lumpur.

interest rates. The resulting higher interest rate from sterilization measures will in fact encourage more capital inflow, and in the end it will become unsustainable, due to its high cost and the expansionary effects of an even larger inflow. Therefore, the measures to stem the huge short-term capital inflow into East Asian countries will, paradoxically, further aggravate the problem. In other words, could this large inflow, which was one of the causes of the 1997–98 East Asian economic and financial crisis, have been policy induced through higher interest rates as a result of the sterilization efforts?

The paper's regression estimates showed that sterilization was effective in limiting the growth of monetary aggregates, but it did not produce a higher level of interest rate. The regression also estimated the effects on monetary aggregates when sterilization was intense and showed that although the sterilization result was stronger during the period of unusually large inflow, the general restraining effects from sterilization were present throughout the entire period of capital inflow. In contrast, the relationship between sterilization and interest rate was found to be insignificant, and this was attributed to the lack of a systematic relationship between the two variables. For better results, the paper suggested that a more appropriate relationship should be between the level of foreign assets and interest rate differentials. The paper also acknowledged that if the adjustment process is completed quickly (which is unlikely because it has to be worked through the banking system), the quarterly data used would not pick up this sterilization effect.

In analyzing the effectiveness of sterilization measures in controlling monetary aggregate and its influence on the movement of interest rate, it is vital to consider other policy objectives that may have prevented interest rates from rising further in line with the larger capital inflow, as well as other measures that were employed to manage capital inflow.

That sterilization measures have not increased the level of interest rate more can be partly explained by the stated policy of many East Asian governments; they target interest rate stability and thus have taken steps to cap large interest rate increases. There are three reasons why East Asian countries resisted high interest rates. Firstly, the East Asian economic growth was predicated on high investment and high leverage, which was made possible only with the availability of relatively cheap credit. In particular, the push for privatized infrastructure projects has significantly increased the level of domestic debt, especially when financing from external sources is restricted: for example, during the period of high investment in Malaysia, domestic private sector loans reached a high of 148.8 percent of the gross domestic product. It is vital that the cost of funding remains low for these projects to be viable. Therefore, it is unlikely that the banking system would fully realize the consequence of sterilization (i.e., raising the level of interest rate) in view of its role as a key supporter of the high-investment, high-leverage growth strategy.

Secondly, many East Asian countries aim for a regime of low inflation as part of their growth strategy, particularly in maintaining export competitiveness. Moreover, it is feared that rising interest rates will heighten consumers' expectation of the future rate of inflation. In the Malaysian case, during the period covered by the paper (1987–1997), the volatility of interest rate was much lower than that of the exchange rate (Malaysia Central Bank 1997). Even in the wake of the East Asian crisis, volatility of the Malaysian interest rate was not unusually high relative to the rest of the 1990s. The Malaysian case of interest rate stability (during the precrisis period) reflects the East Asian policy of ensuring interest rate stability to avoid destabilizing the domestic economy. This interest rate "targeting" may explain the paper's conclusion that although sterilization was effective, it did not increase the level of interest rate; rather, the sterilization measures kept domestic interest rate from falling below the world level.

The importance of the nonbanking route of capital flow can be underestimated in explaining the link between sterilization and the level of interest rate. As is explained in the paper, one possible interpretation of the weak evidence on the lack of causality between sterilization and the level of interest rate is that sterilization is only effective in limiting the growth of monetary aggregates supervised by the banking system. Although the paper focuses on the effect of sterilization on monetary aggregates and interest rate through the banking system, it is useful to consider the impact of capital inflow channeled through the nonbanking sector. A significant part of capital inflow goes into the nonbanking sector—namely, the equity market—with the objective of capturing high returns. These flows are not monitored by the banking system. However, the flow can influence total demand and may affect the price level through increases in asset prices. The effectiveness of the sterilization instruments, including those in the banking sector, will depend on the nonbanking sector's ability to play a substitution role for intermediation. The greater the degree to which these nonbank instruments influence the level of aggregate demand is, the lesser is the ability of the recipient country's government to mitigate the impact of capital flows through the banking system. Hence, even though the total capital inflow is large, the portion that is channeled through the banking system is smaller than that of the nonbank system.

The weak relationship between sterilization measures and movement of interest rate could also be attributed to the shift in the choice of policy instruments. Due to the high costs of sterilization, such as open market operation and increase in statutory requirements, countries have also resorted to other measures, such as indirect capital controls, fiscal adjustment, and trade liberalization. Table 6C.1 summaries the various measures adopted by developing countries and indicates that many Southeast Asian countries had switched their fiscal policy stance from budget deficit to budget surplus in order to counteract the inflationary impact of increased monetary supply from the purchase of foreign assets. As was mentioned

Table 6C.1   **Major Economic Measures Employed**

	Moves Toward a More Flexible Exchange Rate	Fiscal Restraint	Sterilization by Open Market Operations	Sterilization by Other Means	Restriction on Capital Inflows	Liberalization of the Current Account	Selective Liberalization of the Capital Account	Strengthening the Domestic Financial System
Argentina		x				x		x
Chile	x		x		x	x	x	
Colombia	x		x	x	x	x	x	x
Indonesia	x	x	x	x	x	x		x
Korea	x	x	x			x	x	
Malaysia	x	x	x	x	x	x		
Mexico	x	x	x		x	x		
The Philippines		x	x	x	x	x	x	
Thailand	x	x	x	x	x	x	x	

Source: Corbo and Hernández 1996.

earlier, the twin targets of low inflation and reasonable cost of funds have made it necessary for governments to employ fiscal measures to mitigate the pressures on interest rates. In Thailand, for example, capital outflow was encouraged instead of reduction in money supply, through the early servicing of external debt and the easing of restrictions on capital outflow. Other examples include Malaysia's limitations on domestic banks' foreign liabilities as well as restrictions on residents from selling securities to non-residents for a few months in 1994. The paper has taken into account this intense period of management of capital inflow, but it also shows that the sterilization effects are still evidenced even when the intensive sterilization was lifted.

In conclusion, although it is likely that the capital inflow problem is policy induced, other macroeconomic factors also contributed to the large inflow experienced by the East Asian economies. The findings of this paper clearly show that by preventing interest rates from falling, sterilization measures might attract more inflow. Nevertheless, there were other policy instruments that could equally contribute to this problem. The de facto peg exchange rate regime practiced by many East Asian countries—which provided exchange rate stability—may also encourage capital inflow, because in such a system the risk associated with exchange rate volatility was minimized. Stable nominal exchange rates, coupled with high returns, particularly from equity and property markets, have proven to be an attractive combination. Corbo and Hernández (1996) found that the experiences of Chile and Colombia in the 1990s clearly showed that when restrictive monetary policy accompanied an exchange rate target, then sterilized intervention tended to exacerbate, rather than ameliorate, capital flows.

References

Corbo, V., and L. Hernández. 1996. Macroeconomic adjustment to capital inflows: Lessons from recent Latin American and East Asian experience. *World Bank Research Observers* 11 (1): 61–85.
Malaysia Central Bank. *Annual Report 1997.* Kuala Lumpur, Malaysia: Bank Negara Malaysia.

7

Credibility of Hong Kong's Currency Board
The Role of Institutional Arrangements

Yum K. Kwan, Francis T. Lui, and Leonard K. Cheng

7.1 Introduction

Since its introduction in Mauritius in 1849, the currency board as a form of monetary institution has generally been neglected in the economics literature.[1] This is probably due to the fact that currency boards were mainly adopted in relatively small and unimportant economies. In recent years, the situation has changed. Argentina's readoption of the currency board in 1991 and its subsequent impressive economic growth record has contributed to its credibility as a useful monetary system. Its subsequent adoption in Estonia, Lithuania, and Bulgaria further indicates its increasing popularity. Indeed, during the recent global financial turmoil, the currency board had been prescribed for the battered economies of Russia and Indonesia.

There may be another reason why the literature has not paid enough attention to the study of currency boards. Due to the lack of reasonably

Yum K. Kwan is associate professor of economics at the City University of Hong Kong. Francis T. Lui is professor of economics at the Hong Kong University of Science and Technology. Leonard K. Cheng is professor of economics at the Hong Kong University of Science and Technology.

The authors wish to thank Alex Chan, K. C. Chan, Yuk-Shee Chan, Nai-fu Chen, Shinichi Fukuda, Takatoshi Ito, Anne Krueger, Guy Meredith, Merton Miller, and Joseph Yam for discussions and comments. It should be emphasized that they do not necessarily share our views, and all remaining errors are ours. We are especially grateful to an anonymous referee for comments that have led to an improved exposition of our key arguments. The authors would like to acknowledge the following institutions for providing financial support to this research: the Research Grant Council of Hong Kong (grant number HKUST 6217/97H to Francis T. Lui and Yum K. Kwan) and the City University of Hong Kong (small-scale research grant number 9030774 to Yum K. Kwan).

1. Among others, Schuler (1992); Hanke, Jonung, and Schuler (1993); and Williamson (1995) are exceptions.

long and systematic data series, rigorous empirical analyses of their implications were difficult to conduct. Hong Kong, having a long history with the currency board, can readily fill in this gap. Its rich experiences include the abandonment and readoption of the currency board; and, more importantly, it has gone through a series of subtle institutional changes and several episodes of speculative attacks on the Hong Kong dollar. Moreover, systematic data sufficient for implementing meaningful econometric analyses are available.[2] Properly studied, Hong Kong's experiences can offer useful insights for economies interested in adopting a currency board.

The study of Hong Kong's experiences with the currency board is of theoretical interest in its own right. Stimulated by Kydland and Prescott (1977), there have been numerous studies on the relative merit of rules versus discretion in macroeconomic policies. The currency board, in its pure form, is a rule-based system. However, as we shall see in this paper, the Hong Kong Monetary Authority (HKMA), the de facto central bank of Hong Kong, had for some time been deviating from the rules by introducing a number of new tools of intervention. However, the trend of greater reliance on discretion was interrupted toward the end of the Asian financial turmoil in 1998, when the HKMA reverted to the rule-based system again. These changes have, in effect, created natural experiments for us to study the implications of rules versus discretion. The main objective of this paper is to test whether the currency board was more credible under the rule-based regimes or under the discretion regime.

The next section discusses the historical background of Hong Kong's currency board, emphasizing the events during the financial crisis. It shows that the currency board has gone through three regimes as demarcated by the choice of rules versus discretion. Section 7.3 develops and implements empirical tests on the credibility of the currency board under different regimes and interprets our findings. Section 7.4 discusses the effect of rules and discretion on the credibility of Hong Kong's currency board system from the point of view of delegation of functions and the incentive to intervene. The final section concludes.

7.2   An Event Analysis

In this section we briefly outline the history of Hong Kong's currency board. As we shall see, it has not been a static institution. In fact, from October 1983 to the present, the currency board has gone through three major phases: (a) a rule-bound regime, (b) a discretion regime, and (c) a deemphasis of discretion and a return to a rule-based regime with a confidence booster. The primary difference between *rule* and *discretion* is that the former entails commitments about future policy and thus predictability

---

2. See Kwan and Lui (1999) for an early attempt to implement econometric estimations of the implications of the currency board.

of policy measures, whereas the latter exhibits a lack of commitment and a lower degree of predictability. We shall use this defining characteristic to identify the periods of the three regimes. Our empirical analysis in the next section will demonstrate that the currency board's credibility varied significantly across these regimes.

Hong Kong's first currency board was introduced in 1935 when the government decided to abandon the silver standard. From then to 1967, with the exception of four years of interruption during World War II, the Hong Kong dollar was pegged to the pound sterling at the rate of sixteen to one. Before issuing bank notes of sixteen Hong Kong dollars, the authorized note-issuing private banks were obligated to pay the Exchange Fund one pound to purchase the Certificate of Indebtedness (CI). The exchange rate appreciated over time to HK$14.55 per pound sterling by 1967. From 1972 to 1974, the Hong Kong dollar was repegged to the U.S. dollar. After the collapse of the Bretton Woods system, the government decided to let the currency float on 25 November 1974. However, the financial crises caused by anxieties over the future of Hong Kong led to great volatility and considerable downward pressure on the Hong Kong dollar. Eventually, on 17 October 1983, the government reestablished the currency board system, but this time the Hong Kong dollar was pegged to the U.S. dollar at the fixed rate of 7.8, and the peg continues to this day.[3]

In other words, the government promised to buy bank notes at the rate of 7.8 per U.S. dollar. However, despite this promise, currency arbitrage through the purchase and sale of bank notes has played little role in locking the spot rate in the market at or near parity. Instead, proximity of the actual spot rate to the parity depends mostly on the HKMA's active intervention in the spot market and capital flows engendered by the interest rate arbitrage.

During the initial period after the peg's reestablishment, the government by and large was following the fixed rules of the currency board passively, maintaining the stability of the spot rate in the foreign exchange market. In fact, there is no evidence to suggest that the government was pursuing any active monetary policy at the time. A fundamental change in policy took place when the government began to initiate a series of institutional changes. In 1988 some new accounting arrangements, which in effect made open market operations possible, were introduced. Exchange fund bills similar to short-term U.S. Treasury bills have been issued since March 1990. A liquidity adjustment facility (LAF) was also opened in 1990 to provide liquidity to banks, and the HKMA was active in using the LAF. With the new tools in hand, the HKMA acquired some central bank power to intervene in Hong Kong's money market.

The currency board is supposed to be a rule-based monetary system.

---

3. For more details of the history of Hong Kong's currency board, see Nugee (1995) and Kwan and Lui (1999).

The gradual "dilution" of the rules, noted by Schwartz (1993), means greater reliance on discretion. The most significant case that illustrates the exercise of discretion is the change in HKMA's line of defense of the spot rate from 7.8 to 7.75. Even though the official parity is 7.8, beginning in 1992 the HKMA chose a first-line defense at 7.75 (i.e., it would intervene at 7.75 instead of 7.8, to give it a greater sense of security). Figure 7.1 shows that beginning around April 1992 the exchange rate could rarely move above the 7.75 level. However, this has created a new problem. Whenever the exchange rate rose above 7.75, the market could fear that the HKMA would choose not to defend the peg. To restore confidence, the HKMA was forced to intervene at 7.75. In a sense, the HKMA has become the slave of its own discretion. The rationale for a first-line defense is also dubious. If the HKMA fails to maintain the defense of 7.75, it is doubtful that it will be able to maintain the ultimate defense of 7.8. An even more serious implication of greater reliance on discretion is the erosion of the public's belief that the HKMA will always keep the peg. Because it had significantly deviated from the passive rules of the currency board, there would be no guarantee that it would not abandon the peg altogether.

One of our objectives is to test whether discretion is better than rules in strengthening the credibility of currency board. We use 1 April 1992 as a dividing line between a rule-bound regime ("regime 1") and a new regime in which active discretionary interventions were pursued ("regime 2"). As noted earlier, the dilution of rules actually began in 1988. However, the availability of new intervention tools does not necessarily mean that the HKMA had abandoned the rule-based regime. Moreover, it took time for the other policy instruments such as the exchange fund bills and the LAF to come into being and for the market to be convinced that the HKMA was indeed moving towards the discretion regime. We have chosen 1992,

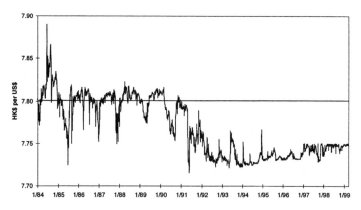

Fig. 7.1   Spot exchange rate, 1 November 1983 to 21 April 1999.

rather than 1988, as the demarcation line, because to us, the strategy of introducing a first-line defense was a clear indication that the HKMA had deviated from an old rule. In implementing the empirical tests, we have also experimented with 1988 as the dividing line between regimes 1 and 2. See section 7.3 for more details.

One may now raise a legitimate question: Is the adoption of a first-line defense a bad rule, instead of the exercise of discretion? We believe it is discretion because despite its actual behavior in the foreign exchange market, the HKMA never made any explicit commitment to the exchange rate of 7.75 for any specified length of time. In addition, its sudden decision effectively to close down the LAF on 23 October 1997 was always an element of its discretion, even though the HKMA never exercised it until that particular date when the Hong Kong dollar came under a major attack. A more detailed description of what happened on that day will be presented later. Again, there was no commitment about the supply of short-term liquidity to facilitate interbank clearing until the beginning of regime 3 (defined in the following paragraph). Nevertheless, one can still raise the question: Was the HKMA's management of the interbank clearing balance during regime 2 the adoption of a bad rule, perhaps due to a lack of understanding of the operation of the interbank clearing system? As will be seen in section 7.5, we leave the question open.

Regime 2 lasted until 7 September 1998, from which time there was a deemphasis of discretion and a return to a rule-based regime, but with new rules ("regime 3"). These were adopted in the midst of the Asian financial turmoil. Until early September 1998, the HKMA relied on interest rate arbitrage (the so-called automatic adjustment mechanism or autopiloting) to defend the Hong Kong dollar. It posited that when there was capital outflow, the resulting drain in Hong Kong dollar liquidity would push up the latter's interest rate, which at a sufficiently high level would restore stability in the exchange rate by attracting capital to return. An interest rate hike was seen as a necessary evil in the Hong Kong dollar's defense against speculation. Although the interest rate arbitrage argument makes intuitive sense, its ineffectiveness as a deliberate policy tool against currency speculation cannot be well understood without knowing the implications of the real-time gross settlement (RTGS) system in conjunction with the HKMA's actions on 23 October 1997, which was known as Black Thursday in Hong Kong.

On 9 December 1996 the HKMA introduced a new interbank payment system, the RTGS.[4] The aggregate balance of the banking system, which can be regarded as the lubricant for interbank settlements, was subject to what the HKMA regarded as an inescapable monetary rule of a currency board. Because the RTGS was very efficient, the aggregate balance typi-

---

4. For details of the RTGS, see Hong Kong Monetary Authority (1998b).

cally stayed at a low level of around roughly HK$2 billion. As the HKMA has recognized, the small size of the balance was conducive to high interest rate volatility. In other words, even a minor capital outflow could cause the interest rate to shoot up significantly under the said monetary rule. To illustrate the mechanics of how the interest rate would rise following a very minor capital outflow, we use the following example.

Suppose that the aggregate balance is equal to HK$2 billion, but there is a capital outflow of HK$3 billion. The banks' clients instruct the banks to sell this amount of Hong Kong dollars for, say, U.S. dollars. If the U.S. dollars cannot be purchased within the banking system, then the banks must buy from the HKMA, and they can do so *only* by using the deposits in their clearing accounts. If a bank does not have enough money in its clearing balance for purchasing the U.S. dollars ordered by its clients, it will have to borrow from the clearing balances of other banks. However, because the total outflow of capital exceeds the aggregate balance, the banks simply cannot settle their committed transactions, and thus the interest rate may rise without limit. This is the case despite the banks' receipt of Hong Kong dollars from their clients' accounts. In fact, even Hong Kong dollar bank notes cannot be used to square their settlement accounts.

This process results from HKMA's deliberate adherence to what it had regarded as an essential monetary rule of a currency board. It believed that it was obliged to drain liquidity from Hong Kong's money market by the same amount as the capital outflow, and it chose to drain it directly from the aggregate balance that serves as the lubricant of the interbank settlement system. After buying Hong Kong dollars in the aggregate balance, the HKMA could delay the injection of Hong Kong dollar liquidity back into the system. In such a situation, the aggregate balance would shrink in size until the interest rate was squeezed up to such an extent that the banks would suffer a smaller loss by using their foreign currency to buy back the Hong Kong dollars from the HKMA to square their accounts. However, since these Hong Kong dollars would not be delivered until one or two days later, the banks still had to borrow from the HKMA at any interest rate set by the latter for clearing purposes.

There was also a second kind of discretion that could raise the interest rate. On the morning of 23 October 1997 the HKMA sent a surprising memorandum to all the licensed banks in Hong Kong, warning them that they might have to pay penalty interest rates if they used the LAF repeatedly. Receiving this memo after several days of volatile interest rates, the banks began to panic. There were even rumors that the penalty rate could be as high as 1,000 percent. The interbank interest rate shot up. At its peak, the rate was close to 300 percent.

Thus, the monetary system in Hong Kong was such that the interest rate was very sensitive to capital flows. In addition, the HKMA might choose to magnify interest rate volatility through such discretionary measures as changing the time of liquidity injection or imposing a penalty interest rate. Until early September 1998, the HKMA's policy making was guided by a belief that high interest was a necessary instrument for dealing with speculative attacks against the Hong Kong dollar. Moreover, a reduction in interest rate volatility was seen as incompatible with the goal of exchange rate stability. It was only after severe public criticism and heavy market pressure during the financial crisis that the HKMA gradually abandoned its high interest rate defense strategy. There are several reasons for the change in its position.

First, a high interest rate was no longer an effective way to deter or punish speculators. Knowing that a small run on the Hong Kong dollar could trigger the monetary mechanism to push up the interest rate, which could be further amplified by the discretion of the HKMA, speculators could either short the Hong Kong dollar forward or short the stock futures index before launching an attack on the spot market of the Hong Kong dollar. Losses in the spot market could easily be outweighed by profits from the currency forward and stock futures if speculators engaged in this double or even triple play.[5]

Second, the volatile high interest rate had caused a serious credit crunch in the banking system. In fact, Hong Kong's real GDP experienced a 5 percent decline in 1998, mainly as a result of the credit crunch. As the harmful effects persisted, people could question the wisdom of keeping the currency board, thus creating further pressure on the currency.

Third, the high interest rate apparently had not led to the interest arbitrage expected by the HKMA. The automatic adjustment mechanism would work well only if people had enough confidence in the Hong Kong dollar. Although Hong Kong's interest rate had been persistently higher than that of the U.S. dollar after the onset of the financial crisis, arbitrage had not occurred. Figure 7.2 highlights such prolonged interest differentials between the one-month Hong Kong Interbank Offered Rate (HIBOR), and the London Interbank Offered Rate (LIBOR) for U.S. dollar, during the crisis period. A plausible explanation is that the interest rate differential represented a risk premium for holding the Hong Kong dollar. If confidence deteriorated, the risk premium, and consequently the interest differential, would simply go up without initiating a process of arbitrage. To restore proper functioning of the automatic adjustment mechanism, the perceived risk of the peg must be lowered.

The devaluation risk of the Hong Kong dollar during the Asian financial crisis, as perceived by the foreign exchange market and measured by the currency's forward premium, indicates a break from the past. More precisely, the forward premium was substantially higher than it was in the

---

5. See Cheng and Lui (1998) and Chan and Kwan (1998) for more detailed discussions.

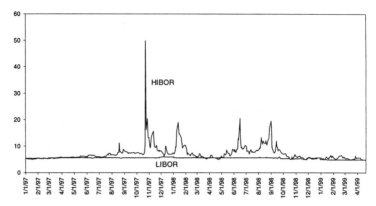

Fig. 7.2   One-month HIBOR and LIBOR, 1 January 1997 to 21 April 1999.

previous period. As reported in Cheng, Kwan, and Lui (1999), as the Hong Kong dollar came under a major speculative attack against the background of the New Taiwan dollar's float, the annualized forward premium shot up to 15 percent on 23 October 1997 (Black Thursday). The forward premium reached 24 percent in the period 12–20 January 1998, when the currency came under another major attack. In the next two attacks in June and August 1998, the forward premium was 6–7.4 percent during 11–19 June and 10 percent between 26 August and 2 September.

Note that the series of speculative attacks against the Hong Kong dollar took place when Hong Kong's fundamental variables were neither very bad nor deteriorating. First, its foreign reserves continued to rise up to October 1997, when a major currency attack occurred. Even with a loss of some reserves between February and October 1998, Hong Kong's foreign reserves ranked the third largest in the world, only after Japan and China at the end of November 1998 (at US$88.6 billion). Second, the unemployment rate in Hong Kong before the Hong Kong dollar crisis (at about 2.5 percent) was low even by historical standards. Thus, there was no pressure from the employment front to suggest a devaluation of the Hong Kong dollar to reduce unemployment. There was indeed deterioration in Hong Kong's international competitiveness as measured by its real exchange rate and by its trade balance (goods and services, but not including investment income). It might potentially be a weak fundamental variable, but the magnitude of the attacks suggests that other factors were at work.

The relationship between the exchange rate of the Hong Kong dollar and the interest rate differential (HIBOR − LIBOR) can be captured by figure 7.3. Line AB denotes the situation when the currency board is completely credible. The exchange rate is exactly 7.8 when the difference between HIBOR and LIBOR is zero. An increase in the difference will make the Hong Kong dollar stronger. In other words, autopiloting works. If con-

Exchange Rate (HK$/US$)

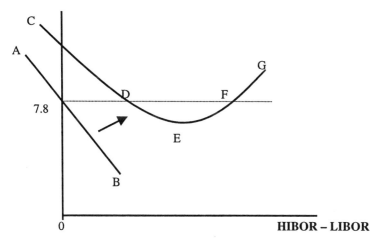

Fig. 7.3   Relationship between exchange rate and interest rate differential

fidence in the Hong Kong dollar deteriorates, the curve moves to CEG. A higher interest rate differential is needed to compensate the risk of holding the Hong Kong dollar or to maintain exchange rate stability (point D). That the HKMA had deviated from the fixed rules of the currency board made its commitment to the peg much less credible. The problem could be worsened if the interest rate were significantly pushed up due to cornering of the market or discretionary measures of the HKMA. The economic and political costs of a very high interest rate could lead more people to believe that the peg would not be sustainable, which would weaken the Hong Kong dollar. This is represented by the positively sloping curve EFG in figure 7.3. Interest rate arbitrage does not work in this case. An increase in the interest rate under such conditions is not conducive to strengthening the Hong Kong dollar.

Believing that confidence was the key to exchange rate and interest rate stability, Alex Chan and Naifu Chen, proposed the issuance of Hong Kong dollar put options, a rule-based exchange rate insurance scheme, as an alternative mechanism of defending the Hong Kong dollar as early as November 1997.[6] After a prolonged public debate, the HKMA finally implemented (on 7 September 1998) some technical measures that were analytically equivalent to the put options. The main features of these measures are as follows.

First, the HKMA provided a clear undertaking to all licensed banks in

6. See Chan and Chen (1999); Cheng, Kwan, and Lui (1999); and Lui, Cheng, and Kwan (2000) for more detailed discussions of the proposal of put options.

Hong Kong to convert Hong Kong dollars in their clearing accounts into U.S. dollars at the fixed exchange rate of HK$7.75 per US$1.

Second, a discount window was established to replace the LAF. Banks can now use the exchange fund bills and notes, which are similar to U.S. Treasury bills, as collateral to borrow overnight Hong Kong dollars from the HKMA. The interest rate of the discount window, called the base rate, is determined by a formula that reflects influences of the HIBOR and the federal fund rate.

Third, on 14 September 1998, due to market pressure, the HKMA introduced a time element into the convertibility undertaking. It specified clearly that within the following six months, the convertibility undertaking would be at the rate of 7.75. Later, the HKMA also announced that this rate would be gradually changed to 7.8 over a period of 500 days.

These elements imply that banks can increase liquidity in their clearing accounts up to an amount equal to the value of the exchange fund bills and notes that they own. Because the convertibility undertaking is applicable to the clearing balances, it is potentially also applicable to all exchange fund bills and notes. Previously, the monetary base consisted of coins in circulation and CI, which backed up the bank notes. Now it includes also the aggregate balance and the outstanding exchange fund bills and notes held by banks. As of the end of 1998, CI and coins amounted to around HK$92 billion, aggregate balance HK$2.5 billion, and outstanding exchange fund bills and notes HK$81 billion (Hong Kong Monetary Authority 1998a). Thus, the monetary base has almost doubled. If all the outstanding exchange fund bills and notes are used as collateral to borrow liquidity, the new aggregate balance can rise from HK$2.5 billion to more than HK$80 billion.

These changes have a number of implications. First, when an attack occurs and capital outflow exceeds the original aggregate balance, banks can restore the aggregate balance for clearing purposes by using the exchange fund bills and notes. The newly established discount window and its associated base rate were an explicit commitment on the part of the HKMA. As a result, short-term liquidity for the purpose of interbank clearing has become predictable. Unlike in the past, relatively small capital outflow is now less likely to cause big interest rate hikes. Second, the exchange fund bills and notes can be interpreted as vehicles embodying the Hong Kong dollar put option.[7] Banks can use them as collateral to borrow from the HKMA to augment their balance, which is covered by the convertibility undertaking. Third, the convertibility undertaking is equivalent to a Hong Kong dollar put option because Hong Kong's common law tradition implies that the undertaking is legally binding. If the HKMA

---

7. Professor Merton Miller, who testified at Hong Kong's Legislative Council in November 1998, also shared this view. See Miller (1998).

abandons the peg, it would be liable to compensate the losses of those who have held the exchange fund bills and notes, which are assets denominated in Hong Kong dollars. In other words, the HKMA has put its money where its mouth is. It has signaled to the market that it has the incentive to follow the fixed rules of the currency board.

Thus, 7 September 1998 can be regarded as the dividing line between regimes 2 and 3. Before this date, the fixed rules of a currency board had been substantially diluted by discretionary measures. The HKMA actively pursued the first line of defense by using its intervention tools without making any commitment to its new target exchange rate. It also artificially amplified interest rate volatility by draining liquidity directly from the RTGS's aggregate balance and imposing penalty interest rates on users of the LAF. After that date, the HKMA established a discount window whose base rate was determined by an explicit formula and both adopted a plan to abandon the first line of defense gradually by moving the central parity of the fixed exchange rate back to the 7.8 over a 500-day period and clarified the nature of its convertibility undertaking. Under these new institutional arrangements, it would be much harder for the HKMA to manipulate the interest rate.

In short, the currency board in Hong Kong, after its readoption in 1983, has experienced three different regimes: from a rule-bound regime to a discretion regime, and then back to a rule-bound regime again. These changes in regimes can be regarded as natural experiments that provide us with an opportunity to test the relative merit of rules versus discretion. The following section implements empirical tests and interprets the results.

7.3   Is Hong Kong's Currency Board a Credible Target Zone?

Our strategy is to infer from financial market data the perceived credibility of the currency board arrangement across the three regimes. In this paper we rely mainly on the forward premium (the annualized percentage deviation of the forward exchange rate from the spot exchange rate) for such a purpose, and the interested reader is referred to Lui, Cheng, and Kwan (2000) for the analysis using HIBOR − LIBOR interest differentials. More precisely, we extract from the forward premium data the implicit risk of devaluation as perceived by the foreign exchange market, using the drift adjustment method developed in the target zone literature. Given the devaluation risk, we can calculate the implicit ex ante probability of devaluation conditional on a given size of realignment. Before we proceed, however, we should emphasize that contrary to the belief of some HKMA officials, the apparent stability of the spot exchange rate is by itself *not* proof of the peg's future credibility. The forward premium, however, does capture the market's expectation of the exchange rate's risk of devaluation.

Let s_t and c_t be the natural logarithms of the spot exchange rate and the central parity, respectively. Then one can write down an identity $s_t \equiv c_t + x_t$, where x_t is by construction the spot rate's (log) deviation from the central parity, or the movement of the exchange rate within the target zone. Let $\Delta c_{t+\tau} = c_{t+\tau} - c_t$ and the average rate of realignment from time t to $t + \tau$ be $\Delta c_{t+\tau}/\tau dt$, and similarly for s_t and x_t. It follows from the identity that

$$(1) \qquad E_t\left[\frac{\Delta c_{t+\tau}}{\tau dt}\right] \equiv E_t\left[\frac{\Delta s_{t+\tau}}{\tau dt}\right] - E_t\left[\frac{\Delta x_{t+\tau}}{\tau dt}\right].$$

The left-hand side in equation (1) is the expected rate of change of the central parity, or the implicit risk of devaluation (revaluation if negative) as perceived by the foreign exchange market, a measure of the credibility of the target zone. It can be recovered from observed data by estimating the two expected rates on the right-hand side in equation (1). First, the expected rate of total depreciation, $E_t\Delta s_{t+\tau}/\tau dt$, is identified with the observed forward premium by appealing to covered interest parity. Second, the expected rate of drift within the target zone, $E_t\Delta x_{t+\tau}/\tau dt$, is estimated by the linear projection of $\Delta x_{t+\tau}/\tau dt$ on a vector of state variables z_t, with the projection standard errors computed from a Newey-West heteroscedasticity autocorrelation consistent matrix of τ lags:

$$(2) \qquad \frac{\Delta x_{t+\tau}}{\tau dt} = z_t'\beta + \varepsilon_{t+\tau}.$$

The state variable vector z_t includes an orthogonal cubic polynomial in x_t, the current forward premium of maturity τ, and a measure of the slope of the yield curve (the difference between twelve-month and one-month forward premium). Our choice of state variables is based on the theoretical target zone literature. Svensson (1991) shows that the expected rate of drift is a negatively sloped nonlinear function of x_t, a well-known property of a credible target zone (Krugman, 1991). We specify a cubic polynomial to capture the possible nonlinearity. The use of orthogonal polynomials, as opposed to simple polynomials, lessens the extent of multicollinearity in the empirical estimation. The remaining two state variables are meant to capture the influence of stochastic devaluation risk on expected exchange rate movements, an extension of the basic target zone model suggested by Bertola and Svensson (1993). As in previous literature (e.g., Lindberg, Soderlind, and Svensson 1993; Lindberg and Soderlind 1994; Rose and Svensson 1994; Svensson 1993), we include the forward premium or the domestic and foreign interest rate differential as a state variable. In addition, we follow Bekaert and Gray's (1998) empirical target zone model by including the forward premium counterpart of the slope of the yield curve to capture the temporal profile of devaluation risk.

The projection equation (2) is run separately for the three policy regimes identified in section 7.2 for the one-month and three-month horizons. The Chow test indicates that there have been significant structural changes across the three regimes, which provides empirical support to our three-regime demarcation scheme. Besides providing an estimate of the expected drift, the projection equations are of interest in their own right. The estimation results reported in tables 7.1 and 7.2 lead to the following conclusions.

First, consider the marginal relationship between the expected drift and the current exchange rate position x_t. In all the linear specifications in which the quadratic and cubic term are excluded, the x_t coefficients are statistically significant and negative, implying that exchange rate movements are mean reverting within the target zone, holding constant the level of devaluation risk proxied by the two remaining state variables. We have also found that omitting the two devaluation risk proxies from the regression weakens the mean-reverting property considerably. Taken together our empirical finding supports the Bertola and Svensson (1993) model with exogenous stochastic devaluation risk, which shifts up and down the negative relationship between the expected drift and x_t.

The evidence for nonlinear mean reversion, a property emphasized in Krugman's (1991) fully credible target zone model, is mixed, however. Nonlinear mean reversion shows up in regimes 1 and 3 in the one-month case, and also in regime 3 in the three-month case, as indicated by the small p-values of Wald tests reported in the rows titled "Exclude P_2 and P_3." Moreover, the sign pattern of the polynomial coefficients indicates that the nonlinearity is not necessarily of the famous S-shaped (smooth pasting) property suggested in fully credible target zone models.

Finally, the coefficients of the two devaluation risk proxies—current forward premium and yield curve slope—exhibit a pattern of cyclical sign reversal across regimes. In regime 1, the two coefficients are significantly negative, suggesting that during the rule-bound period the automatic adjustment mechanism worked well and the peg was most credible. The two coefficients become significantly positive in regime 2, which signals the absence of interest arbitrage and a lack of credibility. Contrary to its own belief, the HKMA had in fact made the currency board less credible, after acquiring all the intervention tools during the discretion period. In regime 3, the two coefficients revert back to the negative zone in most cases, indicating that the board had regained credibility after returning to a rule-bound regime.

As discussed in section 7.2, the transition from the rule-based regime 1 to the discretionary regime 2 was a gradual process. We have argued that it is more reasonable to choose 1992, rather than 1988, as the demarcation line between the two regimes. To test the robustness of the empirical results, we also have performed the same econometric analysis reported in

Table 7.1   Projection Equations (1-month)

	Regime 1		Regime 2		Regime 3	
constant	-0.4399	-0.1238	-0.7131	-0.9980	1.1060	1.1631
	(-2.3576)	(-0.2303)	(-4.3807)	(-3.6382)	(5.4595)	(4.9971)
$P_1(x)$	-4.1977	-6.1672	-1.5886	-2.2604	-0.7686	-0.8879
	(-4.8723)	(-5.7667)	(-5.9402)	(-4.0145)	(-7.5402)	(-10.289)
$P_2(x)$		0.7872		-0.8093		0.1629
		(0.6729)		(-1.5405)		(2.5795)
$P_3(x)$		-3.0409		-0.2892		-0.0270
		(-3.3173)		(-0.8976)		(-0.2489)
1-month forward premium	-0.8020	-0.8561	0.1606	0.1506	0.0164	0.0094
	(-3.4089)	(-3.6923)	(2.9684)	(2.6877)	(0.3829)	(0.2237)
Yield curve slope	-1.1507	-1.1677	0.2213	0.2097	-0.3803	-0.3854
	(-3.0927)	(-3.2887)	(2.5070)	(2.403)	(-3.2233)	(-2.9885)
R^2	0.17	0.20	0.24	0.25	0.58	0.58
Exclude P_2 and P_3		[0.0014]		[0.2967]		[0.0070]
Sample size	2174	2174	1656	1656	141	141

Notes: t-values are in parentheses. Dependent variable $= (x_{t+\tau} - x_t)/\tau dt$, $dt = 1/261$, $\tau = 22$ and 65 (business) days corresponding to one-month and three-month maturities, respectively. $x_t =$ spot exchange rate (as percentage deviation from parity). Within a regime of T days, the dependent variable is defined for $t = 1, 2, \ldots, T - \tau$; i.e., the projection is strictly within regime. Regime 1 = 1983:11:1 to 1992:3:31; Regime 2 = 1992:4:1 to 1998:9:6; and Regime 3 = 1998:9:7 to 1999:4:21, excluding holidays. $P_1(x)$, $P_2(x)$ and $P_3(x)$ are Legendre orthogonal polynomials up to degree 3, with x rescaled to $[-1, 1]$. They are generated by the three-term recurrence relation: $(n + 1)P_{n+1}(x) = (2n + 1)xP_n(x) - nP_{n-1}(x)$, $P_0 = 1$, $P_1 = x$. See Davis and Rabinowitz (1984, p. 34). "Yield curve slope" is the differential between twelve-month and one-month forward premium. "Exclude P_2 and P_3" reports the χ^2 (2) p-value (in squared brackets) from Wald tests for the joint hypothesis of excluding $P_2(x)$ and $P_3(x)$. Evidence of nonlinearity is indicated by a small p-value. All equations are estimated by ordinary least squares with Newey-West covariance matrix of τ lags.

Table 7.2   Projection Equations (3-month)

	Regime 1	Regime 2	Regime 3
constant	-0.2782	-0.4145	-0.5361	0.3110	0.3483
	(2.0050)	(-4.2542)	(-6.4145)	(17.925)	(12.445)
$P_1(x)$	-2.3650	-0.9716	-1.2357	-0.2878	-0.2994
	(-6.0464)	(-5.5789)	(-8.4755)	(-39.782)	(-47.185)
$P_2(x)$	0.9354		-0.3293		0.0428
	(1.9154)		(-2.0863)		(4.0333)
$P_3(x)$	0.0137		-0.0698		0.0368
	(0.0277)		(-0.5068)		(1.5445)
3-month forward premium	-0.3402	0.0971	0.0938	-0.0258	-0.0326
	(-3.5188)	(4.5874)	(4.7023)	(-5.0853)	(-7.1933)
Yield curve slope	-0.2964	0.0651	0.0637	-0.0368	-0.0456
	(-2.4026)	(2.5309)	(2.5866)	(-3.1494)	(-3.5304)
R^2	0.29	0.43	0.44	0.89	0.91
Exclude P_2 and P_3	[0.1496]		[0.1022]		[0.0001]
Sample size	2131	1613	1613	98	98

Note: See table 7.1.

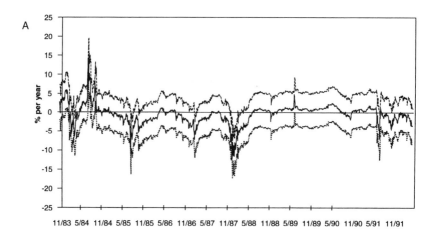

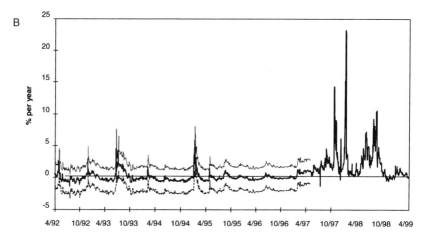

Fig. 7.4   One-month devaluation risk and 2–standard deviation confidence bands:
A, **1 November 1983 to 31 March 1992;** *B,* **1 April 1992 to 21 April 1999;** *C,* **1**
May 1997 to 21 April 1999; *D,* **1 July 1998 to 21 April 1999.**

tables 7.1 and 7.2 on data using 1988 as the dividing line. The general results remain the same, although there is a slight drop in statistical significance.[8]

Panel A of figure 7.4 depicts the estimated one-month devaluation risk together with 2–standard deviation confidence bands for regime 1. The devaluation risk is statistically significant at the 5 percent level if zero lies outside of the bands. We see that most of the time the devaluation risk was not significant, except for a few short intervals during which the deval-

---

8. For lack of space, we do not report details of these results, which are available upon request.

C

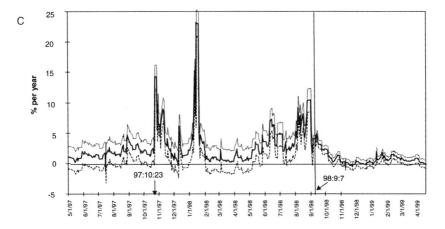

D

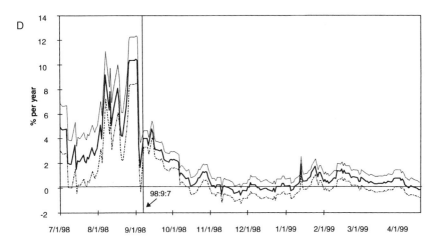

Fig. 7.4   (cont.)

uation risk was significantly different from zero. This shows that the peg was generally credible in the rule-bound regime. In panel B of figure 7.4 we see that the peg had been under occasional devaluation pressure even before the currency crisis period. The crisis period was dramatized by the skyrocketing devaluation risk unseen before, as is shown in panels A and B of figure 7.4. The rapid recovery of credibility after the return to a rule-based currency board in regime 3 was equally dramatic (panel D of figure 7.4): The devaluation risk dropped by half overnight after the announcement on 5 September 1998 and then gradually became insignificant.

The last result can be interpreted from another perspective. During the financial crisis, many people believed that there was a so-called Asian risk premium because Hong Kong was regarded as part of a troubled region.

The dramatic restoration of market confidence in the peg after the return to the rule-based system is not supportive of this assertion. Had a general Asian risk premium existed in Hong Kong, we could hardly witness its disappearance in the matter of just a few days after the announcement of a new policy. Even if one insists on the existence of such a premium in Hong Kong, the evidence in panel D of figure 7.4 can at most allow us to make two different but related interpretations. First, the Asian risk premium was not significant in Hong Kong. Second, Hong Kong could be easily differentiated from the rest of Asia if the HKMA had chosen the rule-based approach, an argument made by some researchers (see Cheng and Lui 1998).

Given an estimate of the devaluation risk, we can recover the implicit probability of devaluation perceived by the market. Let p_t^τ be the probability at time t of a realignment of random size $\Delta c_{t+\tau}$ during the period from time t to $t + \tau$. The expected change in central parity (expected devaluation) can be written as

$$(3) \qquad E_t[\Delta c_{t+\tau}] = (1 - p_t^\tau)0 + p_t^\tau E_t[\Delta c_{t+\tau} | realignment]$$

$$= p_t^\tau E_t[\Delta c_{t+\tau} | realignment].$$

In terms of rate of changes, equation (3) can be rewritten as

$$(4) \qquad E_t\left[\frac{\Delta c_{t+\tau}}{\tau dt}\right] = v_t^\tau E_t[\Delta c_{t+\tau} | realignment],$$

where $v_t^\tau \equiv p_t^\tau / \tau dt$ is by definition the expected average frequency of realignment during the period from time t to $t + \tau$. To illustrate how the devaluation probability can be calculated, suppose that the three-month devaluation risk is 7 percent and the expected devaluation size is 5 percent. In annual terms, $\tau dt = 1/4$ year. Using equation (4), $v_t^\tau = 7/5 = 1.4$, and $p_t^\tau = 1.4/4 = 0.35$. Panel A of figure 7.5 shows the probabilities that the Hong Kong dollar would be devalued by 5 percent within one month and three months throughout the crisis period up to the end of our sample. As can be expected from theory, the probability of devaluation of the same magnitude within a given period is higher the longer the period. Among other things, the figure reveals that the probability of devaluation was highest during January 1998. For instance, the market's predicted probability that the Hong Kong dollar would devalue by 5 percent within three months was as high as 60 percent. An equivalent interpretation is that the probability of a 15 percent devaluation within three months would be 20 percent. Judged by the extent of devaluation by the New Taiwan dollar and Singapore's dollar around that time, a 10–20 percent chance of devaluation in three months was certainly not an unreasonable expectation.

In any event, regardless of the probable size of devaluation in the event of a depegging of the Hong Kong dollar, panel B of figure 7.5 highlights

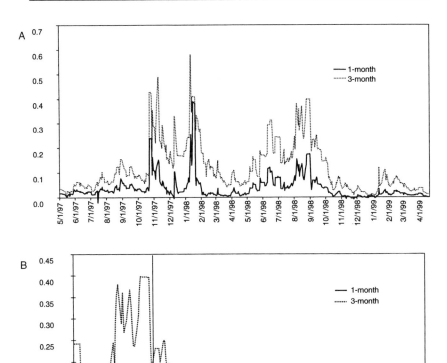

Fig. 7.5   Ex ante devaluation probability (conditional on devaluation size = 5 percent): *A*, 1 May 1997 to 1 April 1999; *B*, 1 July 1998 to 1 April 1999.

the rapid drop in devaluation probability soon after the beginning of regime 3. The following events are particularly revealing: the dramatic fall in probability after the announcement on 5 September of a new regime, the spike before the 14 September clarification of the convertibility undertaking, and the immediate calming in market sentiments right after the clarification.

The relationship between the forward premium and the current position of the exchange rate reveals further information about the credibility of a target zone. As is shown by Bartolini and Bodnar (1992), the relationship can exhibit a variety of shapes depending on the monetary authority's credibility and its intervention policies. If the system is fully credible, then there must be a negative relationship between the forward premium and the deviation of the spot rate from its parity. Low credibility can invert the relationship into a positive one, and asymmetric credibility (i.e., the monetary authority is more credible in preventing appreciation than depreciation) can generate a bimodal pattern.

Figure 7.6 reports scatter plots of one-month forward premium against the spot exchange rate (as percentage deviation from parity). The smooth curve is obtained by fitting a fifth-order orthogonal polynomial, which is flexible enough to accommodate the many shapes suggested by Bartolini and Bodnar (1992). The U-shape pattern in panel A of figure 7.6 is due mainly to the data points of the first year (November 1983 to December 1984), which we highlight by triangles. This is the first year of the newly established currency board, during which the Sino-British negotiation over Hong Kong's future was in full swing and the market was understandably skeptical about the resolve of the monetary authority. After the first year the board started to gain credibility, as indicated by the cloud of points in the northwest and southeast quadrants.

The bimodal curve in panel B of figure 7.6 matches exactly the case of asymmetric credibility and discrete intervention analyzed by Bartolini and Bodnar (1992, fig. 10, p. 388). It can be seen that the hump in the northeast quadrant is due mainly to observations of the crisis period (1 May 1997 to 5 September 1998), whereas the lower branch of the curve is due to the pre- and postcrisis observations. In other words, the crisis works like a natural experiment that provides the observations crucial for us to identify the complete curve, including the upper branch in the northeast quadrant. This empirical pattern suggests that the seeming stability of the discretion regime before the crisis (see figures 7.1 and panel B of 7.4) was not the result of more intervention power as claimed by HKMA; rather, it was because the system had not yet been subject to a shock large enough.

7.4   Rules versus Discretion: Institutions and Incentives for Intervention

One may question the previous interpretation of results, namely that the lower credibility of the currency board during regime 2 was a result of the HKMA's exercise of discretion. An alternative hypothesis is that regime 2 happened to have included a major crisis—namely, the Asian financial crisis. In other words, if a major crisis were to occur during regime 1, then the system would have suffered a similar credibility problem.

There are three answers to the above criticism. First, the demarcation of regimes adopted in the above sections was not based on the appearance of crisis. Rather, it was based on clear changes in institutional arrangements, including the creation of the HKMA, the new accounting arrangements, the issue of exchange fund bills, the adoption of the first line defense, and the deemphasis of discretion and the reversion to rules.

Second, during regime 1 there was also a major crisis in confidence—namely, the Tiananmen Square incident on 4 June 1989. Was the shock to

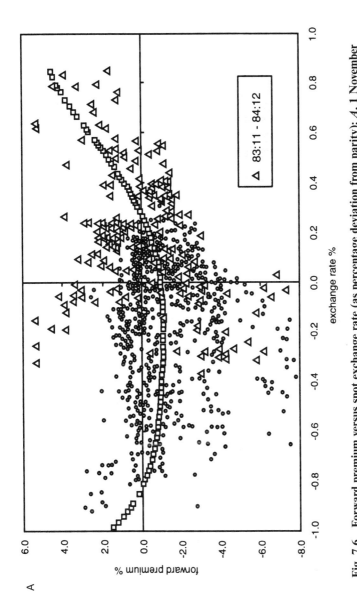

Fig. 7.6 Forward premium versus spot exchange rate (as percentage deviation from parity): *A*, 1 November 1983 to 31 March 1992; *B*, 1 April 1992 to 21 April 1999.

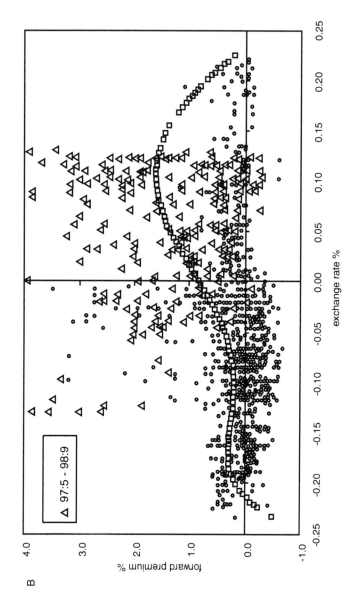

Fig. 7.6 (cont.)

confidence of the Tiananmen incident as bad as the Asian financial crisis? On 5 June 1989 the Hang Seng stock price index fell by 21.75 percent from the previous business day. In comparison, the Hang Seng index fell on 23 October 1997 (Black Thursday) by 10.4 percent from the last business day.[9]

Despite the comparability in the decline of stock and real estates prices, the annualized forward premium during the Tiananmen incident was below 3 percent and lasted only for a brief period. In contrast, the forward premium during the height of the Asian financial crisis was much larger and lasted for a much longer period.

Third, a return to a rule-based system in September 1998 was quickly followed by a substantial reduction in the forward premium, even though the global financial markets continued to be uncertain.

Despite the above arguments, we acknowledge that if the Asian financial crisis is regarded as truly unique, then the counterargument that the Hong Kong currency board's behavior during regime 2 was due to the deterioration in Hong Kong's external environment (i.e., the contagion effect) would remain a viable, though nonrefutable, hypothesis.

Is there any theoretical justification for a more credible system during regime 1? In the currency board literature, there is an emphasis on separating the board from the government. A properly run currency board provides a mechanism that denies the government the option of using the printing press to solve its fiscal problems. The experience of Hong Kong's currency board during regime 1 and regime 2 suggests that the exact institutional arrangements for implementing the currency board also matters. Specifically, their behavior differed under different institutional arrangements.

Before the HKMA took over the interbank clearing function, all commercial banks as well as the HKMA had their transactions cleared at the Hong Kong and Shanghai Banking Corporation (HSBC), a private commercial bank. In those days, when capital flowed out of Hong Kong and interbank liquidity tightened when the exchange fund purchased the corresponding Hong Kong dollars, the HSBC would extend credit to facilitate settlements. That practice not only was consistent with its profit incentive, but also avoided large fluctuations in the interest rate.

The newly created HKMA was not happy with this situation because it felt that a capital outflow should trigger an increase in the interest rate in order to induce capital inflow. Thus, it introduced the new accounting arrangement to exert more effective control over interbank liquidity and

---

9. Real estate property prices adjusted more slowly than did stock prices. Unfortunately, we have not found property price indexes that are more frequent than quarterly indexes. The index for domestic premises for the quarter ending September 1989 dropped by 3 percent from the previous quarter. The same index ending December 1997 dropped by 2.5 percent from the previous quarter.

hence interbank interest rates.[10] Under the RTGS system, the HKMA could engineer interest rate changes when there were capital flows by changing the size of the aggregate balance. In contrast, a private clearing house like the HSBC would only facilitate interbank clearing. Unlike a real central bank, it would not use the clearing function to implement certain monetary operations that central banks regard as essential to managing the monetary system. As we explained in section 7.2, the so-called currency board rule as applied through the aggregate balance of the RTGS system had the unfortunate effect of generating predictable short-term interest rate movements and thus of inadvertently assisting the currency speculators.

Why would the HKMA have managed the aggregate balance the way it did? There are two possible explanations. First, it did not fully understand the implications of its operations. Its complete reversal of its earlier position in September 1998 seems to support this explanation.[11] Second, central banks find it inherently difficult to resist the temptation to preserve and exercise discretion. That is to say, there may be an inherent incentive problem in preserving discretion, the exercise of which may erode credibility. Such an explanation would represent an equilibrium outcome rather than an outcome based on mistakes and misunderstandings. As such, it might be more appealing from certain academic perspectives. However, whether such a theoretical model can be developed is a topic for future research.

7.5   Concluding Remarks

Hong Kong's long history with a currency board has provided us with ample opportunities to better understand the macroeconomic implications of this form of monetary institution. Its experiences in recent years are particularly useful. During the early years after establishing the peg with the U.S. dollar, Hong Kong's currency board was essentially a passive rule-based system. Our empirical results derived using standard methods in the target zone literature show that the automatic adjustment mechanism worked well and that the peg was very credible in this period.

Unfortunately, the ability to intervene in the exchange market appeared to be too much of a temptation for the government. After gradually expanding its set of monetary policy tools, the HKMA engaged in more discretionary intervention in the money and foreign exchange markets. Contrary to the HKMA's own belief, and as the evidence in this paper has

---

10. See Yam (1991) for a detailed description of the mechanics and the rationale behind the arrangement.
11. In the *Report on Financial Market Review* (Hong Kong Special Administrative Region Government 1998), released in April 1998, the HKMA made a rebuttal to the critics of its interest rate hike policy and criticized all alternative policies proposed by the academics.

demonstrated, the expansion of intervention tools and actual intervention made the currency board less, rather than more, credible. The erosion in confidence, as reflected by changes in the forward premium despite an ultrastable spot exchange rate, culminated in even greater intervention during the financial turmoil of 1997 and 1998, including the direct stock market intervention in August 1998.

During the last two weeks of August 1998, the government engaged in an unprecedented and massive buying spree in the stock market, intending to push up the stock index to punish what it called market manipulators. In two weeks the government spent up to US$8.8 billion of Hong Kong's foreign reserves, representing about 9 percent of the total, to fund its HK$118 billion stock purchases. The government has even become the single largest shareholder of HSBC Holdings PLC, one of the world's biggest banks, after acquiring an 8.9 percent stake over these two weeks. The stock market intervention triggered a wave of concern over the government's decision to deviate from its renowned free market policies. Immediately after the stock purchases was over, Standard & Poor's downgraded Hong Kong's credit rating, citing the government's decision to wade into the stock market.

Intense market pressure and public criticism eventually led the HKMA to return to a rule-based regime. The announcement of some new measures, which in substance were equivalent to issuing put options for the Hong Kong dollar, had immediately calmed the market, and the calm remained even during the subsequent Russian debacle and the Long-Term Capital Management (LTCM) event. The empirical analyses show that there had been a dramatic restoration of confidence. The peg once again was a credible system.

This paper suggests that a currency board in actual practice is not necessarily a static institution. Its credibility, however, depends critically on whether the government has a reputation for following fixed rules strictly, rather than relying on discretion. In this sense, this paper may be regarded as an empirical contribution to the debate on rules versus discretion. In the future, we intend to develop a theoretical model to examine the incentive problems of a monetary authority that operates a currency board system.

Finally, we want to point out that we have not dealt with many of the challenges to Hong Kong's currency board. For example, is the U.S. dollar the optimal currency to which the Hong Kong dollar should link? This calls for a cost and benefit analysis along the lines of optimum currency area theory (Mundell, 1961). In the past, because the United States was a much more important importer of Hong Kong goods than other countries such as Japan, business cycles in Hong Kong tended to be synchronized with those in the United States. This eliminated many difficulties associated with a fixed exchange rate. By standard optimum currency area arguments, the cost of losing the exchange rate as an adjustment mechanism can be severe when there are asymmetric shocks affecting the members of a monetary union afflicted with wage and price rigidities, which have no choice but to endure the slow and painful process of internal wage-price adjustment. However, as Hong Kong's economy has become more integrated with China, it is not clear that it will continue to share the same shocks as will the United States.[12] This fact alone may already create pressure on the sustainability of the U.S. dollar peg and raise doubt about the credibility of the currency board system itself.

References

Bartolini, Leonardo, and Gordon M. Bodnar. 1992. Target zones and forward rates in a model with repeated realignments. *Journal of Monetary Economics* 30 (3): 373–408.

Bekaert, Geert, and Stephen F. Gray. 1998. Target zones and exchange rates: An empirical investigation. *Journal of International Economics* 45 (1): 1–35.

Bertola, Giuseppe, and Lars E. Svensson. 1993. Stochastic devaluation risk and the empirical fit of target-zone models. *Review of Economic Studies* 60 (3): 689–712.

Chan, Alex W. H., and Nai-fu Chen. 1999. An intertemporal currency board. *Pacific Economic Review* 4 (2): 215–32.

Chan, Alex W. H., and Yum K. Kwan, eds. 1998. *The Hong Kong dollar crisis revisited* (in Chinese). Hong Kong: Infowide Press.

Cheng, Leonard K., Yum K. Kwan, and Francis T. Lui. 1999. Risk premium, currency board, and attacks on the Hong Kong dollar. Paper presented at American Economic Association Meetings 3–5 January 1999, New York, N.Y.

Cheng, Leonard K., and Francis T. Lui, eds. 1998. *Diagnosis of the Hong Kong dollar crisis* (in Chinese). Hong Kong: Infowide Press.

Davis, Philip, and Philip Rabinowitz. 1984. *Methods of numerical integration,* 2nd ed. New York: Academic Press.

Frankel, Jeffrey, and Andrew Rose. 1997. Is EMU more justifiable ex post than ex ante? *European Economic Review* 41 (3–5): 753–60.

Hanke, Steven H., Lars Jonung, and Kurt Schuler. 1993. *Russian currency and finance: A currency board approach to reform.* London: Routledge Press.

Hong Kong Monetary Authority (HKMA). 1998a. Available at http://www.info.gov.hk/hkma/new/press/monstat/.

———. 1998b. Hong Kong's real time gross settlement. Mimeograph.

Hong Kong Special Administrative Region Government, Financial Services Bureau. 1998. *Report on financial market review.* Hong Kong Government: Printing Department.

Krugman, Paul. 1991. Target zones and exchange rate dynamics. *Quarterly Journal of Economics* 106 (3): 669–82.

12. Frankel and Rose (1997) empirically demonstrated the endogeneity of business cycle symmetry (i.e., as an indicator of the nature of underlying shocks) with respect to trade integration. They found that a closer trade linkage between two countries is strongly and consistently associated with more tightly correlated cyclical fluctuations in the two countries.

Kwan, Yum K., and Francis T. Lui. 1999. Hong Kong's currency board and changing monetary regimes. In *Changes in exchange rates in rapidly developing countries: Theories, practice, and policy issues.* Vol. 7 of NBER East Asian Seminar on Economics, ed. Takatoshi Ito and Anne O. Krueger, chap. 15. Chicago: University of Chicago Press.

Kydland, Finn E., and Edward C. Prescott. 1977. Rules rather than discretion: The inconsistency of optimal plans. *Journal of Political Economy* 85 (3): 473–91.

Lindberg, Hans, and Paul Soderlind. 1994. Testing the basic target zone model on Swedish data 1982–1990. *European Economic Review* 38 (7): 1441–69.

Lindberg, Hans, Paul Soderlind, and Lars E. Svensson. 1993. Devaluation expectations: The Swedish krona 1985–92. *Economic Journal* 103 (September): 1170–79.

Lui, Francis T., Leonard K. Cheng, and Yum K. Kwan. 2000. Currency board, Asian financial crisis, and the case for structured notes. Working Paper, Department of Economics, Hong Kong University of Science and Technology, and City University of Hong Kong, May 2000.

Miller, Merton. 1998. Transcript of testimony at the legislative council. Hong Kong: Legislative Council, 14 November.

Mundell, Robert. 1961. Theory of optimum currency areas. *American Economic Review* 51 (4): 657–65.

Nugee, John. 1995. A brief history of the exchange fund. In *Money and banking in Hong Kong,* 2–24. Hong Kong: Hong Kong Monetary Authority.

Rose, Andrew K., and Lars E. Svensson. 1994. European exchange rate credibility before the fall. *European Economic Review* 38 (6): 1185–216.

Schuler, Kurt. 1992. *Currency boards.* Ph.D. diss. Department of Economics, George Mason University, Fairfax, Va.

Schwartz, Anna J. 1993. Currency boards: Their past, present and possible future role. *Carnegie-Rochester conference series on public policy* 39:147–87.

Svensson, Lars E. 1991. The term structure of interest rate differentials in a target zone. *Journal of Monetary Economics* 28 (1): 87–116.

———. 1993. Assessing target zone credibility: Mean reversion and devaluation expectations in the ERM, 1979–1992. *European Economics Review* 37 (4): 763–802.

Williamson, John. 1995. *What role for currency boards?* Washington, D.C.: Institute for International Economics.

Yam, Joseph. 1991. The development of monetary policy in Hong Kong. In *Monetary management in Hong Kong: The changing role of the exchange fund,* ed. Andrew F. Freris, Y. C. Jao, and Joseph Yam, 54–83. Hong Kong: Chartered Institute of Bankers, Hong Kong Centre.

Comment   Shin-ichi Fukuda

This paper is an interesting case study on credibility and the currency board in Hong Kong. After providing a compact yet comprehensive historical overview on the Hong Kong currency board, the paper presented a sophisticated empirical study of the Hong Kong dollar devaluation risk

Shin-ichi Fukuda is associate professor of economics at the University of Tokyo.

based on the daily data of exchange rates since the early 1980s. The paper makes an important contribution in showing that even under a currency board, a different institutional arrangement has a different effect in establishing governmental credibility.

In order to test whether rules are better than discretion in strengthening the credibility of a currency board, the paper divided the sample period into three regimes: regime 1 (1 November 1983 to 31 March 1992), a rule-bound regime; regime 2 (1 April 1992 to 6 September 1998), a regime with active discretionary interventions; and regime 3 (7 September 1998 to 21 April 1999), a rule-based regime. The paper then demonstrated that switching from a discretionary regime to a rule-based regime—that is, switching from regime 2 to regime 3—reduced devaluation risk suddenly and drastically. The result is interesting in showing that a rule-based system is better for establishing credibility. It also provides important policy implications for the desirability of different currency systems. I have three comments.

My first comment is on the usefulness of the currency board system for East Asian countries. Citing a successful story in Argentina, the introduction of this paper proposed the system's usefulness as a government commitment device. Although it is true that Hong Kong's current currency board system is one possible commitment device for the government, Hong Kong's experience may be different from that of Argentina from the view point of the optimal currency area theory.

That is, in terms of economic integration, the U.S. economy has a dominant effect on Argentina's economy. Thus, it is natural for Argentina to form a U.S. dollar currency block not only from the credibility perspective but also from various economic points of views. However, in the case of Hong Kong, the United States is only one of a number of important foreign partners. In other words, although the U.S. economy has strong impacts on the Hong Kong economy, East Asian economies—particularly those of Japan and China—also have significant effects on the Hong Kong economy. Therefore, putting aside the credibility issue, it is not necessarily clear whether fixing the Hong Kong dollar to the U.S. dollar is a desirable exchange rate system.

For example, suppose that there was a large depreciation of the Japanese yen against the U.S. dollar. In this case, fixing the Hong Kong dollar to the U.S. dollar makes the real effective exchange rate of the Hong Kong dollar appreciate a lot, and may lead to undesirable effects on Hong Kong's trade balance. Similarly, the stability of the Chinese yuan against the U.S. dollar may be an important factor for sustaining Hong Kong's currency board system. If the Chinese yuan devaluates against the U.S. dollar, the sustainability of Hong Kong's currency board system would be difficult even under the current credible system.

My second comment is on what kind of credibility the Hong Kong Monetary Authority (HKMA) needs to establish through the currency board system. In the first-generation currency crisis model, the rule was desirable to establish the credibility such that the government would not create excessive money supplies in response to huge fiscal deficits. Argentina's currency board system was a successful story in establishing this type of credibility. On the other hand, in the second-generation currency crisis model, the rule was desirable to establish the credibility such that the government would not cause excessive inflation to restore macro imbalances such as unemployment.

In Hong Kong, however, what type of credibility does the government need to establish? In a model of time consistency such as Kydland-Prescott, the government's policy objective needs to be different from that of the market equilibrium. Then, what makes Hong Kong's government objective different from the market objective? Because Hong Kong did not have a huge fiscal deficit, the story of the first generation model is not helpful in this sense. Furthermore, because domestic macroeconomic imbalances such as unemployment rates seem not to be large, the story of the second generation model is not useful either.

The paper implicitly assumes that Hong Kong's economic stability can be achieved by stabilizing the Hong Kong dollar against the U.S. dollar. From a practical point of view, this implicit assumption might be true, but it can be tested with actual data by looking at the stability of various macro variables under three alternative currency board regimes. The paper discussed this for interest rate stability and showed that the credible currency board system was actually consistent with the interest rate stability. For other macro variables, however, the paper provided no discussion.

If the only source of economic instability is the loss of HKMA's credibility, the nominal exchange rate stability would be consistent with the stability of other macro variables, such as domestic price level, domestic output level, unemployment rate, and so on. If various external real shocks are sources of economic stability, however, it is highly possible that fixing the Hong Kong dollar to the U.S. dollar may destabilize other macro variables in Hong Kong.

In particular, real shocks in East Asian economies are not necessarily closely correlated to those in the U.S. economy. If real shocks affect East Asian economies and the U.S. economy differently, the credible currency board system can stabilize the nominal exchange rate but may destabilize other macro variables in Hong Kong.

My final comment is on the drastic drop of estimated devaluation risk on 5 September 1998. This is one of the most interesting findings in the paper, and it may imply that a return to a rule-based system can calm the speculative behavior in the market. In fact, looking at the estimated devaluation risk in panel D of figure 7.4 we can see that the devaluation risk dropped by half overnight after 5 September.

Theoretically, the drop can arise either from a shock drop of forward premium or from a drop in the expected rate of drift within the target zone. My question is, which caused such a drastic change of devaluation risk? When we look at HIBOR-LIBOR interest differentials in figure 7.2, we can see a large but relatively gradual decline of interest differentials after September 1998. If there was a sharp drop of forward premium on 5 September 1998, how can we reconcile this with relatively gradual decline in interest differentials? If there was an intensifying drop in the expected rate of drift within the target zone, we probably can give some intuitive interpretation for why this happened in terms of the target zone theory. By contraction, however, the expected rate of drift can change drastically when the regime changes because the coefficients were estimated separately for each regime. Although it is true that there was a big structural change from regime 2 to regime 3, the actual change in coefficients may be more gradual than what was supposed in calculating the devaluation risk in the simulation.

Comment   Takatoshi Ito

This paper combines ideas in the literatures of currency board, target zone, and rule versus discretion, and then applies an empirical model to the case of Hong Kong. The idea of the currency board became a focus of attention in recent years, as currency board economies have ridden currency crises well. Argentina stood well against the tequila crisis in 1995. Hong Kong has maintained the dollar peg despite fierce attacks by speculators in 1997 and 1998. Indonesia's announcement of considering to adopt a currency board became a source of contention between the Indonesian government and the International Monetary Fund (IMF) in February 1998.

In the postcrisis discussion, the so-called two-corner solution became a popular argument. According to this argument, the two corners—that is, a freely floating exchange rate regime and the currency board system—are the only stable exchange rate regimes. Hong Kong and Argentina, both under a currency board arrangement, have survived repeated attacks on their currencies in the second half of the 1990s. Such successes are usually proof that the currency board is stable. This is the first paper, to my knowledge, that looks into details of the workings of a currency board. The reader learns that the currency board in Hong Kong has experienced different regimes within the currency board arrangement.

The paper argues that the Hong Kong Monetary Authority (HKMA)

Takatoshi Ito is professor at the Institute of Economic Research at Hitotsubashi University, Tokyo, and a research associate of the National Bureau of Economic Research.

has been shifting between the rule-based currency board and the discretionary currency board. The authors identify three regimes. In regime 1 (1983:10–1992:3), the HKMA was a rule-bound currency board, whereas in regime 2 (1992:4–1998:9) it was a discretionary currency board; the HKMA switched back to a rule-based currency board in regime 3 (after 1998:9). The peg of HK$7.80 to a US$1.00 has been kept since October 1983. The authors argue that the HKMA's intervention policy with a target zone–like band invited speculative attacks and caused the very high interest rate of regime 2, whereas the rule-based currency board in regime 3 did not experience speculative attacks.

Rules versus Discretion

A narrowly defined currency board is as a rule one in which any currency (monetary base, to be precise) is backed one-to-one by foreign reserves. On the asset side of the currency board, there are no domestic assets, such as government bonds of that country (See Williamson 1995, pp. 2–5.) In order to maintain the fixed exchange rate, the board intervenes in the market. Any net capital inflows mean an increase in foreign assets matched by the equal amount of the increase in the domestic monetary base. As a result, the interest rate will decrease, and capital inflows would stop. Similarly, net capital outflows, either by capital flight or withdrawal of foreign capital, will automatically raise the interest rate, and capital outflows will be deterred.

The original purpose of the currency board is to be a rigid rule to keep the monetary authority from causing inflation. This is the ultimate form of the nominal anchor, or a rule-based monetary policy. A downside of a currency board is that it cannot provide domestic liquidity even if it is needed, unless there is capital inflow. The function of lender of last resort has to be abandoned.

In the wake of currency crises in Mexico and Asia, the currency board has gained another role: that of generating credibility in the currency due to sufficient foreign reserves. By backing every domestic note and coin with foreign reserves, the currency seems to be resilient to a speculative attack. However, for this function the amount of foreign reserves may not be just enough to cover the monetary base. Demand deposits (M1) can be converted quite easily, by domestic residents, to foreign currencies. Even savings accounts (M2) may be quickly converted into foreign assets, if the investors sacrifice some interest payments. Therefore, both Hong Kong and Argentina have foreign reserves that exceed M1. In this regard, the HKMA does not seem to be a pure currency board. Of course, from the viewpoint of preventing currency attacks, having more foreign reserves than monetary base (and even M1) means that HKMA is something more than a pure currency board. It is better from the standpoint of being robust to speculation, but it also invites the criticism of being discretionary.

The paper well describes that discretion combined with the real-time gross settlement (RTGS) system led to high interest rate volatility in 1997 and 1998. The paper argues that it was "only after severe public criticism and heavy market pressure during the financial crisis that the HKMA gradually abandoned its high interest rate defense strategy" (239). Because the currency board is designed to let the interest rate fluctuate as capital comes in and out, the authors' judgment that the interest rate rose more than the normal working of the currency board is a crucial element in evaluating the regime 2. However, a question remains in my mind. What would a "natural" degree of rise in interest rate be under a pure currency board in the time period of regime 2? To what extent was "discretion" responsible for the extra volatility in the interest rate?

I agree that neither the interest rate defense nor interest arbitrage worked in the month of October 1997. I also support the authors' view that "the interest rate differential represented a risk premium for holding the Hong Kong dollar" (239). What I am not convinced of is that a major reason for the apparent lack of credibility of the Hong Kong dollar peg comes from the HKMA's discretionary policy. (The author argues, on page 241, "That the HKMA had deviated from the fixed rules of the currency board made its commitment to the peg much less credible.") It might have been that contagion from Association of Southeast Asian Nations (ASEAN) currency devaluation and speculators' determination based on their success in forcing the Thai authority to abandon a de facto dollar peg was responsible for the situation.

In summary, I like the way authors described the changes of HKMA policies during the crisis period of 1997 and 1998. The description is convincing in that even within the currency board regime, there is room to maneuver in details, especially with respect to the relationship to the domestic interbank market. I am less convinced, however, of regarding regime 2 as discretionary and the regime 3 as rule-based, and making judgments that regime 3 was more successful due to the rule-based policy.

The reasons for my hesitation are threefold. First, the introduction of the first line of defense (regime 2) at 7.75 may not be so significant since the difference between 7.75, and 7.80 is less than 1 percent of the par value. Second, introducing a discount window to replace the liquidity adjustment facility (LAF; regime 3) does not seem to be a rule-based system. The pure currency board should not have a discount window. The difference in opinion may be that I interpret rule-based as a pure currency board, whereas the authors may mean something else. Third, I think that the stability in regime 3 cannot solely be explained by the rule-based approach, but requires namely two other important elements: the HKMA's successful fight by intervening in the stock market (August 1998); and less-active hedge funds, which may be a result of losses from the Russian crisis.

Would the external shocks (speculative attacks) during regime 2 not be more than those during regime 3? The description of the size of the interbank market as opposed to the foreign exchange rate gives a clue. Again, however, if the size of the interbank market is small, then is it not "natural" to see that the interest rate goes up automatically? How could regime 3 be more rule-based if the interest rate did not rise? It seems to me that the answer is based more on institutional details than on quantitative investigation. In fact, according to the description in this paper, the degree of discretion seems to have increased in regime 3.

Target Zone

In this paper the currency board is also expanded to include a target zone. This has the following meaning in the model: because the currency board with a dollar peg is in place, any interest rate differential (HIBOR − LIBOR) is indicative of some devaluation probability ($E\Delta s$). However, adding a target zone feature to this, there is a mean-reverting force. If the current rate (s) deviates from a central rate, then the deviation (x) may be reversed in the future. The mean-reverting force ($E\Delta x$) should be added to any prediction of exchange rate changes. Therefore, even in the existence of an interest rate differential, it may not always signify devaluation (change in the central rate) probability, but may stay in the band of target zone. The key is how to model this mean-reverting process. This is the essence of regressions summarized in tables 7.1 and 7.2.

My comments on this section are twofold. First, the band is quite small, so that the target zone application may be limited. Is more action coming from the interest rate differential (and Δs) than from mean reversion? That is, it may not be necessary to have a target zone framework, but instead to analyze the breakdown of the interest parity as a proxy for devaluation probability. Second, the changes of the signs of coefficients may be due to changes in the speculative force behavior (see the next section) rather than changes in HKMA behavior from discretionary to rule-based. The authors counter my skepticism by saying, "Had a general Asian risk premium existed in Hong Kong, we could hardly witness its disappearance in the matter of just a few days" (250). The judgment is left to the reader.

Assessment of Intervention in the Stock Market

Apparently, the speculation ended in August 1998. The paper seems to attribute this to the regime change in September 1998 (regime 2 to regime 3). However, there may be other explanations. HKMA had conducted unusual operations in August 1998 by purchasing Hong Kong stocks. This was a policy defense against the so-called double play of speculations. This may have been effective finally to quiet down speculative activities. Second, the Russian debacle, and resulting Long-Term Capital Management (LTCM) trouble may have reduced hedge fund activities, and this may have favorably helped the Hong Kong dollar market to become stable.

Although the paper claims that the necessary institutional changes took place well before the LTCM, it is true that a large unwinding of the hedge funds position took place in the fall of 1998, and it was a force behind the sharp appreciation of the yen. The environment of speculative activities seems to be greatly different before and after September 1998. The intervention in the stock market may have been more significant than changes in operating procedure (discretionary to rule-based). However, investigation into the relative importance of each of these phenomena has to be left to future research.

Concluding Remarks

This is an interesting and important paper, documenting how the HKMA works and how the HKMA responded to crises over its currency, mainly caused by large capital inflows and outflows. The aura around currency boards seems to be intact after a battle, because Hong Kong and Argentina are still holding on to dollar pegs with open capital accounts. It is an interesting question whether Hong Kong and Argentina will follow a rigid currency board rule or deviate from the rigid rule. Some of my skepticism is directed to the authors' interpretation of regimes as discretionary and rule-based. Another question I have is the relative importance of HKMA policy changes in the money market versus those in the stock market.

This paper is informative and valuable in examining the question of the two-corner solution, but is the currency board a silver bullet for the emerging market? If so, what kind of operational regimes should the currency board adopt? Only history will tell the answer.

Reference

Williamson, John. 1995. *What role for currency boards?* Washington, D.C.: Institute for International Economics.

How Japanese Subsidiaries in Asia Responded to the Regional Crisis
An Empirical Analysis Based on the MITI Survey

Kyoji Fukao

8.1 Introduction

Japanese manufacturing subsidiaries play an important role in Asian economies. Especially in relatively advanced industries, such as electrical machinery and transport equipment, Japanese subsidiaries sometimes employ more than one-third of the total workforce employed in these industries in the Association of Southeast Asian Nations (ASEAN-4) countries (table 8.1). Japan's foreign direct investment (FDI) has provided Asian countries not only with production technology and managerial know-how but also with stable capital inflows. Therefore, the behavior of Japanese subsidiaries in Asia and the associated consequences for flows of FDI are bound to play a crucial role in shaping the regional recovery process.

Because foreign subsidiaries can rely on their parent firms' support, their operations are likely to be less influenced by the crisis. Moreover, sharp currency devaluations potentially increase affected Asian countries' attractiveness to foreign firms by reducing production costs.[1] However, as of date there is little evidence to prove such optimistic expectations be-

Kyoji Fukao is professor of economics at the Institute of Economic Research at Hitotsubashi University.

This research was conducted as part of the project titled "The Currency and Economic Crisis in Asia" sponsored by the Japanese Ministry of International Trade and Industry (MITI).

1. UNCTAD (1998) stressed the importance of this mechanism. Blomström and Lipsey (1993) found that in Latin America after the debt crisis in the 1980s, foreign subsidiaries increased their exports substantially and contributed to the structural adjustment of host countries.

Table 8.1 **Share of Japan's Manufacturing Subsidiaries in Host-Country Employment, Investment, and International Trade in 1997: The ASEAN-4 Countries and Korea (in percentages)**

	Employment			Investment in Plant and Equipment	Total Exports	Total Imports
	Manufacturing Sector	Electrical Machinery[a]	Transport Equipment[a]			
Korea	1.2	2.9	2.5	0.2	2.0	1.9
Thailand	5.3	n.a.	n.a.	4.3	17.3	12.4
Indonesia	1.8	37.3	34.3	2.8	8.1	10.4
Malaysia	8.8	28.2	30.9	2.8	17.7	17.7
The Philippines	3.6	38.0	n.a.	3.1	18.1	10.4

Sources: MITI (1999a), and Belderbos, Capannelli, and Fukao (1998).

Note: n.a. = not available.

[a]Data for 1995.

cause few empirical studies on foreign subsidiaries' responses to the recent financial crisis in Asia have been carried out.[2] Using subsidiary level data from the Japanese Ministry of International Trade and Industry (MITI) 1996 and 1997, I analyze the response of Japan's manufacturing subsidiaries in the ASEAN-4 countries and Korea to the recent Asian financial crises, which started in the second half of 1997.[3] Because about 90 percent of workers employed by Japanese subsidiaries in this region are employed by manufacturing subsidiaries, I concentrate on manufacturing subsidiaries in this paper.

The paper is organized as follows: In section 8.2 I provide a general overview of the performance of Japan's manufacturing subsidiaries after the crisis. In section 8.3, I study recent trends of Japan's FDI flows to ASEAN-4 countries and Korea. In section 8.4, using microdata of MITI surveys, I compare subsidiaries' performances and responses across industries and host countries. By subdividing subsidiaries into two groups, I also study how different characteristics of subsidiaries affected their performance and response. In section 8.5, I undertake an econometric investigation of Japanese subsidiaries' response using microdata from MITI surveys.

8.2   An Overview of the Performance of Japan's Asian Subsidiaries after the Crisis

The currency crisis had both positive and negative impacts on multinational enterprises' activities in this region. On the one hand, export-oriented subsidiaries may have benefited from the reduction of production costs caused by the sharp currency depreciation. On the other hand, local market–oriented subsidiaries were seriously hit by the decline of local demand and price increases of imported intermediate inputs.

Another consequence of host country currency depreciation are capital losses, which, indeed, a majority of Japanese subsidiaries in this region suffered. An amazingly high percentage of Japanese subsidiaries in this region had not hedged the exchange risk originating from their liabilities

---

2. Dollar and Hallward-Driemeier (1998), Lamberte et al. (1999), and OECF and RIDA (1999) found that both in Thailand and in the Philippines firms with foreign ties performed better than independent local firms after the crisis. There are several reports, written in Japanese, on Japanese subsidiaries' response to the crisis. Among them, JETRO (1999), MITI (1999a,c), Research Institute of International Investment and Development (1999), and Touyou Keizai Sinpou-sha (1999) are informative. Ramstetter (1999) also studies FDI flows in Thailand after the crisis. However, neither Ramstetter nor any of the Japanese studies mentioned here use detailed subsidiary-level data. Until the U.S. Department of Commerce publishes *U.S. Direct Investment Abroad, 1998* I cannot get detailed information on U.S. subsidiaries' 1998 activities in Asia.

3. The 1997 survey accounts for operations during the fiscal year through March 1998.

being denominated mainly in foreign currencies, including yen.[4] According to the MITI's *Comparative Survey of Economic Structure (Keizai Kouzou Hikaku Chousa)*, conducted in December 1998 and January 1999, 50 percent of Japan's manufacturing subsidiaries in the ASEAN-4 countries and Korea had not hedged their exchange risk before the crisis. An additional 32 percent had insufficiently hedged the risk. It seems that they had ignored the exchange risk partly because of relatively stable exchange rates in the region—with the exception of Indonesia and the Philippines—over the past decades.

Critical situations in both the host countries' and the Japanese banking systems may also have had a negative effect on Japanese subsidiaries in this region. Because Japan's foreign subsidiaries borrow primarily from Japanese banks, it seems that the lending behaviors of Japanese banks and their financial subsidiaries abroad have more significant effects on Japan's nonfinancial subsidiaries in Asia than do the lending behaviors of local banks. According to MITI (1998), at the end of fiscal 1995, 64 percent of the total stock of long-term bank loans locally raised by Japan's manufacturing subsidiaries in the ASEAN-4 countries came from local subsidiaries of Japanese banks. Reflecting the financial turmoil and the declining demand for new loans, almost all of Japan's private banks have been reducing their total lending. For example, from fiscal 1996 to 1997, the Industrial Bank of Japan, the Mitsubishi Bank, and the Sakura Bank reduced their total lending by 6.0, 3.0, and 4.8 percent, respectively. In statistics provided by the Bank for International Settlements (BIS), it is reported that Japanese banks reduced their cross-border lending to East Asia by almost 20 percent in the year from June 1997 to June 1998.

Despite the reduction of loans, the majority of Japan's manufacturing subsidiaries in this region registered no complaints about the credit crunch. According to MITI (1998–99), only 28 percent replied that they have faced some difficulties in continuing their borrowing or in getting new loans. Two factors may have mitigated the negative impact of credit contraction. First, since the liberalization of Japan's financial markets in the mid-1980s, large manufacturing firms have increased their direct financing from financial markets and have become more independent from banks.[5] Second, to counter the credit crunch, the Japanese government has let state-owned banks expand their lending. From fiscal 1996 to 1997 the Export-Import Bank of Japan and the Japan Development Bank increased their total lending by 8.9 and 2.5 percent, respectively. Today, quite a number of Japanese parent firms have state-owned banks as their prime lend-

4. For example, Asian subsidiaries of Toray Industries incurred a capital loss of 11 billion yen in fiscal 1997, which is almost equal to its average annual operating profit in the region (Japan Economic Research Institute 1999).
5. However, smaller firms, which still depend on their main banks, might have been affected by the credit crunch.

ers. At the end of fiscal 1997, the Export-Import Bank of Japan was the prime lender for Nissan Motor, Honda Motor, Fujitsu, and major general trading companies, such as Mitsubishi, Mitsui, and Marubeni.

To analyze recent trends in production activity by Japan's manufacturing subsidiaries abroad, MITI's *Survey of Trends of Enterprises (Kigyou Doukou Chousa)*, which is conducted on a quarterly basis, is probably the best source.

Panel A of figure 8.1 shows the change in sales (in yen) of Japan's manufacturing subsidiaries in the ASEAN-4 countries by industry. Subsidiaries in the transport equipment industry, the majority of which are local market–oriented, faced a sharp decline in total sales. According to MITI (1998), Japanese subsidiaries in the transport equipment industry in the ASEAN-4 countries sold 91.9 percent of their total sales in their host country and exported 2.5 percent to Japan, 0.9 percent to other Asian countries, and 4.7 percent outside the region in fiscal 1995. In the case of subsidiaries in the electrical machinery industry, the majority of which are export oriented, the decline in total sales was much smaller. Japanese subsidiaries in this industry in the ASEAN-4 countries sold 29.4 percent of their total sales in their host country and exported 36.2 percent to Japan, 20.3 percent to other Asian countries, and 14.1 percent outside the region in fiscal 1995.

Panel B of figure 8.1 shows changes in employment by industry. Basically, employment trends correspond to those in sales. However, compared to sales, the reduction in employment is moderate. It is interesting that although sales of subsidiaries in the transport equipment industry have dropped more sharply than have sales of subsidiaries in the textiles and garments industry, reductions in employment in the two industries were almost of the same magnitude.

8.3   FDI Flows to Asia after the Crisis

Despite the sharp decline in sales and profits in the region, Japan's FDI flows (on the basis of balance of payment statistics) to this region have increased after the crisis (table 8.2). From the period of July 1996 to June 1997 to the period of July 1997 to June 1998, Japan's FDI flows to the five countries under consideration increased by 49 percent.

According to the standard theory of FDI (Caves 1982; Dunning 1993), it is not surprising to observe increases in FDI inflows to the Asian countries hit by the financial crisis. FDI flows involve not only financial capital but also parent firms' intangible assets, such as the stock of technological knowledge, marketing know-how, and goodwill, on which stable supplier systems are based. Real capital, human resources, location, and other elements of subsidiaries are designed and organized to derive maximum returns from such intangible assets. Large transaction costs are associated

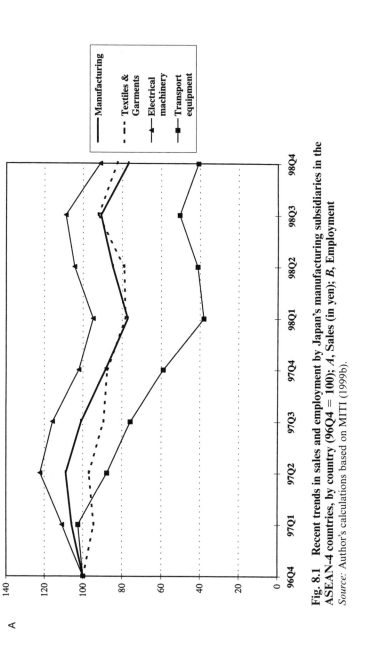

Fig. 8.1 Recent trends in sales and employment by Japan's manufacturing subsidiaries in the ASEAN–4 countries, by country (96Q4 = 100); *A*, Sales (in yen); *B*, Employment
Source: Author's calculations based on MITI (1999b).

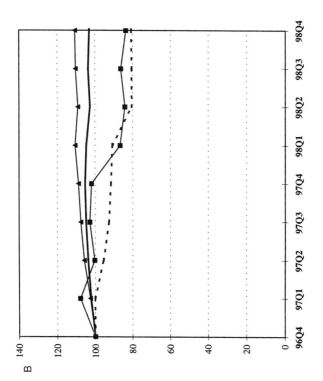

Table 8.2   **Japan's Direct Investment Abroad, Capital Outflows on a BOP Statistics Basis (in billions of yen)**

	1995		1996		1997		1998
	1st half	2nd half	1st half	2nd half	1st half	2nd half	1st half
Korea	19	14	26	18	12	8	53
Thailand	41	47	65	81	91	156	146
Indonesia	32	58	73	90	98	91	93
Malaysia	11	24	31	26	51	69	48
The Philippines	29	72	41	11	16	26	43
Five countries	132	215	236	224	268	351	382
Asia	322	478	535	525	717	870	659
North America	571	302	561	687	489	447	465
Europe	79	237	162	146	215	87	204
All countries	1,049	1,080	1,275	1,273	1,609	1,536	1,835

Source: Bank of Japan, *Balance of Payments (BOP) Monthly,* various issues.

with the transfer of intangible assets among firms by arm's-length transactions. It is also costly to adjust the structure of a subsidiary to another firm's intangible assets. Thus, the resale price of a subsidiary might be much lower than the initial investment. This means that FDI is accompanied by sunk costs. If substantial sunk costs are involved, a parent firm will support its subsidiary under adversary conditions. It is also true that if there is substantial accumulation of firm-specific skills, firms will not drastically cut their employment when their sales decline.[6]

It is sometimes argued that a particular feature of the Japanese production system is a heavy reliance on long-term supplier relationships and the accumulation of firm-specific skills. If this argument is correct, we would expect Japanese parent firms to invest more actively in order to support troubled subsidiaries than do parent firms from other countries. We should also note that if this sunk cost hypothesis is correct, Japanese firms will not easily start new investment projects unless they expect substantial profits.

There are at least two other possible explanations for the increase in FDI inflows to Asia after the crisis. First, currency depreciation and the fall in asset prices in the Asian countries created a kind of a fire-sale situation for foreign firms. If foreign firms expect the Asian countries to recover in the near future, they would not want to miss the bargain. Second, the sharp currency depreciation has potentially increased affected Asian countries' attractiveness to foreign firms by reducing production costs. Foreign firms may therefore consider either establishing new export bases through

6. For a more rigorous theoretical analysis on this issue, see Fukao and Otaki (1993) and Hamermesh (1993).

Table 8.3   The Number of New FDI Cases by Japanese Firms in the ASEAN-4
                   Countries and Korea, Total Number of Greenfield Investments, M&A
                   Purchases, and New Capital Participations: All Industries

	Korea	Thailand	Indonesia	Malaysia	The Philippines	Total
1991	14	51	47	39	16	167
1992	4	35	39	32	12	122
1993	7	28	18	26	4	83
1994	7	39	30	26	7	109
1995	25	63	47	29	43	207
1996	30	99	72	39	40	280
1997	15	65	27	24	30	161
1998	12	18	9	14	16	69

Source: Author's calculations based on Touyou Keizai Shinpou-sha (1999).

greenfield investments or expanding the production capacity of existing export-oriented subsidiaries in order to exploit the decline in production costs.[7] These two explanations, however, are in contradiction with several statistics. According to MITI (1999b), Japan's manufacturing subsidiaries in the ASEAN-4 countries have reduced their investments in tangible fixed assets (excluding land) by 54 percent from the third quarter of 1997 to the third quarter of 1998. Even subsidiaries in the electrical machinery industry, which are the most export oriented and the least hit by the crisis, reduced their investment by 25 percent during this period. According to our data set, average employment in existing subsidiaries in the five countries declined by 5 percent from March 1997 to March 1998.

As table 8.3 shows, the number of new FDI cases by Japanese firms to the ASEAN-4 countries and Korea has declined considerably. It is interesting that although Japanese firms almost stopped new investments, they seem to be reluctant to close or sell their existing subsidiaries. Japanese firms sold or closed fifty-five subsidiaries in 1998 (table 8.6), equivalent to only 1.5 percent of the 3,680 existing subsidiaries in the five countries.

Compared with U.S. and German firms, Japanese firms made a quite limited amount of cross-border mergers and acquisitions (M&A) in the ASEAN-4 countries and Korea (table 8.4). U.S. firms are active in M&A purchases especially in the finance and communication service sectors, in which Japanese firms do not have a comparative advantage (Nikkei 1999b). Even in the manufacturing sector, however, there were only two cases of M&A purchases conducted by Japanese firms in the region in 1998 (table 8.5).

7. Perez-Quiros and Popper (1996) found that FDI is more stable over time compared with short-term investment. Frankel and Rose (1995) found that the accumulation of inward FDI reduces the probability that the host country will be hit by a currency crisis. On this issue, see also Berg and Pattillo (1998).

Table 8.4   The Number of Japanese Subsidiaries in the ASEAN-4 Countries and Korea Which Were Closed or Sold to Local or Other Countries' Firms: All Industries

	Korea	Thailand	Indonesia	Malaysia	The Philippines	Total
1991	4	1	4	2	2	13
1992	3	2	1	5	2	13
1993	6	3	3	3	0	15
1994	4	5	0	8	0	17
1995	8	3	1	5	0	17
1996	3	5	3	4	2	17
1997	6	8	1	5	3	23
1998	7	20	6	14	8	55

Source: Author's calculations based on Touyou Keizai Sinpou-sha (1999).

Table 8.5   Cross-Border M&A Purchases in the ASEAN-4 Countries and Korea by Purchasing Company's Country of Origin, 1997–98 (in millions of U.S. dollars)

	First Half 1997	Second Half 1997	First Half 1998[a]
United States	542	2,066	1,955
Singapore	145	2,001	306
Germany	556	898	872
Japan	648	223	239
Hong Kong	464	180	46
Taiwan	834	274	64
United Kingdom	616	8	252

Source: UNCTAD (1998), original data provided by KPMG Corporate Finance.
[a]Data for the first half of 1998 are preliminary.

It is interesting to note that in the case of U.S. firms, although they actively increased M&A purchases in the five countries, their FDI flows to the five countries declined considerably in 1997 (table 8.7).[8]

Putting the above pieces of evidence together, it appears that Japanese firms increased their FDI flows to the Asian countries mainly in order to financially assist their subsidiaries that were suffering from deteriorating financial conditions. Compared with U.S. and European firms, they made quite limited amounts of cross-border M&A purchases motivated to take advantage of the currency depreciation and the fall of stock prices. Cases of the establishment of new export bases through greenfield investments and capacity expansion of existing export-oriented subsidiaries motivated to exploit the decline in production cost in the Asian countries were also rare.

8. I should note that definitions for FDI flows and M&A purchases differ. For detail on this issue see UNCTAD (1998) and JETRO (1999).

Table 8.6   The Number of New FDI Cases by Japanese Firms in the ASEAN-4 Countries and Korea in 1998, by Entry Mode and by Industry

	Machinery	Other Manufacturing	Finance	Other Nonmanufacturing	Total
Greenfield investments	10	17	2	31	60
M&A purchases	1	1	0	0	2
New capital participations	1	0	0	6	7
Total	12	18	2	37	69

Source: Author's calculations based on Touyou Keizai Shinpou-sha (1999).

Table 8.7   U.S. Direct Investment Abroad, Capital Outflows by Country (in millions of U.S. dollars)

	1994	1995	1996	1997
Korea	390	1,051	766	761
Thailand	703	686	501	−130
Indonesia	2,061	519	686	560
Malaysia	553	1,037	963	637
The Philippines	414	269	716	291
Five countries	4,121	3,562	3,632	2,119
Asia and Pacific	13,437	14,342	12,190	13,815
Europe	34,380	52,275	35,992	60,558
Western hemisphere	17,710	16,040	16,081	23,784
All countries	73,252	92,074	74,833	114,537

Source: U.S. Department of Commerce (1998).

8.4 Detailed Analysis of Japanese Subsidiaries' Response to the Crisis

From the microdata of MITI's *Survey on Trends of Japan's Business Activities Abroad (Kaigai Jigyoukatudou Doukou Chousa)*, we can get more detailed information on activities of Japanese subsidiaries; 2,346 subsidiaries in the ASEAN-4 countries and Korea answered the 1996 MITI survey. I matched individual manufacturing subsidiary data of the 1996 survey with that of the 1997 survey. I also got additional information on parent firms, such as their net profits and total assets, from their financial reports (Japan Ministry of Finance [MOF] 1998). After excluding subsidiaries that did not provide answers regarding basic information, such as sales and employment,[9] I obtained panel data of 1,101 manufacturing subsidiaries that employed 712,000 workers in March 1997.[10] According to Touyou Keizai Shinpou-sha (1999), Japan's manufacturing subsidiaries were employing 857,000 workers in the ASEAN-4 countries and Korea (299,000 in Thailand, 200,000 in Indonesia, 62,000 in Korea, 195,000 in Malaysia, and 101,000 in the Philippines) in October 1998, so our data set covers a substantial percentage of Japan's manufacturing activities in these countries. The data set includes 723 subsidiaries in Korea, Thailand, and Indonesia. Because subsidiaries in these countries were harder hit by the Asian crisis, I will primarily use the latter subset for the analysis in this section.

Table 8.8 compares local market–oriented subsidiaries with export-oriented subsidiaries in Korea, Thailand, and Indonesia. In the case of local market–oriented subsidiaries for which the exports/sales ratio is

9. I have also excluded from the data set subsidiaries suspended before March 1997, started up after April 1996, and employing fewer than twenty workers in March 1997.
10. The data set includes eighteen subsidiaries closed and ten subsidiaries suspended in fiscal 1998.

Table 8.8   Selected Indicators of Japan's Manufacturing Subsidiaries in Korea, Thailand, and Indonesia, by Export Status

	Exports/Sales < 50%			Exports/Sales ≥ 50%		
	N	Mean	Std. Dev.	N	Mean	Std. Dev.
Sales in fiscal 1996 (millions of yen)	350	6129.6	15,357.1	177	5,329.9	10,960.2
Change in sales, fiscal 1996–97 (millions of yen)	350	−1,119.9	5,100.1	177	925.8	4,753.2
Share of subsidiaries for which sales were down	350	67.1%		177	40.1%	
Net profits in fiscal 1996 (millions of yen)	346	329.6	1,031.3	175	92.3	355.6
Change in profits, fiscal 1996–97 (millions of yen)	341	−597.7	2,105.2	172	84.2	859.4
Share of subsidiaries for which profits were down	341	78.9%		172	48.3%	
Employment in fiscal 1996	350	444.0	696.5	177	799.4	1,343.6
Change in employment, March 1997–March 1998	350	−17.6	135.6	177	3.8	339.0
Share of subsidiaries employing fewer workers	350	46.0%		177	41.2%	
Exports/sales ratio in fiscal 1996	350	9.0%	13.9	177	85.6%	16.4
Imports–total procurement ratio in fiscal 1996	276	44.2%	34.5	144	59.3%	34.1
Change in imports–total procurement ratio, fiscal 1996–97	246	−0.9%	27.6	125	−3.9%	24.0
Exports to Japan in fiscal 1996	347	169.3	1,041.7	175	2,716.8	8,681.3
Change in exports to Japan, fiscal 1996–97 (millions of yen)	305	158.6	2,431.7	159	317.0	1,998.4
Capital equity owned by Japanese parent(s), fiscal 1996	350	411.5	742.3	177	1,169.7	4,520.9
Percentage of equity shares owned by Japanese parent(s), March 1997	350	52.8%	21.4	177	75.3%	25.4
Net increase in Japanese capital participation rate, March 1997–March 1998	350	1.5%	10.0	177	1.1%	14.3
Share of subsidiaries in which Japan's capital participation rate was increased	350	11.7%		177	10.7%	

Source: Author's calculations based on the MITI data set.

Note: N = number of observations.

smaller than 50 percent, average sales and profits declined substantially. On average, they also reduced their employment slightly: 79 percent of local market–oriented subsidiaries employ fewer workers. In contrast with this, export-oriented subsidiaries were able to increase their sales by 17 percent and almost doubled their profits. However, compared with their exports before the crisis and with the increase in exports achieved by local market–oriented subsidiaries, the increase in exports by export-oriented subsidiaries does not seem spectacular at all. Moreover, although export-oriented subsidiaries have enjoyed increases in sales and profits, they appear to have hesitated to expand their production capacity, and their average workforce increased by less than 1 percent.

Table 8.9 compares the impact of the crisis across industries in Korea, Thailand, and Indonesia. The table reveals a number of interesting facts. First, as we have already seen, local market–oriented subsidiaries, such as those in the chemical and metal products industry, the transport equipment industry, and in what I have labelled low-tech industries (such as foodstuffs, wood products, etc., but excluding textiles and garments), were hardest hit. It is interesting that the average performance of subsidiaries in the textiles and garments industry was not very good, although their average exports/sales ratio was high. We can partly explain this by the difference in export destinations. According to MITI (1998), ASEAN-4 subsidiaries in this industry sold 35 percent of their total exports within Asia excluding Japan, and exported only 22 percent to Japan in fiscal 1995. In contrast to this, subsidiaries in the electrical machinery industry exported 51 percent of their total exports to Japan. Subsidiaries in the textiles and garments industry might have been hit not only in their local markets but also in their export markets in Asia.

Second, the elasticity of employment to changes of sales, (Δemploy/ employ)/(Δsales/sales), is quite different between industries. In the case of the textiles and garments industry, the chemical and metal products industry, and the low-tech industries, the elasticity was greater than one. In the case of the general machinery and precision instruments industry and the transport equipment industry, the elasticity was smaller than 0.4. Parent firms of subsidiaries in the textiles and garments industry and the low-tech industries are relatively small and have lower profit rates on the whole. In contrast, the majority of subsidiaries in the general machinery and precision instruments industry and the transport equipment industry has large parent firms making a substantial profit. Possibly, subsidiaries in the machinery industry were able to maintain their employment levels because of support from parent firms.[11]

---

11. According to MITI (1998), 62 percent of parent firms of subsidiaries in the textiles and garments and the low-tech industries had paid-in capital of less than one billion yen. In the case of subsidiaries in the transport equipment industry and the general machinery and precision instruments industry, 59 percent of parents had paid-in capital of more than one billion yen.

Table 8.9   Selected Indicators of Japan's Manufacturing Subsidiaries in Korea, Thailand, and Indonesia, by Industry

	Textiles & Garments			Chemical & Metal Products			Electrical Machinery		
	N	Mean	Std. Dev.	N	Mean	Std. Dev.	N	Mean	Std. Dev.
Sales in fiscal 1996 (millions of yen)	71	2,929.9	3,838.2	215	5,641.1	12,495.5	145	8,535.7	12,114.3
Change in sales, fiscal 1996–97 (millions of yen)	71	−95.7	982.8	215	−157.6	2,500.9	145	1,359.7	5,803.8
Share of subsidiaries for which sales were down	71	54.9%		215	61.4%		145	39.3%	
Net profits in fiscal 1996 (millions of yen)	71	−22.2	441.4	206	156.9	742.6	126	280.9	525.1
Change in profits, fiscal 1996–97 (millions of yen)	71	−108.6	541.8	204	−504.6	1,940.3	120	14.8	1,126.7
Share of subsidiaries for which profits were down	71	63.4%		204	71.6%		120	52.5%	
Employment in fiscal 1996	71	642.3	594.7	215	402.8	637.1	145	958.7	1,263.6
Change in employment, March 1997–March 98	71	−44.3	258.7	215	−38.3	259.6	145	−20.6	397.0
Share of subsidiaries employing fewer workers	71	40.8%		215	41.9%		145	44.8%	
Exports-sales ratio in fiscal 1996	43	63.4%	37.6	156	21.6%	30.4	114	55.3%	40.0
Imports–total procurement ratio in fiscal 1996	29	36.7%	35.0	121	47.9%	36.7	97	63.2%	31.2
Change in imports–total procurement ratio, fiscal 1996–97	26	8.9%	20.9	106	1.6%	30.8	86	−5.0%	23.5
Exports to Japan in fiscal 1996	43	502.7	698.7	156	301.3	1,762.3	116	3,186.4	10,363.9

(continued)

Table 8.9   (continued)

	Textiles & Garments			Chemical & Metal Products			Electrical Machinery		
	N	Mean	Std. Dev.	N	Mean	Std. Dev.	N	Mean	Std. Dev.
Change in exports to Japan, fiscal 1996–97 (millions of yen)	40	−27.4	427.5	136	45.5	275.8	100	617.7	1,973.8
Capital equity owned by Japanese parent(s), fiscal 1996	71	309.2	533.7	215	756.8	3,954.2	145	945.4	1,491.3
Percentage of equity shares owned by Japanese parent(s), March 1997	71	57.3%	21.1	215	54.7%	22.9	145	73.0%	26.3
Net increase in Japanese capital participation rate, March 1997–March 98	71	3.4%	14.8	215	0.9%	12.9	145	2.6%	12.4
Share of subsidiaries in which Japan's capital participation rate was increased	71	21.1%		215	11.6%		145	11.0%	

	General Machinery & Precision Instruments			Transport Equipment			Low Tech Industries		
	N	Mean	Std. Dev.	N	Mean	Std. Dev.	N	Mean	Std. Dev.
Sales in fiscal 1996 (millions of yen)	68	3,665.3	6,667.8	114	16,224.4	39,428.8	110	4,475.4	10,109.7
Change in sales, fiscal 1996–97 (millions of yen)	68	−186.4	2,455.2	114	−4,077.4	15,444.1	110	−479.4	2,188.5
Share of subsidiaries for which sales were down	68	55.9%		114	70.2%		110	62.7%	
Net profits in fiscal 1996 (millions of yen)	65	256.9	721.5	110	848.1	2,017.1	103	294.1	−453.0

Change in profits, fiscal 1996–97 (millions of yen)	63	32.4	580.0	109	−731.0	1,788.1	100	−254.7	−21.2
Share of subsidiaries for which profits were down	63	55.6%		109	79.8%		100	59.0%	
Employment in fiscal 1996	68	281.3	413.3	114	820.2	1,531.9	110	571.1	874.3
Change in employment, March 1997–March 98	68	2.5	36.4	114	−74.7	306.2	110	−67.3	7,229.4
Share of subsidiaries employing fewer workers	68	41.2%		114	55.3%		110	31.8%	
Exports-sales ratio in fiscal 1996	46	29.5%	36.6	96	15.5%	27.9	72	42.6%	43.4
Imports–total procurement ratio in fiscal 1996	39	50.2%	34.3	86	52.5%	31.1	56	31.8%	35.8
Change in imports–total procurement ratio, fiscal 1996–97	30	−4.1%	34.8	82	−1.8%	25.1	49	−7.5%	18.8
Exports to Japan in fiscal 1996	47	747.2	2,642.1	97	308.7	1,820.6	72	513.3	915.8
Change in exports to Japan, fiscal 1996–97 (millions of yen)	38	−180.0	2,365.5	95	458.8	4,353.3	63	−33.7	323.6
Capital equity owned by Japanese parent(s), fiscal 1996	68	603.8	1,344.3	114	453.5	625.2	110	508.5	1,182.5
Percentage of equity shares owned by Japanese parent(s), March 1997	68	65.2%	25.4	114	50.6%	21.5	110	57.1%	25.4
Net increase in Japanese capital participation rate, March 1997–March 98	68	3.6%	16.6	114	2.1%	10.8	110	−0.4%	10.6
Share of subsidiaries in which Japan's capital participation was increased	68	11.8%		114	14.0%		110	10.0%	

Source: Author's calculations based on the MITI data set.

Note: N = number of observations.

Third, trends in subsidiaries' exports to Japan are also quite different across industries. Subsidiaries in the transport equipment industry, the electrical machinery industry, and the chemical and metal products industry have increased their exports to Japan considerably. In contrast, exports to Japan by subsidiaries in the other industries have declined.

Fourth, subsidiaries in the electrical machinery, the general machinery and precision instruments industry, and the low-tech industries have reduced their imports/total procurement ratio by more than 4 percent.

Economic conditions in the ASEAN-4 countries and Korea did not deteriorate in the same way. The performance of Japanese subsidiaries was also different across the five host countries. Figures 8.2 and 8.3 show recent trends in these countries' real exchange rates and manufacturing production indexes. The currency crisis spread from Thailand to the other ASEAN-4 countries very quickly in July 1997, whereas the Korean won started depreciating four months later. The sharp decline in production in Thailand preceded the recession in the other four countries. In the case of the Philippines, the impact of currency depreciation on the macroeconomy was relatively moderate in 1997.

Our data set covers subsidiaries' activities of fiscal 1996 and 1997. Therefore, the selected indicators for the subsidiaries in the different countries shown in table 8.10 correspond to macroeconomic trends before March 1998. According to table 8.10, subsidiaries in Thailand have experienced the sharpest decline in sales and profits. Here, 71 percent of all subsidiaries registered a decline in profits. However, subsidiaries in Thailand did not reduce their employment substantially. Subsidiaries in Korea, in contrast, reduced their employment levels considerably while experiencing modest declines in sales and profits. One possible explanation for this difference runs as follows. Japanese subsidiaries in Thailand are generally younger than subsidiaries in Korea.[12] Younger subsidiaries tend to be equipped with more advanced machinery. Changes in economic conditions in host countries also sometimes make locational advantages of old subsidiaries obsolete, so subsidiaries in Thailand may have been better positioned than subsidiaries in Korea. Many Japanese parents seem eager to support their subsidiaries in Thailand. In the case of Thailand, the percentage of subsidiaries in which Japan's capital participation rate increased amounted to 14.7 percent, which was the highest among the five countries.

It is also interesting that subsidiaries in Thailand actively increased their exports to Japan. According to table 8.10, Japanese manufacturing subsidiaries in Thailand increased their exports to Japan by 85 billion yen (371

12. In my data set, the majority of Japan's manufacturing subsidiaries in Korea were established before 1987. In the case of Thailand, about three-fourths of manufacturing subsidiaries were established after 1987.

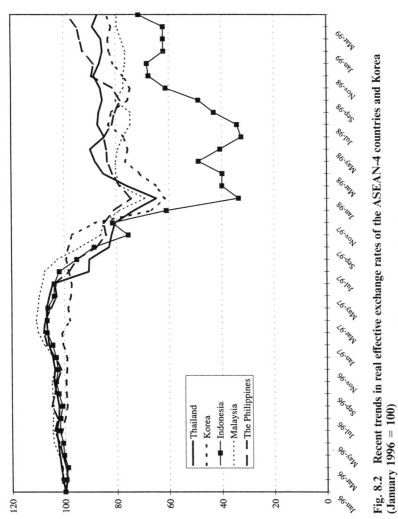

Fig. 8.2 Recent trends in real effective exchange rates of the ASEAN-4 countries and Korea (January 1996 = 100)

Source: Author's calculations based on J. P. Morgan's real "broad" effective exchange rates.

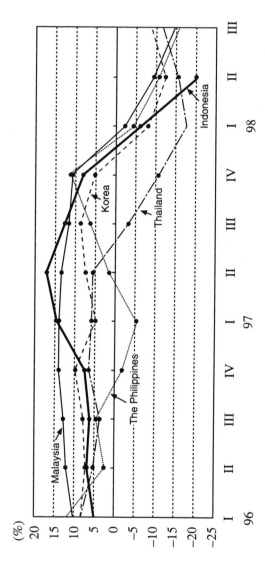

Fig. 8.3   Index of manufacturing production (change over the same quarter of the previous year), by country
Source: MITI (1999c).

Table 8.10   Selected Indicators of Japan's Manufacturing Subsidiaries in the ASEAN-4 Countries and Korea, by Country

	Korea			Thailand			Indonesia		
	N	Mean	Std. Dev.	N	Mean	Std. Dev.	N	Mean	Std. Dev.
Sales in fiscal 1996 (millions of yen)	159	7,657.2	15,394.5	340	8,025.4	23,127.7	224	5,819.3	13,212.9
Change in sales, fiscal 1996–97 (millions of yen)	159	–11.5	3,236.3	340	–1,136.3	9,708.2	224	64.4	3,202.3
Share of subsidiaries for which sales were down	159	57.2%		340	60.6%		224	52.7%	
Net profits in fiscal 1996 (millions of yen)	153	278.1	474.6	319	318.9	1,155.3	209	297.4	1,305.9
Change in profits, fiscal 1996–97 (millions of yen)	152	–23.7	392.3	310	–548.6	2,263.5	205	–177.3	968.1
Share of subsidiaries for which profits were down	152	59.2%		310	71.0%		205	61.0%	
Employment in fiscal 1996	159	342.1	561.2	340	626.7	1,120.4	224	800.0	1,050.4
Change in employment, March 1997–March 98	159	–45.9	236.1	340	–25.6	201.9	224	–63.1	628.3
Share of subsidiaries employing fewer workers	159	50.3%		340	47.9%		224	29.9%	
Exports-sales ratio in fiscal 1996	119	27.1%	35.6	256	35.1%	39.2	152	40.1%	40.9
Imports–total procurement ratio in fiscal 1996	101	43.2%	32.3	215	52.1%	36.0	112	50.8%	35.6
Change in imports–total procurement ratio, fiscal 1996–97	92	–1.5%	25.1	190	–2.3%	29.2	97	–1.0%	22.3
Exports to Japan in fiscal 1996	122	883.5	2,954.8	257	1,261.4	6,912.1	152	712.6	2,497.4

(*continued*)

Table 8.10 (continued)

	Korea			Thailand			Indonesia		
	N	Mean	Std. Dev.	N	Mean	Std. Dev.	N	Mean	Std. Dev.
Change in exports to Japan, fiscal 1996–97 (millions of yen)	111	119.3	1,877.6	228	370.5	2,974.5	133	26.0	465.6
Capital equity owned by Japanese parent(s), fiscal 1996	159	521.0	1,183.1	340	596.7	1,186.8	224	833.3	3,861.2
Percentage of equity shares owned by Japanese parent(s), March 1997	159	57.8%	26.5	340	56.6%	24.7	224	64.7%	23.6
Net increase in Japanese capital participation rate, March 1997–March 98	159	1.7%	10.7	340	2.2%	13.5	224	1.0%	13.1
Share of subsidiaries in which Japan's capital participation rate was increased	159	8.8%		340	14.7%		224	12.1%	

	Malaysia			The Philippines		
	N	Mean	Std. Dev.	N	Mean	Std. Dev.
Sales in fiscal 1996 (millions of yen)	275	8,423.1	13,884.0	103	6,098.2	11,249.7
Change in sales, fiscal 1996–97 (millions of yen)	275	84.8	3,730.2	103	864.7	6,410.1
Share of subsidiaries for which sales were down	275	50.5%		103	31.1%	
Net profits in fiscal 1996 (millions of yen)	260	275.5	1,142.5	92	380.8	966.9

Change in profits, fiscal 1996–97 (millions of yen)	249	−123.3	97.4	90	−200.5	1,042.9
Share of subsidiaries for which profits were down	249	57.4%		90	55.6%	
Employment in fiscal 1996	275	682	924.2	103	763.2	1,527.7
Change in employment, March 1997–March 98	275	−38.5	475.8	103	32.3	282.5
Share of subsidiaries employing fewer workers	275	49.1%		103	35.0%	
Exports-sales ratio in fiscal 1996	208	52.7%	40.5	80	55.7%	46.0
Imports–total procurement ratio in fiscal 1996	173	58.1%	35.8	68	69.7%	35.0
Change in imports–total procurement ratio, fiscal 1996–97	152	−1.5%	24.1	60	−6.2%	20.4
Exports to Japan in fiscal 1996	202	1,676.3	6,123.5	81	1,700.7	5,059.1
Change in exports to Japan, fiscal 1996–97 (millions of yen)	186	209	2,500.3	73	1,103.5	6,482.4
Capital equity owned by Japanese parent(s), fiscal 1996	275	972.7	1,884.4	103	704	978.5
Percentage of equity shares owned by Japanese parent(s), March 1997	275	75.2%	29.7	103	74.7%	30.2
Net increase in Japanese capital participation rate, March 1997–March 98	275	2.0%	14.8	103	2.9%	14.5
Share of subsidiaries in which Japan's capital participation was increased	275	5.5%		103	9.7%	

Source: Author's calculations based on the MITI data set.

Note: N = number of observations.

million yen times 228 subsidiaries). This is a considerable amount compared to the current account deficit of Thailand, which stood at $3 billion in 1997. Even under the serious economic conditions in Thailand, export-oriented subsidiaries were better off. According to my data set, subsidiaries with exports/sales ratios exceeding 50 percent increased their average sales by 20 percent and saw their profits rise by 66 percent. However, they increased their workforce by only 2 percent.

Although their average sales have increased, subsidiaries in Indonesia and Malaysia experienced a decline in profits and cut their workforce substantially. Among the five countries, only subsidiaries in the Philippines increased their average workforce. Seventy-five percent of subsidiaries in the Philippines were employing more workers in March 1998 than in March 1997. They also increased their average exports to Japan by 65 percent.

Subdividing Japan's manufacturing subsidiaries in Korea, Thailand, and Indonesia into two groups, tables 8.11 through 8.14 show how several characteristics of subsidiaries affected their performance and response.

Subsidiaries majority-owned by Japanese firms were generally more export oriented than were minority-owned ones (table 8.11). There is a 19 percent gap in the average exports/sales ratio between the two groups. Many developing countries have linked export performance requirements with restrictions on capital participation rates for foreign investors. Local market–oriented foreign subsidiaries are usually required to be joint ventures with a local partner as the majority owner. According to the Japan Machinery Center for Trade and Investment (1997), many Japanese subsidiaries in Asia reported that they are restricted by such linkage policies. Because of their local market–oriented characteristics, minority-owned subsidiaries were more severely hit by the crisis. After the crisis, all the five countries relaxed their regulations on capital participation rates for foreign firms (Japan External Trade Organization [JETRO] 1999). Such policy changes certainly contributed to the substantial increase in Japan's capital participation rate, especially in the case of minority-owned subsidiaries. In the case of minority-owned subsidiaries, 17 percent of all subsidiaries experienced an increase in the Japanese capital participation rate.

In table 8.12, subsidiaries are subdivided by value added per worker. This shows that the decline in sales was more moderate in the case of subsidiaries with a value added per worker of less than 1.5 million yen. This is probably due to the fact that these subsidiaries were more export oriented. Moreover, despite the stable trend in sales, these subsidiaries reduced their employment more substantially. One possible explanation is that subsidiaries with a high value added per worker are reluctant to lay off workers because these have accumulated considerable firm-specific skills.

Table 8.13 shows that subsidiaries owned by larger parents were hit harder, but these subsidiaries expanded their exports to Japan greatly. Probably, with the help of their large parent firm this type of subsidiary

Table 8.11   Selected Indicators of Japan's Manufacturing Subsidiaries in Korea, Thailand, and Indonesia, by Japan's Capital Participation Rate

	Japan's Participation Rate < 50%			Japan's Participation Rate ≥ 50%		
	N	Mean	Std. Dev.	N	Mean	Std. Dev.
Sales in fiscal 1996 (millions of yen)	361	7,242.7	18,187.8	362	7,279.2	19,644.1
Change in sales, fiscal 1996–97 (millions of yen)	361	−1,021.2	6,059.2	362	−14.1	7,936.5
Share of subsidiaries for which sales were down	361	68.7%		362	46.1%	
Net profits in fiscal 1996 (millions of yen)	340	315.8	1,011.7	341	290.5	1,171.3
Change in profits, fiscal 1996–97 (millions of yen)	331	−552.7	2,077.3	336	−80.6	1,051.0
Share of subsidiaries for which profits were down	331	75.5%		336	55.1%	
Employment in fiscal 1996	361	536.6	864.0	362	698.7	1,137.9
Change in employment, March 1997–March 98	361	−62.6	462.7	362	−20.8	304.6
Share of subsidiaries employing fewer workers	361	46.8%		362	39.0%	
Exports-sales ratio in fiscal 1996	261	19.4%	30.7	266	49.8%	40.6
Imports-total procurement ratio in fiscal 1996	204	39.9%	34.6	224	58.5%	33.4
Change in imports-total procurement ratio, fiscal 1996–97	180	0.3%	26.5	199	−3.7%	26.6
Exports to Japan in fiscal 1996	263	260.8	1,191.4	268	1,760.0	7,134.4
Change in exports to Japan, fiscal 1996–97 (millions of yen)	230	195.2	2,802.5	242	232.5	1,626.2
Capital equity owned by Japanese parent(s), fiscal 1996	361	306.1	590.6	362	999.7	3,253.8
Percentage of equity shares owned by Japanese parent(s), March 1997	361	42.0%	14.6	362	76.6%	21.0
Net increase in Japanese capital participation rate, March 1997–March 98	361	3.7%	13.1	362	−0.2%	12.2
Share of subsidiaries in which Japan's capital participation rate was increased	361	17.2%		362	8.0%	

Source: Author's calculations based on the MITI data set.

Note: N = number of observations.

Table 8.12   Selected Indicators of Japan's Manufacturing Subsidiaries in Korea, Thailand, and Indonesia, by Value Added per Worker

	Value Added per Worker < 1.5 million yen			Value Added per Worker ≥ 1.5 million yen		
	N	Mean	Std. Dev.	N	Mean	Std. Dev.
Sales in fiscal 1996 (millions of yen)	149	2,010.8	4,134.1	364	8,551.1	22,342.4
Change in sales, fiscal 1996–97 (millions of yen)	149	260.2	1,232.2	364	−1,042.0	8,013.2
Share of subsidiaries for which sales were down	149	43.0%		364	61.8%	
Net profits in fiscal 1996 (millions of yen)	145	52.7	468.7	356	343.8	965.2
Change in profits, fiscal 1996–97 (millions of yen)	144	−113.8	451.9	349	−428.7	1,721.4
Share of subsidiaries for which profits were down	144	58.3%		349	68.2%	
Employment in fiscal 1996	149	648.1	980.7	364	590.6	1,037.7
Change in employment, March 1997–March 98	149	−107.5	712.4	364	−26.0	167.3
Share of subsidiaries employing fewer workers	149	43.6%		364	48.6%	
Exports-sales ratio in fiscal 1996	130	52.0%	42.7	326	29.0%	36.4
Imports-total procurement ratio in fiscal 1996	123	45.9%	36.5	305	51.2%	34.6
Change in imports-total procurement ratio, fiscal 1996–97	106	−2.2%	19.5	273	−1.6%	28.9
Exports to Japan in fiscal 1996	130	412.6	1,002.9	330	976.1	3,561.6
Change in exports to Japan, fiscal 1996–97 (millions of yen)	119	129.8	942.5	300	284.2	2,787.2
Capital equity owned by Japanese parent(s), fiscal 1996	149	375.9	712.5	364	782.7	3,195.9
Percentage of equity shares owned by Japanese parent(s), March 1997	149	62.3%	25.8	364	60.5%	24.4
Net increase in Japanese capital participation rate, March 1997–March 98	149	0.9%	12.8	364	1.5%	10.3
Share of subsidiaries in which Japan's capital participation rate was increased	149	11.4%		364	10.7%	

Source: Author's calculations based on the MITI data set.

Note: N = number of observations.

Table 8.13　Selected Indicators of Japan's Manufacturing Subsidiaries in Korea, Thailand, and Indonesia, by Total Assets of the Prime Parent Firm

	Total Assets of the Prime Parent Firm < 100 Billion Yen			Total Assets of the Prime Parent Firm > 100 Billion Yen		
	N	Mean	Std. Dev.	N	Mean	Std. Dev.
Sales in fiscal 1996 (millions of yen)	129	3,011.8	9,181.3	397	10,160.7	23,969.6
Change in sales, fiscal 1996–97 (millions of yen)	129	397.5	5,005.8	397	–1,129.2	8,906.2
Share of subsidiaries for which sales were down	129	55.0%		397	56.9%	
Net profits in fiscal 1996 (millions of yen)	127	73.1	351.7	366	419.8	1,395.7
Change in profits, fiscal 1996–97 (millions of yen)	127	–71.4	1,290.1	358	–453.9	2,011.2
Share of subsidiaries for which profits were down	127	64.6%		358	65.9%	
Employment in fiscal 1996	129	374.3	859.9	397	722.6	947.8
Change in employment, March 1997–March 98	129	1.9	77.2	397	–77.2	515.9
Share of subsidiaries employing fewer workers	129	41.9%		397	43.3%	
Exports-sales ratio in fiscal 1996	115	37.9%	39.7	236	31.5%	37.0
Imports-total procurement ratio in fiscal 1996	94	53.1%	31.7	188	48.3%	36.8
Change in imports-total procurement ratio, fiscal 1996–97	86	–1.0%	21.5	159	–0.6%	30.2
Exports to Japan in fiscal 1996	118	1,353.6	9,116.9	236	1,123.2	3,693.3
Change in exports to Japan, fiscal 1996–97 (millions of yen)	111	46.7	499.7	199	339.7	3,342.9
Capital equity owned by Japanese parent(s), fiscal 1996	129	395.1	824.5	397	717.9	1,313.1
Percentage of equity shares owned by Japanese parent(s), March 1997	129	60.2%	23.9	397	57.8%	24.6
Net increase in Japanese capital participation rate, March 1997–March 98	129	1.0%	11.0	397	2.5%	13.0
Share of subsidiaries in which Japan's capital participation rate was increased	129	9.3%		397	14.9%	

Source: Author's calculations based on the MITI data set.

Note: N = number of observations.

was able to switch from local sales to exports.[13] An increase in the Japanese capital participation rate has also been more common in this group of subsidiaries.

8.5   Econometric Analysis of Subsidiaries' Responses to the Crisis

Because Japanese subsidiaries seem to be characterized not by nimbleness but by perseverance, we study which types of subsidiaries are reluctant to cut their workers when their sales are declining. As we have seen in table 8.9, the elasticity of employment to changes in sales, (Δemploy/ employ)/(Δsales/sales), is quite different across industries. Using the microdata for Japanese subsidiaries in the ASEAN-4 and Korea, as I explained in the previous section, I estimate determinants of subsidiaries' elasticities of employment to a negative change in sales.

In order to estimate determinants of subsidiaries' elasticities of employment to a negative change in sales, I use the following model:

$$(1) \quad GEMP_i = \alpha_0 + \alpha_1 SIGNGSAL_i * GSAL_i + \alpha_2(\beta_0 + \beta_1 CHAR_i)$$
$$* (1 - SIGNGSAL_i) * GSAL_i + \alpha_3 EXCH_i + u_i,$$

where i is the index for subsidiaries; GEMP is the growth rate of employment from March 1997 to March 1998; GSAL is the growth rate of sales from fiscal 1996 to fiscal 1997; SIGNGSAL is a dummy variable which takes the value 1 if and only if GSAL > 0; CHAR denotes a certain characteristic that might affect the elasticity; EXCH is the depreciation rate of the host country's currency against the U.S. dollar from fiscal 1996 to fiscal 1997 (comparison between two annual averages);[14] and u is the usual error term.

As CHAR, I tried the following six variables.

13. According to Nikkei (1999a) and a personal interview, both Toyota Motor Co. and Nissan Motor Co. started exports of their Thai-made pickup trucks "Hilux" and "Dutsan" to Australia, after the crisis, in order to support their Thai subsidiaries. Toyota also increased exports of its Thai-made diesel engine to Japan. We should note that not all the Japanese subsidiaries in the region have easily expanded their exports. For example, in contrast with the case of Thailand, Japanese automobile companies could not substantially increase exports from their Indonesian subsidiaries because of two problems (Fujimoto and Sugiyama 1999). First, since their Indonesian models have low local content compared to their Thai and Malaysian counterparts, improvements of price competitiveness by Indonesian currency depreciation were limited. Second, designs of their Indonesian models, which are mainly van- or minibus-type commercial vehicles, were too adapted to the Indonesian market for export to other regions.

14. All five countries experienced currency depreciation in this period. Theoretically, the relationship between the size of currency depreciation and the growth rate of a subsidiary's employment is ambiguous. Since currency depreciation will increase a subsidiary's optimal employment-sales ratio, it might have a positive effect on the subsidiary's employment. On the other hand, the size of currency depreciation indicates the seriousness of the currency crisis and might have a negative relationship with the subsidiary's employment.

1. ASSET: Total assets of the prime Japanese parent firm, in March 1997 (billion yen).

2. PROF: The net profit/total asset ratio of the prime Japanese parent firm, in fiscal 1996.

3. KEI: Total number of workers employed in the host country by the manufacturing subsidiaries whose parents belong to the same vertical *keiretsu* (corporate group) as subsidiary *i*'s parent divided by subsidiary *i*'s own employment, in March 1997; information on vertical *keiretsu* relationships among parents were taken from Touyou Keizai Shinpou-sha (1998).

4. CAP: Capital participation rate of Japanese firms, in March 1997.

5. LOBO: Subsidiary's long-term local borrowing from non-Japanese banks divided by its owned capital, in March 1996. (The source of this data is MITI 1996).

6. VALUE: Subsidiary's value added per worker in fiscal 1997 (million yen).

A subsidiary owned by a large parent firm, by a parent with higher profit rate, or by a parent with a greater *keiretsu* networks in the same host country is likely to get the parent firm's or *keiretsu*-related subsidiaries' support easily, and tends to keep its employment unchanged. Japanese parents will be more eager to support their subsidiary if their capital participation rate is higher. Thus I expect negative coefficients for ASSET, PROF, KEI, and CAP.

According to Dollar and Hallward-Driemeier (1998) and Lamberte et al. (1999), firms with foreign ties performed better than independent local firms in Thailand and the Philippines after the crisis. Firms with foreign ties tend to have a higher capacity utilization level and keep employment after the crisis. One probable reason for this difference is that firms with foreign ties can get parent firms' support. Another probable reason is that firms with foreign ties tend to be less exposed to the local economy in several aspects. First, firms with foreign ties have a higher exports/sales ratio than independent local firms, on average (Dollar and Hallward-Driemeier 1998) and are likely to be less hard hit by contraction of local demand. In table 8.8, we have already seen that Japanese subsidiaries with higher export/sales ratios performed much better than other subsidiaries.[15] Second, firms with foreign ties are less connected with local banks and local financial markets. They tend to finance their funds from parent firms or from banks of their home countries. In the recent Asian currency crisis, almost all the crisis-hit countries took contracting monetary policy and invited financial crisis. Under such a financial crunch, foreign subsidiaries

15. According to Japan Overseas Economic Cooperation Fund's (OECF's) enterprise survey, which covers both firms with foreign ties and local independent firms, export-oriented firms tend to keep their production after the crisis in Thailand (OECF and Japan Research Institute of Development Assistance [RIDA] 1999).

less connected with local banks are likely to be able to keep their employment. I include LOBO as an explanatory variable to test this hypothesis. It is sometimes argued that the Japanese production system depends more on the accumulation of firm-specific skills. This means that Japanese FDI is accompanied by large sunk cost. If substantial sunk costs are involved, a parent firm will support its subsidiary under adversary conditions. It seems that firm-specific skills play a more important role in subsidiaries with higher value added per worker, so I expect a negative coefficient for VALUE.[16]

Equation (1) can be transformed into the following equation:

$$(2) \quad \text{GEMP}_i = \alpha_0 + \alpha_1 \text{GSAL}_i + (\alpha_2\beta_0 - \alpha_1)(1 - \text{SIGNGSAL}_i)$$
$$* \text{ GSAL}_i + \alpha_2\beta_1\text{CHAR}_i * (1 - \text{SIGNGSAL}_i)$$
$$* \text{ GSAL}_i + \alpha_3\text{EXCH}_i + u_i.$$

Since GSAL and SIGNGSAL are endogenous variables, I estimated equation (2) by the following two-step method. In the first step, I estimated a linear model for GSAL by OLS and two Tobit models for (1 − SIGNGSAL) * GSAL and CHAR * (1 − SIGNGSAL) * GSAL. In the second step, I estimated equation (2) by ordinary least squares (OLS) using the predicted values of GSAL, (1 − SIGNGSAL) * GSAL, and (1 − SIGNGSAL) * CHAR * GSAL in place of actual values of the explanatory variables.

For the linear model and the first Tobit model for (1 − SIGNGSAL) * GSAL, I used the following variables as exogenous explanatory variables: EXP, which equals [subsidiary's exports/sales ratio in fiscal 1996] * EXCH; IMP, which equals [subsidiary's imports/procurement ratio in fiscal 1996] * EXCH; EXPE, which equals number of months of production since start of operations as of March 1996; CAP; country dummies (the dummy for Indonesia was omitted); and thirteen industry dummies (the dummy for the food product industry was omitted).

Equation (1) in table 8.14 is the result of the linear model estimation for GSAL by OLS. It is found that subsidiaries which have a higher exports/total sales ratio and are located in a country experiencing greater currency depreciation tended to have a higher growth rate of sales. It is confirmed that export-oriented subsidiaries were less hit by the Asian currency crisis. It is also found that younger subsidiaries have the higher growth rate of sales. Capital participation rate of Japanese firms has positive effect on the growth rate of sales. The coefficient of the term [subsidiary's imports/

---

16. I should note that there are many other factors, such as the capital-labor ratio, the capacity utilization level, and so on that might affect value added per worker, and VALUE is a quite indirect indicator of the importance of firm-specific skills.

Table 8.14   Determinants of the Growth Rate of Subsidiary's Sales

	Eq. 1	Eq. 2	Eq. 3	Eq. 4	Eq. 5
EXP	0.292	0.545	0.555	0.531	0.387
	(2.594)**	(3.662)***	(3.732)***	(3.607)***	(3.554)***
IMP	0.038	-0.049	-0.045	0.0063	0.105
	(0.324)	(-0.328)	(-0.302)	(0.043)	(0.908)
EXPE	-0.00072	-0.00081	-0.00084	-0.00083	-0.00074
	(-4.292)***	(-3.925)***	(-4.051)***	(-4.078)***	(-4.383)***
CAP	0.210				
	(3.105)***				
ASSET		-0.023			
		(-1.136)			
PROF			0.104		
			(0.143)		
KEI				0.00023	
				(0.096)	
Korea	-0.070	-0.056	-0.043	-0.015	-0.079
	(-1.143)	(-0.704)	(-0.553)	(-0.200)	(-1.260)
Malaysia	-0.099	-0.039	-0.035	-0.047	-0.079
	(-1.947)*	(-0.620)	(-0.552)	(-0.768)	(-1.556)
The Philippines	0.096	0.358	0.354	0.345	0.118
	(1.527)	(4.281)***	(4.231)***	(4.207)***	(1.864)*
Thailand	-0.087	-0.074	-0.072	-0.075	-0.103
	(-1.825)*	(-1.258)	(-1.226)	(-1.276)	(-2.151)**
Textiles	-0.028	0.0032	0.0019	0.040	-0.025
	(-0.233)	(0.022)	(0.013)	(0.273)	(-0.204)
Pulp, Paper, and Paper Products	-0.209	-0.081	-0.129	-0.023	-0.193
	(-1.213)	(-0.375)	(-0.603)	(-0.115)	(-1.112)
Chemicals	0.078	0.104	0.117	0.142	0.081
	(0.679)	(0.785)	(0.886)	(1.048)	(0.701)
Petroleum and Coal Products	-0.219	-0.314	-0.298	-0.303	-0.213
	(-0.878)	(-1.018)	(-0.965)	(-0.978)	(-0.851)

(continued)

Table 8.14 (continued)

	Eq. 1	Eq. 2	Eq. 3	Eq. 4	Eq. 5
Ceramics and Stone Products	0.030	0.042	0.062	0.087	0.032
	(0.239)	(0.288)	(0.419)	(0.577)	(0.249)
Iron and Steel	0.059	0.123	0.111	0.126	0.059
	(0.451)	(0.825)	(0.727)	(0.835)	(0.447)
Non-Ferrous Metals	0.189	0.222	0.236	0.260	0.212
	(1.430)	(1.423)	(1.517)	(1.642)	(1.598)
Metal Products	0.104	0.163	0.167	0.194	0.120
	(0.793)	(1.066)	(1.090)	(1.244)	(0.910)
Industrial Machinery	−0.070	0.086	0.095	0.111	−0.033
	(−0.553)	(0.567)	(0.626)	(0.712)	(−0.264)
Electrical Machinery	0.072	0.171	0.182	0.198	0.102
	(0.666)	(1.359)	(1.438)	(1.519)	(0.930)
Transportation Equipment	0.0052	0.027	0.038	0.052	0.0056
	(0.047)	(0.205)	(0.292)	(0.387)	(0.050)
Precision Instruments	0.034	0.117	0.132	0.203	0.065
	(0.216)	(0.630)	(0.707)	(1.032)	(0.409)
Miscellaneous	−0.080	−0.111	−0.099	−0.069	−0.054
Manufacturing	(−0.701)	(−0.778)	(−0.697)	(−0.467)	(−0.469)
Constant	−0.0062	0.062	0.033	0.0055	0.087
	(−0.053)	(0.473)	(0.249)	(0.041)	(0.763)
N	599	387	387	397	599
F-value	5.01	5.06	4.99	4.95	4.71
Prob > F	0.000	0.000	0.000	0.000	0.000
Adjusted R^2	0.1236	0.1811	0.1782	0.1733	0.1105

Notes: Numbers in parentheses are *t*-values. N = number of observations.

***Significant at the 1 percent level.

**Significant at the 5 percent level.

*Significant at the 10 percent level.

procurement ratio] * EXCH was not significant. Estimated coefficients of country dummies show that subsidiaries in the Philippines and Indonesia performed better than those in the other three countries. After controlling for the subsidiary's characteristics and country-specific factors, there is no significant additional variation in the growth rate of sales across industries. In equations (2)–(4), I tried several different specifications by replacing CAP with other characteristics of subsidiaries, such as, ASSET, PROF, and KEI. However, the coefficients of these variables were not significant, so I used the predicted value of GSAL by equation (1) for the second step. For the first Tobit model for (1 − SIGNGSAL) * GSAL, I used the same explanatory variables as equation (1) of table 8.14, and for the second Tobit model for CHAR * (1 − SIGNGSAL) * GSAL, I used the same explanatory variables as equation (1) of table 8.14 plus CHAR.[17]

Table 8.15 shows the results of the second step of estimating equation (2) for six CHAR variables. Negative and significant estimated coefficients of ASSET and KEI imply that a subsidiary owned by a large parent firm or owned by a parent with a greater *keiretsu* network in the same host country tends to keep its employment unchanged. These findings seem to imply that parent firms' support is important for subsidiaries to keep their employment. Contrary to my hypothesis, it is found that subsidiaries with higher Japanese capital participation rate (CAP) tend to keep their employment. The coefficient of PROF and LOBO were insignificant. The latter result implies that I could not confirm the hypothesis that foreign subsidiaries less connected with local banks are likely to be able to keep their employment. I have also found that if a subsidiary has high value added per worker, it will tend to keep its employment. To check the robustness of the results, I estimated equations that include several CHAR variables at one time (equations [12]–[14]). In these regressions, the estimated coefficients of ASSET, KEI, and VALUE did not change substantially and were still significant, but the coefficient of CAP became insignificant.[18]

8.6   Conclusions

After the financial crisis in Asia, Japanese firms increased their FDI flows to the ASEAN-4 countries and Korea mainly in order to support

17. For PROF * (1 − SIGNGSAL) * GSAL, I estimated a linear model because PROF can take negative values.

18. I also tried reduced-form regressions of linear models directly, with change in employment as the dependent variable. Table 8.16 shows the results of these new regressions. Although the simple linear models do not fit the data well, the results are not inconsistent with my other results, which are summarized in tables 8.14 and 8.15. Positive estimated coefficients of EXP imply that subsidiaries which have higher exports-total sales ratios and are located in countries that experienced greater currency depreciation tend to have higher growth rates of employment. Positive and significant estimated coefficients of KEI and VALUE imply that subsidiaries which are owned by a parent with a greater *keiretu* network in the same host country or have high value added per worker tend to keep their employment.

Table 8.15   Determinants of the Elasticity of Employment to Changes in Sales

	Eq. 6	Eq. 7	Eq. 8	Eq. 9	Eq. 10	Eq. 11	Eq. 12	Eq. 13	Eq. 14
GSAL	0.171	0.174	0.177	0.453	0.426	0.299	0.179	0.233	0.094
	(1.216)	(1.228)	(1.275)	(3.274)***	(3.309)***	(2.364)***	(1.269)	(1.612)	(0.657)
(1 – SIGNGSAL) * GSAL	0.221	0.011	0.272	-0.236	-0.740	-0.025	0.533	0.024	0.773
	(0.821)	(0.042)	(1.084)	(-1.072)	(-2.296)**	(-0.119)	(1.816)*	(0.057)	(2.606)**
EXCH	-0.248	-0.241	-0.172	-0.073	-0.267	-0.120	-0.279	-0.413	-0.203
	(-1.171)	(-1.117)	(-0.850)	(-0.345)	(-1.326)	(-0.630)	(-1.318)	(-1.821)*	(-0.974)
ASSET * (1 – SIGNGSAL) * GSAL	-0.00016						-0.00019	-0.00018	-0.00018
	(-1.943)*						(-2.214)**	(-2.093)**	(-2.160)**
PROF * (1 – SIGNGSAL) * GSAL		-1.864							
		(-0.513)							
KEI * (1 – SIGNGSAL) * GSAL			-0.040				-0.042	-0.036	-0.036
			(-2.644)***				(-2.736)***	(-2.319)**	(-2.025)**
LOBO * (1 – SIGNGSAL) * GSAL				-0.00902					
				(-0.340)					
CAP * (1 – SIGNGSAL) * GSAL					0.826			0.750	
					(2.136)**			(1.625)	
VALUE * (1 – SIGNGSAL) * GSAL						-0.020			-0.030
						(-2.908)***			(-4.296)***
Constant	0.121	0.096	0.096	0.031	0.098	0.059	0.164	0.205	0.141
	(1.330)	(1.053)	(1.099)	(0.318)	(1.168)	(0.727)	(1.775)*	(2.146)**	(1.548)
N	387	387	397	466	599	581	382	382	372
F-value	2.81	1.91	3.61	5.04	4.98	4.81	3.78	3.61	5.29
Prob > F	0.0255	0.1079	0.0066	0.0006	0.0006	0.0008	0.0023	0.0017	0.0000
Adjusted R^2	0.0184	0.0094	0.0257	0.0336	0.0260	0.0256	0.0352	0.0394	0.0799

Notes: Numbers in parentheses are t-values. N = number of observations.

***Significant at the 1 percent level.

**Significant at the 5 percent level.

*Significant at the 10 percent level.

Table 8.16   **Determinants of the Growth Rate of Subsidiary's Employment**

	Eq. 15	Eq. 16	Eq. 17	Eq. 18	Eq. 19
EXP	0.104	0.116	0.134	0.124	0.088
	(1.688)*	(1.632)	(1.895)*	(1.755)*	(1.180)
EXCH	−0.161	−0.221	−0.216	−0.161	−0.209
	(−1.042)	(−1.295)	(−1.296)	(−0.928)	(−1.171)
ASSET		0.00040			
		(0.488)			
KEI			0.0038		
			(2.894)**		
VALUE				0.00470	
				(2.185)**	
IMP					0.0288
					(0.365)
N	743	496	503	626	599
F-value	0.59	0.63	1.14	0.79	0.49
Prob > F	0.886	0.859	0.311	0.697	0.955
Adjusted R^2	−0.0084	−0.0120	0.0046	−0.0054	−0.0140

Notes: Estimated coefficients of industry dummies and constant terms are omitted. $N =$ number of observations.
**Significant at the 5 percent level.
*Significant at the 10 percent level.

their troubled subsidiaries. The number of new FDI cases (including acquisitions), however, declined substantially. Expansions of existing subsidiaries were also very rare. In Korea, Thailand, and Indonesia, export-oriented subsidiaries, which are defined as subsidiaries with exports/sales ratios greater than 50 percent, increased their sales by 17 percent and almost doubled their profits; but they expanded their average employment by less than 1 percent. Although new investments and capacity expansions were rare, Japanese subsidiaries persevered in maintaining employment levels. The persistence of Japanese companies is shown by the fact that even local market–oriented subsidiaries barely reduced employment levels despite sharp declines in sales and profits. Parent firms supported their affiliates by raising their paid-up capital and helped their local market–oriented subsidiaries, such as those in the transport equipment industry, boost their exports substantially.[19] It seems that the prime cause of Japa-

19. Japanese parent firms also took several other measures to support their subsidiaries in the region. Toyota expanded its project to invite workers of developing countries to Japan for on-the-job training after the crisis. In order to keep skilled workers of subsidiaries in ASEAN countries, Toyota doubled the number of invited workers from the region to about 500 in fiscal 1998. This project was supported by the Association for Overseas Technical Scholarship (AOTS), whose activity is partly financed by the Japanese government. According to a personal interview, several parent firms transferred their profit to their subsidiaries in the region by transfer pricing.

nese subsidiaries' export increase is not production expansion by export-oriented subsidiaries but the struggle for survival by previously local market–oriented subsidiaries.

Since Japanese subsidiaries seem to be characterized not by nimbleness but by perseverance, I studied what type of subsidiaries were reluctant to cut their workforces even when their sales were declining. Using econometric analysis on subsidiary-level data, I found that a subsidiary's elasticity of employment to a negative change of sales depends upon several characteristics of the subsidiary. I found that a subsidiary owned by a large parent firm or owned by a parent with a greater *keiretsu* network in the same host country tends to maintain its employment levels. This finding seems to imply that parent firms' support is important for subsidiaries to maintain their employment levels. I also found that if a subsidiary has a high value added per worker, it will tend to keep its employment level.

Probably, Japanese parent firms cannot exploit host countries' currency crisis and the "fire sale" of local firms in part because they themselves are in trouble due to the deep recession in Japan. In order to explain the perseverance of Japanese parent firms, we need another hypothesis. One possible explanation is that they are patient because of sunk costs. It is sometimes argued that the Japanese production system depends more on long-term supplier relationships and the accumulation of firm-specific skills. This means that Japanese FDI is accompanied by large sunk costs. If substantial sunk costs are involved, a parent firm will support its subsidiary under adverse conditions. Long-term commitments inevitably incur larger losses when investments fail. The emphasis on long-term relationships is thought to have made Japanese firms sensitive to risk and wary of making new investments, including corporate acquisitions. Unfortunately, my data set covers too short a period, and statistics on U.S. subsidiaries' activities for 1998 are not yet available. By expanding the time span of my analysis and by comparing Japanese subsidiaries' response with that of U.S. subsidiaries, we may be able to obtain more rigorous results in the future.

What lessons can be learned from these recent experiences? First it was confirmed that direct investment is a much more reliable form of capital movement than quick-at-flight portfolio investment and international bank loans in an economic crisis.[20] Second, optimistic expectations that weak currencies of the host countries would naturally bring about an increase in direct investment have proved to be mistaken. To be able to return to the desirable conditions before the Asian economic crisis, where direct investment was the nucleus around which the intraregional division of labor developed and economic growth continued, Japan and other foreign governments would need to support direct investment actively.

---

20. Analysis by the United Nations Conference on Trade and Development (UNCTAD 1999) also confirms this fact.

References

Belderbos, Rene, Giovanni Capannelli, and Kyoji Fukao. 2000. The local content of Japanese electronics manufacturing operations in Asia. In *The role of foreign investment in East Asian economic development.* Vol. 9 of NBER-East Asian Seminar on Economics, eds. Takatoshi Ito and Anne O. Krueger. Chicago: University of Chicago Press.

Berg, Andrew, and Catherine Pattillo. 1998. Are currency crises predictable? A test. IMF Working Paper no. 98/154. Washington, D.C.: International Monetary Fund.

Blomström, Magnus, and Robert E. Lipsey. 1993. Foreign firms and structural adjustment in Latin America: Lessons from the debt crisis. In *Trade, growth and development: The role of politics and institutions. Proceeding of the 12th Arne Ryde Symposium, 13–14 June 1991, in Honour of Bo Sodersten.* New York: Routledge.

Caves, Richard E. 1982. *Multinational enterprise and economic analysis.* Cambridge: Cambridge University Press.

Dollar, David, and Mary Hallward-Dreimeier. 1998. Crisis, adjustment, and reform: Results from the Thailand industrial survey. Washington, D.C.: World Bank. Unpublished Manuscript.

Dunning, John H. 1993. *Multinational enterprises and the global economy.* Wokingham, U.K.: Addison-Wesley.

Frankel, Jeffrey A., and Andrew K. Rose. 1996. Currency crashes in emerging markets: An empirical treatment. *Journal of International Economics* 41 (3/4): 351–66.

Fujimoto, Takahiro, and Yasuo Sugiyama. 1999. The evolution of Asian Car: A dynamic approach to the global-local trade-off. Paper presented at the Research Institute of International Trade and Industry Symposium, East Asian Economy and Japanese Industry at a Turning Point, 16–17 June 1999, Tokyo, Japan.

Fukao, Kyoji, and Masayuki Otaki. 1993. Accumulation of human capital and the business cycle. *Journal of Political Economy* 101 (1): 73–99.

Hamermesh, Daniel S. 1993. *Labor demand.* Princeton: Princeton University Press.

Japan Economic Research Institute. 1999. Ajia no Keizai/Tuuka Kiki to Nippon no Yakuwari [Economic and currency crisis in Asia and the role of Japan]. Tokyo: Nippon Keizai Chousa Kyougikai. Mimeograph.

Japan External Trade Organization (JETRO). 1999. *JETRO Hakusyo Toushi-hen [White Paper on foreign direct investment].* Tokyo: Maruzen.

Japan Machinery Center for Trade and Investment. 1997. Ajia no Keizai Hatten to Boueki Tousi jou no Mondaiten [Economic growth and government interventions on trade and investments in Asia]. Tokyo: Nippon Kikai Yushutu Kumiai. Mimeograph.

Japan Ministry of Finance (MOF). 1998. *Yuuka Shouken Houkoku-sho [Financial reports of listed firms].* Tokyo: Okura-shou Insatsu-kyoku.

Japan Ministry of International Trade and Industry (MITI). 1996. *Kaigai Jigyou-katudou Kihon Chousa [Survey on Japan's business activities abroad].* Tokyo: MITI.

———. 1996–97. *Kaigai Jigyou Katsudou Doukou Chousa [Survey on trends of Japan's business activities abroad].* Tokyo: MITI.

———. 1998. *Kaigai Tousi Toukei Souran [Basic survey on foreign direct investment],* no. 6. Tokyo: Okura-shou Insatsu-kyoku.

———. 1998–99. *Keizai Kouzou Hikaku Chousa [Comparative survey of economic structure].* Tokyo: MITI.

————. 1999a. *Kaigai Jigyou Katsudou Doukou Chousa Gaiyou [Survey on trends of Japan's business activities abroad]*. Tokyo: MITI.

————. 1999b. *Kigyou Doukou Chousa [Quarterly Survey of Japanese Business Activities]*. Tokyo: Okura-shou Insatsu-kyoku.

————. 1999c. *Tsuushou Hakusyo [White Paper on international trade]*. Tokyo: MITI.

Japan Overseas Economic Cooperation Fund (OECF) and Japan Research Institute of Development Assistance (RIDA). 1999. *OECF's enterprise survey and its policy implications: Thailand, Indonesia, and the Philippines*. Tokyo: OECF.

Lamberte, Mario B., Caesar B. Cororaton, Margarita F. Guerrero, and Aniceto Orbeta. 1999. Impacts of the Southeast Asian financial crisis on the Philippine manufacturing sector. PIDS Discussion Paper no. 99–09. Manila: Philippine Institute for Development Studies.

Nikkei. 1999a. Kaigai Kyoten de Seisan no Jidousha Ikigai Yushutu wo Kakudai: Nissan, Sougyou-ritu no Iji Nerau [Nissan Motor Co. expands its foreign subsidiaries' extra-regional exports in order to keep its operation ratio]. Tokyo: Nihon Keizai Shinbun-sha, 22 July.

————. 1999b. Ajia no M&A Kaifuku [M&A activities in Asia have recovered]. Tokyo, Nihon Keizai Shunbun-sha, 22 July.

Perez-Quiros, Gabriel, and Helen Popper. 1996. International capital flows: Do short-term investment and direct investment differ? Policy Research Working Paper no. 1669. Washington, D.C.: World Bank.

Ramstetter, Eric D. 1999. Foreign multinational corporations in Thailand after the crisis. Kitakyushu, Japan: International Centre for the Study of East Asian Development. Unpublished Manuscript.

Research Institute for International Investment and Development, the Export-Import Bank of Japan. 1999. EXIM JAPAN FY 1998 SURVEY: The outlook of Japanese foreign direct investment—The Asian crisis and the prospect of foreign direct investment by Japanese manufactures. *Journal of Research Institute for International Investment and Development* 25 (1): 4–70.

Touyou Keizai Sinpou-sha. 1998. *Kigyou Keiretu Souran [Directory of corporate groups]*. Tokyo: Touyou Keizai Sinpou-sha.

————. 1999. *Kaigai Shinsyutsu Kigyou Souran [Directory of Japanese subsidiaries abroad]*. Tokyo: Touyou Keizai Sinpou-sha.

United Nations Conference on Trade and Development (UNCTAD). 1998. *World investment report 1998: Trends and determinants.* New York: United Nations.

————. 1999. *World investment report 1999: Trends and determinants.* New York: United Nations.

U.S. Department of Commerce. 1998. U.S. direct investment abroad: Detail for historical-cost position and related capital and income flows, 1997. *Survey of Current Business* 78 (10): 117–56.

Comment   Mario B. Lamberte

Let me start by saying that I learned a lot from this paper. Indeed, there are very few studies that have analyzed the effects of the regional financial

Mario B. Lamberte is president of the Philippine Institute for Development Studies (PIDS).

crisis on firms and their responses to such crisis using microlevel data; one of these is Dr. Fukao's paper. I would like to comment on a few points of his paper to help me better understand his results.

BoP Data versus Microeconomic Level

The paper has pointed out that Japan's FDI flows (on the basis of BoP statistics) to the Asian region increased after the crisis. The reason put forward on page 277 is that "Japanese firms increased their FDI flows to the Asian countries mainly in order to financially assist their subsidiaries that were suffering from deteriorating financial conditions." The FDI flows were not meant for merger and acquisition (M&A) purchases or for "greenfield investment." This explanation seems to be inconsistent with firm-level data. On page 275, the study points out that "according to MITI (1999b), Japan's manufacturing subsidiaries in the ASEAN-4 countries have reduced their investments in tangible fixed assets (excluding land) by 54 percent from the third quarter of 1997 to the third quarter of 1998. Even subsidiaries in the electrical machinery industry, which are the most export oriented and the least hit by the crisis, reduced their investment by 25 percent during this period."

Differences in Behavior between Japanese and U.S./European Firms

The paper has noted that, "Compared with U.S. and European firms, [Japanese firms] made quite limited amounts of cross-border M&A purchases [in the ASEAN-4 countries and Korea]" (277). It could be that Japanese firms are not seizing the investment opportunities available in Asian countries during the financial turmoil. However, one must ask the question: Who is buying firms in Asia? In the case of U.S. and German firms, investment banks and companies could have been acquiring firms in Asia with the intention of unloading them later when their value returns to their precrisis level. In the case of Japanese firms, these may not be investment banks and companies, which I think are currently having financial difficulties with many of their investments turning sour, but manufacturing firms looking for strategic, long-term investment in the Asian region.

Excluding the Philippines

I am a bit disappointed to read that in the detailed microlevel portion of the paper the Philippines was excluded from the analysis because of being the least adversely affected by the it. The analysis could have been enriched had the Philippines been included, because the results could perhaps tell us how Japanese subsidiaries in the least adversely affected countries behaved differently from those hardest hit by the crisis.

The following figures reflect some of our recent findings using the latest firm-level survey data conducted by the National Statistics Office (NSO) with support from the World Bank. Figure 8C.1 shows that there was a

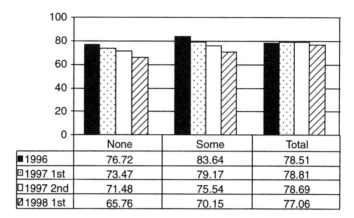

	None	Some	Total
■1996	76.72	83.64	78.51
▣1997 1st	73.47	79.17	78.81
▢1997 2nd	71.48	75.54	78.69
▨1998 1st	65.76	70.15	77.06

Fig. 8C.1   Capacity utilization by foreign control
Source: NSO (1998).

higher proportion of domestically owned firms admitting that they had fewer workers in the wake of the regional crisis than of foreign-owned firms doing so. Figure 8C.2 shows that while the average capacity utilization of wholly domestically owned firms dropped significantly during the period 1996 to the first half of 1998, that of foreign-owned firms had hardly changed at all.

Switching from Local Sales to Exports

The paper found that subsidiaries owned by larger parents were hit harder by the crisis and that they "expanded their exports to Japan greatly. Probably, with the help of their large parent firm this type of subsidiary was able to switch from local sales to exports" (290–94). Is this a temporary measure adopted by parent firms, which are expecting the host countries' market to improve a few months down the line? Did parent companies do something quickly to their subsidiaries to make them internationally competitive? Or were the subsidiaries already internationally competitive, but were simply paying more attention to the domestic market due to huge demand for their products before the onset of the crisis?

Econometric Analysis

In the econometric model, the dependent variable is GEMP, which is the growth of employment from March 1997 to March 1998. During the crisis period, the laying off of workers was only one of the responses of firms. There were other measures, such as cutting down on work hours or the workweek, forced vacation, and so on. In the Philippines, foreign-owned firms took advantage of these measures (see table 8C.1).

The net profit–total asset ratio of the prime Japanese parent firm in

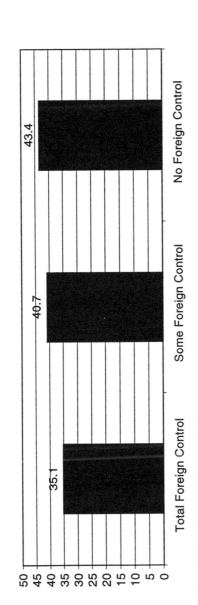

Fig. 8C.2 Percent of firms with fewer workers
Sources: Lamberte et al. (1999); NSO (1998)

Table 8C.1 Responses to Crisis: Labor

	Are Filling Up Vacancies (%)	Laying Off Workers (%)	Pay Severance (%)	Cut Down on Hours (%)	Compressed Work Week (%)	Forced Vacation (%)	Freeze Salary: Rank and File (%)	Freeze Salary: Management (%)	Salary Cut: Rank and File (%)	Salary Cut: Management (%)
By foreign control										
None	36	32	63	40	19	23	30	34	3	5
Some	34	30	57	44	23	23	40	42	6	6
Total	50	21	52	28	16	26	16	17	3	4

Source: NSO (1998).

fiscal year 1996 was used as one of the independent variables in one of the regression runs. Was this based on a consolidated financial statement or did it exclude the contribution of the subsidiaries? These different measurements could have different impacts on the dependent variable.

By estimating equations using different representations of the variable CHAR, the variable in question could have picked up the effects of other variables. Why not estimate an equation using all the variables representing CHAR, except ASSET, which could be highly correlated with PROF or CAP?

References

Lamberte, Mario B., Caesar B. Cororaton, Margarita F. Guerrero, and Aniceto C. Orbeta. 1999. Impacts of the Southeast Asian financial crisis on the Philippine manufacturing sector. PIDS Discussion Paper no. 99-09. Manila: Philippine Institute for Development Studies.
National Statistics Office (NSO). 1998. Survey of Philippine industry and the Asian financial crisis. Manila, Philippines.

Comment   Assaf Razin

An important aspect of FDI is that it is proven to be resilient during financial crises, in situations of international illiquidity, when the country's consolidated financial system has short-term obligations in foreign currency in excess of the amount of foreign currency to which the country has access on short notice. In this context, FDI flows provide the only direct link between the domestic capital market in the host country and the world capital market at large. Indeed, FDI flows to the East Asian countries were remarkably stable during the global financial crises of 1997–98. In sharp contrast, portfolio equity and debt flows, as well as bank loans, dried up almost completely during the same period. The resilience of FDI to financial crisis was also evident in the Mexican crisis of 1994 and the Latin American debt crisis of the early 1980s. This may reflect a unique characteristic of FDI, which is determined by considerations of ownership and control by multinationals of domestic activities, which are more long term in nature, rather than by short-term fluctuations in the value of domestic currency and the availability of credit and liquidity.

Kyoji Fukao has access to a unique data set that can shed light on the resiliency of FDI. He sets himself up to deal with one empirical hypothesis: Due to firm-specific skills and sunk (human and physical capital) in-

Assaf Razin is professor of economics at Tel Aviv University and Stanford University and a research associate of the National Bureau of Economic Research.

vestment costs, employment will not drop as much as sales during the crisis.

Method and Findings

In the typical regression, the dependent variable is employment growth and the explanatory variables are (a) sales growth (interacting with business activity upswing and downswing dummies); (b) parent's firm characteristics; and (c) subsidiary firm's characteristics.

The hypothesis implies the existence of a kink in the employment-sales growth equation. When employment growth is positive, employment responds linearly to sales growth, while the employment response to negative sales growth is inelastic. Since the upswing (downswing) dummy is potentially endogenous, the estimation is carried out in two stages. In the first stage a Tobit model is implemented to estimate interactions between the dummy variable and sales growth. The second stage uses the predicted values of this interaction term in the employment-sales growth equation.

The author finds that the evidence supports a kink-shaped schedule for employment growth and sales growth. He also finds that the characteristics of the parent firm, such as parent firm profits and its ownership share in the subsidiaries (which are related to the incentive of parent firms to support employment in subsidiaries during crisis), are significant statistically in the regressions. He also finds that evidence that new subsidiaries and high-productivity subsidiaries tend to keep employment more than old and low-productivity subsidiaries, in line with the hypothesis.

Critique

My critique is threefold:

1. A key element of the crisis, the huge depreciation of the real exchange rate, is totally ignored. For example, the author does not differentiate between export-oriented and domestic-market-oriented firms, concerning their different behavior when the real exchange rate is stable versus when it is sharply depreciated.

2. Investment data are ignored. A plausible related hypothesis that could have been tested, if investment data were available, concerns the response of the ratio of human to physical capital to real depreciations. When the real exchange rate depreciates and human capital becomes relatively cheap compared to physical capital, there will be a substitution effect away from physical capital, which can help explain the finding of stable employment during the business downswing.

3. Evidently, the employment-sales relationship is a dynamic concept, but the author pursues only contemporaneous relationships between the variables. A longer time series and a dynamic analytical framework of the response of employment to sales is warranted in order to understand the nature of the effect of crises on the employment-sales relationship.

Social Benefits and Losses from FDI
Two Nontraditional Views

Assaf Razin, Efraim Sadka, and Chi-Wa Yuen

9.1 Introduction

It is commonly believed that foreign direct investment (FDI) is beneficial for growth in less developed countries. Among other things, direct investment by multinational corporations in developing countries is considered a major channel for access to advanced technologies owned by the major industrial countries. In particular, technological diffusion can take place through imports of new varieties of inputs. This is in addition to the usual role of FDI as a channel for bringing in foreign savings to augment the stock of domestic capital. Both the technology-transfer and the traditional capital-augmenting roles of FDI translate into greater income growth in the host country. Indeed, in a sample of sixty-nine developing countries over the period 1970–89, Borensztein, De Gregorio, and Lee (1998) provide evidence of (a) complementarity between FDI and human capital on income growth; (b) complementarity between FDI and non-FDI domestic investment; and (c) productivity gains from FDI exceeding those from non-FDI domestic investment.[1]

Assaf Razin is professor of economics at Tel Aviv University and Stanford University and a research associate of the National Bureau of Economic Research. Efraim Sadka is the Henry Kaufman Professor of International Capital Markets at The Eitan Berglas School of Economics, Tel Aviv University, and a research fellow of CESifo, Munich. Chi-Wa Yuen is associate professor of Economics and Finance at the University of Hong Kong.

Financial support from the Hong Kong Research Grants Council through three grants (10200639, 10202090, and 10202893) is gratefully acknowledged. The usual disclaimer applies.

For useful comments, we thank Anne O. Krueger, Mario B. Lamberte, an anonymous referee, and participants of the tenth annual NBER–East Asia Seminar on Economics.

1. The contribution of FDI to growth is evident only when the interaction between human capital and FDI is included in the regression analysis. Their interpretation is that FDI flows

FDI can improve efficiency by promoting competition. The large size of multinational enterprises and the advanced technology they possess often enable them to invest in industries in which barriers to entry (such as large capital requirements) limit the potential access of local competitors.[2]

Overall, the first view of FDI that we shall take in this paper focuses on their effects on technology transfer and promotion of competition. These effects are in addition to the traditional gains from trade afforded by FDI, i.e., the blending of foreign savings with domestic savings to finance domestic investment. We shall formalize these effects in a stylized model and provide a quantitative assessment of the welfare gains from FDI by decomposing them according to their technology transfer effect and competition promotion effect, on top of the traditional gains from intertemporal trade. In doing this, we follow Romer's (1994) argument in relation to the welfare costs of trade barriers: In assuming that the set of goods in an economy never changes, the typical economic model predicts an efficiency loss from a tariff which is second-order small (in the order of the square of the tariff rate). By relaxing this assumption and assuming instead that international trade can bring new goods to the economy, the fraction of national income lost when a tariff is imposed can be much larger (as much as two times the tariff rate).

Another important aspect of FDI is that, in situations of illiquidity associated with global financial crises, FDI provides the only direct link between the domestic capital market in the host country and the world capital market at large. For instance, FDI flows to the East Asian countries were remarkably stable during the global financial crises of 1997–98. In sharp contrast, portfolio equity and debt flows as well as bank loans dried up almost completely during the same period. This resilience of FDI to financial crisis was also evident in the Mexican crisis of 1994 and the Latin American debt crisis of the early 1980s. This may reflect a unique property of FDI, which is determined by considerations of ownership and control by multinationals of domestic activities which are more long term in nature, rather than by short-term fluctuations in the value of domestic currency and the availability of credit and liquidity.[3]

However, the resilience of FDI flows may come at a cost to the host

---

primarily to sectors which use technology similar to that used in the source country. Thus, the interaction of FDI with human capital is important for explaining its role on productivity. By contrast, non-FDI domestic investment may largely follow more traditional activities, and thus the interaction effects between overall domestic investment and human capital are small in their regression. Corroborative evidence found by Feenstra and Hanson (1997) shows that multinational enterprises are active in sectors that use relatively high-skilled workers.

2. In some cases, however, the presence of multinationals may drive out less efficient local firms and ultimately reduce competition.

3. During a crisis, though, foreign direct investors may contribute to capital withdrawals by accelerating profit remittances or reducing the liabilities of affiliates towards their mother companies. While these are not recorded as negative FDI flows, they result from decisions made by foreign investors.

country. Although the foreign direct investors are able to reap their profits from the host country, their investment may exacerbate distortions in the domestic capital market. The distortions originate from the lack of corporate transparency, which gives rise to asymmetric information between "insiders" and "outsiders" of firms operating in the domestic economy, including firms owned and controlled by the foreign direct investors. The domestic capital market could be trapped in a "lemons" situation described by Akerlof (1970): At the price offered by uninformed equity-buyers, which reflects the average productivity of firms whose shares are sold in the market, owners of firms (including FDI-owned firms) which have experienced a higher-than-average value will pull out of the market. This adverse selection problem in the domestic equity market could be magnified by the introduction of FDI flows, resulting in excessive investment by the foreign direct investors and at the same time worsening the misincentives for the domestic savers.[4] These social losses may significantly reduce the attractiveness of FDI to the host country. Typically also, the domestic investment undertaken by FDI establishments is heavily leveraged through the domestic credit market. As a result, the fraction of domestic investment actually financed by foreign savings through FDI flows may not be as big as it may seem, and the size of the traditional gains from FDI may thus be further limited by this domestic leverage.

The second view of FDI that we shall take in this paper focuses on such perverse interactions between FDI and the domestic capital market, which implies that FDI flows may bring losses to the host country. We model this interaction in an asymmetric information framework. Paralleling the welfare assessments of FDI based on the first view, we shall also try to quantify the possible gains and losses from trade based on this second view of FDI and disentangle these nontraditional gains/losses from the traditional gains from trade.

The rest of the paper is organized as follows. We start with an analysis of the second view in section 9.2, followed by a parallel analysis of the first view in section 9.3. Numerical simulations are used to assess the possible welfare gains/losses these two nontraditional aspects of FDI may bring to the host country relative to the traditional gains. Section 9.4 concludes.

9.2   FDI: Interactions with the Domestic Credit Market

In this section and the next, we assume a two-period model of a small, capital-importing country, referred to as the home country. It is assumed

4. There is no direct evidence on the extent of undersaving resulting from these misincentives. A somewhat related study by the World Bank (1999) shows, however, that the correlation between FDI flows and total factor productivity growth in developing countries with high saving rates is positive and significant, whereas in countries with low saving rates the correlation is negative and significant.

that capital imports are channelled solely through FDI. The economy is small enough that, in the absence of any government intervention, it faces a perfectly elastic supply of external funds at a given risk-free world rate of interest, r^*.

Let us begin with the second view of FDI. We follow Gordon and Bovenberg (1996) and Razin, Sadka, and Yuen (1998a, 1999) in modelling the risk in this economy. Suppose there is a very large number (N) of ex ante identical domestic firms. Each firm employs capital input (K) in the first period in order to produce a single composite good in the second period. We assume that capital depreciates at the rate δ. Output in the second period is equal to $F(K)(1 + \varepsilon)$, where $F(\cdot)$ is a production function exhibiting diminishing marginal productivity of capital and ε is a random productivity factor with zero mean and is independent across all firms. (ε is bounded from below by -1, so that output is always non-negative.) We assume that ε is purely idiosyncratic, so that there is no aggregate uncertainty. Through optimal portfolio decisions, consumer-savers will thus behave in a risk-neutral way.

Investment decisions are made by the firms before the state of the world (i.e., ε) is known.[5] Since all firms face the same probability distribution of ε, they all choose the same level of investment. They then seek funds to finance the investment. At this stage, the owner-managers of the firms are better informed than the outside fund-suppliers. There are many ways to specify the degree of this asymmetry in information. In order to facilitate the analysis, however, we simply assume that the owner-managers, being "close to the action," observe ε before they make their financing decisions; but the fund providers, being "far away from the action," do not.

When investment is equity financed, the original owner-managers observe ε while the new potential shareholders of the firm do not. The market will be trapped in the lemons situation described by Akerlof (1970). At the price offered by the new (uninformed) potential equity buyers, which reflects the average productivity of all firms (i.e., the average level of ε) in the market, the owner-manager of a firm experiencing a higher-than-average value of ε will not be willing to sell its shares and will pull out of the market completely. The equity market will fail to serve its investment-financing functions efficiently. Elsewhere (Razin, Sadka, and Yuen 1999), we have shown how another source of equity finance, namely, international capital flows in the form of FDI, may help mitigate this lemons problem by creating an active (albeit distorted) domestic stock market that facilitates the channelling of domestic savings to finance new domestic investment—in addition to its usual role of channelling foreign savings to the domestic capital market to help finance part of the new investment. De-

---

5. For a principal-agent foundation for such an economic structure under which investment is precommitted before the realization of the productivity parameter, see Sosner (1998).

spite the inefficiencies (in the form of foreign overinvestment and domestic undersaving) that may result from the information asymmetry, the gains from trade through FDI can be rather substantial.

However, when a domestic credit market is doing most of the job of channelling domestic savings into domestic investment, the role of FDI diminishes. In fact, it is often observed that FDI is highly leveraged domestically. After gaining control of the domestic firm, a foreign direct investor usually resorts to the domestic credit market to finance new investment and possibly sell (shares of) the firm in the domestic equity market later, after profits from its original investment are realized. We thus extend our analysis in the model below to include a domestic credit market and reassess the gains from trade through FDI.

9.2.1 The FDI-Equity-Credit Equilibrium

In a formal sense, foreign acquisition of shares in domestic firms is classified as FDI when the shares acquired exceed a certain fraction of ownership (say, 10–20 percent). From an economic point of view, we look at FDI not just as ownership of a sizable share in a company but, more importantly, as an actual exercise of control and management and acquisition of inside information (the value of ε in our model).

The sequencing of firm decisions is as follows. Before ε is revealed to anyone (i.e., under symmetric information), foreign investors bid up domestic firms from their original domestic owners, investment decisions are made, and full financing through domestic credit is secured. Then, ε is revealed to the owner-managers (who are all foreigners), but not to domestic equity investors. At this stage, shares are offered in the domestic equity market and the ownership in some of the firms is transferred to the domestic investors. In the initial stage (i.e., before ε is revealed to anyone), the foreign direct investors are able to outbid the domestic savers because the latter lack access to the large amounts of funds necessary to seize control of the firms, while the former, by assumption, are not liquidity constrained.[6]

Since credit is extended ex ante, before ε is revealed, firms cannot sign default-free loan contracts with the lenders. We therefore consider loan contracts which allow for the possibility of default. We adopt the "costly state verification" framework á la Townsend (1979) in assuming that lenders make firm-specific loans, charging an interest rate of r^j to firm $j(j =$

---

6. The existence of wealthy individuals or families in the home country may limit the scope of our analysis to the extent that they can compete with the foreign direct investors on control over these greenfield investment sites. Our analysis will carry over, however, if they form joint ventures with the foreign direct investors. On the other hand, the foreign direct investors need not be excessively resourceful. Even a small technological advantage they may enjoy over the domestic investors will enable them to bid up all these investment sites from the domestic investors and to gain control of these industries.

1,2, . . . ,N) (see also Stiglitz and Weiss 1981). The interest and principal payment commitment will be honored when the firms encounter relatively good shocks, and defaulted when they encounter relatively bad shocks. The loan contract is characterized by a loan rate (r^j), with possible default, and a threshold value ($\bar{\varepsilon}^j$) of the productivity parameter as follows:

(1) $F(K_j)(1 + \bar{\varepsilon}^j) + (1 - \delta)K^j = [K^j - (1 - \delta)K_0^j](1 + r^j).$

When the realized value of ε^j is larger than $\bar{\varepsilon}^j$, the firm is solvent and will thus pay the lenders the promised amount, consisting of the principal $K^j - (1 - \delta)K_0^j$ plus the interest $r^j[K^j - (1 - \delta)K_0^j]$ as given by the right-hand side of equation (1). If, however, ε^j is smaller than $\bar{\varepsilon}^j$, the firm will default. In the case of default, the lenders can incur a cost in order to verify the true value of ε^j and to seize the residual value of the firm. This cost, interpretable as the cost of bankruptcy, is assumed to be proportional to the firm's realized gross return, $\mu[F(K^j)(1 + \varepsilon^j) + (1 - \delta)K^j]$, where $\mu \leq 1$ is the factor of proportionality. Net of this cost, the lenders will receive $(1 - \mu)[F(K^j)(1 + \varepsilon^j) + (1 - \delta)K^j]$.

Since there is no aggregate risk, the expected rate of return required by domestic consumer-savers, denoted by $\bar{r}$, can be secured by sufficient diversification. Therefore, the "default" rate of interest, r^j, must offer a premium over and above the default-free rate, $\bar{r}$, according to

(2') $[1 - \Phi(\bar{\varepsilon}^j)][K^j - (1 - \delta)K_0^j](1 + r^j) + \Phi(\bar{\varepsilon}^j)(1 - \mu)$

$\{F(K^j)[1 + e^-(\bar{\varepsilon}^j)] + (1 - \delta)K^j\} = [K^j(1 - \delta)K_0^j](1 + \bar{r}),$

where $\Phi(\cdot)$ is the cumulative probability distribution of ε, i.e., $\Phi(\bar{\varepsilon}^j) = $ prob($\varepsilon \leq \bar{\varepsilon}^j$), and $e^-(\bar{\varepsilon}^j)$ is the mean value of ε realized by the low-productivity firms, i.e., $e^-(\bar{\varepsilon}^j) \equiv E(\varepsilon|\varepsilon \leq \bar{\varepsilon}^j)$. For later use, we also denote by $e^+(\bar{\varepsilon}^j)$ the mean value of ε realized by the high-productivity firms, i.e., $e^+(\varepsilon^0) \equiv E(\varepsilon|\varepsilon \geq \bar{\varepsilon}^j)$.[7]

The first term on the left-hand side of equation (2') is the contracted principal and interest payment, weighted by the no-default probability. The second term measures the net residual value of the firm, weighted by the default probability. The right-hand side is the no-default return required by the domestic lender. Observe that equations (1) and (2') together imply that

$$[1 - \Phi(\bar{\varepsilon}^j)] + \frac{\Phi(\bar{\varepsilon}^j)(1 - \mu)\{F(K^j)[1 + e^-(\bar{\varepsilon}^j)] + (1 - \delta)K^j\}}{F(K^j)(1 + \bar{\varepsilon}^j) + (1 - \delta)K^j} = \frac{1 + \bar{r}}{1 + r^j}.$$

---

7. The weighted average of $e^-(\bar{\varepsilon}^j)$ and $e^+(\bar{\varepsilon}^j)$ must yield the average value of ε, i.e., $\Phi(\bar{\varepsilon}^j)e^-(\bar{\varepsilon}^j) + [1 - \Phi(\bar{\varepsilon}^j)]e^+(\bar{\varepsilon}^j) = E(\varepsilon) = 0$. This in turn implies that $e^-(\bar{\varepsilon}^j) < 0$ while $e^+(\bar{\varepsilon}^j) > 0$, i.e., the expected value of ε for the "bad" ("good") firm is negative (positive).

Since $e^-(\bar{\varepsilon}^j) < \bar{\varepsilon}^j$ and $0 \leq \mu \leq 1$, it follows that $r^j > \bar{r}$, the difference being a risk premium (which depends, among other things, on K^j, $\bar{\varepsilon}^j$, and μ).

The firm in this setup is competitive (i.e., a price taker) only with respect to $\bar{r}$, the market default-free rate of return. This $\bar{r}$ cannot be influenced by the firm's actions. However, r^j, K^j, and $\bar{\varepsilon}^j$ are firm specific and must satisfy equations (1) and (2'). In making its investment (i.e., choosing $K^j - [1 - \delta]K_0^j$) and its financing (loan contract) decisions, the firm takes these constraints into account. Since these decisions are made before ε is known, i.e., when all firms are (ex ante) identical, they all make the same decision. We henceforth drop the superscript j.

In the equity market which opens after ε is revealed to the (foreign) owner-managers, there is a cutoff level of ε, denoted by ε^0, such that all firms experiencing a value of ε above ε^0 will be retained by the foreign direct investors and all other firms (with ε below ε^0) will be sold to domestic savers. This cutoff level of ε is given by

$$(3') \quad \frac{[F(K)(1 + \varepsilon^0) + (1 - \delta)K] - [K - (1 - \delta)K_0](1 + r)}{1 + r^*}$$

$$= \left[\frac{\Phi(\bar{\varepsilon})}{\Phi(\varepsilon^0)}\right] \cdot 0 + \left[\frac{\Phi(\varepsilon^0) - \Phi(\bar{\varepsilon})}{\Phi(\varepsilon^0)}\right]$$

$$\cdot \left[\frac{\{F(K)[1 + \hat{e}(\bar{\varepsilon}, \varepsilon^0)] + (1 - \delta)K\} - [K - (1 - \delta)K_0])1 + r)}{1 + \bar{r}}\right].$$

where $\hat{e}(\bar{\varepsilon}, \varepsilon^0) \equiv E(\varepsilon|\bar{\varepsilon} \leq \varepsilon \leq \varepsilon^0)$ is the conditional expectation of ε given ε lies between $\bar{\varepsilon}$ and ε^0.

Notice that firms that experience a value of ε below $\bar{\varepsilon}$ default and have zero value. These firms are not retained by the foreign direct investors; hence $\varepsilon^0 \geq \bar{\varepsilon}$. All other firms generate in the second period a *net* cash flow of $[F(K)(1 + \varepsilon) + (1 - \delta)K] - [K - (1 - \delta)K_0](1 + r)$. The left-hand side of equation (3') represents the marginal (from the bottom of the distribution) firm retained by foreign investors. The right-hand side of equation (3') is the expected value of the firms that are purchased by domestic savers. With a conditional probability of $[\Phi(\varepsilon^0) - \Phi(\bar{\varepsilon})]/\Phi(\varepsilon^0)$, they generate a net expected cash flow of $\{F(K)[1 + \hat{e}(\bar{\varepsilon}, \varepsilon^0)] + (1 - \delta)K\} - [K - (1 - \delta)K_0](1 + r)$; and with a probability of $\Phi(\bar{\varepsilon})/\Phi(\varepsilon^0)$, they generate a zero net cash flow. This explains equation (3').

We can substitute equation (1) into equations (2') and (3') in order to eliminate r and then rearrange terms to obtain

$$(2) \quad [1 - \Phi(\bar{\varepsilon})]F(K)(1 + \bar{\varepsilon}) + \Phi(\bar{\varepsilon})(1 - \mu)F(K)[1 + e^-(\bar{\varepsilon})]$$

$$+ [1 - \Phi(\bar{\varepsilon})\mu](1 - \delta)K = [K - (1 - \delta)K_0](1 + \bar{r}),$$

and

$$
(3) \qquad \frac{\varepsilon^0 - \bar{\varepsilon}}{1 + r^*} = \left[\frac{\Phi(\varepsilon^0) - \Phi(\bar{\varepsilon})}{\Phi(\varepsilon^0)} \right] \cdot \left[\frac{\hat{e}(\bar{\varepsilon}, \varepsilon^0) - \bar{\varepsilon}}{1 + \bar{r}} \right].
$$

Consider now the capital investment decision of the firm that is made before ε becomes known, while it is still owned by foreign direct investors. With a probability of $\Phi(\varepsilon^0) - \Phi(\bar{\varepsilon})$, it will be sold to domestic savers who pay a positive price equalling

$$
\frac{\{F(K)[1 + \hat{e}(\bar{\varepsilon}, \varepsilon^0)] + (1 - \delta)K - [K - (1 - \delta)K_0](1 + r)\}}{(1 + \bar{r})}
$$

$$
= \frac{F(K)[\hat{e}(\bar{\varepsilon}, \varepsilon^0) - \bar{\varepsilon}]}{(1 + \bar{r})},
$$

by using equation (1). With a probability of $1 - \Phi(\varepsilon^0)$, it will be retained by the foreign investors, for whom it is worth

$$
\frac{\{F(K)[1 + e^+(\varepsilon^0)] + (1 - \delta)K - [K - (1 - \delta)K_0](1 + r)\}}{(1 + r^*)}
$$

$$
= \frac{F(K)[e^+(\varepsilon^0) - \bar{\varepsilon}]}{(1 + r^*)},
$$

by using equation (1). Hence, the firm seeks to maximize

$$
(4) \qquad V = [1 - \Phi(\varepsilon^0)] \cdot \left\{ \frac{F(K)[e^+(\varepsilon^0) - \bar{\varepsilon}]}{1 + r^*} \right\} + \Phi(\bar{\varepsilon}) \cdot 0
$$

$$
+ [\Phi(\varepsilon^0) - \Phi(\bar{\varepsilon})] \cdot \left\{ \frac{F(K)[\hat{e}(\bar{\varepsilon}, \varepsilon^0) - \bar{\varepsilon}]}{1 + \bar{r}} \right\}
$$

subject to constraint (equation [2]), by choice of K and $\bar{\varepsilon}$, given ε^0.[8] The first-order conditions are spelled out in the appendix.

The (maximized) value of V in equation (4) is the price paid by the foreign direct investors at the greenfield stage of investment. Since the value of ε is not known at this point, the same price is paid for all firms. The low-ε firms are then (after ε is revealed to the foreign direct investors) resold to domestic savers, all at the same price, because ε is not observed by these savers. Net capital inflows through FDI are given by

---

8. The ε^0-condition, as given by equation (3), is determined by equilibrium in the equity market. As such, it will not be taken into account by the price-taking firms when choosing their investment levels.

$$(5) \qquad \text{FDI} = \frac{N[1 - \Phi(\varepsilon^0)]F(K)[e^+(\varepsilon^0) - \bar{\varepsilon}}{(1 + r^*)}$$

(see equation [4]). Unlike the case with no domestic credit (in which the foreign direct investors have to bring in their own capital to finance the domestic investment projects), all capital outlays are financed domestically and FDI consists only of the price paid for the ownership and control of the high-ε firms.

The remainder of the equilibrium conditions is standard. The first-period resource constraint is given by

$$(6) \qquad \text{FDI} = N[K - (1 - \delta)K_0] - [NF(K_0) - c_1].$$

The second-period resource constraint is

$$(7) \qquad c_2 = N[F(K) + (1 - \delta)K] - \text{FDI}(1 + r^*)$$
$$- N\mu\Phi(\bar{\varepsilon})\{F(K)[1 + e^-(\bar{\varepsilon})] + (1 - \delta)K\}.$$

Note that the last term on the left-hand side of equation (7) reflects the existence of real default costs. Finally, the consumer-savers do not have access to the world capital market and can only borrow/lend from the domestic market. As a result, in maximizing utility, they will equate their intertemporal marginal rate of substitution to the domestic risk-free rate of return as follows:

$$(8) \qquad \frac{u_1(c_1, c_2)}{u_2(c_1, c_2)} = 1 + \bar{r}.$$

In this model, the eight equations (i.e., [2], [3], [5]–[8] together with the two first-order conditions associated with the choice of K and $\bar{\varepsilon}$) determine the eight endogenous variables, i.e., K, r, $\bar{r}$, $\bar{\varepsilon}$, ε^0, c_1, c_2, FDI, and the LaGrange multiplier λ associated with the constraint (equation [2]).

9.2.2 Gains from Trade

To flesh out in a simplified manner the kind of gains or losses brought about by FDI, we compare the laissez-faire allocation in the presence of FDI with the closed economy laissez-faire allocation.

In the autarky case, the lemons problem will drive the equity market out of existence. Firms will have to rely solely on the provision of domestic credit in financing its investment projects. The firm-specific debt contract for any firm j continues to be characterized by a default-risky interest rate (r^j) and a threshold productivity level ($\bar{\varepsilon}^j$) that satisfy the cutoff condition (equation [1]). The default-free interest rate ($\bar{r}$) is still defined implicitly by equation (2′). Again, since all firms are ex ante identical, we can drop the superscript j. The firm's investment decision is to choose K, r, and $\bar{\varepsilon}$ to solve the following problem:

$$(4')\quad \max_{(K,r,\bar{\varepsilon})} F(K) - \Phi(\bar{\varepsilon})\{F(K)[1 + e^-(\bar{\varepsilon})] + (1 - \delta)K\}$$
$$- [1 - \Phi(\bar{\varepsilon})][K - (1 - \delta)K_0](1 + r)$$

subject to equations (1) and (2'). We can use equation (1) to substitute out the risky interest rate (r) in equation (2') as well as in the objective function above. The first order conditions with respect to K and $\bar{\varepsilon}$ for this reduced problem are laid out in the appendix. Utility maximization by the consumer-savers continues to yield the same intertemporal condition (equation [8]). In the absence of capital flows, FDI $\equiv 0$ in the two resource constraints (equations [6] and [7]). Together, these five conditions determine the five endogenous variables, i.e., K, $\bar{r}$, $\bar{\varepsilon}$, c_1, and c_2.

In the open economy case with domestic credit, FDI has conflicting effects on welfare. Its first role (discussed in detail in Razin, Sadka, and Yuen 1999) is to facilitate the channelling of domestic saving into domestic investment by getting around a lemons problem and sustaining a domestic equity market. This, by itself, is welfare enhancing; but, as we have already indicated, FDI is driven also by distorted incentives, and its traditional role of directing foreign savings into domestic investment may generate an excessive stock of domestic capital (either when capital inflows are not needed at all or, when they are needed to start with, too much of them take place). This foreign overinvestment (coupled with possible domestic over- or undersaving)—i.e., $F'(K) - \delta < r^*$ (and $\gtrless \bar{r}$)—tends to reduce welfare.

We use numerical examples to illustrate the total effect of FDI on welfare. In these examples, we employ a logarithmic utility function ($u[c_1, c_2] = \ln[c_1] + \gamma \ln[c_2]$), with a subjective discount factor γ, a Cobb-Douglas production function ($F[K] = AK^\alpha$), and a uniform distribution of ε defined over the interval $(-a, a)$. The welfare gain (loss) is measured by the uniform percentage change (in c_1 and c_2) which is needed in order to lift the autarkic utility level to the FDI utility level. We set the parameter values as $\gamma = 0.295$, $\alpha = 0.333$, $\delta = 0.723$, $N = 1$, $A = 1$, $K_0 = 1$, $a = 0.99$, and $\mu = 0.05$. This set of values yields a normalized output level of unity in the initial period. Since we think of each period as constituting half the lifetime of a generation (i.e., about twenty-five years), the values of γ and δ are chosen in such a way as to reflect an annual time preference rate of 5 percent and an annual depreciation rate of 5 percent.

Unlike the case where domestic credit is not available (as analyzed in Razin, Sadka, and Yuen 1999), an autarkic economy with a domestic credit market can utilize domestic savings to debt-finance domestic investment. The crucial role of FDI as a vehicle for sustaining a domestic equity

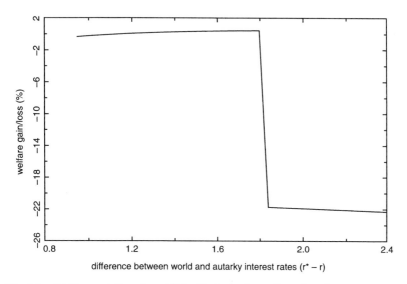

Fig. 9.1   Welfare gain/loss from FDI with domestic credit and equity

market through which domestic savings are channelled into domestic investment is thus substantially diminished. Consequently, the negative effect of FDI associated with the distorted incentives emanating from the domestic equity market dominates, and altogether there may exist a net welfare loss from trade.[9] Figure 9.1 illustrates the welfare gains and losses occurring at various levels of the world rate of interest, r^*, relative to the autarky risk-free rate $\bar{r}$. Among other things, three points are worth noting from this figure. First, except for levels of $r^* - \bar{r}$ ranging from 1.2 to 1.8 (equivalent to an annual real rate differential of 3.2 percent to 4.2 percent) where some minimal welfare gains of 0.04 percent to 0.55 percent are re-corded, welfare losses are prominent (about -2 percent at lower levels of $r^* - \bar{r}$ and increasing to more than -20 percent when $r^* - \bar{r}$ exceeds 1.8). Second, observe that there is a discrete jump in the welfare levels around $r^* - \bar{r} = 1.8$. Below that level, we have a low investment, low FDI equilibrium, with an investment rate of about 17 percent and a FDI/GDP ratio of 6–8 percent. Above that, the investment rate surges to 25–26 percent and the FDI/GDP ratio to 11–13 percent. The saving rate is relatively stable, though—only slightly higher in the latter case (around 13 percent) than in the former (around 10 percent). This suggests the possibility of multiple equilibria driven by self-fulfilling expectations. Although the role of FDI in financing domestic investment is much less important relative

9. This possibility of losses from trade in an originally distorted economy can be viewed as a corroboration of the earlier findings of Brecher and Diaz-Alejandro (1977) and Helpman and Razin (1983).

to the scenario with no domestic credit (not shown here; see Razin, Sadka, and Yuen 1999), foreign overinvestment (i.e., $F'[K] - \delta < r^*$) prevails in all these cases. So also does domestic oversaving (i.e., $F'[K] - \delta > \bar{r}$). Third, note that the autarkic default-free interest rate $\bar{r}$ ($= 2.9$) falls short of all the values of r^* considered here. So here we have the possibility that although the FDI flows are not fundamentally needed, they do nevertheless flow in.

9.3   FDI: Technology Transfer and Promotion of Competition

We now return to discuss in detail the second view of FDI. We start with an autarkic situation in the host country where only traditional inputs are used for domestic production and the domestic input markets are plagued by perils of imperfect competition. In this section, we assume that FDI can bring new inputs to an economy and can promote competition in the domestic input market. We view technology transfer as the introduction of new inputs brought in by the foreign direct investors in the sense that productivity can be raised by the addition of more varieties of inputs. Alternatively, we can view these new inputs as tradable goods and the traditional inputs as nontradable goods. To illustrate the possible gains from FDI in a partial equilibrium setting, we show in figures 9.2 and 9.3 the gains from the increase in the use of traditional inputs brought about by increased competition (area B in figure 9.2)[10] and from the introduction of new inputs (area C in figure 9.3).

As in the previous section, the economy is producing a single, all-purpose (consumption and capital) good with a composite capital input through a Cobb-Douglas technology:

$$(9) \qquad Y = AK^{\alpha}, \text{ where } K = \left(\sum_{j=1}^{M} k_j^{\theta} \right)^{1/\theta}, \qquad 0 < \theta < 1.$$

That is, capital is a composite of a number of varieties of individual inputs ($k_j, j = 1, 2, \ldots, M$). The elasticity of substitution among these inputs is given by ($1/(1 - \theta)$). In the absence of uncertainty, we can interpret the production technology specified in section 9.2.2 as a special case of equation (9), with $M = 1$.

It is easy to show that, holding the cost of production constant, a mere increase in the number of inputs can generate more output. In particular, suppose that either $\hat{k}$ units each of M kinds of inputs or $\tilde{k}$ units each of $M + m$ kinds of inputs can be used to compose the same aggregate level of

---

10. Area A of figure 9.2 does not constitute any welfare gain or loss from increased competition because the gain in consumer surplus due to the fall in the input price from w (its imperfectly competitive level) to 1 (its competitive level) is exactly offset by the loss in producer surplus.

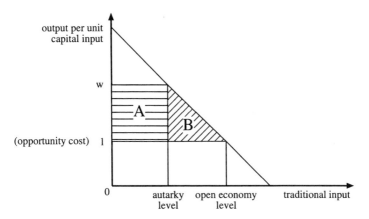

Fig. 9.2   Gains from increase in competition in the use of traditional inputs

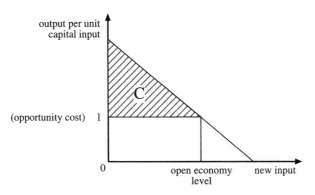

Fig. 9.3   Gains from the introduction of new inputs

capital stock $(\overline{K})$, i.e., $M\hat{k} = (M + m)\tilde{k} = \overline{K}$, and hence incur the same input costs. Then

$$Y(M, \hat{k}) = A\left(\sum_{j=1}^{M} \hat{k}^\theta\right)^{\alpha/\theta} = A\left[M\left(\frac{\overline{K}}{M}\right)^\theta\right]^{\alpha/\theta} = AM^{\alpha(1-\theta)/\theta}\overline{K}^\alpha,$$

and

$$Y(M + m, \tilde{k}) = A\left(\sum_{j=1}^{M+m} \tilde{k}^\theta\right)^{\alpha/\theta} = A\left[(M + m)\left(\frac{\overline{K}}{M + m}\right)^\theta\right]^{\alpha/\theta}$$

$$= A(M + m)^{\alpha(1-\theta)/\theta}\overline{K}^\alpha.$$

Obviously, $Y(M + m, \tilde{k}) > Y(M, \hat{k})$ for $m > 0$; i.e., there exist productivity gains from an increase in the variety of inputs. From the growth accounting perspective, a 1 percent growth in the variety of inputs will translate into a $\alpha(1 - \theta)/\theta$ percent growth in total output.

9.3.1 Autarky with Traditional Inputs and Imperfect Competition

We view the market structure for capital inputs as monopolistically competitive. There are M symmetric input-coordinating firms. Each firm will buy each specific input (k_j) from the households at the competitive price of unity and sell the aggregate stock to the final producers at a monopolistically competitive price of w_j.

Taking these input prices w_i and the interest rate r as given, the final good producer chooses its quantities demanded for the capital inputs (k_j) to solve the following investment problem

(10)
$$\max_{(k_j)} \frac{Y + (1 - \delta)\sum_{j=1}^{M} k_j}{1 + r} - \sum_{j=1}^{M} w_j k_j$$

subject to equation (9). Solution to the problem yields the following inverse demand function

(11)
$$w_i(k_i) = \frac{mpk_i + (1 - \delta)}{1 + r},$$

where mpk_i is the marginal product of the ith capital input, defined as

(11a)
$$mpk_i \equiv \alpha A K^{\alpha-\theta} k_i^{\theta-1}.$$

As a monopoly supplier of capital inputs to the final producers, the ith input-coordinating firm will take the inverse demand functions $w_i(k_i)$ (and the competitive return of unity to be paid to the households) as given and choose the quantities supplied of capital inputs k_i to maximize its profit

$$\max_{(k_i)} \pi_i(k_i) \equiv [w_i(k_i) - 1]k_i.$$

Solution to this problem yields the markup condition

(12)
$$w_i(k_i)[1 - \eta_i(k_i)] = 1,$$

where $\eta_i(k_i)$ is the reciprocal of the elasticity of the inverse demand function, defined as

(12a) $\eta_i(k_i) \equiv - \dfrac{w_i'(k_i)k_i}{w_i(k_i)}$

$$= -\left[\frac{mpk_i}{mpk_i + (1 - \delta)}\right]\left[(\theta - 1) + (\alpha - \theta)\left(\frac{k_i^\theta}{\sum_{j=1}^{M} k_j^\theta}\right)\right].$$

Note that with full depreciation ($\delta = 1$) and when the number of capital inputs is infinitely large ($M \to \infty$), $\eta_i(k_i) = \theta - 1$ so that the markup, $1/[1 - \eta_i(k_i)]$, becomes a constant equal to $1/\theta$ (> 1).

The problem of the consumer-saver (competitive supplier of domestic savings) is the same as the one spelled out in section 9.2 above—except that, instead of K_0, he or she now takes $\Sigma_{j=1}^{M} k_{j0}$ as the initial endowment. Solution to his or her utility maximization problem yields the standard intertemporal condition (equation [8]), where (in the absence of default risk here) $\bar{r}$ is simply the autarky interest rate.

Assuming symmetry in the capital inputs across firms, the economy-wide resource constraints are given by

(6') $$c_1 = N\{AM^{\alpha/\theta}k_0^{\alpha} - M[k - (1 - \delta)k_0]\},$$

and

(7') $$c_2 = N[AM^{\alpha/\theta}k^{\alpha} + (1 - \delta)Mk].$$

In this model, the five equations (i.e., [11], [12], [6'], [7'], [8]) determine the five endogenous variables (c_1, c_2, k, w, $\bar{r}$).

9.3.2   FDI with New Inputs and Increased Competition

The opening-up of the economy involves three features. First, because of the difference between the world rate of interest r^* and the autarky interest rate $\bar{r}$, capital will flow in. Second, bundled with FDI, m new types of capital inputs will be imported.[11] Third, the increase in competition (given the perfectly elastic supply of inputs from abroad) will drive w_i to its competitive level of unity.

In the presence of imported capital inputs and under a competitive input market structure, the maximization problem facing the producer-investors becomes the following:

(10') $$\max_{(k_i)} \frac{Y + (1 + \delta)\sum_{j=1}^{M+m} k_j}{1 + r^*} - \sum_{j=1}^{M+m} k_j,$$

subject to

(9') $$Y = AK^{\alpha}, \quad \text{where } K = \left(\sum_{j=1}^{M+m} k_j^{\theta}\right)^{1/\theta}.$$

Solution to the problem yields the standard marginal productivity condition

$$mpk_i = r^* + \delta,$$

---

11. See also a similar setup in Borensztein, De Gregorio, and Lee (1998).

where, as in equation (11a), $mpk_i \equiv \alpha A K^{\alpha-\theta} k_i^{\theta-1}$ except that K now includes both traditional and new inputs.

The consumer-saver's problem remains unchanged, except that the autarky interest rate $\bar{r}$ is now replaced by the world rate of interest r^*. As a result, the intertemporal condition becomes

$$(8') \qquad \frac{u_1(c_1, c_2)}{u_2(c_1, c_2)} = 1 + r^*.$$

The two economy-wide resource constraints are modified as follows:

$$(6'') \quad \text{FDI} = N[(M + m)k - (1 - \delta)Mk_0] - (NAM^{\alpha/\theta}k_0^\alpha - c_1),$$

and

$$(7'') \quad c_2 = N[A(M + m)^{\alpha/\theta}k^\alpha + (1 - \delta)(M + m)k] - \text{FDI}(1 + r^*).$$

In this model, the four equations (i.e., [11'], [8'], [6''], and [7'']) determine the four endogenous variables (c_1, c_2, k, FDI).

9.3.3   Gains from Trade

As is clear from the discussion above, there are three possible sources of gains from FDI flows: (a) traditional gains (from the use of foreign savings to augment the domestic capital stock), (b) gains from technology transfer, and (c) gains from the promotion of competition in the input market. The two nontraditional types (b) and (c) both result from the importation of increased variety of capital inputs.

In the simulations reported below, we choose the same set of parameter values as in section 9.2.2 above, i.e., $\gamma = 0.295$, $\alpha = 0.333$, $\delta = 0.723$, $N = 1$, and $K_0 = 1$. In the benchmark model with both the technology-transfer and competition-promotion features, we set $\theta = 0.314$, $M = 0.05$, and $m/M = 0.1$. The value of the production coefficient A is reset from 1 to 24 so as to generate a normalized output level of unity in the initial period in the presence of input variety M. The values of θ and M are chosen in such a way as to produce a markup of input price over its marginal cost of 1.4 as in Rotemberg and Woodford (1995). Our values of α and θ also imply a contribution of input variety to output growth (i.e., $\partial \ln[Y]/\partial \ln[M] = \alpha[1 - \theta]/\theta$) of 0.728. In the alternative traditional model with perfectly competitive input markets and without technology transfer, we set $\theta = 0.298$ and $m/M = 0$ so as to yield a unit markup.

The welfare gains from FDI between the benchmark and traditional cases are compared in figure 9.4. In the latter case (solid line), the welfare gains are positive as long as the interest differential between the world rate and the autarky rate ($r^* - r$) is nonzero. However, the relevant range for our purpose (i.e., positive rather than negative capital inflows) is the downward-sloping segment, when $r^* < r$ ($= 3.051$, or an annual rate of

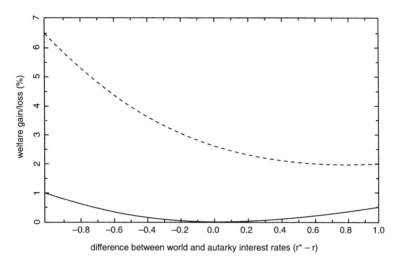

Fig. 9.4   **Welfare gains from FDI with technology transfer and promotion of competition vs. traditional gains from FDI**

5.76 percent). In comparison, the former case (dashed line) generates much bigger welfare gains—as big as a 6 percent or greater difference in lifetime consumption with a FDI/GDP ratio of 27 percent when $r^* - r = -1$ (or an annual rate differential of 2.81 percent)—because of the technology transfer and competition promotion effects. At $r^* = r$ (when the traditional gains are absent), we still have a positive FDI/GDP ratio of 9 percent, producing a gain of 2.6 percent that represents a measure of these nontraditional effects.

In order to disentangle the two nontraditional effects (b) and (c), we use in figures 9.5 and 9.6 the traditional case as a frame of reference (solid line) and consider variations in the technology transfer effect and competition promotion effect. The former effect is examined in figure 9.5 by varying the m/M ratio from 0 percent (solid line) to 10 percent (dashed line) to 20 percent (dotted line). The latter effect is studied in figure 9.6 by varying the markup from unity (solid line) to 1.4 (dashed line; the Rotemberg-Woodford 1995 number) to 2.0 (dotted line; Hall's 1988 estimate). These two figures are not easily comparable, but one message is clear: Both effects can generate large welfare gains through FDI inflows even in the absence of traditional gains from FDI. In addition, when $r^* = r$, the technology transfer effect delivers a welfare gain of 1.9 percent when the m/M ratio equals the benchmark value of 0.1 while the competition promotion effect induces a gain of 0.7 percent when the markup equals the benchmark value of 1.4. These two welfare numbers together make up the overall nontraditional gains of 2.6 percent found in the mixed case depicted by figure 9.4.

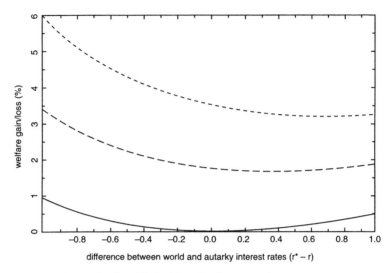

Fig. 9.5 Welfare gains from FDI with technology transfer

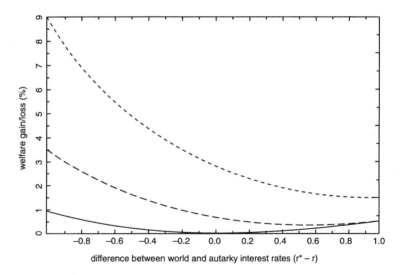

Fig. 9.6 Welfare gains from FDI with promotion of competition

9.4 Conclusion

International capital flows typically fall into three major categories—i.e., portfolio flows, loans, and FDI—and perform a variety of functions in the world economy. Their common traditional role lies in the blending of foreign savings with domestic savings to finance domestic investment.

FDI, distinct from other types of capital flows, performs two important additional functions. First, FDI can be viewed not only as an exchange of the ownership of domestic investment sites from domestic residents to foreign residents, but also as a corporate governance mechanism in which the foreign investor exercises management and control over the host-country firm. In so doing, the foreign direct investors gain crucial inside information about the productivity of the firm under their control—an obvious advantage over the uninformed domestic savers, who are offering to buy shares in the firm. Taking advantage of their superior information, the foreign direct investors will tend to retain the high-productivity firms under their ownership and control and sell the low-productivity firms to these uninformed savers. This adverse selection problem, which plagues the domestic stock market, leads to overinvestment by the foreign direct investors and, at the same time, to undersaving by the domestic residents.

A second view focuses on the effects of FDI in facilitating technology transfer through the importation of new varieties of factor inputs and in promoting competition in the input market. We nest the two theories into a calibrated model and use numerical simulations to reassess the welfare gains/losses FDI may generate for the host country and compare them to the more traditional gains. We also provide a quantitative assessment of the magnitudes of the potential gains/losses arising separately from the two views of the role of FDI.

In accordance with the first view, our simulation results show that substantial welfare losses can indeed be brought about by FDI in the presence of adverse selection in the domestic equity market. These losses can nonetheless be dominated by the gains induced by the technology transfer and competition promotion effects of FDI, i.e., the second view (cf. figures 9.1 and 9.2 at a common level of interest rate differential of, say, 1, where the net gain is 1.8 percent of permanent consumption). A more rigorous assessment of the net gains/losses from these two views taken together requires blending the two models into a unified framework and redoing the simulation exercise in that context. This more difficult task is left for future research.

Drawing on the efficiency implications of the two nontraditional roles, corrective government policies are called for. Enforcement of better disclosure rules for corporations and fiscal measures that will subsidize domestic saving and that will tax excessive FDI may serve to counteract the adverse selection problem triggered by FDI in the domestic stock market. Removing policy and institutional barriers, which may hinder other types of international capital flows, can potentially mitigate the adverse selection problems in the domestic stock market as well.

Evidently, allowing the host country to use nontraditional new inputs—as specified in this paper as a form of technology transfer or as a side benefit from FDI—is not affected by the magnitude of FDI, whether big or small. Thus, there is no reason to subsidize FDI on this ground.[12]

Appendix

Derivation of First-Order Conditions for the Firm's Investment Problem in the FDI-Equity-Credit Equilibrium and the Autarky Equilibrium

In the open economy case, the maximization of firm value V as specified in equation (4) with respect to K and $\bar{\varepsilon}$ yields the following first-order conditions:

$$(A1)\quad 0 = \left\{ \frac{[1 - \Phi(\varepsilon^0)][e^+(\varepsilon^0) - \bar{\varepsilon}]}{1 + r^*} + \frac{[\Phi(\varepsilon^0) - \Phi(\bar{\varepsilon})][\hat{e}(\bar{\varepsilon}, \varepsilon^0) - \bar{\varepsilon}]}{1 + \bar{r}} \right\} F'(K)$$

$$+ \lambda\{[1 - \Phi(\bar{\varepsilon})](1 + \bar{\varepsilon}) + \Phi(\bar{\varepsilon})(1 - \mu)[1 + e^-(\bar{\varepsilon})]\} F'(K)$$

$$- \lambda(\bar{r} + \delta) - \lambda\Phi(\bar{\varepsilon})\mu(1 - \delta),$$

and

$$(A2)\quad 0 = -\frac{1 - \Phi(\varepsilon^0)}{1 + r^*} - \frac{\Phi'(\bar{\varepsilon})[\hat{e}(\bar{\varepsilon}, \varepsilon^0) - \bar{\varepsilon}]}{1 + \bar{r}}$$

$$+ \frac{[\Phi(\varepsilon^0) - \Phi(\bar{\varepsilon})]\left[\dfrac{\partial\hat{e}}{\partial*}(\bar{\varepsilon}, \varepsilon^0) - 1\right]}{1 + \bar{r}} - \lambda\Phi'(\bar{\varepsilon})(1 + \bar{\varepsilon})$$

$$+ \lambda[1 - \Phi(\bar{\varepsilon})] + \lambda\Phi'(\bar{\varepsilon})(1 - \mu)[1 + e^-(\bar{\varepsilon})]$$

$$+ \lambda\Phi(\bar{\varepsilon})(1 - \mu)\frac{de^-(\bar{\varepsilon})}{d\bar{\varepsilon}} F(K) - \lambda\mu\Phi'(\bar{\varepsilon})(1 - \delta)K,$$

where λ is a Lagrange multiplier. Our numerical simulations suggest that, in this case as well as in the case without domestic credit, there will be domestic undersaving and foreign overinvestment, i.e., $\bar{r} < F'(K) - \delta < r^*$.

In the autarky case, the first-order conditions for the maximization problem as stated in equation (4') with respect to K and $\bar{\varepsilon}$ are

---

12. Naturally, policy intervention may be called for if the set of goods available in the economy as well as the degree of competition in the domestic input market are positively related to the amount of FDI flows. The latter involves, however, an antitrust issue that should more appropriately be tackled through regulations rather than Pigouvian taxes/subsidies.

$$0 = F'(K) - \Phi(\bar{\varepsilon})\{F'(K)[1 + e^-(\bar{\varepsilon})] + (1 - \delta)\}$$
$$- [1 - \Phi(\bar{\varepsilon})][F'(K)(1 + \bar{\varepsilon}) + (1 - \delta)]$$
$$+ \lambda[1 - \Phi(\bar{\varepsilon})][F'(K)(1 + \bar{\varepsilon}) + (1 - \delta)]$$
$$+ \lambda\Phi(\bar{\varepsilon})(1 - \mu)\{F'(K)[1 + e^-(\bar{\varepsilon})] + (1 - \delta)\}$$
$$- \lambda(1 + \bar{r}),$$

and

$$0 = -\Phi'(\bar{\varepsilon})\{F(K)[1 + e^-(\bar{\varepsilon})] + (1 - \delta)K\}$$
$$- \Phi(\bar{\varepsilon})F(K)[de^-(\bar{\varepsilon})/d\bar{\varepsilon}] - [1 - \Phi(\bar{\varepsilon})]F(K)$$
$$+ \Phi'(\bar{\varepsilon})[F(K)(1 + \bar{\varepsilon}) + (1 - \delta)K] + \lambda[1 - \Phi(\bar{\varepsilon})]F(K)$$
$$- \lambda\Phi'(\bar{\varepsilon})[F(K)(1 + \bar{\varepsilon}) + (1 - \delta)K]$$
$$+ \lambda\Phi'(\bar{\varepsilon})(1 - \mu)\{F(K)[1 + e^-(\bar{\varepsilon})] + (1 - \delta)K\}$$
$$+ \lambda\Phi(\bar{\varepsilon})(1 - \mu)\{F(K)[de^-(\bar{\varepsilon})/d\bar{\varepsilon}]\}.$$

References

Akerlof, George. 1970. The market for "lemons": Qualitative uncertainty and the market mechanism. *Quarterly Journal of Economics* 89:488–500.

Borensztein, Eduardo, Jose De Gregorio, and Jong-wha Lee. 1998. How does foreign direct investment affect economic growth? *Journal of International Economics* 45:115–35.

Brecher, Richard A., and Carlos F. D\az-Alejandro. 1977. Tariffs, foreign capital, and immiserizing growth. *Journal of International Economics* 7:317–22.

Feenstra, Robert C., and Gordon H. Hanson. 1997. Foreign direct investment and relative wages: Evidence from Mexico's *maquiladoras. Journal of International Economics* 42:371–93.

Gordon, Roger H., and A. Lans Bovenberg. 1996. Why is capital so immobile internationally? Possible explanations and implications for capital income taxation. *American Economic Review* 86:1057–75.

Hall, Robert E., 1988. The relation between price and marginal Cost in U.S. industry. *Journal of Political Economy* 96:921–948.

Helpman, Elhanan, and Assaf Razin. 1983. Increasing returns, monopolistic competition and factor movements: A welfare analysis. *Journal of International Economics* 14:263–76.

Razin, Assaf, Efraim Sadka, and Chi-Wa Yuen. 1998a. A pecking order of capital inflows and international tax principles. *Journal of International Economics* 44: 45–68.

———. 1998b. Capital flows with debt- and equity-financed investment: equilibrium structure and efficiency implications. IMF Working Paper no. WP/98/159. Washington, D.C.: International Monetary Fund.

———. 1999. An information-based model of foreign direct investment: The gains from trade revisited. *International Tax and Public Finance* 6 (November): 579–

96. Reprinted in Peter Isard, Assaf Razin, and Andrew K. Rose, eds. *International finance and financial crises: Essays in honor of Robert P. Flood, Jr.*, 95–112. Boston: Kluwer Academic, 1999.

Romer, Paul M. 1994. New goods, old theory, and the welfare costs of trade restrictions. *Journal of Development Economics* 43:5–38.

Rotemberg, Julio J., and Michael Woodford. 1995. Dynamic general equilibrium models with imperfectly competitive product markets. In *Frontiers of business cycle research,* ed. Thomas F. Cooley, 243–93. Princeton: Princeton University Press.

Sosner, Nathan. 1998. The sequence of investment decisions as a solution of an agency problem. The Eitan Berglas School of Economics, Tel Aviv University. Mimeograph.

Stiglitz, Joseph E., and Andrew Weiss. 1981. Credit rationing in markets with imperfect information. *American Economic Review* 71:393–410.

Townsend, Robert M. 1979. Optimal contracts and competitive markets with costly state verification. *Journal of Economic Theory* 21:265–93.

World Bank. 1999. *Global development finance.* Washington, D.C.: World Bank.

Comment   Anne O. Krueger

This paper is a well-done and interesting exercise in which the authors develop an asymmetric information model of foreign direct investment (FDI). The driving factor in the model is the assumption that foreigners have inside information about the prospects of the domestic firms into which they buy. They then retain equity shares in firms with good prospects, but sell shares in firms with less satisfactory prospects. Domestic investors do not have this information, and buy shares on the domestic capital market.

Because foreigners have selectively retained shares, the average return on the domestic share market is less than it would have been had there been less (or no) FDI. There is overinvestment by foreigners (who get above-average rates of return because of their superior knowledge) and undersavings by domestic residents (who are receiving below-average rates of return), with a consequent welfare loss (which could be offset by increased competition, technology transfer, and other benefits of FDI in their model). Razin, Sadka, and Yuen (RSY) then simulate their model, and conclude that welfare losses may well result from FDI based on plausible estimates for the parameters.

The model is ingenious and well developed. It has long been known that capital inflows in the presence of distortions could be immiserizing (see

Anne O. Krueger is the Herald L. and Caroline L. Ritch Professor of Economics, senior fellow of the Hoover Institution, director of the Center for Research on Economic Development and Policy Reform at Stanford University, and a research associate of the National Bureau of Economic Research.

Brecher and Diaz-Alejandro 1977 for an early demonstration), and the RSY result is another instance of that outcome. In the RSY specification, all firms are alike except that, in the production function for each firm, there is a stochastic element which is not known ex ante. Once there is a specific shock, insiders know about it and outsiders do not, so there is a distortion. The result as modeled by RSY is a "lemons" problem for the domestic capital market, as "good firms" are ones in which foreigners retain their investments while "bad firms" are ones they remove from their portfolios. FDI is thus a firm-specific equity investment on the part of foreigners.

While the model generates that result, one can question how applicable it is to the real world. One might first ask, if there is asymmetric information, who is likely to be better informed: domestic residents or foreigners? For the RSY model, the timing of who knows what and when is crucial to the outcome: If domestic residents know, or sense, that there are problems before foreigners do, the outcome could easily be reversed.

A second question relates to the behavior of domestic entrepreneurs who know they have a good outcome. In the RSY model, they cannot finance with equity because domestic residents will underprice their prospects. From this specification, a question arises as to what domestic entrepreneurs do, and where domestic savings go. Does this imply that good investments are not made at all? Why cannot domestic entrepreneurs attract foreign capital?

While these questions are specific to the model, there are some more general issues that give rise to concern. All production functions are assumed to be alike, with the difference only in the stochastic element. In the real world, managers differ in their abilities: The same physical assets may yield significantly different returns when placed in the hands of a competent manager. If foreigners are competent managers, the benefits of FDI (as takeovers from incompetent managers) would be much greater than can be modeled within the RSY framework.

Related to that consideration, FDI might be regarded as a mechanism with which foreigners identify (and perhaps improve) domestic managers. If the quality of domestic management increases as a result of FDI, the welfare results would be quite different than those that emanate from the asymmetric information framework.

Finally, RSY find that FDI goes to countries where there is good growth, which they believe is consistent with their hypothesis. In fact, it is equally consistent with the view that FDI goes to countries whose overall economic policy framework is conducive to efficient resource allocation; and, countries with such policy frameworks achieve superior growth performance.

Overall, then, I find the paper interesting and useful in demonstrating one mechanism through which FDI might interact with domestic distortions. I question, however, whether the sort of asymmetric information assumed in the model is the type most frequently found in developing countries, and believe that other alternatives—with the opposite implications for the impact of FDI—are at least as plausible as the RSY mechanism.

Reference

Brecher, Richard, and Carlos Diaz-Alejandro. 1977. Tariffs, foreign capital and immiserizing growth. *Journal of International Economics* 7 (4): 317–22.

Comment   Mario B. Lamberte

The issues raised in this paper are indeed timely, especially since most governments in Asia are now reviewing their policies on foreign capital flows in light of the Asian financial crisis. There is currently much talk about favoring foreign direct investment (FDI) more than portfolio inflows; however, the results of this paper suggest that an appropriate policy for FDI is needed for a country to benefit fully from it.

The paper attempts to formalize, in models, two nontraditional views on FDI. I will comment on each model in order.

First Model

There is a need to remind ourselves of the difference between FDI and portfolio inflows. Usually, FDI investors go to a developing country not to buy an existing firm but to establish a new one, bringing with them their capital and technology. Unlike portfolio investment inflows, FDI inflows stay much longer. Foreign direct investments typically go into areas where domestic investors do not go for lack of access to capital and technology. All this implies that

1. FDI investors know already the productivity levels of the firms before they establish them as subsidiaries in developing countries;

2. Unlike short-term portfolio investments, FDI subsidiaries are kept by parent firms because they confer strategic advantages to the parent firms; and

3. As the paper suggests, local investors are facing liquidity constraint and, given the huge amount of capital required to acquire the shares of FDI investor in a firm, they cannot possibly afford to buy and take over the subsidiaries of foreign corporations. Aside from financial constraint,

Mario B. Lamberte is president of the Philippine Institute for Development Studies (PIDS).

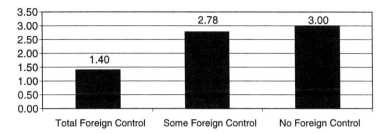

Fig. 9C.1   Average debt-equity ratio of firms according to the extent of foreign participation

local investors are unlikely to have access to the technology and the management system to manage it. It is to be noted that subsidiaries are dependent on their parent companies for so many things, one of which is research and product development. Given the cost of R&D, the local investors will not be on equal footing with FDI investors when they acquire subsidiaries of foreign companies.

The paper assumes that in the presence of a domestic credit market, "it is often observed that FDI is highly leveraged domestically" (315). I tried to check the situation in the Philippines and found that wholly foreign-owned firms are the least leveraged firms (see fig. 9C.1). The most highly leveraged firms are the wholly domestically-owned firms.

There are several reasons for this. First, banks in host countries are usually subject to several regulations, one of which is the single-borrower's limit. Given that banks in developing countries are small, subsidiaries of foreign corporations that normally have huge capital requirement easily hit the single-borrower's limit; thus they cannot borrow from domestic banks as much as they want to. Secondly, developing countries usually have laws limiting the amount that subsidiaries of foreign corporations can borrow from the domestic market so as not to crowd out local firms as well as to encourage them to bring in more capital. For example, in the Philippines, subsidiaries of foreign corporations are allowed to borrow from local banks up to only 50 percent of their capital.

If, indeed, FDI investors unload their shares in their subsidiaries in the local market because their productivity is later found to be lower than their "reservation" productivity level, then what will they do with the proceeds? Will they repatriate them? If so, then how will the process of FDI inflows suggested by the model be affected?

Second Model

The second model banks on the assumption that an increase in competition in the input market brought about by FDI inflows (given the perfectly elastic supply of inputs from abroad) will drive w, the price of intermediate inputs, to its competitive level. This implies that inputs brought in by FDI and domestic inputs are perfect substitutes. This may not be an appropriate assumption because, typically, inputs brought in by FDI are different from those that are locally available. If so, then w will not be driven down to its competitive level.

Finally, near the end of the paper, the authors state that their ". . . simulation results show that substantial welfare losses can indeed be brought about by FDI in the presence of adverse selection in the domestic equity market. These losses can nonetheless be dominated by the gains induced by the technology transfer and competition promotion effects of FDI" (329). This assertion is not clear to me from the analyses presented in the paper. It seems to me that the two models have not yet been integrated.

Currency Crisis of Korea
Internal Weakness or External Interdependence?

Dongchul Cho and Kiseok Hong

10.1 Introduction

During the 1997–98 period, the international capital market experienced arguably the most severe turmoil since the Great Depression. Many economists as well as international investors were greatly surprised by the magnitude and abruptness of capital flow reversals from the emerging markets.

This surprise was possibly amplified by the fact that the crisis took place in East Asia, which has long been regarded as a model economy; it exhibited rapid growth combined with macrostability. To the economists and policy makers who sought the causes of the remarkable achievements in this region (e.g., World Bank 1993), the Asian Crisis came as a shock. Even to those who were skeptical about the Asian Miracle, the abrupt collapse of the region may not be a natural implication of their skepticism. The main implication of input-driven growth (e.g., Krugman 1994 and Young 1995) is the erosion of efficiency, and thus the natural prediction would be a long-term slowdown of growth instead of an immediate collapse. For this reason, many have been led to pay more attention to the effects of contagion (e.g., Agenor and Aizenman 1997 and Perry and Lederman 1998).

This paper examines the currency crisis of Korea—a key country in the Asian Crisis as well as the Asian Miracle—in the context of this upheaval

Dongchul Cho and Kiseok Hong are research fellows at the Korea Development Institute.

The authors are grateful to Deockhyun Ryu, Sungchul Hong, Jin-Myon Lee, and Byung-Sun Lee at the Korean Development Institute for their research assistance. We also appreciate the help of Dosup Kwon at Korean Trade Information Services (KOTIS) and Youngwoo Lee at Korean International Institute for Economic Policy (KIEP) for collecting data.

in the international capital market. In particular, this paper attempts to provide some clues to the question of whether Korea was a poor victim of or a major contributor to the crisis in the global capital market. As is expected from this sort of formidable question, the answer will be indefinite.

Nevertheless, this paper tries to distinguish quantitatively the effects of weaknesses in domestic fundamentals from the effects of external interdependence (called *contagion effects* in this paper). We found that the magnitudes of contagion effects were huge, but the Korean crisis could not be completely attributable to these effects alone. Weak domestic fundamentals and poor management of the government appeared to play significant roles as well, particularly at the triggering moment of the crisis.

More specifically, the following three conclusions summarize this paper's analyses. First, the outbreak of the Korean crisis may not be completely attributable to the contagion effects alone, although the crises of other countries substantially worsened the situation. Second, Korea's fundamentals prior to the crisis were not so strong that economists were astonished with the outbreak of the crisis of Korea, although they were not so weak that investors should have been able to anticipate the crisis. Third, if one considered the structural vulnerability of Korea's financial market in addition to the conventional macrofundamentals, and if one could have foreseen the stubborn policies of the government in coping with financial turmoil, the Korean crisis might have been easier to anticipate.

This paper is organized as follows. Employing the conventional probit model methodology for data from approximately 100 developing countries, section 10.2 evaluates the position of Korea's fundamentals, which are usually considered important in explaining currency crises in developing countries. Among those fundamental factors, Korea's domestic macroeconomic fundamentals were strong (high growth, low inflation, and mild current account deficits), whereas its external finance structure was fragile (low reserve to short-term debt ratios and low FDI to GDP ratios). Overall, Korea's fundamentals were not particularly strong, but not particularly weak either. It is true that Korea's fundamentals sharply deteriorated in 1996 (thus raising the probability of a crisis in 1997) compared to the 1994–95 period, but the overall condition in 1996 was not terrible relative to its historical average, except for the contagion effects. In this section, we also examine the effect of neighbor countries (or contagion effect) using our own index of geographical proximity as well as the trade linkage index developed by Glick and Rose (1998). An important finding is that our geographical proximity index dominates the trade linkage index, which may suggest that investors' perceptions and expectations really matter in transmitting currency crises.

Section 10.3 takes a further look at the contagion issue, using daily-frequency data of the exchange rates and sovereign spreads on the U.S.

dollar–denominated debts for selected countries. We use standard time-series methodologies, and similar analyses can be found in Baig and Gold-fajn (1998). Unlike Baig and Goldfajn, however, we extend the sample to non-Asian countries such as Latin American countries, Russia, China, and Japan, while focusing on the case of Korea. By doing so, we are able to provide a more complete picture and to decompose explicitly the contribution of the contagion effects from other parts of the world. We also relate the chronology of daily news on Korea's financial market to the shocks identified by the time series analyses giving us a sense of the sort of news which would negatively impact the financial market at the triggering moment of the crisis. Overall, we found that the news about the series of *chaebol* bankruptcies and the government's continued bailout policies for these *chaebols* and financial institutions appeared to operate negatively in preventing foreign investors from fleeing.

Section 10.4 notes some additional weaknesses in Korea's financial market structure that deserve mention. In this section, we do not provide a formal analysis to the degree we did in sections 10.2 and 10.3. Instead, we briefly summarize several points made by other researchers in Korea, so that readers do not miss important aspects of the Korean crisis simply because the effects of those aspects cannot be easily quantified. In particular, we note the facts that the corporate sector of Korea had long suffered from low profitability and high leverage ratios, whereas a small number of *chaebols* had extraordinarily high influence in the financial system. Section 10.5 offers some concluding remarks.

10.2 Domestic Fundamentals versus Contagion: Cross-Country Analysis

In this section we examine Korea's economic fundamentals during the precrisis period in comparison with other developing countries as well as the role of the contagion effect in the outbreak of Korea's currency crisis. To this end, we employ a probit model using a data set of roughly 100 developing countries.

10.2.1 Theory

Existing theories on currency crises are often classified into two generations of models.[1] Whereas the first-generation model stresses economic fundamentals such as domestic credit expansion and liquidity (Krugman 1979), the second-generation model puts more emphasis on investors' expectations and inherent instability in the international capital market (Obstfeld 1995). In empirical investigations of a currency crisis, however, it is hard to distinguish between the two classes of models. Although the second-generation model emphasizes the role of expectations, expectations

---

1. See Eichengreen, Rose, and Wyplosz (1995) for a detailed survey on the literature.

are likely to be systematically related to economic fundamentals. Thus, in practice, both classes of models commonly predict that the probability of a currency crisis increases with deterioration of economic fundamentals. The only way to distinguish between the two classes of models is to prove that some crisis episodes are actually generated by self-fulfilling expectations. Clearly, this is a difficult task. Referring to this difficulty, Garber (1996) has concluded that the two classes of models are observationally equivalent.

Similar argument applies to the so-called contagion effect. Contagion effect refers to the phenomenon that a currency crisis spreads contagiously from one country to another, for whatever reasons.[2] Because contagion can take place due either to cross-country correlation in economic fundamentals or to pure investor psychology, the existence of contagion itself cannot be used as evidence for self-fulfilling expectations. For more concrete evidence, one needs to prove the existence of contagion after controlling for all relevant economic fundamentals. In practice, however, it is not feasible to control for every relevant variable.[3]

For this reason, this section does not intend to test the relevance of a particular model. The goal of this section is simply to estimate a probit equation that relates crisis episodes to standard macroeconomic fundamentals along with contagion measures, and to evaluate how well Korea's currency crisis episode fits in the model.

10.2.2   Dependent Variable

The dependent variable for our probit estimation is a crisis index, which has a value of 1 if a currency crisis occurs and 0 otherwise. Specifically, following Frankel and Rose (1996), we define a currency crisis as a depreciation of the nominal exchange rate (with respect to the U.S. dollar) of at least 25 percent that is also at least a 10 percent increase in the rate of depreciation.[4]

2. For discussion on various channels of contagion effects, see Calvo and Reinhart (1996) and Valdes (1996).

3. Nevertheless, there exists pioneering research that attempts to identify fundamental channels of contagion effects. For example, see Doukas (1999) for the channel through co-movements of major macrovariables; Glick and Rose (1998) for the channel through trade; and Frankel and Schmukler (1998) for the channel through the New York investor fund community. For more microdata analyses that particularly stress the role of incomplete information, see Aharony and Swary (1983, 1996); Park (1991); Karafiath, Mynatt, and Smith (1991); Calomiris and Mason (1994).

4. Ideally, definition of a currency crisis should be comprehensive enough to incorporate various events fully, such as violent depreciation of the exchange rate, sharp reduction in foreign exchange reserves, and rapid increase in interest rates. For developing countries, however, it is hard to find an interest rate measure that is consistent across countries and free from direct government control. Also, developing countries with weak fundamentals tend eventually to develop a currency crisis regardless of their efforts to defend their currencies using foreign exchange reserves. Thus, we use only the nominal exchange rate in constructing our crisis index.

10.2.3   Explanatory Variables

For possible causes of a currency crisis, we consider the following three sets of variables:

1. Macroeconomic indicators: GDP growth rate, real domestic credit growth, inflation rate, fiscal deficit/GDP ratio.
2. External variables: current account/GDP ratio, changes in the terms of trade, changes in the real exchange rate, foreign reserves/short-term debt ratio, FDI/GDP ratio, total foreign debt/GDP ratio, short-term debt/total foreign debt ratio.
3. Foreign conditions: GDP growth rate and interest rate in developed countries, crisis incidents of foreign countries.

A decrease in the GDP growth rate increases the possibility of a crisis by weakening general solvency of the country or by engendering expansionary monetary policy. Also, rapid expansion of domestic credit or fiscal deficit increases the possibility of a crisis by generating inflationary pressures in the goods market and depreciation pressures in the foreign exchange market. Factors such as deterioration in the terms of trade, appreciation of the real exchange rate, and current account deficits can produce a crisis by reducing both profitability of the exporting sector and net foreign assets of the economy. Lastly, whereas a high foreign debt/GDP ratio increases the probability of a crisis by making the country vulnerable to a negative shock, high foreign reserves/short-term debt or FDI/GDP ratios reduce the probability of a crisis by providing greater liquidity.

In addition to domestic fundamentals, foreign conditions can also play a key role in the outbreak of a currency crisis. Because developed countries are the net creditors in the international capital market, economic booms in developed countries can lead to reductions in capital supply for developing countries. Among developing countries, a currency crisis in one country may increase the possibility of crisis in another country. As was mentioned earlier, this contagion effect may reflect either cross-country correlation in economic fundamentals or merely investors' psychology. In this section, we simply define the contagion index for each country as a weighted average of the crisis index of all other countries, with the weights given by either the inverse of geographical distance between the country in question and other countries or the trade linkage used in Glick and Rose (1998).[5] Because currency crises appear to be regionally concentrated, we suspect that geographical distance is perhaps the most important determinant of the contagion effect. Glick and Rose, on the other hand, argue

---

5. Because distributions of thus-constructed indexes are close to lognormal, we prevent influence of potential outliers by taking logarithms of the indexes. Main results remain unaffected by the use of the original indexes.

that contagion takes place mainly through trade channels. This section considers both our own contagion index and the trade contagion index.[6] Detailed definitions of explanatory variables are provided in the appendix.

10.2.4 Data

Our data set covers 103 developing countries, including the Asian and Latin American countries hit by the crisis, mostly for the years 1980–96. The nominal exchange rate, however, covers the period 1980–97. As we will show, this enables us to relate the dependent variable to one-year-lagged values of explanatory variables. Using lags of explanatory variables better serves our goal of identifying the "causes" of a currency crisis. Unlike other explanatory variables, however, we let the contagion index take contemporaneous values with the dependent variable, because the contagion effect is expected to be coincident with currency crises. According to our definition of currency crisis, about 10 percent of the total country-years are classified as crisis episodes.

10.2.5 Probit Estimation Results

Probit estimation results using the aforementioned variables are reported in table 10.1. Because coefficients from probit estimation are hard to interpret, we calculate the marginal contribution of each regressor to the probability of a crisis, using historical means of the variables. We first report in columns 1 and 2 of the table the estimation results without the contagion effect. For most variables, the estimated coefficients are significant and of the correct signs. This suggests that incidence of a currency crisis is not randomly distributed across countries but is systematically related to economic fundamentals. Variables such as government deficit, current account, and total foreign debt, however, are insignificant or of the wrong signs. Frankel and Rose (1996) have reported similar findings. As column 2 shows, when these insignificant variables are excluded from the regression, coefficients on the remaining regressors change only slightly.

In columns 3 and 4, we add a contagion index to the equation. We find that the trade contagion index and our contagion index each have significantly positive effects.[7] As was mentioned earlier, however, it is not clear what the correlation between the crisis index and the contagion index truly implies. Although we have included standard macroeconomic variables in

6. One may argue that contagion of crises may take place through financial linkages as well (see, for example, Kaminsky and Reinhart 2000). In a separate paper, Hong (2000) has constructed a financial contagion index using the BIS data on international claims, and compared it with the regional and trade contagion indexes of this paper. Hong has found that the main result of this section still holds: The regional contagion index dominates the trade and financial contagion indexes.

7. According to the estimates, a one-unit increase in the trade contagion index and our contagion index (100 percent increase in the original contagion indexes) increases the probability of a currency crisis by 4 and 6 percentage points, respectively.

Table 10.1   Cross-Country Probit Analyses: Causes of Currency Crises

	(1)	(2)	(3)	(4)	(5)
Per capita GDP growth	-0.346 (-2.05)	-0.282 (-2.11)	-0.195 (-1.36)	-0.205 (-1.61)	-0.254 (-1.23)
Fiscal deficit/GDP	-0.001 (-0.61)				
Inflation rate	0.043 (2.02)	0.039 (2.10)	0.040 (2.08)	0.036 (2.12)	0.059 (2.14)
Real domestic credit growth	0.110 (2.32)	0.055 (1.40)	0.068 (1.64)	0.063 (1.74)	0.105 (1.80)
Current account/GDP	-0.002 (-0.93)				
Terms of trade changes	-0.160 (-1.89)	-0.136 (-1.97)	-0.145 (-1.98)	-0.123 (-1.90)	-0.210 (-2.02)
Real exchange rate depreciation	-0.216 (-3.19)	-0.175 (-2.92)	-0.189 (-2.96)	-0.195 (-3.34)	-0.295 (-3.16)
Reserves/short-term debt	-0.015 (-2.24)	-0.008 (-2.27)	-0.009 (-2.05)	-0.008 (-2.47)	-0.015 (-2.34)
FDI/GDP	-0.017 (-2.51)	-0.015 (-2.66)	-0.014 (-2.17)	-0.011 (-2.01)	-0.017 (-1.86)
Total foreign debt/GDP	-0.058 (-2.82)				
Short-term debt/total foreign debt	0.001 (0.86)				
Foreign GDP growth	0.021 (2.52)				
Foreign interest rate	-0.001 (-0.37)				
Trade contagion index			0.043 (3.07)	0.069 (4.98)	0.018 (0.82)
Our contagion index					0.095 (3.70)
Sample size	675	1,028	999	1,028	999
Unconditional probability of crisis	0.114	0.117	0.118	0.117	0.118
Average estimated probability of crisis countries	0.198	0.157	0.165	0.184	0.181
Average estimated probability of no-crisis countries	0.103	0.111	0.111	0.107	0.109

Note: Numbers in parentheses are z-statistics.

the regression, the possibility of important excluded variables still remains. In addition, using one index without the other may produce biased estimates because the two indexes are likely to be correlated.[8] Only by considering both indexes at the same time, will one be able to properly evaluate the independent contribution of each index to the probability of a currency crisis.

We report the results from this experiment in column 5 of table 10.1. Note that when the two indexes are included in one regression, our index dominates the trade contagion index and the latter becomes insignificant. This result suggests that the trade contagion index works only as a proxy for our contagion index, and thus the trade linkage is probably not the main channel of regional contagion of crises.[9] For this reason, we will use column 3 as our benchmark estimates for the rest of this section. Under the benchmark estimates, the average of the fitted probability for all actual crisis episodes is 0.18.

10.2.6   Korea's Currency Crisis and Contagion

In this section, we focus on Korea's currency crisis based on results from previous sections. First, we report the fitted values for Korea and other countries hit by crisis, such as Mexico, Thailand, Malaysia, and Indonesia. As column 1 of table 10.2 shows, when only economic fundamentals in 1996 are considered, the fitted value was 0.127 for Korea and below 0.1 for the other Asian countries. Considering the fact that the unconditional probability of a currency crisis is 0.1 in our sample, the Asian crisis as a whole was rather unanticipated. The only exception is Korea, whose economic fundamentals in 1996 appear to have been weak enough to imply a possible crisis in the following year.[10] The finding that the crisis probability of Korea in 1996 was relatively high may be surprising, because many people have argued that Korea's economic fundamentals were sound before the crisis. Column 1 of table 10.2 does not support this popular claim.[11]

The crisis potential of Asia in 1997 was small, not only by international standards, but also by its own historical trends. As shown in column 2 of table 10.2, the fitted probability for the Asian countries was not substantially greater in 1997 than it was in the earlier years. For example, Korea's

---

8. It is obvious that trade is more active among countries in geographical proximity. In fact, correlation of the two indexes in our pooled data set is 0.7.

9. One problem is that due to data availability, we used only the 1997 international trade matrix, assuming that the trade linkage is constant over time. For more rigorous results, we need to construct the trade linkage for every year. However when the sample period is restricted to 1992–97, however, our index still dominates the trade linkage.

10. Rigorously speaking, the estimated probability is not ex ante, because the contagion index takes contemporaneous values. For countries like Korea where a crisis took place at the end of the year, however, the probability may well be considered as ex ante.

11. Table 10.3 (heading C) is not a true out-of-sample exercise, because observations in 1997 are used in the estimation. An out-of-sample exercise, however, changes the results only slightly.

Table 10.2   **Cross-Country Probit Analyses: Probability of a Currency Crisis**

	With Contagion Index (from eq. [2] in table 10.1)		With Contagion Index (from eq. [3] in table 10.1)		With Contagion Index (from eq. [4] in table 10.1)	
	(1)	(2)	(3)	(4)	(5)	(6)
Mexico						
(1987–93)		0.133		0.100		0.140
(1994)	0.132		0.115		0.168	
Thailand						
(1987–96)		0.088		0.093		0.082
(1997)	0.084		0.106		0.182	
Malaysia						
(1987–96)		0.041		0.043		0.040
(1997)	0.081		0.075		0.138	
Indonesia						
(1987–96)		0.111		0.114		0.102
(1997)	0.070		0.101		0.171	
Korea						
(1987–96)		0.112		0.100		0.102
(1997)	0.127		0.148		0.208	

crisis potential was about 0.1 even before 1996. Although we find that the Korean economy in 1996 was in fact much weaker than it was during the economic boom of 1994 and 1995, 1996 was not the worst year of the decade.

In columns 3–6 of table 10.2, we examine whether the crisis probability increases for Asian countries when the contagion effect is included as an additional regressor. Depending upon which contagion index is used the results vary substantially. When the trade linkage index is used, the estimated probabilities of the Asian countries change only slightly. However, our geographical linkage index substantially increases the estimated probability for the Asian countries from the range of 0.08–0.13 to the average level of ex post crisis countries, 0.19! According to this result, one could naturally have predicted the Korean crisis after the outbreak of the Southeast Asian turmoil.

Next, we examine which variables were particularly important in Korea's currency crisis compared with other crisis episodes. To this end, we calculate the contribution of each explanatory variable to the incidence of each crisis by multiplying the benchmark coefficient estimates in column 4 of table 10.1 with the corresponding values of explanatory variables. Deviation of each crisis from a reference-group mean of similarly constructed contribution measures can be used to illustrate distinguishing features of each crisis episode. Before examining each individual country's episode in detail, however, we first compare the average values of the crisis countries with those of the whole sample in table 10.3. This table clearly shows that, on average, the crisis countries exhibit weaknesses in all of the considered fundamentals. Apart from the contagion, in particular, the reserves to short-term debt ratio makes the greatest contribution to the crisis probability.

Table 10.3 also reports the results from the same experiment for each individual country's episode, using all crisis countries (column 1) as our reference group to be compared. A negative number in the table implies that the contribution of the variable to the corresponding crisis episode is smaller than to the whole crisis group in our data set. In Korea's crisis, for example, external factors (such as the terms-of-trade shock, low reserves, and low FDI) have been particularly important, whereas domestic macro-

Table 10.3   Cross-Country Probit Analyses: Contribution of Each Explanatory Variable to the Asian Crisis

	Deviations from Average Values of the Whole Sample		
	Sample Mean		
	Whole Sample (1)	Crisis Countries (2)	Marginal Contribution[a]
Per capita GDP growth	0.00477	−0.01056	0.00314
Inflation	0.18787	0.30629	0.00429
Real domestic credit growth	0.01930	0.03707	0.00113
Terms of trade changes	−0.00804	−0.03552	0.00337
Real exchange rate depreciation	−0.01699	−0.05357	0.00715
Reserves/short-term debt	3.39132	1.27950	0.01752
FDI/GDP	1.25291	0.71543	0.00600
Our contagion index	−2.39022	−2.10817	0.01946
Sum of deviations			0.06206

	Deviations from Average Values of Crisis Countries				
	Mexico (1994)	Thailand (1997)	Malaysia (1997)	Indonesia (1997)	Korea (1997)
Per capita GDP growth	−0.00106	−0.00987	−0.01049	−0.01150	−0.01154
Inflation	−0.00772	−0.00904	−0.00985	−0.00831	−0.00935
Real domestic credit growth	−0.00046	−0.01887	0.00525	0.00575	0.00561
Terms of trade changes	−0.00398	−0.00484	−0.00710	−0.00879	0.00549
Real exchange rate depreciation	0.00641	−0.00275	−0.00466	−0.00346	−0.00930
Reserves/short-term debt	0.00492	0.00241	−0.00898	0.00602	0.00609
FDI/GDP	−0.00416	−0.00610	−0.04260	−0.03133	0.00263
Our contagion index	0.00724	0.05687	0.05392	0.04985	0.03376
Sum of deviations	0.00118	0.00781	−0.02452	−0.00176	0.02339

[a]Marginal Contribution to Crisis Probability = $x[(b) − (a)]$.

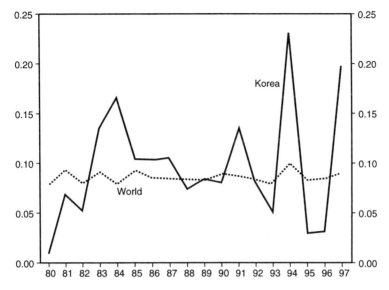

Fig. 10.1   Distance contagion index of Korea (1980–97)

conditions (such as GDP growth and inflation) had limited effects. Also, in most Asian countries the growth rate of real domestic credit has had a positive impact, supporting the popular view that overlending and overinvestment were critical factors in the Asian crisis.

Table 10.3 also indicates that the role of the contagion effect has been more important in the Asian crisis than in other crisis episodes. Even for Korea, which was the least affected by contagion of the Asian countries, the contagion effect appears to have played a key role. Figure 10.1 plots the contagion index of Korea along with the world average of the index.

We have so far examined Korea's currency crisis on the basis of a general probit model. In short, the results suggest that the role of the contagion effect in Korea's crisis was significant, but economic fundamentals of Korea (particularly external factors) were not sound prior to the crisis, relative to the other Asian countries in particular. Although the above exercises produce many interesting results, one should acknowledge many limitations as well. Perhaps the most important limitation is that our exercise was performed for virtually a single observation out of more than 2,000 sample points, and thus the related error margin is potentially very large.

10.3   Country Shock versus Contagion: Further Analysis with Daily Data

The previous section of cross-country analyses suggests that the contagion effect may have been a major cause of the Korean crisis as well as the Asian crises in general. However, the cross-country analyses cannot examine dynamic diffusion processes of shocks across countries. With respect to the analysis of contagion effects, this seems to be an important limitation. For example, when many countries fall into crises in the same year, it is impossible to investigate whether one country's crisis causes another or whether they altogether generate a vicious circle of crises through mutual interactions. With the binary definition of the crisis, it becomes even harder to examine to what extent the crises of other countries worsened the situation of one country. In addition, it seems persuasive to argue that shocks in financial markets are transmitted so rapidly that analyses with annual data can hardly capture the complete picture.

In this section, therefore, we analyze the high-frequency data of the relevant variables, namely, daily data of the exchange rates (against the U.S. dollar) and the spreads (over the Treasury bill rate) of the U.S. dollar–denominated sovereign debts. When high-frequency data are used, the limitation of data coverage across countries as well as the relevant macrovariables that can help identify the sources of contagion are obvious disadvantages. For this reason, we will not seriously question the ultimate sources of the contagion effects in this section. Instead, we will attribute the whole magnitude "explained" by the shocks of other countries in the regressions to contagion effects, and the remaining parts to effects from domestic shocks.[12]

Considering data availability and its importance in the recent crisis, we selected ten countries: Brazil, Argentina, Mexico, Russia, China, Korea, Malaysia, Thailand, Indonesia, and Japan. Japan is included in order to check whether we can find any systematic evidence for the popular argument that the weakness of the Japanese economy played a significant role in triggering the Asian crisis. The sample period was chosen from 19 June 1997 to 31 December 1998, so that we can cover the situation right before Thailand's crisis. The sample size is approximately 400 for each country. The recent paper by Baig and Goldfajn (1998) presents similar analyses to those in this section, but we examine data largely from Korea's viewpoint using a wider set of countries. Details of the data sources can be found in the appendix.

10.3.1 Exchange Rates

A serious difficulty with using the exchange rate data is that the government, implicitly or explicitly, controls this variable in many countries. For example, the exchange rates of the three Latin American countries, Russia, and China are virtually uncorrelated with the exchange rates of other countries (not reported) because the governments of these countries managed their exchange rates. We dropped these five countries from our sample

---

12. Put more precisely, *domestic shock* is defined as the component that is orthogonal to shocks to other countries in the sample. Therefore, it is likely that more variations are attributed to domestic shocks when a smaller number of countries are included in the sample.

Table 10.4   **Analyses for the Exchange Rate**

	Korea	Malaysia	Thailand	Indonesia	Japan
A. ADF Test for Unit Root (daily data, lag = 2, including intercept)[a]					
Test statistic	−2.24	−2.31	−2.62	−1.71	−1.52
B. Pair-wise Correlation Coefficients (daily data, log-difference)[b]					
Korea	1.00				
Malaysia	0.10	1.00			
Thailand	0.09	0.41	1.00		
Indonesia	0.22	0.49	0.27	1.00	
Japan	0.08	0.12	0.20	0.11	1.00
C. Pair-wise Correlation Coefficients (daily data, log-level)[b]					
Korea	1.00				
Malaysia	0.81	1.00			
Thailand	0.82	0.82	1.00		
Indonesia	0.67	0.83	0.56	1.00	
Japan	0.51	0.68	0.56	0.77	1.00
D. p-Value for the Granger Causality Test (daily data, log-difference)[c]					
Korea		0.07	0.40	0.25	0.13
Malaysia	0.01		0.00	0.48	0.01
Thailand	0.00	0.02		0.01	0.77
Indonesia	0.00	0.00	0.00		0.16
Japan	0.82	0.26	0.65	0.87	

[a]1% critical value −3.45, 5% critical value −2.87, 10% critical value −2.57.

[b]Asymptotic standard error 0.05.

[c]Numbers are p-values of the tests for the nulls of no Granger causality from the country in the column to the country in the row.

for this reason and analyzed the five Asian countries, even though it is known that the governments in these countries also intervened in the foreign exchange markets from time to time. A more accurate reading of the pure market responses probably can be found from the sovereign spread data in secondary markets, the results for which we will discuss in the next section.

Cross-Country Correlation

Having confirmed that the null hypotheses of unit roots in the log of the exchange rates are not rejected (see heading A of table 10.4), heading B of table 10.4 reports the pair-wise correlation coefficients of the log differences for the five Asian countries. This table shows that the daily fluctuations are closely correlated with one another.[13] However, the correlation coefficients of Korea with other countries are far smaller than those among

13. All of the exchange rates are against the U.S. dollar, and correlation across countries may be spurious in that it may reflect the common fluctuation of the U.S. dollar. In this sense, an interpretation about the absolute degree of the correlation coefficient should be made with caution. However, comparison of the coefficient with other countries is largely immune to this problem.

the three Association of Southeast Asian Nations (ASEAN) countries. This result may be regarded as consistent with the finding from the cross-country data that the contagion effect was small for Korea relative to the ASEAN countries.

In addition, Japan's exchange rate does not appear to be significantly correlated with that of Korea; it is more correlated with the exchange rates of the ASEAN countries. At least from the daily variations for the sample period used in this paper, it appears difficult to justify the casual argument that the weakness of the Japanese yen was a major cause of the Asian crisis, particularly the crisis of Korea.

The relatively low frequency data or the level data shows a slightly different picture. For example, the correlation coefficients of Korea with the other countries are significant for the first differences of the weekly averages (not reported) and for the levels under heading C of table 10.4, although the degrees are still smaller than other coefficients. This may indicate that sizable lagged effects exist in transmitting one country's shock to another country, and if so, the Granger causality test exercise can be meaningful.

Granger Causality Test

Heading D of table 10.4 reports the *p*-values of the test statistic under the null of no Granger causality for each pair of countries, using two days of time lags. It may not be surprising that shocks in many countries Granger-cause movements in many other countries. What is impressive, however, is that Korea Granger-caused devaluations of the ASEAN countries far more significantly than vice versa. In addition, it is hard to find any causality connections between Japan and Korea, which is consistent with the result from the contemporaneous correlation coefficients.

VAR Simulation

How much of Korea's devaluation can be attributed to the contagion, and how much to the country's own shock? In order to provide a mechanical answer to this question, we applied the vector autoregression (VAR) technique for these five countries' data, using two lagged variables and no drift terms.[14] As for the ordering of the countries, we used the Granger causality results of table 10.4: Korea → Malaysia → Thailand → Indonesia → Japan. Because the VAR results are usually sensitive to the orderings, however, we tried the other extreme case for Korea: Malaysia → Thailand → Indonesia → Japan → Korea. Figure 10.1 plots the actual exchange rate of Korea, along with the two simulated paths by the respec-

---

14. Experiments with more than two lagged variables did not greatly change the simulation results, and the null of no drift term was accepted for all of the regressions.

tive VAR estimations that would have been realized if the shocks to other countries had not occurred. That is, the two dotted lines depict the exchange rate variations that can be attributed to the domestic shocks of Korea and its repercussions through the other four countries in the VAR models.

From these experiments, one can see that the contagion effects on Korea's exchange rate were large throughout the whole sample period, which is consistent with the results from the cross-country analyses. According to the lower dotted line that attributes Korea's variation wholly to the contagion effects, the exchange rate would have returned to the precrisis level during the second half of 1999 if there had been no foreign shocks. Also, the decomposition of the variation between domestic shocks and foreign shocks is rather insensitive to the ordering of the equations; that is, the two dotted lines are close to each other. This robustness of the results for Korea may have been expected from the above results for the correlation coefficients and the Granger causality tests.

Perhaps a more important message of figure 10.2 is, however, that the domestic shock must have played a critical role at least in triggering the explosion during the period of November and December 1998. Of course, this experiment has many limitations. As was noted earlier, for example, the exchange rate data are contaminated by the government intervention, and thus the analysis of the contagion effects was performed for only a limited number of countries. In particular, the redevaluation of the Asian exchange rates in the second half of 1998 was often attributed to the crises of Russia and Brazil, but the above analysis could not give support to this conjecture. In section 10.3.2, therefore, we present the results for the sovereign spread data in the secondary market for a wider set of countries.

10.3.2   Sovereign Spreads

The general methodology employed here is virtually identical to that in the previous section except for the coverage of the sample countries: For the sovereign spread data, we can include three Latin American countries (Brazil, Argentina, Mexico), Russia, and China, in addition to the previous Asian five. Parallel to the previous section, we focus on the results for the first differences. This is different from Baig and Goldfajn (1998), whose study analyzed the results for the levels of the sovereign spreads. It is not clear to us which one of the two is a superior concept in the context of contagion effects. Our choice of the first difference is based on the test results that do not reject the nulls of the unit roots in the data (see heading A of table 10.5). However, we also report some of the results for the level data as well because the correlation of the first differences only shows the contemporaneous daily contagion, whereas the correlation of the levels may indicate that the contagion cumulated over time with time lags.

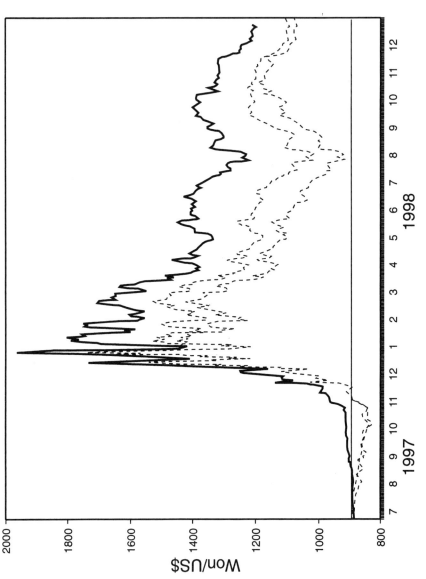

Fig. 10.2 Decomposition of Korea's exchange rate: Domestic versus foreign shock–driven components

Notes: The solid line is the actual won–dollar exchange rate, and the dotted lines are generated using the VAR estimation results with the foreign shocks set to be zeros. The upper dotted line is from the VAR with Korea at the highest in the

Table 10.5 **Analyses for the Sovereign Spreads**

	Brazil	Argentina	Mexico	Russia	China	Korea	Malaysia	Thailand	Indonesia	Japan
	A. ADF Test for Unit Root (daily data, lag = 2, including intercept)[a]									
Test statistic	-1.65	-1.53	-1.74	-0.16	-1.47	-1.70	-0.99	-1.72	-1.59	-3.01
	B. Pair-wise Correlation Coefficients (daily data, first difference)[b]									
Brazil	1.00									
Argentina	0.71	1.00								
Mexico	0.76	0.79	1.00							
Russia	0.35	0.45	0.49	1.00						
China	0.08	0.08	-0.02	0.05	1.00					
Korea	0.30	0.36	0.24	0.18	0.17	1.00				
Malaysia	-0.09	0.09	-0.02	0.03	0.09	0.22	1.00			
Thailand	-0.03	0.07	-0.02	0.06	0.03	0.05	0.12	1.00		
Indonesia	0.20	0.14	0.16	0.07	-0.06	0.01	0.04	0.01	1.00	
Japan	-0.10	-0.12	-0.18	-0.16	0.07	0.09	0.12	-0.01	-0.03	1.00
	C. Pair-wise Correlation Coefficients (daily data, level)[b]									
Brazil	1.00									
Argentina	0.93	1.00								
Mexico	0.95	0.97	1.00							
Russia	0.80	0.86	0.80	1.00						
China	0.81	0.90	0.85	0.87	1.00					

(*continued*)

Table 10.5 (continued)

	Brazil	Argentina	Mexico	Russia	China	Korea	Malaysia	Thailand	Indonesia	Japan
Korea	0.81	0.88	0.88	0.83	0.74	1.00				
Malaysia	0.86	0.90	0.88	0.84	0.93	0.93	1.00			
Thailand	0.85	0.88	0.88	0.84	0.67	0.81	0.92	1.00		
Indonesia	0.66	0.70	0.70	0.62	0.80	0.80	0.81	0.89	1.00	
Japan	0.01	0.08	0.08	0.05	-0.26	-0.03	0.19	-0.15	0.22	1.00

D. p-Value for the Granger Causality Test (daily data, first difference)[c]

	Brazil	Argentina	Mexico	Russia	China	Korea	Malaysia	Thailand	Indonesia	Japan
Brazil		0.00	0.00	0.03	0.08	0.01	0.00	0.02	0.39	0.42
Argentina	0.00		0.06	0.79	0.12	0.09	0.00	0.01	0.39	0.34
Mexico	0.00	0.00		0.00	0.16	0.00	0.01	0.00	0.16	0.92
Russia	0.00	0.00	0.00		0.00	0.92	0.00	0.00	0.61	0.36
China	0.00	0.00	0.00	0.00		0.00	0.70	0.03	0.99	0.81
Korea	0.00	0.00	0.01	0.00	0.33		0.02	0.98	0.23	0.07
Malaysia	0.00	0.12	0.00	0.01	0.06	0.00		0.00	0.48	0.19
Thailand	0.00	0.00	0.01	0.01	0.08	0.00	0.00		0.02	0.16
Indonesia	0.00	0.12	0.04	0.30	0.65	0.42	0.89	0.55		0.45
Japan	0.00	0.00	0.00	0.01	0.00	0.06	0.01	0.02	0.28	

[a] 1% critical value −3.45, 5% critical value −2.87, 10% critical value −2.57.
[b] Asymptotic standard error 0.05.
[c] Numbers are p-values of the tests for the nulls of no Granger causality from the country in the column to the country in the row.

Cross-Country Correlation

Heading B of table 10.5 reports the pair-wise correlation coefficients of the first differences of the sovereign spreads for the ten countries. First, the correlation coefficients among the three Latin American countries are extremely high: They are over 0.7! One may be able to argue that the three countries are taken to be virtually a single market in the international capital market.

In contrast, the correlation coefficients among the three ASEAN countries are far smaller: The correlation coefficient between Malaysia and Thailand is barely significant at the 5 percent level, whereas the coefficients between Indonesia and the other two countries are not significant at all. In fact, Indonesia appears to be more correlated with Latin American countries than with other Asian countries. Russia is also more correlated with Latin American countries than with the Asian countries, and China is not significantly correlated with any other countries. It is interesting that Japan shows negative correlation with Latin American countries, which seems to indicate that the international capital market perceives the crises in Latin America as positive shocks to Japan (or negative shocks to the United States; recall that we use the spreads over the U.S. Treasury bill rate).

Finally, it is surprising that Korea shows stronger correlation with the Latin American countries than with Asian countries. As in the exchange rate analyses, however, the cross-country correlation appears to be far more significant when the first differences of the weekly average or the levels of the daily data are used.[15] For the first differences of the weekly average data (not reported) or for the levels under heading C in table 10.5, for example, Korea turns out to be significantly correlated with all other countries except Indonesia. Again, this divergence of results when the data frequency is varied seems to suggest that substantial time lags exist in the contagion effects that cannot be captured by the contemporaneous daily correlation.

Granger Causality Test

This argument is confirmed by the Granger causality test results reported under heading D in table 10.5. Allowing for just two days of time lags, the nulls of no causality were rejected in many pairs for which the contemporaneous daily correlation did not appear to be significant. For example, Thailand appeared to be significantly correlated only with Malaysia in the daily difference correlation, but it appeared to Granger-cause, as well as to be Granger-caused by, many other countries. The passive role of Japan is confirmed again: It was Granger-caused by most of the sample

---

15. For example, Valdes (1996) used the average of weekly data for the sovereign spreads for Latin American countries.

countries, but it did not Granger-cause the crisis countries. As in the previous section, the role of Japan in triggering the crises appeared to be minimal.

Finally, Korea was Granger-caused by the Latin American countries as well as it Granger-caused them, but it Granger-caused the other Asian countries and was not Granger-caused by them. All of these results are not in accordance with the casual assertion that the ASEAN or Japanese financial crises triggered the Korean crisis. Instead, these results seem to support the hypothesis that the Korean crisis was largely triggered by domestic weaknesses and that it was deepened by the crises of Russia and Brazil later on.

VAR Simulation

Using similar methodology as described in the previous section, figure 10.3 plots the actual sovereign spread of Korea, along with the simulated paths by the VAR estimations (two lagged variables and no drift terms) that would have been realized if the shocks to other countries had not occurred.[16] As for the ordering of the countries, again, we referred to the Granger causality test results (Brazil → Argentina → Mexico → Russia → China → Korea → Malaysia → Thailand → Indonesia → Japan). In order to check the sensitivity of the result, we also report an additional simulation result that placed Korea at the bottom in the ordering of the countries.

A literal interpretation of this graph is that the spike in Korea's spread in mid-1998 would not have occurred if there had been no crises in other countries (Brazil in particular): The simulated spread does not exceed 400 basis points, whereas the actual spread peaked at 1,000 basis points. This is somewhat different from the result for the exchange rate in figure 10.2 in which Russia and Latin American countries were not considered. That is, this difference indicates that Korea's crisis was significantly affected by the contagion effects from the Russian and Latin American crises in the second half of 1998. Nevertheless, the rise of Korea's spread in 1997 cannot be fully attributed to contagion effects, which is the same conclusion as in the analyses with the exchange rates.

10.3.3 News

An important result from the analyses of both the exchange rates and sovereign spreads is that the outbreak of the Korean crisis at the end of 1997 is hardly attributable to contagion effects. In this section, therefore, we examine more closely what happened inside Korea during this critical period from October to December 1997. For this purpose, we collect major news on the financial market and examine how the market reacted to each incident.

---

16. Experiments with more than two lagged variables did not greatly change the simulation results, and the constant terms appeared to be insignificant for most countries.

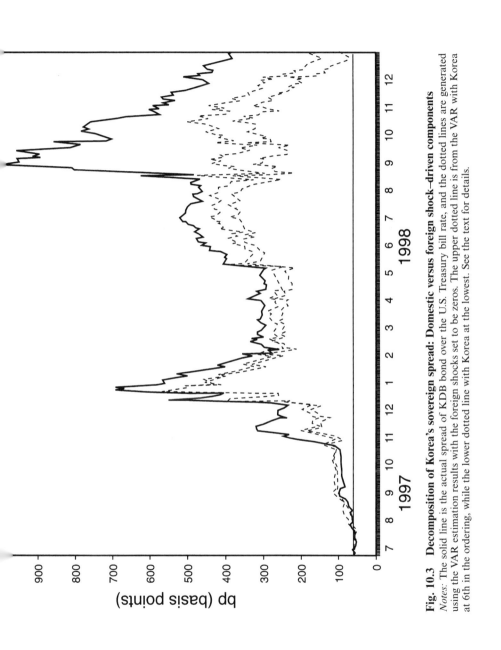

Fig. 10.3 Decomposition of Korea's sovereign spread: Domestic versus foreign shock–driven components

Notes: The solid line is the actual spread of KDB bond over the U.S. Treasury bill rate, and the dotted lines are generated using the VAR estimation results with the foreign shocks set to be zeros. The upper dotted line is from the VAR with Korea at 6th in the ordering, while the lower dotted line with Korea at the lowest. See the text for details.

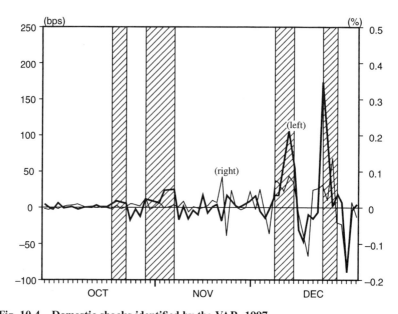

Fig. 10.4   Domestic shocks identified by the VAR, 1997

Note: The thick line is the shock on the sovereign spread; the thin line is the shock on the exchange rate.

Figure 10.4 reports Korea's residuals that were identified from the VAR estimation of the exchange rate and sovereign spreads (with Korea at the fifth position from the bottom in the ordering). From this figure, one may find the four subperiods that experienced serious negative shocks (or the positive residuals), which we highlighted with the shaded areas: 10/21–10/25, 10/30–11/8, 12/8–12/13, and 12/22–12/24.

Table 10.6 reports the relevant news that we collected from several Korean newspapers (Maeil Economic Daily, Hankuk Economic Daily, and so forth) and Bloomberg. In order to reduce possible selection bias, we tried to collect only the headline news of the financial sections in domestic newspapers, and simply skipped the dates on which the headline news were mere descriptions of the financial market situation. From Bloomberg, in contrast, we included the comments on Korea's situations and government policies.

One can notice that the news for the International Monetary Fund's (IMF) rescue plan was not a big shock to the market; it may have been anticipated. Rather, the news that stirred the financial market was the bankruptcies of several *chaebols* and financial institutions and the bailout policies of the government. Readers can also refer to table 10.11 to see how many conglomerates of Korea had gone bankrupt right before the crisis and how large they were in the Korean financial market. The first

Table 10.6	News on the Korean Financial Market, October–December 1997	
	Korean Newspapers	Bloomberg
3 October	Standard & Poor's downgrades commercial banks.	
4 October	Euromoney downgrades Korea.	
14 October	Bank of Korea makes special loans of 1 trillion won to merchant banks.	
20 October	Government leads commercial banks to syndicated loans to ailing *chaebols*.	
23 October	**Government decides to undertake Kia Motors as a public enterprise through KDB's debt-equity swap.**	
24 October		**Standard & Poor's downgrades Korea because the government rescued Korea First Bank and "nationalized" the near-bankrupt Kia.**
25 October	**Standard & Poor's downgrades Korea.**	
27 October		Free-fall of currency raises concern Korea will follow other Asian nations in seeking IMF assistance, although government denies it.
29 October	Moody's downgrades Korea.	
29 October	Bond market will be opened from 1998.	Korea accelerates opening bond market, but it is too late to allure foreign investors.
30 October		Government orders banks and companies to stop hoarding dollars, and investors suspect that BOK's official reserve of $30 billion does not include dollars borrowed through forward transactions.
3 November	**Haitai group applies for composition.**	
4 November	**Newcore group applies for composition.**	
5 November		**A costly—and probably futile—attempt to stabilize the currency value increases systemic risks. Many estimate actual reserves could be as low as $15 billion. The focus of Korean banks' lending to a handful of customers, or *chaebol*, could make matters even worse.**

(continued)

Table 10.6 (continued)

	Korean Newspapers	Bloomberg
8 November	**Government requests foreign press to stop spreading "groundless" bad rumors about Korea.**	
10 November		Foreign investors dismiss government optimism in coping with the turmoil.
11 November	Government will support 1.3 trillion won for Kia group.	
12 November	Financial Reform Amendment is rejected by the National Assembly.	
18 November	BOK makes $1 billion in emergency loans to the five major commercial banks on the brink of bankruptcies.	Korea may need IMF assistance, although IMF and government deny it.
19 November		Finance minister is replaced to clear the way for the government to seek $40 billion from the IMF.
20 November	Government guarantees all deposits and interest for three years.	
20 November	Exchange rate band is widened from 2.5 to 10 percent per day.	
21 November	Government asks for IMF support.	
26 November	Foreign exchange treatments of eight merchant banks are suspended.	
28 November	IBRD and ADB decide to support Korea.	
2 December		Government orders nine crippled finance companies to suspend business.
3 December	Halla group asks for syndicated loan.	
3 December	Nine merchant banks are closed.	Korea agrees to a $55 billion international bailout.
4 December	IMF and government agree upon a $55 billion rescue package.	
6 December	Korea Securities Co. goes bankrupt.	
8 December	**Daewoo group acquires Ssangyong Motors with syndicated loans.**	
8 December	**BOK injects 1.2 trillion won to ailing merchant banks, and will make more special loans if necessary.**	
9 December	**Government invests 1.8 trillion won in Seoul Bank and Korea First Bank.**	

11 December	**Five more merchant banks are closed.**	
11 December	**BOK makes 5 trillion won in special loans to commercial banks.**	
11 December	**Dongseo Securities Co. is closed.**	
13 December	**BOK will inject 11 trillion won to nonbank financial institutions.**	
15 December	Government will allow for redundant layoffs.	Government ends limits on foreign exchange trading.
16 December	Exchange rate band is abolished.	Government will cancel plans to inject capital into six banks because of objections from IMF officials.
16 December		Government delays plans to bolster banks and offers aid to brokerages, resisting the reform package of the IMF.
17 December		Finance and Economy Ministry says financial institutions have "less than $10 billion" in short-term foreign currency debt maturing in January, but independent economists say the government figure is optimistic.
18 December	Dae-Jung Kim is elected as the new president.	
23 December	**Moody's downgrades Korea to a junk-bond level.**	**Korea is pushed closer to the economic brink as Moody's cuts the country's credit rating to junk status.**
23 December	**IMF is discontent with the government treatment of the ailing financial institutions.**	
23 December	**Vice minister of Finance Department acknowledges that there exist more than $100 billion in offshore borrowings.**	**U.S. officials deny a report that the Clinton administration offered $5 billion in "emergency credits."**
24 December		**BOK asks Japan banks to roll over debts.**
25 December	IMF and G7 promise to support $10 billion early.	
25 December	Financial market will be completely opened.	Korea will allow bank layoffs.
26 December		Korea's courts reject applications from Koryo and Dongsuh Securities Co. for court receivership, making it likely the brokerages will be sold or shut down.
26 December		
27 December	Cheongku Group applies for composition.	
30 December		Korea's external debt totals $156.9 billion at the end of November, according to IMF standards.
30 December		National Assembly passes a package of economic reform bills.

period matches the news about the bailout policy for Kia, whereas the second period coincides with the bankruptcy news of Haitai and New-Core. The third period matches the news on the acquisition of Ssangyong Autos by Daewoo and the unconditional rescues of many distressed financial institutions, including two major bankrupt banks (First Korea and Seoul) by the government (and the Bank of Korea). Finally, the last period was driven by the news that Moody's downgraded Korea's sovereign debt to a junk-bond level and the finance department vice minister's acknowledgment that Korea's foreign debt may exceed $250 billion instead of the official $100 billion.

In short, the news that the Korean government still tried to stick to old-fashioned bailout policies appears to have operated as bad shocks. At least at the triggering moment of the Korean crisis, the market's reaction appeared to be most negative to the series of *chaebol* bankruptcies and the government's bailout policies.

10.4   Further Discussion on the Korean Crisis

The previous section suggests that the Korean crisis was triggered more by domestic shocks than by contagion effects, although the contagion effects substantially deepened the crisis. This is basically in accordance with the result from the probit analyses, with more emphasis on domestic weaknesses. Yet, the probit analyses indicate that the domestic fundamentals were not extremely bad. This section, therefore, adds some discussion about some important weaknesses of Korea's financial market structure that we could not systematically analyze due to the limitations of comparable cross-country data availability. Instead of providing formal analysis results, we will briefly sketch the crucial points that have been made by other researchers.

10.4.1   Bank Runs rather than Currency Speculation

Table 10.7 shows Korea's balance-of-payment situation during the 1997–98 period. From this table, one can be astonished at how abrupt the capital flow reversal was during the fourth quarter in 1997. The usable foreign reserve, which had been fluctuating around $30 billion until the third quarter, abruptly decreased by $15 billion during just one month, November 1997. In fact, the foreign reserve would have been completely depleted by the end of December had there not been the emergency loan of $16 billion through the public sector institutions, such as the IMF and the World Bank.

An important point of this table, however, is that the major component of this abrupt capital flow reversal was the withdrawal of foreign debt rather than the shift of portfolio investment. Private external debt decreased by $6.5 billion in November and by $11.3 billion in December,

Table 10.7   Trends of the Balance-of-Payment Components (in US$ billions)

	1997							1998			
	First Quarter	Second Quarter	Third Quarter	Fourth Quarter	October	November	December	First Quarter	Second Quarter	Third Quarter	Fourth Quarter
Foreign reserve decrease[a]	8.28	−4.17	2.89	13.55	0.12	15.04	−1.61	−15.28	−12.89	−6.33	−5.14
Private foreign asset decrease[a]	−1.88	−1.44	−1.76	−10.00	−1.14	2.37	−11.23	−5.87	−0.80	2.84	3.83
Total	6.40	−5.61	1.13	3.55	−1.02	17.41	−12.84	−21.15	−13.69	−3.49	−1.31
Decrease in external debt[b]	−5.59	−6.47	−2.94	−1.10	−2.95	6.55	−4.70	4.26	−0.83	3.23	2.06
(public)	0.07	0.17	0.06	−15.92	0.04	0.05	−16.01	−6.69	−5.67	−1.42	−0.47
(private)	−5.66	−6.64	−3.00	14.82	−2.99	6.50	11.31	10.95	4.83	4.64	2.53
Increase in deposit at overseas branches[b]	4.20	0.00	0.00	3.33	0.00	8.91	−5.58	−5.93	−1.74	−0.26	−0.07
Net direct investment outflow[a]	0.51	0.23	0.66	0.21	0.10	−0.05	0.16	0.34	−0.34	−0.47	0.08
Net equity securities outflow[a]	−0.54	−2.54	−0.50	1.38	0.76	1.07	−0.46	−2.99	−0.01	0.22	−1.31
Errors and omission	0.02	−0.15	1.17	4.03	0.50	2.35	1.18	0.50	1.25	1.16	2.16
Current account deficit[a]	7.35	2.72	2.05	−3.96	0.49	−0.86	−3.59	−10.83	−10.91	−9.62	−8.69

Sources: Bank of Korea, *Balance of Payments* (various issues), and the data for external debt are from the Ministry of Finance and Economy.

[a] Negative numbers denote increase, inflows, or surplus.

[b] External debt is reckoned based on IBRD standards, and deposit at overseas branches denotes the deposit of the Bank of Korea at the overseas branches of the domestic banks.

whereas the magnitude of equity securities outflow was rather small. If one includes the emergency loan of the Bank of Korea to the overseas branches of the Korean banks that were on the brink of bankruptcies, the decrease of private foreign debt in November was over $15 billion!

Based on this inspection, Shin (1998) argues that the triggering mechanism of the currency crisis in Korea fits the bank-run theories (e.g., Cole and Kehoe 1996; Goldfajn and Valdes 1997; Chang and Velasco 1998) better than the speculative attack hypotheses (e.g., Krugman 1979; and Obstfeld 1995). Somewhat arbitrarily, table 10.8 decomposes the demand for foreign reserves into two parts: the component that was not affected by the exchange rate movement from the creditor's point of view, and the other component that was subject to the capital loss from currency depreciation. According to this decomposition, one can confirm that the first component outweighs the second in magnitude. This finding seems to support the hypothesis that the abrupt reversal of the capital flow in Korea was triggered by the bankruptcy risks of the major Korean banks, rather than the hypothesis that currency speculation in pursuit of capital gain triggered massive capital outflow.

This argument appears to be reinforced by the external liability rollover rate of the seven major Korean banks in table 10.9, cited from Shin (1998). That is, the rollover rate of the major Korean banks, which already remained below 100 percent before November, sharply declined in November and further in December.

In relation to the contagion issue and the contagious effects from the weak financial system of Japan in particular, table 10.10 shows that Japan's role was not particularly prominent. That is, the absolute amount of credit withdrawn by Japan was large because of its high exposure to the Korean market, but the flight from Korean banks was a general phenomenon regardless of the creditors' region. This information is also consistent with the result of the above section that Japan's role appears to be minimal in triggering the Korean crisis.

10.4.2 Fragile Financial Market Structure That Was Not Considered Above

We argued that the Korean crisis appeared to be triggered by bank runs rather than speculative currency attacks. We also argued that the critical news triggering the crisis seemed to be the *chaebol* bankruptcies and the bail out policies of the government. In relation to these arguments, this section briefly mentions the fragile aspects of Korea's financial system that were not considered in the probit model analyses.

Perhaps the most important weaknesses in Korea's financial structure that were overlooked in the probit analyses were the low profitability and the high leverage ratios of the corporate sector. Figure 10.5 shows that the corporate sector of Korea had the lowest profitability and the highest debt/

Table 10.8   Demand Factors of the Foreign Reserves

	1997							1998			
	First Quarter	Second Quarter	Third Quarter	Fourth Quarter	October	November	December	First Quarter	Second Quarter	Third Quarter	Fourth Quarter
Outflow of foreign currency denominated assets[a]	-1.30	-6.47	-2.93	2.24	-2.95	15.46	-10.28	-1.68	-2.57	2.97	1.99
Outflow of domestic currency denominated assets 1[b]	-0.51	-2.69	0.66	5.41	1.27	3.42	0.72	-2.49	1.24	1.38	0.85
Outflow of domestic currency denominated assets 2[c]	6.84	0.03	2.71	1.45	1.75	2.56	-2.87	-13.32	-9.66	-8.24	-7.83

Sources: All numbers are from table 10.7.

Note: Negative numbers denote capital inflow.

[a]Sum of the decrease in external debt and the increase in the deposit at the overseas branches of the domestic banks.

[b]Sum of net equity securities outflow, and errors and omissions.

[c]Sum of the net equity securities outflow, errors and omissions, and current account deficit.

Table 10.9   Weekly Rollover Rate of Foreign Loans: Seven Major Commercial Banks, 1997

	July	August	September	October	November	December
First week	157.3	64.1	82.2	83.7	70.0	23.7
Second week	95.5	84.9	82.8	83.9	67.2	26.8
Third week	83.6	86.9	84.1	80.5	55.9	26.2
Fourth week	76.1	76.2	89.8	84.9	48.7	31.9
Fifth week	87.5		127.3			53.3
Average	89.1	79.2	85.5	86.5	58.8	32.2

Table 10.10   Trend of Regional Composition of Foreign Loans: Thirteen Major Banks[a]

	96.12	97.3	97.6	97.9	97.12
Japan	259.7 (50.2)	212.8 (42.0)	220.9 (44.8)	206.3 (45.8)	139.5 (47.6)
United States	70.1 (13.5)	88.3 (17.4)	86.4 (17.5)	70.5 (15.7)	46.3 (15.8)
Europe	187.6 (36.3)	205.4 (40.6)	185.8 (37.7)	173.0 (38.5)	107.1 (36.6)
Total[b]	517.4 (100.0)	506.4 (100.0)	493.1 (100.0)	449.8 (100.0)	292.9 (100.0)

[a] Seven commercial banks and six specialized banks.
[b] This figure excludes foreign loans extended by creditor banks in regions other than Japan, the United States, and Europe.

(Unit: %)

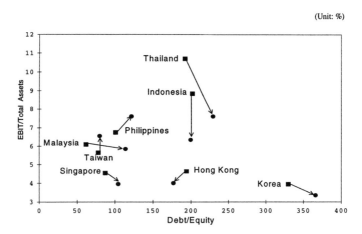

Fig. 10.5   Debt equity ratio and EBIT-total assets for East Asian countries (1991–96)
Source: Nam, Kang, and Kim (1999).
Note: The solid square denotes average for 1991–92; the solid circle denotes average for 1995–96.

equity ratio among the eight Asian countries. This financial structure was a large potential threat to the solvency of the banking sector of Korea.

In addition, the high concentration of financial assets in a small number of *chaebols* was perceived to be another factor causing vulnerability in the financial system. Table 10.11 shows that the top thirty *chaebols* governed almost 50 percent of the total assets in Korea. Under this high concentration ratio, a small negative shock to the *chaebols* could develop into sys-

Table 10.11   **Thirty Largest *Chaebols:* April 1996 (in trillions of won)**

	Total Assets	Leverage (debt/equity)	Number of Subsidiaries	Date of Bankruptcy
1. Hyundai	43.7 (6.94)	440%	46	
2. Samsung	40.8 (6.48)	279%	55	
3. LG	31.4 (4.99)	345%	48	
4. Daewoo	31.3 (4.97)	391%	25	
5. SK	14.6 (2.32)	352%	32	
6. Ssangyong	13.9 (2.21)	310%	23	
7. Hanjin	12.2 (1.94)	559%	24	
8. Kia	11.4 (1.81)	522%	16	07/16/97*
9. Hanhwa	9.2 (1.46)	712%	31	12/17/97***
10. Lotte	7.1 (1.13)	191%	28	
11. Kumho	6.4 (1.02)	480%	27	
12. Doosan	5.8 (0.92)	907%	26	
13. Daelim	5.4 (0.86)	424%	18	
14. Hanbo	5.1 (0.81)	648%	21	01/18/97*
15. Dongah	5.1 (0.81)	362%	16	01/10/98***
16. Halla	4.8 (0.76)	2,457%	17	12/03/97***
17. Hyosung	3.6 (0.57)	362%	16	
18. Dongkuk	3.4 (0.54)	223%	16	
19. Jinro	3.3 (0.52)	4,836%	14	09/09/97**
20. Kolon	3.1 (0.49)	340%	19	
21. Tongyang	3.0 (0.48)	305%	22	
22. Hansol	3.0 (0.48)	291%	19	
23. Dongbu	2.9 (0.46)	219%	24	
24. Kohap	2.9 (0.46)	603%	11	01/30/98***
25. Haitai	2.9 (0.46)	669%	14	08/26/97*
26. Sammi	2.5 (0.40)	3,333%	8	03/20/97*
27. Hanil	2.2 (0.35)	581%	8	12/31/97***
28. Keukdong	2.2 (0.35)	516%	11	
29. Newcore	2.0 (0.32)	1,253%	18	05/23/97**
30. Byucksan	1.9 (0.30)	473%	16	
Total	286.9 (45.6)		669	

Source: Data from the Fair Trade Commission.

Note: Figures in parentheses are the share of total assets in percentages of the corporate sector in Korea (629.8 trillion won as of the end of 1996).

*denotes bankruptcy.

**denotes standstill agreement.

***denotes syndicated loan.

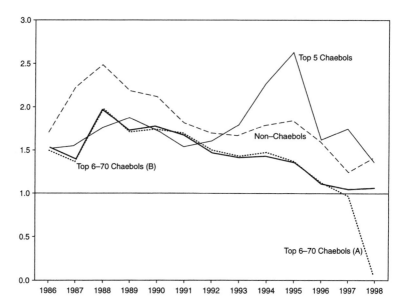

Fig. 10.6   Interest payment coverage ratios for listed firms
Source: National Information and Credit Evaluation, Inc.
Notes: Figures for 1998 are those for the first half of 1998. (A) includes all subsidiaries of the top 6–70 *chaebols;* (B) excludes Kia and Asia automobile companies among the top 6–70 *chaebols.*

temic risk affecting the whole banking sector. In this regard, the severe deterioration in the profitability of the top six to seventy *chaebols* since 1995 as shown in figure 10.6 was a growing threat to the whole banking system of Korea. In table 10.11 we also report the bankruptcy dates to show how many *chaebols* went bankrupt during 1997. Recognizing this aspect of Korea's financial system may help readers better understand why the financial market reacted so drastically to the news of *chaebol* bankruptcies.

10.5   Concluding Remarks

This paper examines the Korean currency crisis, focusing on the weaknesses in domestic fundamentals as opposed to the contagious external effects. The results of this paper appear to suggest that the contagion effects were large, but not sufficient enough to explain Korea's crisis. In particular, the triggering moment of the crisis did not appear to be attributable to the contagion effects.

As for the conventional factors that are considered important in explaining the currency crisis, Korea's fundamentals were weak, but not extreme enough to generate such a deep crisis. While external transactions were loosely managed, domestic macrofundamentals appeared to be sound. Nevertheless, the Korean currency crisis seems to have been triggered by runs on the major banks, with the triggering moment associated with the bankruptcies of *chaebols* and the nontransparent bailout policies of the government. This observation seems to suggest that additional fragile aspects of the financial system were important in explaining Korea's crisis. Examples of such aspects are the low profitability and high leverage ratio of the corporate sector, the high concentration ratio of financial assets in a small number of *chaebols,* and so forth.

A crucial question that arises here is why the bank runs were triggered by foreign investors while domestic investors were less worried. A possible explanation is the divergence of expectations about conventional practices of the government policies. That is, among Korean investors, expectations about bailout policies for *chaebol* and financial institutions were largely expected while foreign investors were surprised. If this proposition is true, Korea's crisis was a more fundamental crisis for the whole financial system of Korea rather than a simple liquidity crisis for foreign exchanges. In other words, the crisis may have been an inevitable outcome when the implicit bailout expectation among Korean investors (or the crony capitalism of Krugman 1998) was broken by foreign investors. This is a complex issue that should be further investigated.

Appendix
Data Sources

Cross-Country Data

Most of the data used in section 10.2 are extracted from the *World Development Indicators on CD-ROM 1998* by the World Bank (hereafter WDI98), unless otherwise indicated.

Crisis index. The crisis index takes value 1 for a currency crisis and value 0 otherwise. A crisis is defined as annual depreciation of the nominal exchange rate (with respect to the U.S. dollar) of at least 25 percent that is also at least a 10 percent increase in the rate of depreciation.

Growth rate of per capita GDP. The per capita GDP growth rate is constructed by taking the log difference of per capita GDP.

Growth rate of real domestic credit. Real domestic credit denotes domestic credit extended to the private sector by the banking sector divided by the consumer price index (CPI). The banking sector comprises monetary authorities, depository banks, and other financial institutions (e.g., mutual credit unions and housing financial cooperatives).

Ratio of foreign exchange reserve to short-term foreign debt. The data for foreign exchange reserves are from the *International Finance Statistics CD-ROM March 1999* (hereafter IFS), and short-term foreign debt is obtained by multiplying total foreign debt by the share of short-term foreign debt in total foreign debt. Total foreign debt includes foreign borrowings by the government sector, government-guaranteed foreign borrowings, non–government-guaranteed private borrowings, and credit and short-term debt provided by the International Monetary Fund.

Depreciation of the real exchange rate. The real exchange rate depreciation is the log difference of the nominal exchange rate over CPI. The nominal exchange rate is the year-end market exchange rate from IFS, whereas CPI is from WDI98.

Changes in the terms of trade. Changes in the terms of trade are constructed by taking the log difference of the ratio of export price to import price. The export and import prices are export and import values (in current U.S. dollars) divided by export and import volumes (in constant local currency), respectively.

FDI/GDP. FDI denotes net foreign direct investment inflow.

Growth rate of foreign GDP. The foreign GDP growth rate is the log difference of the total sum of GDPs of OECD economies.

Foreign interest rates. Foreign interest rates are the weighted average of lending rates in the United States, Japan, the United Kingdom, Germany, and France. The weights are given by the currency composition of the long-term debt in each country. The currency composition ratios are from the World Bank (1997, 1998) and World Bank (various issues).

Regional contagion index. The regional contagion index is a weighted average of the crisis indexes of other countries. The weights are given by the inverse of the geographical distance between the country in question and other countries. For the geographical distance between two countries, latitude and longitude of the corresponding capital cities are used.

   Trade linkage index: The trade linkage index in section 10.2 is the same as the one used by Glick and Rose (1998). The trade linkage between two countries 0 and i are given by the following:

$$\text{Trade}_i \equiv \sum_k \left[\left(\frac{X_{0k} + X_{ik}}{X_0 + X_i} \right) \cdot \left(\frac{1 - |(X_{ik} - X_{0k})|}{X_{ik} + X_{0k}} \right) \right],$$

where X_{ik} denotes aggregate bilateral exports from country i to k ($k \neq i$, 0) and X_i denotes aggregate exports from country i.

Daily Data

Sovereign Spreads. The spread is defined by subtracting the yield rate on the U.S. Treasury bill from the yield rate on each sovereign bond in the secondary market. We collected the yield rate of each country's sovereign bond from Bloomberg Online. The following are the CUSIP numbers of the sovereign bonds, along with the specific name of the bond and due date.

> Argentina: 040114AN0, ARGENT 11, 10/06, USD, GOVT.
> Brazil: 105756AG5, BRAZIL 9 3/8, 04/08, USD, GOVT.
> Mexico: 593048bf7, MEX 8 5/8, 03/12/08, GOVT.
> Malaysia: PETRONAS 7 1/8, 10/06, USD, PETRONAS.
> China: 712219AE4, CHINA 7 3/4, 07/06, USD, GOVT.
> Indonesia: 455780AB2, INDO 7 3/4, 08/06, USD, GOVT.
> Thailand: 88322kac5, Thailand Kingdom, Thai, 3/4, 04/07.
> Korea: Korea Development Bank due to 2003, 10 years, Global.
> Japan: TOKYO MISTZUBISHI, BOT, 7 3/4, 11/02/02.
> Russia: XS0077745163, RUSSIA 10, 06/07, USD, GOVT.
> Treasury Bill: T 5 1/4, 02/15/29, 30 years.

References

Agenor, Pierre-Richard, and Joshua Aizenman. 1997. *Contagion and volatility with imperfect credit markets.* Cambridge, Mass.: International Monetary Fund.

Aharony, Joseph, and Itzhak Swary. 1983. Contagion effects of bank failures: Evidence from capital markets. *Journal of Business* 56 (3): 305–22.

———. 1996. Additional evidence on the information-based contagion effects of bank failures. *Journal of Banking and Finance* 20:57–69.

Baig, Taimur, and Ilan Goldfajn. 1998. *Financial market contagion in the Asian crisis.* Washington, D.C.: International Monetary Fund.

Bank of Korea. Various issues. *Balance of payments* (in Korean). Available at http://www.bok.or.kr.

Calomiris, Charles W., and Joseph R. Mason. 1994. Contagion and bank failures during the Great Depression: The June 1932 Chicago banking panic. NBER Working Paper no. 4934. Cambridge, Mass.: National Bureau for Economic Research, November.

Calvo, Sara, and Carmen Reinhart. 1996. Capital flows to Latin America: Is there evidence of contagion effects? Policy Research Working Paper no. 1619. Washington, D.C.: Institute for International Economics.

Chang, Robert, and Andres Velasco. 1998. Financial crises in emerging markets: A canonical model. NBER Working Paper no. 6606. Cambridge, Mass.: National Bureau of Economic Research, June.

Chari, V. V., and Ravi Jagannathan. 1998. Banking panics, information, and rational expectations equilibrium. *Journal of Finance* 43 (3): 749–63.

Cohen, Daniel. 1993. A valuation formula for LDC debt. *Journal of International Economics* 34 (1–2): 167–80.

Cole, Harold, and Timothy Kehoe. 1996. A self-fulfilling model of Mexico's 1994–95 debt crisis. Staff Report 210. Federal Reserve Bank of Minneapolis.

Corbo, Vittorio, and Leonardo Hernandez. 1994. Macroeconomic adjustment to capital inflows: Latin American style versus East Asian style. World Bank Policy Research Working Paper no. 1377. Washington, D.C.: World Bank, November.

Doukas, John. 1989. Contagion effect on sovereign interest rate spreads. *Economics Letters* 29 (3): 237–41.

Eichengreen, Barry, Andrew K. Rose, and Charles Wyplosz. 1995. Exchange market mayhem: The antecedents and aftermath of speculative attacks. *Economic Policy* 21 (October): 251–312.

Flood, R., and P. Garber. 1984. Collapsing exchange rate regimes: Some linear examples. *Journal of International Economics* 17 (1–2): 1–13.

Forbes, Kristin, and Roberto Rigobon. 1998. No contagion, only interdependence: Measuring stock market co-movements. MIT–Sloan School of Management, Unpublished Manuscript, November.

Frankel, Jeffrey A., and Andrew K. Rose. 1996. Currency crashes in emerging markets: An empirical treatment. *Journal of International Economics* 41 (3–4): 351–66.

Frankel, Jeffrey A., and Sergio L. Schmukler. 1998. Crisis, contagion, and country funds. In *Managing capital flows and exchange rates,* ed. R. Glick, 1–47. Cambridge: Cambridge University Press.

Garber, Peter. 1996. Are currency crises self-fulfilling? In *NBER Macroeconomics Annual 1996,* ed. Ben S. Bernanke and Julio Rotemberg, 403–06. Cambridge: MIT Press.

Glick, Reuven, and Andrew K. Rose. 1998. Contagion and trade: Why are currency crises regional? University of California at Berkeley, Unpublished Manuscript, August 12. Available at http://haas.berkeley.edu/~arose.

Goldfajn, Ilan, and Rodrigo O. Valdes. 1997. Capital flows and the twin crises: The role of liquidity. IMF Working Paper no. 9787. Washington, D.C.: International Monetary Fund, July.

Haque, Nadeem U., Manmohan S. Kumar, Nelson Mark, and Donald J. Mathieson. 1996. The economic content of indicators of developing country creditworthiness. IMF Working Paper, January.

Hong, Kiseok. 2000. Channels of contagion effects in currency crises. Mimeograph.

Kaminsky, Graciela L., and Carmen M. Reinhart. 2000. On crises, contagion, and confusion. *Journal of International Economics,* forthcoming.

Karafiath, Imre, Ross Mynatt, and Kenneth L. Smith. 1991. The Brazilian default announcement and the contagion effect hypothesis. *Journal of Banking and Finance* 15 (3): 699–716.

Krugman, Paul. 1979. A model of balance of payment crisis. *Journal of Money, Credit, and Banking* 11 (3): 311–25.

———. 1994. The myth of Asia's miracle. *Foreign Affairs* 73 (6): 62–78.

———. 1998. What happened to Asia? Unpublished Manuscript. Cambridge, Mass.: MIT. Available at http://web.mit.edu/krugman/www/DISINTER.html.

Nam, Il-Chong, Yeongjae Kang, and Joon-Kyung Kim. 1999. Comparative corporate governance trends in Asia. Paper submitted to conference, Corporate governance in Asia: A comparative perspective, sponsored by OECD and KDI, Seoul, Korea, 3–5 March 1999.

National Information and Credit Evaluation, Inc. [http://www.nice.co.kr.].
Obstfeld, Maurice. 1995. Models of currency crisis with self-fulling features. NBER Working Paper no. 5285. Cambridge, Mass.: National Bureau of Economic Research, October.
Park, Sangkyun. 1991. Bank failure contagion in historical perspective. *Journal of Monetary Economics* 28 (2): 271–86.
Perry, Guillermo E., and Daniel Lederman. 1998. *Financial vulnerability, spillover effects, and contagion: Lessons from the Asian crises for Latin America.* World Bank Latin American and Caribbean Studies, World Bank.
Rigobon, Roberto. 1998. On the measurement of contagion. MIT-Sloan School of Management, Unpublished Manuscript, December.
Sachs, Jeffrey D., Aaron Tornell, and Andres Velasco. 1996a. Financial crises in emerging markets: The lessons from 1995. *Brookings Papers on Economic Activity,* issue no. 0: 147–98. Washington, D.C.: Brookings Institution.
———. 1996b. The Mexican peso crisis: Sudden death or death foretold? *Journal of International Economics* 41 (3–4): 265–83.
Shin, In-seok. 1998. Currency crisis of Korea: A thought on the triggering mechanism. *KDI Policy Studies* 20 (3–4): 3–55.
Tornell, Aaron. 1999. Common fundamentals in the tequila and Asian crises. NBER Working Paper no. 7139. Cambridge, Mass.: National Bureau of Economic Research, June.
Valdes, Rodrigo O. 1996. Essays on capital flows and exchange rates. Ph.D. diss. Department of Economics, MIT.
World Bank. 1993. *The East Asian miracle: Economic growth and public policy.* New York: Oxford University Press.
———. 1997. *Global development finance.* Washington, D.C.: World Bank.
———. 1998. *Global development finance.* Washington, D.C.: World Bank.
———. Various issues. *World debt tables.* Washington, D.C.: World Bank.
Young, Alwyn. 1995. The tyranny of numbers: Confronting the statistical realities of the East Asian growth experience. *Quarterly Journal of Economics* 110 (3): 641–80.

Comment   Nouriel Roubini

This paper presents an empirical study of the causes of the Korean crisis of 1997–98. The authors analyze whether the crisis was due to domestic fundamentals or external interdependence (or contagion). They present a variety of evidence, both econometric and more qualitative.

There has been a broad debate on whether the Korean crisis was due to fundamentals or rather was caused by a liquidity run (with foreign banks suddenly withdrawing interbank lines) exacerbated by international contagion. In a sense, these alternative explanations are not contradictory but rather complementary. Seriously weak fundamentals may have initially triggered the crisis, but international contagion from East Asia to Korea

Nouriel Roubini is professor of economics at the Stern School of Business, New York University, and a research associate of the National Bureau of Economic Research.

(and vice versa) and a self-fulfilling bank-run psychology and panic may have exacerbated it. So, the issue is more one of the relative weight of alternative explanations. My reading of this paper and of the overall evidence for Korea is that fundamentals certainly played an important role. Although traditional fundamentals were not important in Korea (as public deficits and debt were low; inflation low; and savings and investment rates high), other structural weaknesses related to the financial system and distorted investment and borrowing incentives were very important. To summarize, the fundamental weaknesses of Korea, even before the onset of the currency crisis at the end of 1997, were as follows:

1. A severe recession in early 1997, well before the currency crisis.

2. Severe corporate distress (with seven out of the top thirty *chaebols* being effectively bankrupt by the middle of 1997). The distress of the corporations led to significant distress for a wide range of financial institutions (merchant and commercial banks).

3. Large current account deficits in 1996 driven by excessive investment and severe terms of trade shock (the fall in semiconductor prices) and a moderate amount of real appreciation of the currency.

4. Current account deficits mostly financed by short-term unhedged foreign currency loans (mostly cross-border interbank loans).

5. Short-term debt to foreign reserves (an important early warning signal) was high at the onset of the crisis and inward FDI very low given restrictions and regulations to FDI.

6. Dominance of the economy by "empire maximizing" *chaebols* that were overinvesting and inefficient.

7. Excessive investment was partly driven by "connected lending" and "directed lending" policies. Moral hazard-inducing implicit and explicit guarantees also distorted investment and borrowing and lending decisions of *chaebols* and financial institutions. Poor supervision and regulation of the financial system worsened such distortions.

8. High leverage of the *chaebols* with debt-to-equity ratios being on average over 300 percent even before the crisis, and devaluation further increased the burden of foreign currency debt.

9. Low profitability of investment with two-thirds of *chaebols* having losses in 1996 and the return on capital being low in the 1990s.

The qualitative and quantitative evidence presented in the paper is consistent with this assessment, suggesting an important role for fundamentals in triggering the crisis. The authors find some role for both contagion and domestic fundamentals.

The econometric analysis of the role of fundamentals and contagion is performed in sections 10.2 and 10.3. In section 10.2, using a standard probit model with data from about 100 countries, the authors find that fundamental weaknesses played a role, although contagion channels were also important (more geographic proximity than trade). A few comments on these results: First, traditional probit models are unable to capture non-traditional fundamentals because data on variables other than standard macro ones are not easily available. As the previous discussion suggests, the weaknesses of Korea were in its financial system and corporate structure rather than just traditional macro weaknesses. However, such structural variables are hard to measure and are not usually included in empirical models of the likelihood of a currency crisis. This may explain why the predictive power of the model is good but statistically not very large. Second, because proxies for geographic proximity and trade are highly correlated, it is not clear whether the stronger statistical significance of "proximity" relative to trade links is driven by such trade links. Third, it would have been useful to derive some direct proxies of financial contagion (such as common creditor links) rather than rely on proximity as a proxy for such contagion links. Fourth, the decomposition in table 10.3 of the contribution of various variables to the crisis probability is qualitatively interesting and sensible, but the quantitative contribution of significant factors (e.g., FDI, high debt to reserves, and terms of trade shocks) is modest. Given the significant contribution of the contagion variable, more could be done to figure out what this variable really proxies for: Is it "rational" contagion or "irrational" contagion?

Section 10.3 considers in more detail the contagion question by studying daily data on exchange rates and sovereign spreads for a set of emerging market economies. Interestingly, the authors relate these asset prices to news on Korea's economy and financial markets. They find that negative news about financial distress of *chaebols* and financial institutions drives such asset prices. The analysis is interesting and the results sensible. There are a number of general limitations to this approach: The country sample is small; there are missing macro variables in the regressions, given the use of daily data; and other asset prices such as stock prices and domestic interest rates could also have been analyzed.

Some remarks on the exchange rate results: First, the correlation between the value of the won and the yen may be spurious and driven by movement of the U.S. dollar; i.e., statistical correlation may occur even if the two exchange rates are statistically independent. One could use a numeraire to deal with this issue. Second, high correlation may be due to heteroscedasticity (high variance in turbulent times). Third, some correlations are low (as for the Japan correlations), but splitting the sample into subperiods (such as those in 1998 when the yen was weak and falling) may provide better results. Fourth, the VAR results on the contagion from East Asia to the Korean currency are interesting; conversely, one may argue that the free fall of the won in the fall of 1997 led to another round of contagious effects from Korea to the rest of the region.

The results on sovereign spreads are somewhat surprising: Korea's spreads seem to be more correlated with those of Latin America than those of Asia. This may be due to some "cross-hedging" across markets. Also, the robustness of this result in subsamples of turbulent periods may have to be tested. Also, the results of the Granger causality tests showing causality going from Korea to East Asia but not vice versa are a bit at odds with the exchange rate results suggesting contagion from East Asia to Korea.

The results on the effects of news on asset prices are novel and interesting; they confirm the view that negative domestic news about *chaebols* and financial distress of commercial and merchant banks as well as government bailout policies negatively affected asset markets. Two issues here: Although bailout news signals that there are serious distress problems, they should reduce panic and runs as long as the bailout commitment is credible. The results instead seem to suggest that bailout news is perceived as negative by investors. Second, finding a significant effect of bad news on asset prices does not rule out the possibility that such prices overreacted to the news; it is one thing to find that news matters, and another to infer that such significant relations between news and prices imply no overshooting of such prices to the news. In the absence of a fundamental model of the quantitative effect of such news, it is again hard to assess whether Korean financial markets and foreign investors overreacted to the negative news that came out of the Korean economy at the end of 1997. Although fundamentals played a strong role, as the paper convincingly argues, at the end of 1997 some run psychology and panic may have been triggered by such negative developments and may have led Korea to the brink of default. Only the negotiated agreement at the end of 1997 between Korea and its international creditor banks to roll over short term cross-border lines avoided this potentially disastrous outcome.

In conclusion, this is an interesting empirical study of the causes of the Korean crisis; it confirms the view that fundamentals mattered in triggering the crisis but that external interdependence (contagion) also mattered. The results appear to be convincing. Perhaps the authors could have tried to probe a little more the alternative view that Korea's crisis was caused by a self-fulfilling bank run and panic.

Comment   Ponciano S. Intal, Jr.

I would like to congratulate Dongchul Cho and Kiseok Hong for their admirable effort in analyzing the causes of the recent currency crisis in Korea. I start my comments on a few technical points. Afterwards, I will

Ponciano S. Intal, Jr. is professor of economics at De La Salle University.

focus on the real sector to complement Cho and Hong's "fundamentals" story. Of course, Cho and Hong, being Koreans, know the real sector aspects much more than I do. My aim is primarily to nudge the authors to consider somewhat more fully the real sector aspects in their paper. Clearly, no single paper can ever do justice to such a complex phenomenon as a currency or economic crisis. Nevertheless, I feel that the authors will end up with a more insightful paper if they give more space in the paper on the real sector aspects of the Korean crisis.

Some Technical Points

One technical point I would like to highlight is that the contagion index in the Cho and Hong paper does not measure the usual meaning of contagion as presented in Kaminsky and Reinhart (chap. 3, this volume). Given that the data used is annual, thereby raising issues of simultaneity/endogeneity, the geography-based contagion index can proxy more neatly the trade, financial, and investment linkages among neighboring countries, i.e., akin to an index of economic integration or economic interdependence. Viewed this way, Cho and Hong's contagion index supports better the authors' view that the Korean crisis was primarily determined by Korea's fundamentals but was substantially aggravated by the crisis in Southeast Asia. (There may be some quibbling here, in the sense that what could have been an economic turbulence in Korea ended up being a full-blown crisis because of the regional contagion effect.)

The second point is that some of the results are counterintuitive. For example, in the case of Thailand and Indonesia, the results indicate that the probability of a currency crisis in Thailand and Indonesia was historically higher during the late 1980s and early 1990s than in 1997. In view of the modest results, Cho and Hong might like to consider modifying the specification of the probit model. For example, like in Corsetti, Pesenti, and Roubini (chap. 1, this volume), Tornell (chap. 2, this volume), and Kaminsky and Reinhart (chap. 3, this volume), it may be that some variables need to pass some threshold levels or be conditional upon other relevant variables before they significantly contribute to the occurrence of a crisis. Cho and Hong may also like to use the sharp increase in the "foreign exchange market pressure" à la Girton and Roper instead of a sharp drop in the exchange rate as the measure of currency crisis. The foreign exchange market pressure is a weighted sum of the exchange rate change and the change in foreign exchange reserves similar to those in Corsetti, Pesenti, and Roubini and Tornell. This is the more analytically satisfactory measure, especially in developing countries that do not have free and flexible foreign exchange markets. Finally, the authors may also include direct measures of financial sector vulnerability in the probit model, given the prominence of Korea's financial sector in the unraveling of Korea's crisis.

The last technical point is related to the Granger causality tests. Using daily data of log differences of exchange rates, the authors found minimal pair-wise correlation between the won and the Southeast Asian currencies. Moreover, the Korean won Granger-caused the Southeast Asian currencies, which is somewhat surprising. Except for the possible sample size requirement of a Granger causality test, it does not seem persuasive that daily data need to be used especially in the light of the counterintuitive results and the fact that the South Korean won and the Southeast Asian currencies are not freely floating.

Some Real Sector Underpinnings

Cho and Hong show the importance of terms of trade changes and real exchange rate changes as contributing factors to the occurrence of currency crises. The authors did not discuss them; nevertheless, the two factors appear to be important for the Korean crisis story because they bring out some of the real economy underpinnings of the financial sector fragility in Korea. Specifically, the decline in Korea's corporate profit rate to its lowest level ever (Smith 1998) may have stemmed in large part from the appreciation of the won vis-à-vis the yen (resulting in the loss of price competitiveness of Korea's exports vis-à-vis Japan's exports in third markets), the sharp fall in the export prices of Korea's semiconductor exports, and the significant slowdown in Korea's exports.

The drop in export prices was partly of Korea's doing because Korea is a major player in the world's semiconductor chips industry. The drop in export prices resulted from the serious overcapacity in the industry brought about by the slowdown in world demand on the one hand and, to some extent, the investment binge of Korea's *chaebols* on the other. The increased commodity concentration of Korea's exports, which led to Korea's greater vulnerability to terms of trade changes, may have stemmed in part from the *chaebols'* bias for economies of scale as the source of international competitiveness (rather than manufacturing flexibility in niches followed by Taiwanese firms), the real appreciation of the won, and the sharp rise in real wages in Korea.

It must be noted that the *chaebols'* corporate strategy is fundamentally a high-wire act. Focusing on economies of scale as a source of competitive advantage means building large, capital-intensive plants, which in the case of Korea's *chaebols* were largely debt financed. Highly leveraged with historically low corporate profit rates compared to a number of East Asian countries, the *chaebols* need robust growth in exports and the Korean economy as well as low wages in labor-efficiency terms in order to stay afloat. However, the sharp rise in the real wages in the 1990s and the sharp slowdown in exports and economic growth in 1996 substantially raised the probability of corporate failures and, given the debt-financed nature of Korean investments, also of bank failures.

The 1997–98 Korean economic crisis has a precedent in Korea: the 1980 crisis, which was caused as much by debt-financed overinvestment in the late 1970s as by an external shock (the world oil price hike). A major difference between the 1980 crisis and the 1997–98 crisis, however, is the sharply higher rate of Korean bank-intermediated, variable-rate, and short-term external debt in the recent episode. Cho and Hong show the significance of short-term debt as a predictor of a currency crisis. Why there was a sharp rise in short-term external debt in Korea is an interesting issue by itself. What is worth noting here is that it has been the less regulated merchant banks that triggered Korea's recent financial crisis, just as it was the less regulated finance companies that did it for Thailand in 1997 and for the Philippines in the early 1980s. Although this points to the issue of prudential regulations, it may also indicate problems related to the pace and pattern of the liberalization and deregulation of Korea's financial market.

Finally, it may be noted that within two years after the 1980 crisis, the Korean economy recovered as Korea reflated and as the triple lows (i.e., low won, low interest rate, and low world oil price) eventually led to surging exports. A low won (i.e., depreciation of the won and appreciation of the yen relative to the dollar) and a recovery in world semiconductor chip prices may lead to an export-led recovery of the Korean economy. Nevertheless, the success story of the 1980s may not be totally replicated in the recent episode. The drastically changed industrial relations environment in Korea and the increasing competition from Southeast Asia and China may constrain the recovery and growth potentials of the Korean economy. Thus, the basis for optimism for sustained recovery from the crisis would have to come from something else. Specifically, just as the 1980 crisis led to Korea's trade policy reforms, the 1997–98 crisis provides the impetus for Korea's financial sector and corporate restructuring and governance reforms. This seems to be happening despite much difficulty, as indicated by the Daewoo case.

Reference

Smith, H. 1998. *Korea.* In *East Asia in crisis: From a miracle to needing one?* ed. R. H. Mcleod and R. Garnaut, 66–84. London: Routledge.

Contributors

Leonard K. Cheng
Department of Economics
Hong Kong University of Science and
  Technology
Clearwater Bay
Kowloon
Hong Kong

Dongchul Cho
Research Fellow
Korea Development Institute
P.O. Box 113, Cheongryang
Seoul 113
Korea

Giancarlo Corsetti
Department of Economics
University of Rome III
Viale Ostiense 139
00154 Rome
Italy

Taro Esaka
c/o Shinji Takagi
Faculty of Economics
Osaka University
1-7 Machikaneyama
Toyonaka, Osaka 560-0043
Japan

Yukiko Fukagawa
8-828, 4-4-25, Aoyama Gakuin
  University
Shibuya, Shibuya-ku
Tokyo 150-8366
Japan

Kyoji Fukao
The Institute of Economic Research
Hitotsubashi University
Naka 2-1, Kunitachi-shi
Tokyo 186
Japan

Shin-ichi Fukuda
Faculty of Economics
University of Tokyo
7-3-1 Hongo Bunkyo-ku
Tokyo 113-0033
Japan

Kiseok Hong
Macroeconomics Division
Korea Development Institute
P.O. Box 113, Cheongryang
Seoul 130-012
Korea

Ponciano S. Intal, Jr.
DLSU Angelo King Institute for
    Economics and Business Studies
De La Salle University
2401 Taft Avenue
1004 Manila
Philippines

Takatoshi Ito
Institute of Economic Research
Hitotsubashi University
Naka 2-1, Kunitachi
186-8603 Tokyo
Japan

Graciela L. Kaminsky
Department of Economics
George Washington University
Washington, DC 20052

Anne O. Krueger
Department of Economics
Stanford University
579 Serra Mall
Landau Economics Bldg., Room 153
Stanford, CA 94305-6072

Yum K. Kwan
Department of Economics and
    Finance
City University of Hong Kong
Tat Chee Avenue
Kowloon
Hong Kong

Mario B. Lamberte
Philippine Institute for Development
    Studies
NEDA sa Makati Bldg., 106
    Amorsolo St.
Legaspi Village, Makati City, 1229
Philippines

Francis T. Lui
Department of Economics
Hong Kong University of Science and
    Technology
Clearwater Bay
Kowloon
Hong Kong

Eiji Ogawa
Department of Commerce
Hitotsubashi University
Kunitachi, Tokyo 186-8601
Japan

Paolo Pesenti
Federal Reserve Bank of New York
International Research Function
33 Liberty Street
New York, NY 10045

Assaf Razin
Eitan Berglas School of Economics
Tel Aviv University
Tel Aviv, 69978
Israel

Carmen M. Reinhart
University of Maryland
School of Public Affairs
Van Munching Hall, Room 4113D
College Park, MD 20742

Nouriel Roubini
Leonard M. Stern School of Business
New York University
Henry Kaufman Management Center
44 W 4th Street, 7-83
New York, NY 10012-1126

Efraim Sadka
The Eitan Berglas School of
    Economics
Tel Aviv University
Tel Aviv 69978
Israel

Lijian Sun
Fudan University
Shanghai
People's Republic of China

Shinji Takagi
Faculty of Economics
Osaka University
1-7 Machikaneyama
Toyonaka, Osaka 560-0043
Japan

Pranee Tinakorn
Thailand Development Research
   Institute
565 Ramkhamhaeng Soi 39,
   (Thepleela 1)
Wangthonglang
Bangkok, 10310
Thailand

Aaron Tornell
Department of Economics
University of California, Los Angeles
Box 951477
Los Angeles, CA 90095-1477

Chi-Wa Yuen
School of Economics and Finance
University of Hong Kong
Hong Kong

Mahani Zainal-Abidin
Faculty of Economics and
   Administration
University of Malaya
50603 Kuala Lumpur
Malaysia

Author Index

Ministry of International Trade and Industry (MITI), 268t, 269n2, 270, 271, 273f, 275, 280, 286f, 295, 305
Mishkin, Frederic, 11n1
Montiel, Peter, 44, 197, 198, 199n2, 202, 213, 219t, 224
Morris, Stephen, 32n32
Mundell, Robert, 257
Mynatt, Ross, 340n3

Nakamura, A., 121n6
Nam, Il-Chong, 366f
National Statistics Office, the Philippines, 306f, 307f, 308f
Nikkei Index, Japan, 294n13
Nugee, John, 235n3

Obstfeld, Maurice, 15n7, 48, 339, 364
Ogawa, Eiji, 151n1, 188
Organisation for Economic Cooperation and Development (OECD), 13
Otaki, Masayuki, 274n6

Park, Sangkyun, 340n3
Patrick, Hugh, 120n3
Pattillo, Catherine, 17n9, 275n7
Pazarbasioglu, Ceyla, 31
Perez-Quiros, Gabriel, 275n7
Perry, Guillermo, 337
Pesenti, Paolo, 11n1, 12, 13n4, 14, 15, 17n10, 21, 28, 29, 30, 36, 48, 117n1, 377
Phillips, Peter C. B., 210–11n11
Pill, Huw, 13n4, 131
Pomerleano, Michael, 13
Popper, Helen, 275n7
Prescott, Edward C., 234
Pyle, D. H., 120

Rabinowitz, Philip, 246t
Radelet, Steven, 12n2, 30, 48, 117n1, 198
Raghavan, C., 112
Rajan, R. G., 121n6
Ramstetter, Eric D., 269n2
Razin, Assaf, 11n1, 314, 320, 321n9, 322
Rebelo, Sergio, 14
Reinhart, Carmen, 11n1, 15n8, 17, 42, 44, 48, 50n1, 73–74, 76, 77n6, 79, 81, 83n11, 85, 86n12, 88, 92n13, 152, 166, 197, 199n2, 202, 213, 219t, 224, 340n2, 342n6, 377
Reinhart, Vincent, 202, 213, 219t

Research Institute of International Investment and Development, 269n2
Rodrik, Dani, 121n5
Romer, Paul M., 312
Rose, Andrew, 17, 48, 50n1, 73, 75, 81n9, 157n2, 244, 258n12, 275n7, 338, 339n1, 340, 341, 342, 370
Rotemberg, Julio, 326, 327
Roubini, Nouriel, 11n1, 12, 13n4, 14, 15, 17n10, 21, 28, 29, 30, 36, 48, 81, 117n1, 377

Sachs, Jeffrey, 11n1, 12n2, 15n7, 17, 20, 30, 42, 48, 50n1, 54, 117n1, 120n4, 198
Sadka, Efraim, 314, 320, 322
Sasaki, Yuri N., 151n1, 188
Scharfstein, D., 120
Schmukler, S., 75, 340n3
Schuler, Kurt, 233n1
Schwartz, Anna J., 236
Seng, Lim Choon, 197, 198, 202, 203, 205, 213, 219t
Shaw, E. S., 120n3
Shin, Hyun Song, 32n32
Shin, In-seok, 364
Smets, F., 75, 81
Smith, H., 378
Smith, Kenneth L., 340n3
Soderlind, Paul, 244
Sosner, Nathan, 314n5
Spiegel, Mark M., 204, 224
Stiglitz, Joseph E., 117n1, 206, 220, 316
Sugiyama, Yasuo, 294n13
Svensson, Lars E., 244, 245
Swary, Itzhak, 340n3

Takagi, Shinji, 206
Toda, Hito T., 210nn9,11
Tornell, Aaron, 11n1, 15n7, 17, 20, 29, 42, 48, 50n1, 54, 120n4, 377
Touyou Keizai Sinpou-sha, 269n2, 275t, 276t, 277t, 295
Townsend, Robert M., 315
Turner, Philip, 31

United Nations Conference on Trade and Development (UNCTAD), 267n1, 277, 302n20

Valdes, Rodrigo O., 11n1, 15n8, 152, 340n2, 355n15, 364
Vegh, Carlos, 14n6

Subject Index